REVERSE ENGINEERING – RECENT ADVANCES AND APPLICATIONS

Edited by **Alexandru C. Telea**

Reverse Engineering – Recent Advances and Applications
Edited by Alexandru C. Telea

Published by InTech
Janeza Trdine 9, 51000 Rijeka, Croatia

Publishing Process Manager Danijela Duric

Technical Editor Teodora Smiljanic

Cover Designer InTech Design Team

Additional hard copies can be obtained from orders@intechopen.com

Reverse Engineering – Recent Advances and Applications, Edited by Alexandru C. Telea
p. cm.
ISBN 978-953-51-0158-1

For EU product safety concerns:
IN TECH d.o.o., Prolaz Marije Krucifikse Kozulić 3, 51000 Rijeka, Croatia,
info@intechopen.com or visit our website at intechopen.com.

Meet the editor

Prof. dr. Alexandru C. Telea has obtained his PhD in 2000 in software architectures for data visualization from the Eindhoven University, the Netherlands. Until 2007, he worked as assistant professor in data and information visualization at the same university. Since 2007, he is professor of visualization and computer graphics at the Faculty of Mathematical and Natural Sciences, Institute Johann Bernoulli, University of Groningen, the Netherlands. He is the author of 150 papers in international journals, conferences, and books. His main research interests are software reverse engineering, software and information visualization, and multiscale 3D shape processing, with a strong focus on applications in the IT and data analysis industries. He is a member of the ACM.

Contents

Preface

Introduction

In the recent decades, the amount of data produced by scientific, engineering, and life science applications has increased with several orders of magnitude. In parallel with this development, the applications themselves have become increasingly complex in terms of functionality, structure, and behaviour. In the same time, development and production cycles of such applications exhibit a tendency of becoming increasingly shorter, due to factors such as market pressure and rapid evolution of supporting and enabling technologies.

As a consequence, an increasing fraction of the cost of creating new applications and manufacturing processes shifts from the creation of new artifacts to the *adaption* of existing ones. A key component of this activity is the *understanding* of the design, operation, and behavior of existing manufactured artifacts, such as software code bases, hardware systems, and mechanical assemblies. For instance, in the software industry, it is estimated that maintenance costs exceed 80% of the total costs of a software product's lifecycle, and software understanding accounts for as much as half of these maintenance costs.

Reverse engineering encompasses the set of activities aiming at (re)discovering the functional, structural, and behavioral semantics of a given artifact, with the aim of leveraging this information for the efficient usage or adaption of that artifact, or the creation of related artifacts. Rediscovery of information is important in those cases when the original information is lost, unavailable, or cannot be efficiently processed within a given application context. Discovery of new information, on the other hand, is important when new application contexts aim at reusing information which is inherently present in the original artifact, but which was not made explicitly available for reuse at the time of creating that artifact.

Reverse engineering has shown increasing potential in various application fields during the last decade, due to a number of technological factors. First, advances in data analysis and data mining algorithms, coupled with an increase of cheap computing power, has made it possible to extract increasingly complex information from raw data, and to structure this information in ways that make it effective for answering specific questions on the function, structure, and behavior of the artifact under study. Secondly, new data sources, such as 3D scanners, cell microarrays, and a large variety of sensors, has made new types of data sources available from which detailed insights about mechanical and living structures can be extracted.

Given the above factors, reverse engineering applications, techniques, and tools have shown a strong development and diversification. However, in the same time, the types of questions asked by end users and stakeholders have become increasingly complex. For example, while a decade ago the reverse engineering of a software application would typically imply extracting the static structure of an isolated code base of tens of thousands of lines of code written in a single programming language, current software reverse engineering aims at extracting structural, behavioral, and evolutionary patterns from enterprise applications of millions of lines of code written in several programming languages, running on several machines, and developed by hundreds of individuals over many years. Similarly, reverse engineering the geometric and mechanical properties of physical shapes has evolved from the extraction of coarse surface models to the generation of part-whole descriptions of complex articulated shapes with the submillimeter accuracy required for manufacturing processes. This has fostered the creation of new reverse engineering techniques and tools.

This book gives an overview of recent advances in reverse engineering techniques, tools, and application domains. The aim of the book is, on the one hand, to provide the reader with a comprehensive sample of the possibilities that reverse engineering currently offers in various application domains, and on the other hand to highlight the current research-level and practical challenges that reverse engineering techniques and tools are faced.

Structure of this book

To provide a broad view on reverse engineering, the book is divided into three parts: software reverse engineering, reverse engineering shapes, and reverse engineering in medical and life sciences. Each part contains several chapters covering applications, techniques, and tools for reverse engineering relevant to specific use-cases in the respective application domain. An overview of the structure of the book is given below.

Part 1: Software Reverse Engineering

In part 1, we look at reverse engineering the function, structure, and behavior of large *software-intensive applications*. The main business driver behind software reverse engineering is the increased effort and cost related to maintainting existing software applications and designing new applications that wish to reuse existing legacy software. As this cost increases, getting detailed information on the structure, run-time behavior, and quality attributes of existing software applications becomes highly valuable.

In **Chapter 1**, Kienle *et al.* Give a comprehensive overview of reverse engineering tools and techniques applied to embedded software. Apart from detailing the various pro's and con's related to the applicability of existing reverse engineering technology to embedded software, they also discuss the specific challenges that embedded software poses to classical reverse engineering, and outline potential directions for improvement.

In **Chapter 2**, Campos *et al.* Present an example of reverse engineering aimed at facilitating the development and maintenance of software applications that include a substantial user interface source code. Starting from the observation that understanding (and thus maintenance) of user interface code is highly challenging due to the typically non-modular structure of such code and its interactions with the remainder of the application, they present a technique and tool that is able to extract user interface behavioral models from the source code of Java applications, and show how these models can be used to reason about the application's usability and implementation quality.

In **Chapter 3**, Favre presents a model-driven architecture approach aimed at supporting program understanding during the evolution and maintenance of large software systems and modernization of legacy systems. Using a combination of static and dynamic analysis, augmented with formal specification techniques, and a new metamodeling language, they show how platform-independent models can be extracted from object-oriented (Java) source code and refined up to the level that they can be reused in different development contexts.

In **Chapter 4**, Rama *et al.* Show how platform-independent models can be extracted from large, complex business applications. Given that such applications are typically highly heterogeneous, *e.g.* involve several programming languages and systems interacting in a distributed manner, fine-grained reverse engineering as usually done for desktop or embedded applications may not be optimal. The proposed approach focuses on information at the service level. By reusing the platform-independent models extracted, the authors show how substantial cost savings can be done in the development of new applications on the IBM WebSphere and SAP NetWeaver platforms.

In **Chapter 5**, Li *et al.* present a different aspect of software reverse engineering. Rather than aiming to recover information from source code, they analyze the behavior of several peer-to-peer (P2P) protocols, as implemented by current P2P applications. The aim is to reverse engineer the high-level behavior of such protocols, and how this behavior depends on various parameters such as user behavior and application settings, in order to optimize the protocols for video streaming purposes. As compared to the previous chapters, the target of reverse engineering is here the behavior of an entire set of distributed P2P applications, rather than the structure or behavior of a single program.

Part 2: Reverse Engineering Shapes

In part 2, our focus changes from software artifacts to *physical shapes*. Two main use-cases are discussed here. First, methods and techniques for the reverse-engineering of the geometry and topology of complex shapes from low-level unorganized 3D scanning data, such as point clouds, are presented. The focus here is on robust extraction of shape information with guaranteed quality properties from such 3D scans, and also on the efficient computation of such shapes from raw scans involving millions of sample points. Secondly, methods and techniques are presented which help the process of *manufacturing* 3D shapes from information which is reverse engineered from previously manufactured shapes. Here, the focus is on guaranteeing required quality and cost related metrics throughout the entire mechanical manufacturing process.

In **Chapter 6**, Keller *et al.* present a multiresolution method for the extraction of accurate 3D surfaces from unorganized point clouds. Attractive aspects of the method are its simplicity of implementation, ability to capture the shape of complex surface structures with guaranteed connectivity properties, and scalability to real-world point clouds of millions of samples. The method is demonstrated for surface reconstruction of detail object scans as well as for spatially large point clouds obtained from environmental LiDaR scans.

In **Chapter 7**, Kaisarlis presents a systematic approach for geometric and dimensional tolerancing in reverse engineering mechanical parts. Tolerancing is a vital component of the accurate manufacturing process of such parts, both in terms of capturing such variability in a physical model and in terms of extracting tolerancing-related information from existing models and design artifacts using reverse engineering. A methodology is presented where tolerancing is explicitly modeled by means of a family of parameterizable tolerancing elements which can be assembled in tolerance chains. Applications are presented by means of three case studies related to the manufacturing of complex mechanical assemblies for optical sensor devices.

In **Chapter 8**, Chang presents a review of shape design and parameterization in the context of shape reverse engineering. Extracting 3D parameterizable NURBS surfaces from low-level scanned information, also called auto-surfacing, is an important modeling tool, as it allows designers to further modify the extracted surfaces on a high level. Although several auto-surfacing tools and techniques exist, not all satisfy the same requirements and up to the same level. The review discusses nine auto-surfacing tools from the viewpoint of 22 functional and non-functional requirements, and presents detailed evaluations of four such tools in real-world case studies involving auto-surfacing.

In **Chapter 9**, Mello *et al.* present a model for integration of mechanical reverse engineering (RE) with design for manufacturing and assembly (DFMA). Their work is motivated by the perceived added value in terms of lean development and manufacturing for organizations that succeed in combining the two types of activities. Using action research, they investigate the use of integrated RE and DFMA in two companies involved in manufacturing home fixture assemblies and machine measuring instruments respectively. Their detailed studies show concrete examples of the step-by-step application of integrated RE and DFMA and highlight the possible cost savings and related challenges.

Part 3: Reverse Engineering in Medical and Life Sciences

In part 3, our focus changes from industrial artifacts to artifacts related to *medical and life sciences*. Use-cases in this context relate mainly to the increased amounts of data acquired from such application domains which can support more detailed and/or accurate modeling and understanding of medical and biological phenomena. As such, reverse engineering has here a different flavor than in the first two parts of the book: Rather than recovering information lost during an earlier design process, the aim is to extract new information on natural processes in order to best understand the dynamics of such processes.

In **Chapter 10**, Yuji *et al.* present a method to reverse engineer the structure and dynamics of gene regulatory networks (GRNs). High amounts of gene-related data are available from various information sources, *e.g.* gene expression experoments, molecular interaction, and gene ontology databases. The challenges is how to find relationships between transcription factors and their potential target genes, given that one has to deal with noisy datasets containing tens of thousands of genes that act according to different temporal and spatial patterns, strongly interact among each others, and exhibit subsampling. A computational data mining framework is presented which integrates all above-mentioned information sources, and uses genetic algorithms based on particle swarm optimization techniques to find relationships of interest. Results are presented on two different cell datasets.

In **Chapter 11**, Mayo *et al.* present a reverse engineering activity that aims to create a predictive model of the dynamics of gas transfer (oxygen uptake) in mammalian lungs. The solution involves a combination of geometric modeling of the mammalian lung coarse-scale structure (lung airways), mathematical modeling of the gas transport equations, and an efficient way to solve the emerging system of diffusion-reaction equations by several modeling and numerical approximations. The proposed model is next validated in terms of predictive power by comparing its results with actual experimental measurements. All in all, the reverse engineering of the complex respiratory physical process can be used as an addition or replacement to more costly measuring experiments.

In **Chapter 12**, Cernescu *et al.* present a reverse engineering application in the context of dental engineering. The aim is to efficiently and effectively assess the mechanical quality of manufactured complete dentures in terms of their behavior to mechanical stresses *e.g.* detect areas likely to underperform or crack in normal operation mode. The reverse engineering pipeline presented covers the steps of 3D model acquisition by means of scanning and surface reconstruction, creation of a finite element mesh suitable for numerical simulations, and the actual computation of stress and strain factors in presence of induced model defects.

Challenges and Opportunities

From the material presented in this book, we conclude that reverse engineering is an active and growing field with an increasing number of applications. Technological progress is making increasingly more data sources of high accuracy and data volume available. There is also an increased demand across all application domains surveyed for cost-effective techniques able to reduce the total cost of development, operation, and maintenance of complex technical solutions. This demand triggers the need for increasingly accurate and detailed information of the structure, dynamics, and semantics of processes and artifacts involved in such solutions.

Reverse engineering can provide answers in the above directions. However, several challenges still exist. Numerous reverse engineering technologies and tools are still in the research phase, and need to be refined to deliver robust and detailed results on real-world datasets. Moreover, the increase in types of datasets and technologies available to reverse engineering poses challenges in terms of the cost-effective development of end-to-end solutions able to extract valuable insights from such data.

Prof. Dr. Alexandru C. Telea
Faculty of Mathematical and Natural Science
Institute Johann Bernoulli
University of Groningen
The Netherlands

Part 1

Software Reverse Engineering

1

Software Reverse Engineering in the Domain of Complex Embedded Systems

Holger M. Kienle[1], Johan Kraft[1] and Hausi A. Müller[2]
[1]*Mälardalen University*
[2]*University of Victoria*
[1]*Sweden*
[2]*Canada*

1. Introduction

This chapter focuses on tools and techniques for software reverse engineering in the domain of complex embedded systems. While there are many "generic" reverse engineering techniques that are applicable across a broad range of systems (e.g., slicing (Weiser, 1981)), complex embedded system have a set of characteristics that make it highly desirable to augment these "generic" techniques with more specialized ones. There are also characteristics of complex embedded systems that can require more sophisticated techniques compared to what is typically offered by mainstream tools (e.g., dedicated slicing techniques for embedded systems (Russell & Jacome, 2009; Sivagurunathan et al., 1997)). Graaf et al. (2003) state that "the many available software development technologies don't take into account the specific needs of embedded-systems development ... Existing development technologies don't address their specific impact on, or necessary customization for, the embedded domain. Nor do these technologies give developers any indication of how to apply them to specific areas in this domain." As we will see, this more general observations applies to reverse engineering as well.

Specifically, our chapter is motivated by the observation that the bulk of reverse engineering research targets software that is outside of the embedded domain (e.g., desktop and enterprise applications). This is reflected by a number of existing review/survey papers on software reverse engineering that have appeared over the years, which do not explicitly address the embedded domain (Canfora et al., 2011; Confora & Di Penta, 2007; Kienle & Müller, 2010; Müller & Kienle, 2010; Müller et al., 2000; van den Brand et al., 1997). Our chapter strives to help closing this gap in the literature. Conversely, the embedded systems community seems to be mostly oblivious of reverse engineering. This is surprising given that maintainability of software is an important concern in this domain according to a study in the vehicular domain (Hänninen et al., 2006). The study's authors "believe that facilitating maintainability of the applications will be a more important activity to consider due to the increasing complexity, long product life cycles and demand on upgradeability of the [embedded] applications."

Embedded systems are an important domain, which we opine should receive more attention of reverse engineering research. First, a significant part of software evolution is happening in this domain. Second, the reach and importance of embedded systems are growing with emerging trends such as ubiquitous computing and the Internet of Things. In this chapter we specifically focus on *complex embedded systems*, which are characterized by the following properties (Kienle et al., 2010; Kraft, 2010):

- large code bases, which can be millions of lines of code, that have been maintained over many years (i.e., "legacy")
- rapid growth of the code base driven by new features and the transition from purely mechanical parts to mechatronic ones
- operation in a context that makes them safety- and/or business-critical

The rest of the chapter is organized as follows. We first introduce the chapter's background in Section 2: reverse engineering and complex embedded systems. Specifically, we introduce key characteristics of complex embedded systems that need to be taken into account by reverse engineering techniques and tools. Section 3 presents a literature review of research in reverse engineering that targets embedded systems. The results of the review are twofold: it provides a better understanding of the research landscape and a starting point for researchers that are not familiar with this area, and it confirms that surprisingly little research can be found in this area. Section 4 focuses on timing analysis, arguably the most important domain-specific concern of complex embedded systems. We discuss three approaches how timing information can be extracted/synthesized to enable better understanding and reasoning about the system under study: executing time analysis, timing analysis based on timed automata and model checking, and simulation-based timing analysis. Section 5 provides a discussion of challenges and research opportunities for the reverse engineering of complex embedded systems, and Section 6 concludes the chapter with final thoughts.

2. Background

In this section we describe the background that is relevant for the subsequent discussion. We first give a brief introduction to reverse engineering and then characterize (complex) embedded systems.

2.1 Reverse engineering

Software reverse engineering is concerned with the analysis (not modification) of an existing (software) system (Müller & Kienle, 2010). The IEEE Standard for Software Maintenance (IEEE Std 1219-1993) defines reverse engineering as "the process of extracting software system information (including documentation) from source code." Generally speaking, the output of a reverse engineering activity is synthesized, higher-level information that enables the reverse engineer to better reason about the system and to evolve it in a effective manner. The process of reverse engineering typically starts with lower levels of information such as the system's source code, possibly also including the system's build environment. For embedded systems the properties of the underlying hardware and interactions between hardware and software may have to be considered as well.

When conducting a reverse engineering activity, the reverse engineer follows a certain process. The workflow of the reverse engineering process can be decomposed into three subtasks: extraction, analysis, and visualization (cf. Figure 1, middle). In practice, the reverse engineer has to iterate over the subtasks (i.e., each of these steps is repeated and refined several times) to arrive at the desired results. Thus, the reverse engineering process has elements that make it both ad hoc and creative.

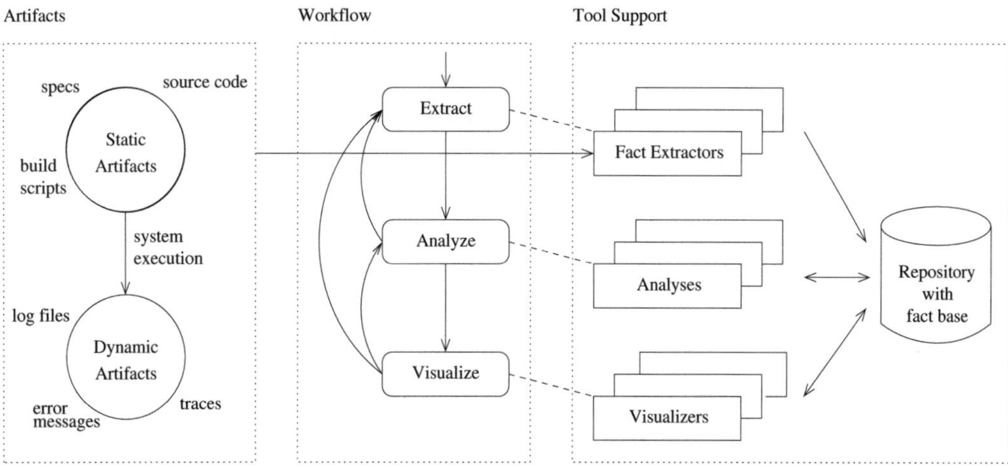

Fig. 1. High-level view of the reverse engineering process workflow, its inputs, and associated tool support.

For each of the subtasks tool support is available to assist the reverse engineer (cf. Figure 1, right). From the user's point of view, there may exist a single, integrated environment that encompasses all tool functionality in a seamless manner (tight coupling), or a number of dedicated stand-alone tools (weak coupling) (Kienle & Müller, 2010). Regardless of the tool architecture, usually there is some kind of a (central) repository that ties together the reverse engineering process. The repository stores information about the system under scrutiny. The information in the repository is structured according to a model, which is often represented as a data model, schema, meta-model or ontology.

When extracting information from the system, one can distinguish between static and dynamic approaches (cf. Figure 1, left). While static information can be obtained without executing the system, dynamic information collects information about the running system. (As a consequence, dynamic information describes properties of a single run or several runs, but these properties are not guaranteed to hold for all possible runs.) Examples of static information are source code, build scripts and specs about the systems. Examples of dynamic information are traces, but content in log files and error messages can be utilized as well. It is often desirable to have both static and dynamic information available because it gives a more holistic picture of the target system.

2.2 Complex embedded systems

The impact and tremendous growth of embedded systems is often not realized: they account for more than 98% of the produced microprocessors (Ebert & Jones, 2009; Zhao et al., 2003). There is a wide variety of embedded systems, ranging from RFID tags and household appliances over automotive components and medical equipment to the control of nuclear power plants. In the following we restrict our discussion mostly to complex embedded systems.

Complex embedded software systems are typically special-purpose systems developed for control of a physical process with the help of sensors and actuators. They are often mechatronic systems, requiring a combination of mechanical, electronic, control, and computer engineering skills for construction. These characteristics already make it apparent that complex embedded systems differ from desktop and business applications. Typical non-functional requirements in this domain are safety, maintainability, testability, reliability and robustness, safety, portability, and reusability (Ebert & Salecker, 2009; Hänninen et al., 2006). From a business perspective, driving factors are cost and time-to-market (Ebert & Jones, 2009; Graaf et al., 2003).

While users of desktop and web-based software are accustomed to software bugs, users of complex embedded systems are by far less tolerant of malfunction. Consequently, embedded systems often have to meet high quality standards. For embedded systems that are safety-critical, society expects software that is free of faults that can lead to (physical) harm (e.g., consumer reaction to cases of unintended acceleration of Toyota cars (Cusumano, 2011)). In fact, manufacturers of safety-critical devices have to deal with safety standards and consumer protection laws (Åkerholm et al., 2009). In case of (physical) injuries caused by omissions or negligence, the manufacturer may be found liable to monetarily compensate for an injury (Kaner, 1997). The Economist claims that "product-liability settlements have cost the motor industry billions" (The Economist, 2008), and Ackermann et al. (2010) say that for automotive companies and their suppliers such as Bosch "safety, warranty, recall and liability concerns ... require that software be of high quality and dependability."

A major challenge is the fact that complex embedded systems are becoming more complex and feature-rich, and that the growth rate of embedded software in general has accelerated as well (Ebert & Jones, 2009; Graaf et al., 2003; Hänninen et al., 2006). For the automotive industry, the increase in software has been exponential, starting from zero in 1976 to more than 10 million lines of code that can be found in a premium car 30 years later (Broy, 2006). Similar challenges in terms of increasing software are faced by the avionics domain (both commercial and military) as well; a fighter plane can have over 7 million lines of code (Parkinson, n.d.) and alone the flight management system of a commercial aircraft's cockpit is around 1 million lines of code (Avery, 2011). Software maintainers have to accommodate this trend without sacrificing key quality attributes. In order to increase confidence in complex embedded systems, verification techniques such as reviews, analyses, and testing can be applied. According to one study "testing is the main technique to verify functional requirements" (Hänninen et al., 2006). Ebert and Jones say that "embedded-software engineers must know and use a richer combination of defect prevention and removal activities than other software domains" Ebert & Jones (2009).

Complex embedded systems are *real-time systems*, which are often designed and implemented as a set of tasks[1] that can communicate with each other via mechanisms such as message queues or shared memory. While there are off-line scheduling techniques that can guarantee the timeliness of a system if certain constraints are met, these constraints are too restrictive for many complex embedded systems. In practice, these systems are implemented on top of a real-time operating system that does online scheduling of tasks, typically using preemptive fixed priority scheduling (FPS).[2] In FPS scheduling, each task has a scheduling priority, which typically is determined at design time, but priorities may also change dynamically during

[1] A task is "the basic unit of work from the standpoint of a control program" RTCA (1992). It may be realized as an operating system process or thread.

[2] An FPS scheduler always executes the task of highest priority being ready to execute (i.e., which is not, e.g., blocked or waiting), and when preemptive scheduling is used, the executing task is immediately preempted when a higher priority task is in a ready state.

run-time. In the latter case, the details of the temporal behavior (i.e., the exact execution order) becomes an emerging property of the system at run-time. Worse, many complex embedded systems are *hard real-time systems*, meaning that a single missed deadline of a task is considered a failure. For instance, for Electronic Control Units (ECUs) in vehicles as much as 95% of the functionality is realized as hard real-time tasks (Hänninen et al., 2006). The deadline of tasks in an ECU has a broad spectrum: from milliseconds to several seconds.

The real-time nature of complex embedded systems means that maintainers and developers have to deal with the fact that the system's correctness also depends on *timeliness* in the sense that the latency between input and output should not exceed a specific limit (the deadline). This is a matter of timing predictability, not average performance, and therefore poses an additional burden on verification via code analyses and testing. For example, instrumenting the code may alter its temporal behavior (i.e., probing effect (McDowell & Helmbold, 1989)). Since timing analysis arguably is the foremost challenge in this domain, we address it in detail in Section 4.

The following example illustrates why it can be difficult or infeasible to automatically derive timing properties for complex embedded systems (Bohlin et al., 2009). Imagine a system that has a task that processes messages that arrive in a queue:

```
do {
  msg = receive_msg(my_msg_queue);
  process_msg(msg);
} while (msg != NO_MESSAGE);
```

The loop's execution time obviously depends on the messages in the queue. Thus, a timing analysis needs to know the maximum queue length. It also may have to consider that other tasks may preempt the execution of the loop and add messages to the queue.

Besides timing constraints there are other resource constraints such as limited memory (RAM and ROM), power consumption, communication bandwidth, and hardware costs (Graaf et al., 2003). The in-depth analysis of resource limitations if often dispensed with by over-dimensioning hardware (Hänninen et al., 2006). Possibly, this is the case because general software development technologies do not offer features to effectively deal with these constraints (Graaf et al., 2003).

Even though many complex embedded systems are safety-critical, or at least business-critical, they are often developed in traditional, relatively primitive and unsafe programming languages such as C/C++ or assembly.[3] As a general rule, the development practice for complex embedded systems in industry is not radically different from less critical software systems; formal verification techniques are rarely used. Such methods are typically only applied to truly safety-critical systems or components. (Even then, it is no panacea as formally proven software might still be unsafe (Liggesmeyer & Trapp, 2009).)

Complex embedded systems are often legacy systems because they contain millions of lines of code and are developed and maintained by dozens or hundreds of engineers over many years.

[3] According to Ebert & Jones (2009), C/C++ and assembly is used by more than 80 percent and 40 percent of companies, respectively. Another survey of 30 companies found 57% use of C/C++, 20% use of assembly, and 17% use of Java (Tihinen & Kuvaja, 2004).

Thus, challenges in this domain are not only related to software development per se (i.e., "green-field development"), but also in particular to software maintenance and evolution (i.e., "brown-field development"). Reverse engineering tools and techniques can be used—also in combination with other software development approaches—to tackle the challenging task of evolving such systems.

3. Literature review

As mentioned before, surprisingly little research in reverse engineering targets embedded systems. (Conversely, one may say that the scientific communities of embedded and real-time systems are not pursuing software reverse engineering research.) Indeed, Marburger & Herzberg (2001) did observe that "in the literature only little work on reverse engineering and re-engineering of embedded systems has been described." Before that, Bull et al. (1995) had made a similar observation: "little published work is available on the maintenance or reverse engineering specific to [safety-critical] systems."

Searching on IEEE Xplore for "software reverse engineering" and "embedded systems" yields 2,702 and 49,211 hits, respectively.[4] There are only 83 hits that match both search terms. Repeating this approach on Scopus showed roughly similar results:[5] 3,532 matches for software reverse engineering and 36,390 for embedded systems, and a union of 92 which match both. In summary, less than 4% of reverse engineering articles found in Xplore or Scopus are targeting embedded systems.

The annual IEEE Working Conference on Reverse Engineering (WCRE) is dedicated to software reverse engineering and arguably the main target for research of this kind. Of its 598 publication (1993–2010) only 4 address embedded or real-time systems in some form.[6] The annual IEEE International Conference on Software Maintenance (ICSM) and the annual IEEE European Conference on Software Maintenance and Reengineering (CSMR) are also targeted by reverse engineering researchers even though these venues are broader, encompassing software evolution research. Of ICSM's 1165 publications (1993–2010) there are 10 matches; of CSMR's 608 publications (1997-2010) there are 4 matches. In summary, less than 1% of reverse engineering articles of WCRE, ICSM and CSMR are targeting embedded systems.

The picture does not change when examining the other side of the coin. A first indication is that overview and trend articles of embedded systems' software (Ebert & Salecker, 2009; Graaf et al., 2003; Hänninen et al., 2006; Liggesmeyer & Trapp, 2009) do not mention reverse engineering. To better understand if the embedded systems research community publishes reverse engineering research in their own sphere, we selected a number of conferences and journals that attract papers on embedded systems (with an emphasis on software, rather than hardware): Journal of Systems Architecture – Embedded Systems Design

[4] We used the advanced search feature (`http://ieeexplore.ieee.org/search/advsearch.jsp`) on all available content, matching search terms in the metadata only. The search was performed September 2011.

[5] Using the query string `TITLE-ABS-KEY(reverse engineering) AND SUBJAREA(comp OR math)`, `TITLE-ABS-KEY(embedded systems) AND SUBJAREA(comp OR math)` and `TITLE-ABS-KEY(reverse engineering embedded systems) AND SUBJAREA(comp OR math)`. The search string is applied to title, abstract and keywords.

[6] We used FacetedDBLP (`http://dblp.l3s.de`), which is based on Michael Ley's DBLP, to obtain this data. We did match "embedded" and "real-time" in the title and keywords (where available) and manually verified the results.

(JSA); Languages, Compilers, and Tools for Embedded Systems (LCTES); ACM Transactions on Embedded Computing Systems (TECS); and International Conference / Workshop on Embedded Software (EMSOFT). These publications have a high number of articles with "embedded system(s)" in their metadata.[7] Manual inspection of these papers for matches of "reverse engineering" in their metadata did not yield a true hit.

In the following, we briefly survey reverse engineering research surrounding (complex) embedded systems. Publications can be roughly clustered into the following categories:

- summary/announcement of a research project:
  - Darwin (van de Laar et al., 2011; 2007)
  - PROGRESS (Kraft et al., 2011)
  - E-CARES (Marburger & Herzberg, 2001)
  - ARES (Obbink et al., 1998)
  - Bylands (Bull et al., 1995)
- an embedded system is used for
  - a comparison of (generic) reverse engineering tools and techniques (Bellay & Gall, 1997) (Quante & Begel, 2011)
  - an industrial experience report or case study involving reverse engineering for
    - design/architecture recovery (Kettu et al., 2008) (Eixelsberger et al., 1998) (Ornburn & Rugaber, 1992)
    - high-level language recovery (Ward, 2004) (Palsberg & Wallace, 2002)
    - dependency graphs (Yazdanshenas & Moonen, 2011)
    - idiom extraction (Bruntink, 2008; Bruntink et al., 2007)
- a (generic) reverse engineering method/process is applied to—or instantiated for—an embedded system as a case study (Arias et al., 2011) (Stoermer et al., 2003) (Riva, 2000; Riva et al., 2009) (Lewis & McConnell, 1996)
- a technique is proposed that is specifically targeted at—or "coincidentally" suitable for—(certain kinds of) embedded systems:
  - slicing (Kraft, 2010, chapters 5 and 6) (Russell & Jacome, 2009) (Sivagurunathan et al., 1997)
  - clustering (Choi & Jang, 2010) (Adnan et al., 2008)
  - object identification (Weidl & Gall, 1998)
  - architecture recovery (Marburger & Westfechtel, 2010) (Bellay & Gall, 1998) (Canfora et al., 1993)
  - execution views (Arias et al., 2008; 2009)
  - tracing (Kraft et al., 2010) (Marburger & Westfechtel, 2003) (Arts & Fredlund, 2002)
  - timing simulation models (Andersson et al., 2006) (Huselius et al., 2006) (Huselius & Andersson, 2005)
  - state machine reconstruction (Shahbaz & Eschbach, 2010) (Knor et al., 1998)

[7] According to FacetedDBLP, for EMSOFT 121 out of 345 articles (35%) match, and for TECS 125 out of 327 (38%) match. According to Scopus, for JSA 269 out of 1,002 (27%) and for LCTES 155 out of 230 (67%) match.

For the above list of publications we did not strive for completeness; they are rather meant to give a better understanding of the research landscape. The publications have been identified based on keyword searches of literature databases as described at the beginning of this section and then augmented with the authors' specialist knowledge.

In Section 5 we discuss selected research in more detail.

4. Timing analysis

A key concern for embedded systems is their timing behavior. In this section we describe static and dynamic timing analyses. We start with a summary of software development—i.e., forward engineering from this chapter's perspective—for real-time systems. For our discussion, forward engineering is relevant because software maintenance and evolution intertwine activities of forward and reverse engineering. From this perspective, forward engineering provides input for reverse engineering, which in turn produces input that helps to drive forward engineering.

Timing-related analyses during forward engineering are state-of-the-practice in industry. This is confirmed by a study, which found that "analysis of real-time properties such as response-times, jitter, and precedence relations, are commonly performed in development of the examined applications" (Hänninen et al., 2006). Forward engineering offers many methods, technique, and tools to specify and reason about timing properties. For example, there are dedicated methodologies for embedded systems to design, analyze, verify and synthesize systems (Åkerholm et al., 2007). These methodologies are often based on a component model (e.g., AUTOSAR, BlueArX, COMDES-II, Fractal, Koala, and ProCom) coupled with a modeling/specification language that allows to specify timing properties (Crnkovic et al., 2011). Some specification languages extend UML with a real-time profile (Gherbi & Khendek, 2006). The OMG has issued the UML Profile for Schedulability, Performance and Time (SPL) and the UML Profile for Modeling and Analysis of Real-time and Embedded Systems (MARTE).

In principle, reverse engineering approaches can target forward engineering's models. For example, synthesis of worst-case execution times could be used to populate properties in a component model, and synthesis of models based on timed automata could target a suitable UML Profile. In the following we discuss three approaches that enable the synthesis of timing information from code. We then compare the approaches and their applicability for complex embedded systems.

4.1 Execution time analysis

When modeling a real-time system for analysis of timing related properties, the model needs to contain execution time information, that is, the amount of CPU time needed by each task (when executing undisturbed). To verify safe execution for a system the *worst-case execution time* (WCET) for each task is desired. In practice, timing analysis strives to establish a tight upper bound of the WCET (Lv et al., 2009; Wilhelm et al., 2008).[8] The results of the WCET Tool Challenge (executed in 2006, 2008 and 2011) provide a good starting point for understanding the capabilites of industrial and academic tools (`www.mrtc.mdh.se/projects/WCC/`).

[8] For a non-trivial program and execution environment the true WCET is often unknown.

Static WCET analysis tools analyze the system's source or binary code, establishing timing properties with the help of a hardware model. The accuracy of the analysis greatly depends on the accuracy of the underlying hardware model. Since the hardware model cannot precisely model the real hardware, the analysis has to make conservative, worst case assumptions in order to report a save WCET estimate. Generally, the more complex the hardware, the less precise the analysis and the looser the upper bound. Consequently, on complex hardware architectures with cache memory, pipelines, branch prediction tables and out-of-order execution, tight WCET estimation is difficult or infeasible. Loops (or back edges in the control flow graph) are a problem if the number of iterations cannot be established by static analysis. For such case, users can provide annotations or assertions to guide the analyses. Of course, to obtain valid results it is the user's responsibility to provide valid annotations. Examples of industrial tools are AbsInt's aiT (`www.absint.com/ait/`) and Tidorum's Bound-T (`www.bound-t.com`); SWEET (`www.mrtc.mdh.se/projects/wcet`) and OTAWA (`www.otawa.fr`) are academic tools.

There are also *hybrid approaches* that combine static analysis with run-time measures. The motivation of this approach is to avoid (or minimize) the modeling of the various hardware. Probabilistic WCET (or pWCET), combines program analysis with execution-time measurements of basic-blocks in the control flow graph (Bernat et al., 2002; 2003). The execution time data is used to construct a probabilistic WCET for each basic block, i.e., an execution time with a specified probability of not being exceeded. Static analysis combines the blocks' pWCETs, producing a total pWCET for the specified code. This approach is commercially available as RapiTime (`www.rapitasystems.com/products/RapiTime`). AbsInt's TimeWeaver (`www.absint.com/timeweaver/`) is another commercial tool that uses a hybrid approach.

A common method in industry is to obtain timing information by performing measurements of the real system as it is executed under realistic conditions. The major problem with this approach is the coverage; it is very hard to select test cases which generate high execution times and it is not possible to know if the worst case execution time (WCET) has been observed. Some companies try to compensate this to some extent through a "brute force" approach, where they systematically collect statistics from deployed systems, over long periods of real operation. This is however very dependent on how the system has been used and is still an "optimistic" approach, as the real WCET might be higher than the highest value observed.

Static and dynamic approaches have different trade-offs. Static approaches have, in principle, the benefit that results can be obtained without test harnesses and environment simulations. On the other hand, the dependence on a hardware timing model is a major criticism against the static approach, as it is an abstraction of the real hardware behavior and might not describe all effects of the real hardware. In practice, tools support a limited number of processors (and may have further restrictions on the compiler that is used to produce the binary to be analyzed). Bernat et al. (2003) argues that static WCET analysis for real complex software, executing on complex hardware, is "extremely difficult to perform and results in unacceptable levels of pessimism." Hybrid approaches are not restricted by the hardware's complexity, but run-time measurements may be also difficult and costly to obtain.

WCET is a prerequisite for *schedulability or feasibility analysis* (Abdelzaher et al., 2004; Audsley et al., 1995). (Schedulability is the ability of a system to meet all of its timing constraints.)

While these analyses have been successively extended to handle more complex (scheduling) behavior (e.g., semaphores, deadlines longer than the periods, and variations (jitter) in the task periodicity), they still use a rather simplistic system model and make assumptions which makes them inapplicable or highly pessimistic for embedded software systems which have not been designed with such analysis in mind. Complex industrial systems often violate the assumptions of schedulability analyses by having tasks which

- trigger other tasks in complex, often undocumented, chains of task activations depending on input
- share data with other tasks (e.g., through global variables or inter-process communication)
- have radically different behavior and execution time depending on shared data and input
- change priorities dynamically (e.g., as on-the-fly solution to identified timing problems during operation)
- have timing requirements expressed in functional behavior rather than explicit task deadline, such as availability of data in input buffers at task activation

As a result, schedulability analyses are overly pessimistic for complex embedded systems since they do not take behavioral dependencies between tasks into account. (For this reason, we do not discuss them in more detail in this chapter.) Analyzing complex embedded systems requires a more detailed system model which includes relevant behavior as well as resource usage of tasks. Two approaches are presented in the following where more detailed behavior models are used: model checking and discrete event simulation.

4.2 Timing analysis with model checking

Model checking is a method for verifying that a model meets formally specified requirements. By describing the behavior of a system in a model where all constructs have formally defined semantics, it is possible to automatically verify properties of the modeled system by using a model checking tool. The model is described in a modeling language, often a variant of finite-state automata. A system is typically modeled using a network of automata, where the automata are connected by synchronization channels. When the model checking tool is to analyze the model, it performs a *parallel composition*, resulting in a single, much larger automaton describing the complete system. The properties that are to be checked against the model are usually specified in a temporal logic (e.g., CTL (Clarke & Emerson, 1982) or LTL (Pnueli, 1977)). Temporal logics allow specification of safety properties (i.e., "something (bad) will never happen"), and liveness properties (i.e., "something (good) must eventually happen").

Model checking is a general approach, as it can be applied to many domains such as hardware verification, communication protocols and embedded systems. It has been proposed as a method for software verification, including verification of timeliness properties for real-time systems. Model checking has been shown to be usable in industrial settings for finding subtle errors that are hard to find using other methods and, according to Katoen (1998), case studies have shown that the use of model checking does not delay the design process more than using simulation and testing.

SPIN (Holzmann, 2003; 1997) is a well established tool for model checking and simulation of software. According to SPIN's website (`wwww.spinroot.com`), it is designed to scale well and can perform exhaustive verification of very large state-space models. SPIN's modeling language, Promela, is a guarded command language with a C-like syntax. A Promela model roughly consists of a set of sequential processes, local and global variables and communication channels. Promela processes may communicate using communication channels. A channel is a fixed-size FIFO buffer. The size of the buffer may be zero; in such a case it is a synchronization operation, which blocks until the send and receive operations can occur simultaneously. If the buffer size is one or greater, the communication becomes asynchronous, as a send operation may occur even though the receiver is not ready to receive. Formulas in linear temporal logic (LTL) are used to specify properties that are then checked against Promela models.[9] LTL is classic propositional logic extended with temporal operators (Pnueli, 1977). For example, the LTL formula `[] (l U e)` uses the temporal operators always (`[]`) and strong until (`U`). The logical propositions l and e could be electrical signals, e.g., in a washing machine, where l is true if the door is locked, and e is true if the machine is empty of water, and thereby safe to open. The LTL formula in the above example then means "the door must never open while there is still water in the machine."

Model checkers such as SPIN do not have a notion of quantitative time and can therefore not analyze requirements on timeliness, e.g., "if x, then y must occur within 10 ms". There are however tools for model checking of real-time systems that rely on timed automata for modeling and Computation Tree Logic (CTL) (Clarke & Emerson, 1982) for checking.

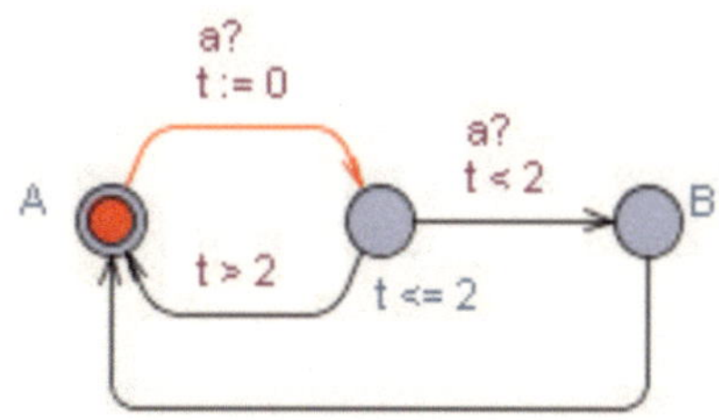

Fig. 2. Example of a timed automaton in UppAal.

A *timed automata* may contain an arbitrary number of clocks, which run at the same rate. (There are also extensions of timed automata where clocks can have different rates (Daws & Yovine, 1995).) The clocks may be reset to zero, independently of each other, and used in conditions on state transitions and state invariants. A simple yet illustrative example is presented in Figure 2, from the UppAal tool. The automaton changes state from A to B if event a occurs twice within 2 time units. There is a clock, t, which is reset after an initial occurrence of event a. If the clock reaches 2 time units before any additional event a arrives, the invariant on the middle state forces a state transition back to the initial state A.

CTL is a branching-time temporal logic, meaning that in each moment there may be several possible futures, in contrast to LTL. Therefore, CTL allows for expressing possibility properties such as "in the future, x may be true", which is not possible in LTL.[10] A CTL formula consists of a state formula and a path formula. The state formulae describe properties of individual states, whereas path formulae quantify over paths, i.e., potential executions of the model.

[9] Alternatively, one can insert "assert" commands in Promela models.

[10] On the other hand, CTL cannot express fairness properties, such as "if x is scheduled to run, it will eventually run". Neither of these logics fully includes the other, but there are extensions of CTL, such as CTL* (Emerson & Halpern, 1984), which subsume both LTL and CTL.

Both the UppAal and KRONOS model checkers are based on timed automata and CTL. **UppAal** (`www.uppaal.org` and `www.uppaal.com`) (David & Yi, 2000) is an integrated tool environment for the modeling, simulation and verification of real-time systems. UppAal is described as "appropriate for systems that can be modeled as a collection of non-deterministic processes with finite control structure and real-valued clocks, communicating through channels or shared variables." In practice, typical application areas include real-time controllers and communication protocols where timing aspects are critical. UppAal extends timed automata with support for, e.g., automaton templates, bounded integer variables, arrays, and different variants of restricted synchronization channels and locations. The query language uses a simplified version of CTL, which allows for reachability properties, safety properties and liveness properties. Timeliness properties are expressed as conditions on clocks and state in the state formula part of the CTL formulae.

The **Kronos** tool[11] (`www-verimag.imag.fr/DIST-TOOLS/TEMPO/kronos/`) (Bozga et al., 1998) has been developed with "the aim to verify complex real-time systems." It uses an extension of CTL, Timed Computation Tree Logic (TCTL) (Alur et al., 1993), allowing to express quantitative time for the purpose of specifying timeliness properties, i.e., liveness properties with a deadline.

For model checking of complex embedded systems, the *state-space explosion* problem is a limiting factor. This problem is caused by the effect that the number of possible states in the system easily becomes very large as it grows exponentially with the number of parallel processes. Model checking tools often need to search the state space exhaustively in order to verify or falsify the property to check. If the state space becomes too large, it is not possible to perform this search due to memory or run time constraints.

For complex embedded systems developed in a traditional code-oriented manner, no analyzable models are available and model checking therefore typically requires a significant modeling effort.[12] In the context of reverse engineering, the key challenge is the construction of an analysis model with sufficient detail to express the (timing) properties that are of interest to the reverse engineering effort. Such models can be only derived semi-automatically and may contain modeling errors. A practical hurdle is that different model checkers have different modeling languages with different expressiveness.

Modex/FeaVer/AX (Holzmann & Smith, 1999; 2001) is an example of a model extractor for the SPIN model checker. Modex takes C code and creates Promela models by processing all basic actions and conditions of the program with respect to a set of rules. A case study of Modex involving NASA legacy flight software is described by Glück & Holzmann (2002). Modex's approach effectively moves the effort from manual modeling to specifying patterns that match the C statements that should be included in the model (Promela allows for including C statements) and what to ignore. There are standard rules that can be used, but the user may add their own rules to improve the quality of the resulting model. However, as explained before, Promela is not a suitable target for real-time systems since it does not have a notion of quantitative time. Ulrich & Petrenko (2007) describe a method that synthesizes models from traces of a UMTS radio network. The traces are based on test case executions

[11] Kronos is not longer under active development.

[12] The model checking community tends to assume a model-driven development approach, where the model to analyze also is the system's specification, which is used to automatically generate the system's code (Liggesmeyer & Trapp, 2009).

and record the messages exchanged between network nodes. The desired properties are specified as UML2 diagrams. For model checking with SPIN, the traces are converted to Promela models and the UML2 diagrams are converted to Promela never-claims. Jensen (1998; 2001) proposed a solution for automatic generation of behavioral models from recordings of a real-time systems (i.e. model synthesis from traces). The resulting model is expressed as UppAal timed automata. The aim of the tool is verification of properties such as response time of an implemented system against implementation requirements. For the verification it is assumed that the requirements are available as UppAal timed automata which are then parallel composed with the synthesized model to allow model checking.

While model checking itself is now a mature technology, reverse engineering and checking of timing models for complex embedded system is still rather immature. Unless tools emerge that are industrial-strength and allow configurable model extraction, the modeling effort is too elaborate, error-prone and risky. After producing the model one may find that it cannot be analyzed with realistic memory and run time constraints. Lastly, the model must be kept in sync with the system's evolution.

4.3 Simulation-based timing analysis

Another method for analysis of response times of software systems, and for analysis of other timing-related properties, is the use of *discrete event simulation*,[13] or simulation for short. Simulation is the process of imitating key characteristics of a system or process. It can be performed on different levels of abstraction. At one end of the scale, simulators such as Wind River Simics (`www.windriver.com/products/simics/`) are found, which simulates software and hardware of a computer system in detail. Such simulators are used for low-level debugging or for hardware/software co-design when software is developed for hardware that does not physically exist yet. This type of simulation is considerably slower than normal execution, typically orders of magnitudes slower, but yields an exact analysis which takes every detail of the behavior and timing into account. At the other end of the scale we find scheduling simulators, who abstract from the actual behavior of the system and only analyzes the scheduling of the system's tasks, specified by key scheduling attributes and execution times. One example in this category is the approach by Samii et al. (2008). Such simulators are typically applicable for strictly periodic real-time systems only. Simulation for complex embedded systems can be found in the middle of this scale. In order to accurately simulate a complex embedded system, a suitable simulator must take relevant aspects of the task behavior into account such as aperiodic tasks, triggered by messages from other tasks or interrupts. Simulation models may contain non-deterministic or probabilistic selections, which enables to model task execution times as probability distributions.

Using simulation, rich modeling languages can be used to construct very realistic models. Often ordinary programming languages, such as C, are used in combination with a special simulation library. Indeed, the original system code can be treated as (initial) system model. However, the goal for a simulation models is to abstract from the original system. For example, atomic code blocks can be abstracted by replacing them with a "hold CPU" operation.

---

[13] Law & Kelton (1993) define discrete event simulation as "modeling of a system as it evolves over time by a representation in which the state variables change instantaneously at separate points in time." This definition naturally includes simulation of computer-based systems.

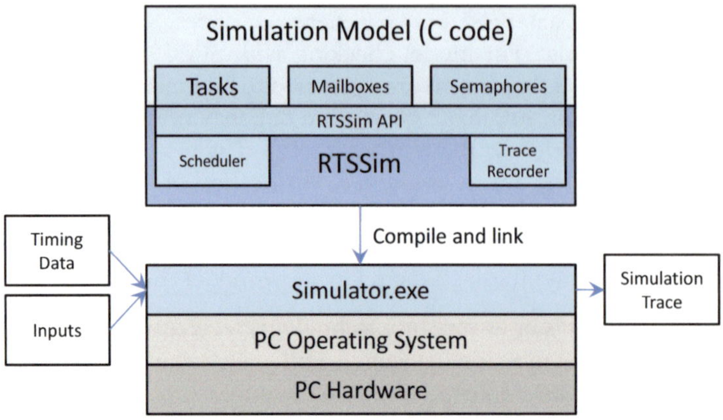

Fig. 3. Architecture of the RTSSim tool.

Examples of simulation tools are ARTISST (`www.irisa.fr/aces/software/artisst/`) (Decotigny & Puaut, 2002), DRTSS (Storch & Liu, 1996), RTSSim (Kraft, 2009), and VirtualTime (`www.rapitasystems.com/virtualtime`). Since these tools have similar capabilites we only describe RTSSim in more detail. **RTSSim** was developed for the purpose of simulation-based analysis of run-time properties related to timing, performance and resource usage, targeting complex embedded systems where such properties are otherwise hard to predict. RTSSim has been designed to provide a generic simulation environment which provides functionality similar to most real-time operating systems (cf. Figure 3). It offers support for tasks, mailboxes and semaphores. Tasks have attributes such as priority, periodicity, activation time and jitter, and are scheduled using preemptive fixed-priority scheduling. Task-switches can only occur within RTSSim API functions (e.g., during a "hold CPU"); other model code always executes in an atomic manner. The simulation can exhibit "stochastic" behavior via random variations in task release time specified by the jitter attribute, in the increment of the simulation clock, etc.

To obtain timing properties and traces, the simulation has to be driven by suitable input. A typical goal is to determine the highest observed response time for a certain task. Thus, the result of the simulation greatly depends on the chosen sets of input. Generally, a random search (traditional Monte Carlo simulation) is not suitable for worst-case timing analysis, since a random subset of the possible scenarios is a poor predictor for the worst-case execution time. *Simulation optimization* allows for efficient identification of extreme scenarios with respect to a specified measurable run-time property of the system. MABERA and HCRR are two heuristic search methods for RTSSim. MABERA (Kraft et al., 2008) is a genetic algorithm that treats RTSSim as a black-box function, which, given a set of simulation parameters, outputs the highest response-time found during the specified simulation. The genetic algorithm determines how the simulation parameters are changed for the next search iteration. HCRR (Bohlin et al., 2009), in contrast, uses a hill climbing algorithm. It is based on the idea of starting at a random point and then repeatedly taking small steps pointing "upwards", i.e., to nearby input combinations giving higher response times. Random restarts are used to avoid getting stuck in local maxima. In a study that involved a subset of an industrial complex embedded system, HCRR performed substantially better than both Monte Carlo simulation and the MABERA (Bohlin et al., 2009).

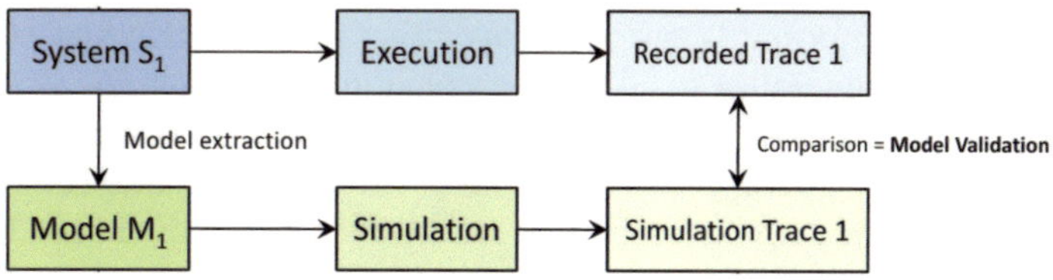

Fig. 4. Conceptual view of model validation with tracing data.

It is desirable to have a model that is substantially smaller than the real system. A smaller model can be more effectively simulated and reasoned about. It is also easier to evolve. Since the simulator can run on high-performance hardware and the model contains only the characteristics that are relevant for the properties in focus, a simulation run can be much faster than execution of the real system. Coupled with simulator optimization, significantly more (diverse) scenarios can be explored. A simulation model also allows to explore scenarios which are difficult to generate with the real system, and allows impact analyses of hypothetical system changes.

Reverse engineering is used to construct such simulation models (semi-)automatically. The **MASS** tool (Andersson et al., 2006) supports the semi-automatic extraction of simulation models from C code. Starting from the entry function of a task, the tool uses dependency analysis to guide the inclusion of relevant code for that task. For so-called model-relevant functions the tool generates a code skeleton by removing irrelevant statements. This skeleton is then interactively refined by the user. Program slicing is another approach to synthesize models. The Model eXtraction Tool for C (MTXC) (Kraft, 2010, chapter 6) takes as input a set of model focus functions of the real system and automatically produces a model via slicing. However, the tool is not able to produce an executable slice that can be directly used as simulation input. In a smaller case study involving a subset of an embedded system, a reduction of code from 3994 to 1967 (49%) lines was achieved. Huselius & Andersson (2005) describe a dynamic approach to obtain a simulation model based on tracing data containing interprocess communications from the real system. The raw tracing data is used to synthesize a probabilistic state-machine model in the ART-ML modeling language, which can be then run with a simulator.

For each model that abstracts from the real system, there is the concern whether the model's behavior is a reasonable approximation of the real behavior (Huselius et al., 2006). This concern is addressed by *model validation*, which can be defined as the "substantiation that a computerized model within its domain of applicability possesses a satisfactory range of accuracy consistent with the intended application of the model" (Schlesinger et al., 1979). Software simulation models can be validated by comparing trace data of the real system versus the model (cf. Figure 4). There are many possible approaches, including statistical and subjective validation techniques (Balci, 1990). Kraft describes a five-step validation process that combines both subjective and statistical comparisons of tracing data (Kraft, 2010, chapter 8).

4.4 Comparison of approaches

In the following we summarize and compare the different approaches to timing analysis with respect to three criteria: soundness, scalability and applicability to industrial complex embedded systems. An important concern is *soundness* (i.e., whether the obtained timing results are guaranteed to generalize to all system executions). Timing analysis via executing the actual system or a model thereof cannot give guarantees (i.e., the approach is unsound), but heuristics to effectively guide the runs can be used to improve the confidence into the obtained results.[14] A sound approach operates under the assumptions that the underlying model is valid. For WCET the tool is trusted to provide a valid hardware model; for model checking the timing automata are (semi-automatically) synthesized from the system and thus model validation is highly desirable.[15]

Since both model synthesis and validation involve manual effort, scalability to large systems is a major concern for both model checking and simulation. However, at this time simulation offers better tool support and less manual effort. Another scalability concern for model checking is the state-space explosion problem. One can argue that improvements in model checking techniques and faster hardware alleviate this concern, but this is at least partially countered by the increasing complexity of embedded systems. Simulation, in contrast, avoids the state-space explosion problem by sacrificing the guaranteed safety of the result. In a simulation, the state space of the model is sampled rather than searched exhaustively.

With respect to applicability, execution time analysis (both static and hybrid) are not suitable for complex embedded systems and it appears this will be the case for the foreseeable future. The static approach is restricted to smaller systems with simple hardware; the hybrid approach does overcome the problem to model the hardware, but is still prohibitive for systems with nontrivial scheduling regimes and data/control dependencies between tasks. Model checking is increasingly viable for model-driven approaches, but mature tool support is lacking to synthesize models from source code. Thus, model checking may be applicable in principle, but costs are significant and as a result a more favorable cost-to-benefit ratio likely can be obtained by redirection effort elsewhere. Simulation arguably is the most attractive approach for industry, but because it is unsound a key concern is quality assurance. Since industry is very familiar with another unsound technique, testing, expertise from testing can be relatively easily transferred to simulation. Also, synthesis of models seems feasible with reasonable effort even though mature tool support is still lacking.

5. Discussion

Based on the review of reverse engineering literature (cf. Section 3) and our own expertise in the domain of complex embedded system we try to establish the current state-of-the-art/practice and identify research challenges.

It appears that industry is starting to realize that approaches are needed that enable them to maintain and evolve their complex embedded "legacy" systems in a more effective and predictable manner. There is also the realization that reverse engineering techniques are one important enabling factor to reach this goal. An indication of this trend is the Darwin

[14] This is similar to the problems of general software testing; the method can only be used to show the presence of errors, not to prove the absence of errors. Nonetheless, a simulation-based analysis can identify extreme scenarios, e.g., very high response-times which may violate the system requirements, even though worst case scenarios are not identified.

[15] The simulation community has long recognized the need for model validation, while the model checking community has mostly neglected this issue.

project (van de Laar et al., 2011), which was supported by Philips and has developed reverse engineering tools and techniques for complex embedded systems using a Philips MRI scanner (8 million lines of code) as a real-world case study. Another example is the E-CARES project, which was conducted in cooperation with Ericsson Eurolab and looked at the AXE10 telecommunications system (approximately 10 millions of lines of PLEX code developed over about 40 years) (Marburger & Herzberg, 2001; Marburger & Westfechtel, 2010).

In the following we structure the discussion into static/dynamic fact extraction, followed by static and dynamic analyses.

5.1 Fact extraction

Obtaining facts from the source code or the running system is the first step for each reverse engineering effort. Extracting static facts from complex embedded systems is challenging because they often use C/C++, which is difficult to parse and analyze. While C is already challenging to parse (e.g., due to the C preprocessor) , C++ poses additional hurdles (e.g., due to templates and namespaces). Edison Design Group (EDG) offers a full front-end for C/C++, which is very mature and able to handle a number of different standards and dialects. Maintaining such a front end is complex; according to EDG it has more than half a million lines of C code of which one-third are comments. EDG's front end is used by many compiler vendors and static analysis tools (e.g., Coverity, CodeSurfer, Axivion's Bauhaus Suite, and the ROSE compiler infrastructure). Coverity's developers believe that the EDG front-end "probably resides near the limit of what a profitable company can do in terms of front-end gyrations," but also that it "still regularly meets defeat when trying to parse real-world large code bases" (Bessey et al., 2010). Other languages that one can encounter in the embedded systems domain—ranging from assembly to PLEX and Erlang—all have their own idiosyncratic challenges. For instance, the Erlang language has many dynamic features that make it difficult to obtain precise and meaningful static information.

Extractors have to be robust and scalable. For C there are now a number of tools available with fact extractors that are suitable for complex embedded system. Examples of tools with fine-grained fact bases are Coverity, CodeSurfer, Columbus (`www.frontendart.com`), Bauhaus (`www.axivion.com/`), and the Clang Static Analyzer (`clang-analyzer.llvm.org/`); an example of a commercial tool with a course-grained fact base is Understand (`www.scitools.com`). For fine-grained extractors, scalability is still a concern for larger systems of more than half a million of lines of code; coarse-grained extractors can be quite fast while handling very large systems. For example, in a case study the Understand tool extracted facts from a system with more than one million of lines of C code in less than 2 minutes (Kraft, 2010, page 144). In another case study, it took CodeSurfer about 132 seconds to process about 100,000 lines of C code (Yazdanshenas & Moonen, 2011).

Fact extractors typically focus on a certain programming language per se, neglecting the (heterogeneous) environment that the code interacts with. Especially, fact extractors do not accommodate the underlying hardware (e.g., ports and interrupts), which is mapped to programming constructs or idioms in some form. Consequently, it is difficult or impossible for down-stream analyses to realize domain-specific analyses. In C code for embedded systems one can often find embedded assembly. Depending on the C dialect, different constructs are used.[16] Robust extractors can recognize embedded assembly, but analyzing it is beyond their capabilites (Balakrishnan & Reps, 2010).

Extracting facts from the running system has the advantage that generic monitoring functionality is typically provided by the hardware and the real-time operating system. However, obtaining finer-grained facts of the system's behavior is often prohibitive because of the monitoring overhead and the probing effect. The amount of tracing data is restricted by the hardware resources. For instance, for ABB robots around 10 seconds (100,000 events) of history are available, which are kept in a ring buffer (Kraft et al., 2010). For the Darwin project, Arias et al. (2011) say "we observed that practitioners developing large and complex software systems desire minimal changes in the source code [and] minimal overhead in the system response time." In the E-CARES project, tracing data could be collected within an emulator (using a virtual time mode); since tracing jobs have highest priority, in the real environment the system could experience timing problems (Marburger & Herzberg, 2001).

For finer-grained tracing data, strategic decisions on what information needs to be traced have to be made. Thus, data extraction and data use (analysis and visualization) have to be coordinated. Also, to obtain certain events the source code may have to be selectively instrumented in some form. As a result, tracing solutions cannot exclusively rely on generic approaches, but need to be tailored to fit a particular goal. The Darwin project proposes a tailorable architecture reconstruction approach based on logging and run-time information. The approach makes "opportunistic" use of existing logging information based on the assumption that "logging is a feature often implemented as part of large software systems to record and store information of their specific activities into dedicated files" (Arias et al., 2011).

After many years of research on scalable and robust static fact extractors, mature tools have finally emerged for C, but they are still challenged by the idiosyncracies of complex embedded systems. For C++ we are not aware of solutions that have reached a level of maturity that matches C, especially considering the latest iteration of the standard, C++11. Extraction of dynamic information is also more challenging for complex embedded systems compared to desktop applications, but they are attractive because for many systems they are relatively easy to realize while providing valuable information to better understand and evolve the system.

5.2 Static analyses

Industry is using static analysis tools for the evolution of embedded systems and there is a broad range of them. Examples of common static checks include stack space analysis, memory leakage, race conditions, and data/control coupling. Examples of tools are PC-lint (Gimpel Software), CodeSurfer, and Coverity Static Analysis. While these checkers are not strictly reverse engineering analyses, they can aid program understanding.

Static checkers for complex embedded systems face several adoption hurdles. Introducing them for an existing large system produces a huge amount of diagnostic messages, many of which are false positives. Processing these messages requires manual effort and is often prohibitively expensive. (For instance, Boogerd & Moonen (2009) report on a study where

[16] The developers of the Coverity tool say (Bessey et al., 2010): "Assembly is the most consistently troublesome construct. It's already non-portable, so compilers seem to almost deliberately use weird syntax, making it difficult to handle in a general way."

30% of the lines of code in an industrial system triggered non-conformance warnings with respect to MISRA C rules.) For complex embedded systems, analyses for concurrency bugs are most desirable. Unfortunately, Ornburn & Rugaber (1992) "have observed that because of the flexibility multiprocessing affords, there is an especially strong temptation to use ad hoc solutions to design problems when developing real-time systems." Analyses have a high rate of false positives and it is difficult to produce succinct diagnostic messages that can be easily confirmed or refuted by programmers. In fact, Coverity's developers says that "for many years we gave up on checkers that flagged concurrency errors; while finding such errors was not too difficult, explaining them to many users was" (Bessey et al., 2010).

Generally, compared to Java and C#, the features and complexity of C—and even more so of C++—make it very difficult or impossible to realize robust and precise static analyses that are applicable across all kinds of code bases. For example, analysis of pointer arithmetic in C/C++ is a prerequisite to obtain precise static information, but in practice pointer analysis is a difficult problem and consequently there are many approaches that exhibit different trade-offs depending on context-sensitivity, heap modeling, aggregate modeling, etc. (Hind, 2001). For C++ there are additional challenges such as dynamic dispatch and template metaprogramming. In summary, while these general approaches to static code analysis can be valuable, we believe that they should be augmented with more dedicated (reverse engineering) analyses that take into account specifically the target system's peculiarities (Kienle et al., 2011).

Architecture and design recovery is a promising reverse engineering approach for system understanding and evolution (Koschke, 2009; Pollet et al., 2007). While there are many tools and techniques very few are targeted at, or applied to, complex embedded systems. Choi & Jang (2010) describe a method to recursively synthesize components from embedded software. At the lowest level components have to be identified manually. The resulting component model can then be validated using model simulation or model checking techniques. Marburger & Westfechtel (2010) present a tool to analyze PLEX code, recovering architectural information. The static analysis identifies blocks and signaling between blocks, both being key concepts of PLEX. Based on this PLEX-specific model, a higher-level description is synthesized, which is described in the ROOM modeling language. The authors state that Ericssons' "experts were more interested in the coarse-grained structure of the system under study rather than in detailed code analysis." Research has identified the need to construct architectural viewpoints that address communication protocols and concurrency as well as timing properties such as deadlines and throughput of tasks (e.g., (Eixelsberger et al., 1998; Stoermer et al., 2003)), but concrete techniques to recover them are missing.

Static analyses are often geared towards a single programming language. However, complex embedded system can be heterogenous. The Philips MRI scanner uses many languages, among them C, C++/STL, C#, VisualBasic and Perl (Arias et al., 2011); the AXE10 system's PLEX code is augmented with C++ code (Marburger & Westfechtel, 2010); Kettu et al. (2008) talk about a complex embedded system that "is based on C/C++/Microsoft COM technology and has started to move towards C#/.NET technology, with still the major and core parts of the codebase remaining in old technologies." The reverse engineering community has neglected (in general) multi-language analyses, but they would be desirable—or are often necessary—for complex embedded systems (e.g., recovery of communication among tasks implemented in different languages). One approach to accommodate heterogenous systems with less tooling effort could be to focus on binaries and intermediate representations rather than source code (Kettu et al., 2008). This approach is most promising if source code is transformed to an underlying intermediate representation or virtual machine (e.g., Java bytecode or .NET CIL code) because in this case higher-level information is often preserved. In contrast, if source code is translated to machine-executable binaries, which is typically the case for C/C++, then most of the higher-level information is lost. For example, for C++ the binaries often do not allow to reconstruct all classes and their inheritance relationships (Fokin et al., 2010).

Many complex embedded systems have features of a product line (because the software supports a portfolio of different devices). Reverse engineering different configurations and variablity points would be highly desirable. A challenge is that often ad hoc techniques are used to realize product lines. For instance, Kettu et al. (2008) describe a C/C++ system that uses a number different techniques such as conditional compilation, different source files and linkages for different configurations, and scripting. Generally, there is research addressing product lines (e.g., (Alonso et al., 1998; Obbink et al., 1998; Stoermer et al., 2003)), but there are no mature techniques or tools of broader applicability.

5.3 Dynamic analyses

Research into dynamic analyses have increasingly received more attention in the reverse engineering community. There are also increasingly hybrid approaches that combine both static and dynamic techniques. Dynamic approaches typically provide information about a single execution of the system, but can also accumulate information of multiple runs.

Generally, since dynamic analyses naturally produce (time-stamped) event sequences, they are attractive for understanding of timing properties in complex embedded systems. The Tracealyzer is an example of a visualization tool for embedded systems focusing on high-level runtime behavior, such as scheduling, resource usage and operating system calls (Kraft et al., 2010). It displays task traces using a novel visualization technique that focuses on the task preemption nesting and only shows active tasks at a given point in time. The Tracealyzer is used systematically at ABB Robotics and its approach to visualization has proven useful for troubleshooting and performance analysis. The E-CARES project found that "structural [i.e., static] analysis ... is not sufficient to understand telecommunication systems" because they are highly dynamic, flexible and reactive (Marburger & Westfechtel, 2003). E-CARES uses tracing that is configurable and records events that relate to signals and assignments to selected state variables. Based on this information UML collaboration and sequence diagrams are constructed that can be shown and animated in a visualizer. The Darwin project relies on dynamic analyses and visualization for reverse engineering of MRI scanners. Customizable mapping rules are used to extract events from logging and run-time measurements to construct so-called execution viewpoints. For example, there are visualizations that show with different granularity the system's resource usage and start-up behavior in terms of execution times of various tasks or components in the system (Arias et al., 2009; 2011).

Cornelissen et al. (2009) provide a detailed review of existing research in dynamic analyses for program comprehension. They found that most research focuses on object-oriented software and that there is little research that targets distributed and multi-threaded applications. Refocusing research more towards these neglected areas would greatly benefit complex embedded systems. We also believe that research into hybrid analyses that augment static information with dynamic timing properties is needed.

Runtime verification and monitoring is a domain that to our knowledge has not been explored for complex embedded systems yet. While most work in this area addresses Java, Havelund (2008) presents the RMOR framework for monitoring of C systems. The idea of runtime verification is to specify dynamic system behavior in a modeling language, which can then be checked against the running system. (Thus, the approach is not sound because conformance is always established with respect to a single run.) In RMOR, expected behavior is described as state machines (which can express safety and liveness properties). RMOR then instruments the system and links it with the synthesized monitor. The development of RMOR has been driven in the context of NASA embedded systems, and two case studies are briefly presented, one of them showing "the need for augmenting RMOR with the ability to express time constraints."

6. Conclusion

This chapter has reviewed reverse engineering techniques and tools that are applicable for complex embedded systems. From a research perspective, it is unfortunate that the research communities of reverse engineering and embedded and real-time systems are practically disconnected. As we have argued before, embedded systems are an important target for reverse engineering, offering unique challenges compared to desktop and business applications.

Since industry is dealing with *complex* embedded systems, reverse engineering tools and techniques have to scale to larger code bases, handle the idiosyncracies of industrial code (e.g., C dialects with embedded assembly), and provide domain-specific solutions (e.g., synthesis of timing properties). For industrial practitioners, adoption of research techniques and tools has many hurdles because it is very difficult to assess the applicability and suitability of proposed techniques and the quality of existing tools. There are huge differences in quality of both commercial and research tools and different tools often fail in satisfying different industrial requirements so that no tool meets all of the minimum requirements. Previously, we have argued that the reverse engineering community should elevate adoptability of their tools as a key requirement for success (Kienle & Müller, 2010). However, this needs to go hand in hand with a change in research methodology towards more academic-industrial collaboration as well as a change in the academic rewards structure.

Just as in other domains, reverse engineering for complex embedded systems is facing adoption hurdles because tools have to show results in a short time-frame and have to integrate smoothly into the existing development process. Ebert & Salecker (2009) observe that for embedded systems "research today is fragmented and divided into technology, application, and process domains. It must provide a consistent, systems-driven framework for systematic modeling, analysis, development, test, and maintenance of embedded software in line with embedded systems engineering." Along with other software engineering areas, reverse engineering research should take up this challenge.

Reverse engineering may be able to profit from, and contribute to, research that recognizes the growing need to analyze systems with multi-threading and multi-core. Static analyses and model checking techniques for such systems may be applicable to complex embedded systems as well. Similarly, research in runtime-monitoring/verification and in the visualization of streaming applications may be applicable to certain kinds of complex embedded systems.

Lastly, reverse engineering for complex embedded systems is facing an expansion of system boundaries. For instance, medical equipment is no longer a stand-alone system, but a node in the hospital network, which in turn is connected to the Internet. Car navigation and driver assistance can be expected to be increasingly networked. Similar developments are underway for other application areas. Thus, research will have to broaden its view towards software-intensive systems and even towards systems of systems.

7. References

Abdelzaher, L. S. T., Arzen, K.-E., Cervin, A., Baker, T., Burns, A., Buttazzo, G., Caccamo, M., Lehoczky, J. & Mok, A. K. (2004). Real time scheduling theory: A historical perspective, *Real-Time Systems* 28(2–3): 101–155.

Ackermann, C., Cleaveland, R., Huang, S., Ray, A., Shelton, C. & Latronico, E. (2010). *1st International Conference on Runtime Verification (RV 2010)*, Vol. 6418 of *Lecture Notes in Computer Science*, Springer-Verlag, chapter Automatic Requirements Extraction from Test Cases, pp. 1–15.

Adnan, R., Graaf, B., van Deursen, A. & Zonneveld, J. (2008). Using cluster analysis to improve the design of component interfaces, *23rd IEEE/ACM International Conference on Automated Software Engineering (ASE'08)* pp. 383–386.

Åkerholm, M., Carlson, J., Fredriksson, J., Hansson, H., Håkansson, J., Möller, A., Pettersson, P. & Tivoli, M. (2007). The SAVE approach to component-based development of vehicular systems, *Journal of Systems and Software* 80(5): 655–667.

Åkerholm, M., Land, R. & Strzyz, C. (2009). Can you afford not to certify your control system?, *iVTinternational* p. 16. http://www.ivtinternational.com/legislative_focus_nov.php.

Alonso, A., Garcia-Valls, M. & de la Puente, J. A. (1998). Assessment of timing properties of family products, *Development and Evolution of Software Architectures for Product Families, Second International ESPRIT ARES Workshop*, Vol. 1429 of *Lecture Notes in Computer Science*, Springer-Verlag, pp. 161–169.

Alur, R., Courcoubetis, C. & Dill, D. L. (1993). Model-checking in dense real-time, *Information and Computation* 104(1): 2–34. http://citeseer.ist.psu.edu/viewdoc/versions?doi=10.1.1.26.7610.

Andersson, J., Huselius, J., Norström, C. & Wall, A. (2006). Extracting simulation models from complex embedded real-time systems, *1st International Conference on Software Engineering Advances (ICSEA 2006)*.

Arias, T. B. C., Avgeriou, P. & America, P. (2008). Analyzing the actual execution of a large software-intensive system for determining dependencies, *15th IEEE Working Conference on Reverse Engineering (WCRE'08)* pp. 49–58.

Arias, T. B. C., Avgeriou, P. & America, P. (2009). Constructing a resource usage view of a large and complex software-intensive system, *16th IEEE Working Conference on Reverse Engineering (WCRE'09)* pp. 247–255.

Arias, T. B. C., Avgeriou, P., America, P., Blom, K. & Bachynskyyc, S. (2011). A top-down strategy to reverse architecting execution views for a large and complex software-intensive system: An experience report, *Science of Computer Programming* 76(12): 1098–1112.

Arts, T. & Fredlund, L.-A. (2002). Trace analysis of Erlang programs, *ACM SIGPLAN Erlang Workshop (ERLANG'02)*.

Audsley, N. C., Burns, A., Davis, R. I., Tindell, K. W. & Wellings, A. J. (1995). Fixed priority pre-emptive scheduling: An historical perspective, *Real-Time Systems* 8(2–3): 173–198.

Avery, D. (2011). The evolution of flight management systems, *IEEE Software* 28(1): 11–13.

Balakrishnan, G. & Reps, T. (2010). WYSINWYX: What you see is not what you eXecute, *ACM Transactions on Programming Languages and Systems* 32(6): 23:1–23:84.

Balci, O. (1990). Guidelines for Successful Simulation Studies, *Proceedings of the 1990 Winter Simulation Conference*, Department of Computer Science, Virginia Polytechnic Institute and State University, Blacksburg, Virginia 2061-0106, USA.

Bellay, B. & Gall, H. (1997). A comparison of four reverse engineering tools, *4th IEEE Working Conference on Reverse Engineering (WCRE'97)* pp. 2–11.

Bellay, B. & Gall, H. (1998). Reverse engineering to recover and describe a system's architecture, *Development and Evolution of Software Architectures for Product Families, Second International ESPRIT ARES Workshop*, Vol. 1429 of *Lecture Notes in Computer Science*, Springer-Verlag, pp. 115–122.

Bernat, G., Colin, A. & Petters, S. (2002). WCET Analysis of Probabilistic Hard Real-Time Systems, *Proceedings of the 23rd IEEE International Real-Time Systems Symposium (RTSS'02), Austin, TX, USA*.

Bernat, G., Colin, A. & Petters, S. (2003). pWCET: a Tool for Probabilistic Worst Case Execution Time Analysis of Real-Time Systems, *Technical Report YCS353*, University of York, Department of Computer Science, United Kingdom.

Bessey, A., Block, K., Chelfs, B., Chou, A., Fulton, B., Hallem, S., Henri-Gros, C., Kamsky, A., McPeak, S. & Engler, D. (2010). A few billion lines of code later: Using static analysis to find bugs in the real world, *Communications of the ACM* 53(2): 66–75.

Bohlin, M., Lu, Y., Kraft, J., Kreuger, P. & Nolte, T. (2009). Simulation-Based Timing Analysis of Complex Real-Time Systems, *Proceedings of the 15th IEEE International Conference on Embedded and Real-Time Computing Systems and Applications (RTCSA'09)*, pp. 321–328.

Boogerd, C. & Moonen, L. (2009). Evaluating the relation between coding standard violations and faults within and across software versions, *6th Working Conference on Mining Software Repositories (MSR'09)* pp. 41–50.

Bozga, M., Daws, C., Maler, O., Olivero, A., Tripakis, S. & Yovine, S. (1998). Kronos: A Model-Checking Tool for Real-Time Systems, *in* A. J. Hu & M. Y. Vardi (eds), *Proceedings of the 10th International Conference on Computer Aided Verification, Vancouver, Canada*, Vol. 1427, Springer-Verlag, pp. 546–550.

Broy, M. (2006). Challenges in automotive software engineering, *28th ACM/IEEE International Conference on Software Engineering (ICSE'06)* pp. 33–42.

Bruntink, M. (2008). Reengineering idiomatic exception handling in legacy C code, *12th IEEE European Conference on Software Maintenance and Reengineering (CSMR'08)* pp. 133–142.

Bruntink, M., van Deursen, A., D'Hondt, M. & Tourwe, T. (2007). Simple crosscutting concerns are not so simple: analysing variability in large-scale idioms-based implementations, *6th International Conference on Aspect-Oriented Software Development (AOSD'06)* pp. 199–211.

Bull, T. M., Younger, E. J., Bennett, K. H. & Luo, Z. (1995). Bylands: reverse engineering safety-critical systems, *International Conference on Software Maintenance (ICSM'95)* pp. 358–366.

Canfora, G., Cimitile, A. & De Carlini, U. (1993). A reverse engineering process for design level document production from ada code, *Information and Software Technology* 35(1): 23–34.

Canfora, G., Di Penta, M. & Cerulo, L. (2011). Achievements and challenges in software reverse engineering, *Communications of the ACM* 54(4): 142–151.

Choi, Y. & Jang, H. (2010). Reverse engineering abstract components for model-based development and verification of embedded software, *12th IEEE International Symposium on High-Assurance Systems Engineering (HASE'10)* pp. 122–131.

Clarke, E. M. & Emerson, E. A. (1982). Design and synthesis of synchronization skeletons using branching-time temporal logic, *Logic of Programs, Workshop*, Springer-Verlag, London, UK, pp. 52–71.

Confora, G. & Di Penta, M. (2007). New frontiers of reverse engineering, *Future of Software Engineering (FOSE'07)* pp. 326–341.

Cornelissen, B., Zaidman, A., van Deursen, A., Moonen, L. & Koschke, R. (2009). A systematic survey of program comprehension through dynamic analysis, *IEEE Transactions on Software Engineering* 35(5): 684–702.

Crnkovic, I., Sentilles, S., Vulgarakis, A. & Chaudron, M. R. V. (2011). A classification framework for software component models, *IEEE Transactions on Software Engineering* 37(5): 593–615.

Cusumano, M. A. (2011). Reflections on the Toyota debacle, *Communications of the ACM* 54(1): 33–35.

David, A. & Yi, W. (2000). Modelling and analysis of a commercial field bus protocol, *Proceedings of 12th Euromicro Conference on Real-Time Systems*, IEEE Computer Society Press, pp. 165–172.

Daws, C. & Yovine, S. (1995). Two examples of verification of multirate timed automata with kronos, *Proceedings of the 16th IEEE Real-Time Systems Symposium (RTSS'95)*, IEEE Computer Society, Washington, DC, USA, p. 66.

Decotigny, D. & Puaut, I. (2002). ARTISST: An extensible and modular simulation tool for real-time systems, *5th IEEE International Symposium on Object-Oriented Real-Time Distributed Computing (ISORC'02)* pp. 365–372.

Ebert, C. & Jones, C. (2009). Embedded software: Facts, figures and future, *IEEE Computer* 42(4): 42–52.

Ebert, C. & Salecker, J. (2009). Embedded software—technologies and trends, *IEEE Software* 26(3): 14–18.

Eixelsberger, W., Kalan, M., Ogris, M., Beckman, H., Bellay, B. & Gall, H. (1998). Recovery of architectural structure: A case study, *Development and Evolution of Software Architectures for Product Families, Second International ESPRIT ARES Workshop*, Vol. 1429 of *Lecture Notes in Computer Science*, Springer-Verlag, pp. 89–96.

Emerson, E. A. & Halpern, J. Y. (1984). Sometimes and Not Never Revisited: on Branching Versus Linear Time, *Technical report*, University of Texas at Austin, Austin, TX, USA.

Fokin, A., Troshina, K. & Chernov, A. (2010). Reconstruction of class hierarchies for decompilation of C++ programs, *14th IEEE European Conference on Software Maintenance and Reengineering (CSMR'10)* pp. 240–243.

Gherbi, A. & Khendek, F. (2006). UML profiles for real-time systems and their applications, *Journal of Object Technology* 5(4). `http://www.jot.fm/issues/issue_2006_05/article5`.

Glück, P. R. & Holzmann, G. J. (2002). Using SPIN model checking for flight software verification, *IEEE Aerospace Conference (AERO'02)* pp. 1–105–1–113.

Graaf, B., Lormans, M. & Toetenel, H. (2003). Embedded software engineering: The state of the practice, *IEEE Software* 20(6): 61–69.

Hänninen, K., Mäki-Turja, J. & Nolin, M. (2006). Present and future requirements in developing industrial embedded real-time systems – interviews with designers in the vehicle domain, *13th Annual IEEE International Symposium and Workshop on Engineering of Computer Based Systems (ECBS'06)* pp. 139–147.

Havelund, K. (2008). *Runtime Verification of C Programs*, Vol. 5047 of *Lecture Notes in Computer Science*, Springer-Verlag, chapter Testing of Software and Communicating Systems (TestCom/FATES'08), pp. 7–22.

Hind, M. (2001). Pointer analysis: Haven't we solved this problem yet?, *ACM SIGPLAN/SIGSOFT Workshop on Program Analysis for Software Tools and Engineering (PASTE'01)* pp. 54–61.

Holzmann, G. (2003). *The SPIN Model Checker: Primer and Reference Manual*, Addison-Wesley.

Holzmann, G. J. (1997). The Model Checker SPIN, *IEEE Trans. Softw. Eng.* 23(5): 279–295.

Holzmann, G. J. & Smith, M. H. (1999). A practical method for verifying event-driven software, *Proceedings of the 21st international conference on Software engineering (ICSE'99)*, IEEE Computer Society Press, Los Alamitos, CA, USA, pp. 597–607.

Holzmann, G. J. & Smith, M. H. (2001). Software model checking: extracting verification models from source code, *Software Testing, Verification and Reliability* 11(2): 65–79.

Huselius, J. & Andersson, J. (2005). Model synthesis for real-time systems, *9th IEEE European Conference on Software Maintenance and Reengineering (CSMR 2005)*, pp. 52–60.

Huselius, J., Andersson, J., Hansson, H. & Punnekkat, S. (2006). Automatic generation and validation of models of legacy software, *12th IEEE International Conference on Embedded and Real-Time Computing Systems and Applications (RTCSA 2006)*, pp. 342–349.

Jensen, P. K. (1998). Automated Modeling of Real-Time Implementation, *Technical Report BRICS RS-98-51*, University of Aalborg.

Jensen, P. K. (2001). *Reliable Real-Time Applications. And How to Use Tests to Model and Understand*, PhD thesis, Aalborg University.

Kaner, C. (1997). Software liability. `http://www.kaner.com/pdfs/theories.pdf`.

Katoen, J. (1998). Concepts, algorithms and tools for model checking, lecture notes of the course Mechanised Validation of Parallel Systems, Friedrich-Alexander University at Erlangen-Nurnberg.

Kettu, T., Kruse, E., Larsson, M. & Mustapic, G. (2008). *Architecting Dependable Systems V*, Vol. 5135 of *Lecture Notes in Computer Science*, Springer-Verlag, chapter Using Architecture Analysis to Evolve Complex Industrial Systems, pp. 326–341.

Kienle, H. M., Kraft, J. & Nolte, T. (2010). System-specific static code analyses for complex embedded systems, *4th International Workshop on Software Quality and Maintainability (SQM 2010), sattelite event of the 14th European Conference on Software Maintenance and Reengineering (CSMR 2010)*. `http://holgerkienle.wikispaces.com/file/view/KKN-SQM-10.pdf`.

Kienle, H. M., Kraft, J. & Nolte, T. (2011). System-specific static code analyses: A case study in the complex embedded systems domain, *Software Quality Journal*. Forthcoming, `http://dx.doi.org/10.1007/s11219-011-9138-7`.

Kienle, H. M. & Müller, H. A. (2010). The tools perspective on software reverse engineering: Requirements, construction and evaluation, *Advances in Computers* 79: 189–290.

Knor, R., Trausmuth, G. & Weidl, J. (1998). Reengineering C/C++ source code by transforming state machines, *Development and Evolution of Software Architectures for Product Families, Second International ESPRIT ARES Workshop*, Vol. 1429 of *Lecture Notes in Computer Science*, Springer-Verlag, pp. 97–105.

Koschke, R. (2009). Architecture reconstruction: Tutorial on reverse engineering to the architectural level, *in* A. De Lucia & F. Ferrucci (eds), *ISSSE 2006–2008*, Vol. 5413 of *Lecture Notes in Computer Science*, Springer-Verlag, pp. 140–173.

Kraft, J. (2009). RTSSim – a simulation framework for complex embedded systems, *Technical Report*, Mälardalen University. `http://www.mrtc.mdh.se/index.php?choice=publications&id=1629`.

Kraft, J. (2010). *Enabling Timing Analysis of Complex Embedded Systems*, PhD thesis no. 84, Mälardalen University, Sweden. `http://mdh.diva-portal.org/smash/get/diva2:312516/FULLTEXT01`.

Kraft, J., Kienle, H. M., Nolte, T., Crnkovic, I. & Hansson, H. (2011). Software maintenance research in the PROGRESS project for predictable embedded software systems, *15th IEEE European Conference on Software Maintenance and Reengineering (CSMR 2011)* pp. 335–338.

Kraft, J., Lu, Y., Norström, C. & Wall, A. (2008). A Metaheuristic Approach for Best Effort Timing Analysis targeting Complex Legacy Real-Time Systems, *Proceedings of the IEEE Real-Time and Embedded Technology and Applications Symposium (RTAS'08)*.

Kraft, J., Wall, A. & Kienle, H. (2010). *1st International Conference on Runtime Verification (RV 2010)*, Vol. 6418 of *Lecture Notes in Computer Science*, Springer-Verlag, chapter Trace Recording for Embedded Systems: Lessons Learned from Five Industrial Projects, pp. 315–329.

Law, A. M. & Kelton, W. D. (1993). *Simulation, Modeling and Analysis*, ISBN: 0-07-116537-1, McGraw-Hill.

Lewis, B. & McConnell, D. J. (1996). Reengineering real-time embedded software onto a parallel processing platform, *3rd IEEE Working Conference on Reverse Engineering (WCRE'96)* pp. 11–19.

Liggesmeyer, P. & Trapp, M. (2009). Trends in embedded software engineering, *IEEE Software* 26(3): 19–25.

Lv, M., Guan, N., Zhang, Y., Deng, Q., Yu, G. & Zhang, J. (2009). A survey of WCET analysis of real-time operating systems, *2009 IEEE International Conference on Embedded Software and Systems* pp. 65–72.

Marburger, A. & Herzberg, D. (2001). E-CARES research project: Understanding complex legacy telecommunication systems, *5th IEEE European Conference on Software Maintenance and Reengineering (CSMR'01)* pp. 139–147.

Marburger, A. & Westfechtel, B. (2003). Tools for understanding the behavior of telecommunication systems, *25th Internatinal Conference on Software Engineering (ICSE'03)* pp. 430–441.

Marburger, A. & Westfechtel, B. (2010). Graph-based structural analysis for telecommunication systems, *Graph transformations and model-driven engineering*, Vol. 5765 of *Lecture Notes in Computer Science*, Springer-Verlag, pp. 363–392.

McDowell, C. E. & Helmbold, D. P. (1989). Debugging concurrent programs, *ACM Computing Surveys* 21(4): 593–622.

Müller, H. A. & Kienle, H. M. (2010). *Encyclopedia of Software Engineering*, Taylor & Francis, chapter Reverse Engineering, pp. 1016–1030. http://www.tandfonline.com/doi/abs/10.1081/E-ESE-120044308.

Müller, H., Jahnke, J., Smith, D., Storey, M., Tilley, S. & Wong, K. (2000). Reverse engineering: A roadmap, *Conference on The Future of Software Engineering* pp. 49–60.

Obbink, H., Clements, P. C. & van der Linden, F. (1998). Introduction, *Development and Evolution of Software Architectures for Product Families, Second International ESPRIT ARES Workshop*, Vol. 1429 of *Lecture Notes in Computer Science*, Springer-Verlag, pp. 1–3.

Ornburn, S. B. & Rugaber, S. (1992). Reverse engineering: resolving conflicts between expected and actual software designs, *8th IEEE International Conference on Software Maintenance (ICSM'92)* pp. 32–40.

Palsberg, J. & Wallace, M. (2002). Reverse engineering of real-time assembly code. http://www.cs.ucla.edu/~palsberg/draft/palsberg-wallace02.pdf.

Parkinson, P. J. (n.d.). The challenges and advances in COTS software for avionics systems. http://blogs.windriver.com/parkinson/files/IET_COTSaviation_PAUL_PARKINSON_paper.pdf.

Pnueli, A. (1977). The temporal logic of programs, *18th IEEE Annual IEEE Symposium on Foundations of Computer Science (FOCS'77)*, pp. 46–57.

Pollet, D., Ducasse, S., Poyet, L., Alloui, I., Cimpan, S. & Verjus, H. (2007). Towards a process-oriented software architecture reconstruction taxonomy, *11th IEEE European Conference on Software Maintenance and Reengineering (CSMR'07)* pp. 137–148.

Quante, J. & Begel, A. (2011). ICPC 2011 industrial challenge. http://icpc2011.cs.usask.ca/conf_site/IndustrialTrack.html.

Riva, C. (2000). Reverse architecting: an industrial experience report, *7th IEEE Working Conference on Reverse Engineering (WCRE'00)* pp. 42–50.

Riva, C., Selonen, P., Systä, T. & Xu, J. (2009). A profile-based approach for maintaining software architecture: an industrial experience report, *Journal of Software Maintenance and Evolution: Research and Practice* 23(1): 3–20.

RTCA (1992). Software considerations in airborne systems and equipment certification, *Standard RTCA/DO-17B*, RTCA.

Russell, J. T. & Jacome, M. F. (2009). Program slicing across the hardware-software boundary for embedded systems, *International Journal of Embedded Systems* 4(1): 66–82.

Samii, S., Rafiliu, S., Eles, P. & Peng, Z. (2008). A Simulation Methodology for Worst-Case Response Time Estimation of Distributed Real-Time Systems, *Proceedings of Design, Automation, and Test in Europe (DATE'08)*, pp. 556–561.

Schlesinger, S., Crosbie, R. E., Gagne, R. E., Innis, G. S., Lalwani, C. S. & Loch, J. (1979). Terminology for Model Credibility, *Simulation* 32(3): 103–104.

Shahbaz, M. & Eschbach, R. (2010). Reverse engineering ECUs of automotive components, *First International Workshop on Model Inference In Testing (MIIT'10)* pp. 21–22.

Sivagurunathan, Y., Harman, M. & Danicic, S. (1997). Slicing, I/O and the implicit state, *3rd International Workshop on Automatic Debugging (AADEBUG'97)* pp. 59–67. http://www.ep.liu.se/ea/cis/1997/009/06/.

Stoermer, C., O'Brien, L. & Verhoef, C. (2003). Moving towards quality attribute driven software architecture reconstruction, *10th IEEE Working Conference on Reverse Engineering (WCRE'03)* pp. 46–56.

Storch, M. & Liu, J.-S. (1996). DRTSS: A Simulation Framework for Complex Real-Time Systems, *2nd IEEE Real-Time Technology and Applications Symposium (RTAS'96)*, pp. 160–169.

The Economist (2008). Driven to distraction: Why autonomous cars are still a pipe-dream. April 25, `http://www.economist.com/node/11113185`.

Tihinen, M. & Kuvaja, P. (2004). Embedded software development: State of the practice. `http://www.vtt.fi/moose/docs/oulu/embedded_sw_development_tihinen_kuvaja.pdf`.

Ulrich, A. & Petrenko, A. (2007). *3rd European conference on Model driven architecture-foundations and applications (ECMDA-FA'07)*, Vol. 4530 of *Lecture Notes in Computer Science*, Springer-Verlag, chapter Reverse Engineering Models from Traces to Validate Distributed Systems – An Industrial Case Study, pp. 184–193.

van de Laar, P., Douglas, A. U. & America, P. (2011). *Views on the Evolvability of Embedded Systems*, Springer-Verlag, chapter Researching Evolvability, pp. 1–20.

van de Laar, P., van Loo, S., Muller, G., Punter, T., Watts, D., America, P. & Rutgers, J. (2007). The Darwin project: Evolvability of software-intensive systems, *3rd IEEE Workshop on Software Evolvability (EVOL'07)* pp. 48–53.

van den Brand, M. G. J., Klint, P. & Verhoef, C. (1997). Reverse engineering and system renovation–an annotated bibliography, *SIGSOFT Software Engineering Notes* 22(1): 57–68.

Ward, M. P. (2004). Pigs from sausages? reengineering from assembler to C via FermaT transformations, *Science of Computer Programming* 52(1–3): 213–255.

Weidl, J. & Gall, H. (1998). Binding object models to source code: An approach to object-oriented re-architecting, *22nd IEEE International Computer Software and Applications Conference (COMPSAC'98)* pp. 26–31.

Weiser, M. (1981). Program Slicing, *5th International Conference on Software Engineering (ICSE'81)*, pp. 439–449.

Wilhelm, R., Engblom, J., Ermedahl, A., Holst, N., Thesing, S. et al. (2008). The worst-case execution-time problem—overview of methods and survey of tools, *Transactions on Embedded Computing Systems* 7(3): 36:1–36:50.

Yazdanshenas, A. R. & Moonen, L. (2011). Crossing the boundaries while analyzing heterogeneous component-based software systems, *27th IEEE International Conference on Software Maintenance (ICSM'11)* pp. 193–202.

Zhao, M., Childers, B. & Soffa, M. L. (2003). Predicting the impact of optimizations for embedded systems, *ACM SIGPLAN conference on Language, compiler, and tool for embedded systems (LCTES'03)* pp. 1–11.

2

GUIsurfer: A Reverse Engineering Framework for User Interface Software

José Creissac Campos[1], João Saraiva[1], Carlos Silva[1] and João Carlos Silva[2]
[1]*Departamento de Informática, Universidade do Minho*
[2]*Escola Superior de Tecnologia, Instituto Politécnico do Cávado e do Ave*
Portugal

1. Introduction

In the context of developing tool support to the automated analysis of interactive systems implementations, this chapter proposal aims to investigate the applicability of reverse engineering approaches to the derivation of user interfaces behavioural models. The ultimate goal is that these models might be used to reason about the quality of the system, both from an usability and an implementation perspective, as well as being used to help systems' maintenance, evolution and redesign.

1.1 Motivation

Developers of interactive systems are faced with a fast changing technological landscape, where a growing multitude of technologies (consider, for example, the case of web applications) can be used to develop user interfaces for a multitude of form factors, using a growing number of input/output techniques. Additionally, they have to take into consideration non-functional requirements such as the usability and the maintainability of the system. This means considering the quality of the system both from the user's (i.e. external) perspective, and from the implementation's (i.e. internal) perspective. A system that is poorly designed from a usability perspective will most probably fail to be accepted by its end users. A poorly implemented system will be hard to maintain and evolve, and might fail to fulfill all intended requirements. Furthermore, when subsystems are subcontracted, the problem is faced of how to guarantee the quality of the implemented system during acceptance testing. The generation of user interface models from source code has the potential to mitigate these problems. The analysis of these models enables some degree of reasoning about the usability of the system, reducing the need to resort to costly user testing (cf. (Dix et al., 2003)), and can support acceptance testing processes. Moreover, the manipulation of the models supports the evolution, redesign and comparison of systems.

1.2 Objectives

Human-Computer interaction is an important and evolving area. Therefore, it is very important to reason about GUIs. In several situations (for example the mobile industry) it is the quality of the GUI that influences the adoption of certain software.

In order for a user interface to have good usability characteristics it must both be adequately designed and adequately implemented. Tools are currently available to developers that allow for the fast development of user interfaces with graphical components. However, the design of interactive systems does not seem to be much improved by the use of such tools.

Interfaces are often difficult to understand and use by end users. In many cases users have problems in identifying all the supported tasks of a system, or in understanding how to achieve their goals (Loer & Harrison, 2005).

Moreover, these tools produce *spaghetti* code which is difficult to understand and maintain. The generated code is composed by call-back procedures for most widgets like buttons, scroll bars, menu items, and other widgets in the interface. These procedures are called by the system when the user interacts with the system through widget's event. Graphical user interfaces may contains hundreds of widgets, and therefore many call-back procedures which makes difficult to understand and maintain the source code (Myers, 1991).

At the same time it is important to ensure that GUI based applications behave as expected (Memon, 2001). The correctness of the GUI is essential to the correct execution of the software (Berard, 2001). Regarding user interfaces, correctness is usually expressed as usability: the effectiveness, efficiency, and satisfaction with which users can use the system to achieve their goals (Abowd et al., 1989; SC4, 1994).

The main objective of this Chapter consists in developing tools to automatically extract models containing the GUI behaviour. We call this reverse engineering the GUI source code. Models allow designers to analyse systems and could be used to validate system requirements at reasonable cost (Miller et al., 2004). Different types of models can be used for interactive systems, like user and task models. Models must specify which GUI components are present in the interface and their relationship, when a particular GUI event may occur and the associated conditions, which system actions are executed and which GUI state is generated next. Another goal of this Chapter is to be able to reason about in order to analyse aspects of the original application's usability, and the implementation quality.

This work will be useful to enable the analysis of existing interactive applications and to evolve/update existing applications (Melody, 1996). In this case, being able to reason at a higher level of abstraction than that of code will help in guaranteeing that the new/updated user interface has the same characteristics of the previous one.

1.3 Structure of the chapter

This Chapter is structured into three main parts. Part 1 (Section 2) presents the reverse engineering area relating it to the GUI modelling area. Reverse engineering techniques' state of the art, related work and additional methodologies used within this research are firstly described. Then, the Section follows with a review of the approaches to model GUIs. A graphical user interface representation is exposed, and the aspects usually specified by graphical user interfaces are described.

Part 2 (Sections 3, 4, 5 and 6) presents the approach proposed in this Chapter. Section 3 presents methodologies to retargetable GUI reverse engineering. Section 4 presents the GUISURFER: the developed reverse engineering tool. It describes the GUISURFER architecture, the techniques applied for GUI reverse engineering and respective generated models. Then, Section 5, describe the research about GUI reasoning through behavioural models of interactive applications. Section 6 describes the application of GUISURFER to a realistic third-party application.

Finally, the last part (Section 7) presents conclusions, discussing the contributions achieved with this research, and indicating possible directions for future work.

2. Reverse engineering applied to GUI modelling

In the Software Engineering area, the use of reverse engineering approaches has been explored in order to derive models directly from existing systems. Reverse engineering is a process that helps understand a computer system. Similarly, user interface modelling helps designers and software engineers understand an interactive application from a user interface perspective. This includes identifying data entities and actions that are present in the user interface, as well as relationships between user interface objects.

In this Section, reverse engineering and user interface modelling aspects are described (Campos, 2004; Duke & Harrison, 1993). Section 2.1 provides details about the reverse engineering area. Then, the type of GUIs models to be used is discussed in Section 2.2. Finally, the last Section summarizes the Section presenting some conclusions.

2.1 Reverse engineering

Reverse engineering is useful in several tasks like documentation, maintenance, and re-engineering (E. Stroulia & Sorenson, 2003).

In the software engineering area, the use of reverse engineering approaches has been explored in order to derive models directly from existing interactive system using both static and dynamics analysis (Chen & Subramaniam, 2001; Paiva et al., 2007; Systa, 2001). Static analysis is performed on the source code without executing the application. Static approaches are well suited for extracting information about the internal structure of the system, and about dependencies among structural elements. Classes, methods, and variables information can be obtained from the analysis of the source code. On the contrary, dynamic analysis extracts information from the application by executing it (Moore, 1996). Within a dynamic approach the system is executed and its external behaviour is analysed.

Program analysis, plan recognition and redocumentation are applications of reverse engineering (Müller et al., 2000). Source code program analysis is an important goal of reverse engineering. It enables the creation of a model of the analysed program from its source code. The analysis can be performed at several different levels of abstraction. Plan recognition aims to recognize structural or behavioural patterns in the source code. Pattern-matching heuristics are used on source code to detect patterns of higher abstraction levels in the lower level code. Redocumentation enables one to change or create documentation for an existing system from source code. The generation of the documentation can be considered as the generation of a higher abstraction level representation of the system.

2.2 Types of GUI relevant models

Model-based development of software systems, and of interactive computing systems in particular, promotes a development life cycle in which models guide the development process, and are iteratively refined until the source code of the system is obtained. Models can be used to capture, not only the envisaged design, but also its rational, thus documenting the decision process undertook during development. Hence, they provide valuable information for the maintenance and evolution of the systems.

User interface models can describe the domain over which the user interface acts, the tasks that the user interface supports, and others aspects of the graphical view presented to the user. The use of interface models gives an abstract description of the user interface, potentially allowing to:

- express the user interfaces at different levels of abstraction, thus enabling choice of the most appropriate abstraction level;
- perform incremental refinement of the models, thus increasing the guarantee of quality of the final product;
- re-use user interface specifications between projects, thus decreasing the cost of development;
- reason about the properties of the models, thus allowing validation of the user interface within its design, implementation and maintenance processes.

One possible disadvantage of a model based approach is the cost incurred in developing the models. The complexity of today's systems, however, means that controlling their development becomes very difficult without some degree of abstraction and automation. In this context, modelling has become an integral part of development.

Two questions must be considered when thinking of modelling an interactive system:

- which aspects of the system are programmers interested in modelling;
- which modelling approach should programmers use.

These two issues will now be discussed.

In order to build any kind of model of a system, the boundaries of such system must be identified. Therefore the following kinds of models may be considered of interest for user interface modelling:

- *Domain models* are useful to define the domain of discourse of a given interactive system. Domain models are able to describe object relationships in a specific domain but do not express the semantic functions associated with the domain's objects.
- *User models* are a first type of model. In its simplest form, they can represent the different characteristics of end users and the roles they are playing. (Blandford & Young, 1993). In their more ambitious form, user models attempt to mimic user cognitive capabilities, in order to enable prediction of how the interaction between the user and the device will progress (Duke et al., 1998; Young et al., 1989);
- *Task models* express the tasks a user performs in order to achieve goals. Task models describe the activities users should complete to accomplish their objectives. The goal of a task model is not to express how the user interface behaves, but rather how a user will use it. Task models are important in the application domain's analysis and comprehension phase because they capture the main application activities and their relationships. Another of task models applications is as a tool to measure the complexity of how users will reach their goals;
- *Dialogue models* describe the behaviour of the user interface. Unlike task models, where the main emphasis is the users, dialogue model focus on the device, defining which actions are made available to users via the user interface, and how it responds to them. These models capture all possible dialogues between users and the user interface. Dialog models express the interaction between human and computer;

- *Presentation models* represent the application appearance. They describe the graphical objects in the user interface. Presentation models represent the materialization of widgets in the various dialog states. They define the visual appearance of the interface;
- *Navigation models* defines how objects can be navigated through the user interface from a user view perspective. These models represent basically a objects flow graph with all possible objects's navigation;
- And, finally, *Platform models* define the physical devices that are intended to host the application and how they interact with each other.

This Chapter will focus in generating dialogue models. On the one hand they are one of the more useful type of models to design or analyse the behaviour of the system. On the other hand, they are one of type of models that is closest to the implementation, thus reducing the gap to be filled by reverse engineering.

2.3 Summarizing GUI reverse engineering

This Section introduced Reverse Engineering, a technique which is useful in several software engineering tasks like documentation, maintenance and reengineering. Two kinds of reverse engineering processes were described: static and dynamic analysis. Several approaches exist, each aiming at particular systems and objectives. One common trend, however, is that the approaches are not retargetable, i.e. in all cases it is not possible to apply the approach to a different language than that it was developed for. Considering the plethora of technological solutions currently available to the development of GUIs, retargetability is an helpful/important feature. As a solution, this research proposes that static analysis can be used to develop a retargetable tool for GUI analysis from source code.

Several models may be considered for user interface modelling. *Task models* describe the tasks that an end user can performs. *Dialogue models* represent all possible dialogues between users and the user interface. *Domain models* define the objects that a user can view, access and manipulate through the user interface. *Presentation models* represent the application appearance. *Platform models* define the physical system used to host the application. The goal of the approach will be the generation of *dialogue models*.

With the above in mind, this Chapter is about the development of tools to automatically extract models from the user interface layer of interactive computing systems source code. To make the project manageable the Chapter will focus on event-based programming toolkits for graphical user interfaces development (*Java/Swing* being a typical example).

3. GUISURFER: A reverse engineering tool

This Section describes GUISURFER, a tool developed as a testbed for the reverse engineering approach proposed in the previous Section. The tool automatically extracts GUI behavioural models from the applications source code, and automates some of the activities involved in the analisys of these models.

This Section is organized as follows: Section 3.1 describes the architecture of the GUISURFER tool. A description about the retargetability of the tool is provided in Section 3.2. Finally, Section 3.3 presents some conclusions.

3.1 The architecture of GUISURFER

One of GUISURFER's development objectives is making it as easily retargetable as possible to new implementation languages. This is achieved by dividing the process in two phases: a language dependent phase and a language independent phase, as shown in Figure 1. Hence, if there is the need of retargeting GUISURFER into another language, ideally only the language dependent phase should be affected.

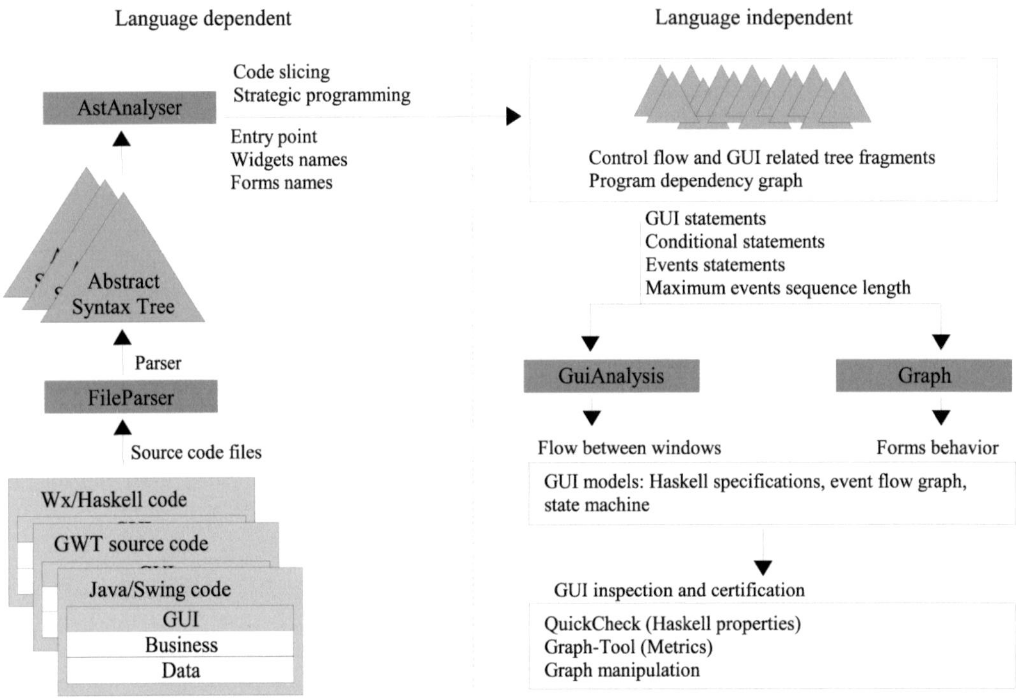

Fig. 1. GUISURFER architecture and retargetability

To support these two phases process, the GUISURFER architecture is composed of four modules:

- *FileParser*, which enables parsing the source code;
- *AstAnalyser*, which performs code slicing;
- *Graph*, which support GUI behavioural modelling;
- *GUIAnalysis*, which also support also GUI behavioural modelling;

The *FileParser* and *AstAnalyser* modules are implementation language dependent. They are the front-end of the system. The *Graph* and *GUIAnalysis* modules are independent of the implementation language.

3.1.1 Source code slicing

The first step GUISURFER performs is the parsing of the source code. This is achieved by executing a parser and generating an abstract syntax tree. An AST is a formal representation of the abstract syntactical structure of the source code. Moreover, the AST represents the entire code of the application. However, the tool's objective is to process the GUI layer of interactive systems, not the entire source code. To this end, GUISURFER was built using two generic techniques: strategic programming and code slicing. On the one hand, the use of strategic programming enables transversing heterogeneous data structures while aggregating uniform and type specific behaviours. On the other hand, code slicing allows extraction of relevant information from a program source code, based on the program dependency graph and a slicing criteria.

3.1.2 GUI behavioural modelling

Once the AST has been created and the GUI layer has been extracted, GUI behavioural modelling can be processed. It consists in generating the user interface behaviour. The relevant abstractions are user inputs, user selections, user actions and output to user. In this phase, behavioural GUI models are created. Therefore, a GUI intermediate representation is created in this phase.

3.1.3 GUI reasoning

It is important to perform reasoning over the generated models. For example, GUISURFER models can be tested by using the *Haskell QuickCheck* tool (Claessen & Hughes, 2000), a tool that tests *Haskell* programs automatically. Thereby, the programmer defines certain properties functions, and afterwards tests those properties through the generation of random values.

GUISURFER is also capable of creating event-flow graph models. Models that abstract all the interface widgets and their relationships. Moreover, it also features the automatic generation of finite state machine models of the interface. These models are illustrated through state diagrams in order to make them visually appealing. The different diagrams GUISURFER produces are a form of representation of dialog models.

GUISURFER's graphical models are created through the usage of *GraphViz*, an open source set of tools that allows the visualization and manipulation of abstract graphs (Ellson et al., 2001). GUI reasoning is also performed through the use of *Graph-Tool*[1] for the manipulation and statistical analysis of graphs. In this particular case an analogy is considered between state machines and graphs.

3.2 A language independent tool

A particular emphasis has been placed on developing tools that are, as much as possible, language independent. Although *Java/Swing* was used as the target language during initial development, through the use of generic programming techniques, the developed tool aims at being retargetable to different user interface toolkits, and different programming languages. Indeed, the GUISURFER tool has already been extended to enable *GWT* and *WxHaskell* based applications analysis.

Google Web Toolkit (*GWT*) is a Google technology (Hanson & Tacy, 2007). GWT provides a *Java*-based environment which allows for the development of *JavaScript* applications using the *Java* programming language. *GWT* enables the user to create rich Internet applications. The fact that applications are developed in the *Java* language allows *GWT* to bring all of *Java*'s benefits to web applications development. *GWT* provides a set of user interface widgets that can be used to create new applications. Since *GWT* produced a *JavaScript* application, it does not require browser plug-ins additions.

[1] see, http://projects.skewed.de/graph-tool/, last accessed 27 July, 2011

WxHaskell is a portable and native GUI library for *Haskell*. The library is used to develop a GUI application in a functional programming setting.

3.3 Summarizing GUISURFER approach

In this Section a reverse engineering tool was described. The GUISURFER tool enables extraction of different behavioural models from application's source code. The tool is flexible, indeed the same techniques has already been applied to extract similar models from different programming paradigm.

The GUISURFER architecture was presented and important parameters for each GUISURFER's executable file were outlined. A particular emphasis was placed on developing a tool that is, as much as possible, language independent.

This work will not only be useful to enable the analysis of existing interactive applications, but can also be helpful in a re-engineering process when an existing application must be ported or simply updated (Melody, 1996). In this case, being able to reason at a higher level of abstraction than that of code, will help in guaranteeing that the new/updated user interface has the same characteristics of the previous one.

4. GUI Reasoning from reverse engineering

The term GUI reasoning refers to the process of validating and verifying if interactive applications behave as expected (Berard, 2001; Campos, 1999; d'Ausbourg et al., 1998). Verification is the process of checking whether an application is correct, i.e. if it meets its specification. Validation is the process of checking if an application meets the requirements of its users (Bumbulis & Alencar, 1995). Hence, a verification and validation process is used to evaluate the quality of an application. For example, to check if a given requirement is implemented (Validation), or to detect the presence of bugs (Verification) (Belli, 2001).

GUI quality is a multifaceted problem. Two main aspects can be identified. For the Human-Computer Interaction (HCI) practitioner the focus of analysis is on Usability, how the system supports users in achieving their goals. For the Software Engineer, the focus of analysis is on the quality of the implementation. Clearly, there is an interplay between these two dimensions. Usability will be a (non-functional) requirement to take into consideration during development, and problems with the implementation will create problems to the user.

In a survey of usability evaluation methods, Ivory and Hearst (Ivory & Hearst, 2001) identified 132 methods for usability evaluation, classifying them into five different classes: (User) Testing; Inspection; Inquiry; Analytical Modelling; and Simulation. They concluded that automation of the evaluation process is greatly unexplored. Automating evaluation is a relevant issue since it will help reduce analysis costs by enabling a more systematic approach.

The reverse engineering approach described in this Chapter allows for the extraction of GUI behavioural models from source code. This Section describes an approach to GUI reasoning from these models. To this end, the *QuickCheck Haskell* library (Claessen & Hughes, 2000), graph theory, and the *Graph-Tool*[2] are used.

The analysis of source code can provide a means to guide the development of the application and to certify software. Software metrics aim to address software quality by measuring

[2] see, http://projects.skewed.de/graph-tool/, last accessed 27 July, 2011.

software aspects, such as lines of code, functions' invocations, etc. For that purpose, adequate metrics must be specified and calculated. Metrics can be divided into two groups: internal and external (ISO/IEC, 1999).

External metrics are defined in relation to running software. In what concerns GUIs, external metrics can be used as usability indicators. They are often associated with the following attributes (Nielsen, 1993):

- Easy to learn: The user can carry out the desired tasks easily without previous knowledge;
- Efficient to use: The user reaches a high level of productivity;
- Easy to remember: The re-utilization of the system is possible without a high level of effort;
- Few errors: The system prevents users from making errors, and recovery from them when they happen;
- Pleasant to use: The users are satisfied with the use of the system.

However, the values for these metrics are not obtainable from source code analysis, rather through users' feedback.

In contrast, internal metrics are obtained from the source code, and provide information to improve software development. A number of authors have looked at the relation between internal metrics and GUI quality.

Stamelos et al. (Stamelos et al., 2002) used the Logiscope[3] tool to calculate values of selected metrics in order to study the quality of open source code. Ten different metrics were used. The results enable evaluation of each function against four basic criteria: testability, simplicity, readability and self-descriptiveness. While the GUI layer was not specifically targeted in the analysis, the results indicated a negative correlation between component size and user satisfaction with the software.

Yoon and Yoon (Yoon & Yoon, 2007) developed quantitative metrics to support decision making during the GUI design process. Their goal was to quantify the usability attributes of interaction design. Three internal metrics were proposed and defined as numerical values: complexity, inefficiency and incongruity. The authors expect that these metrics can be used to reduce the development costs of user interaction.

While the above approaches focus on calculating metrics over the code, Thimbleby and Gow (Thimbleby & Gow, 2008) calculate them over a model capturing the behaviour of the application. Using graph theory they analyse metrics related to the user's ability to use the interface (e.g., strong connectedness ensure no part of the interface ever becomes unreachable), the cost of erroneous actions (e.g., calculating the cost of undoing an action), or the knowledge needed to use the system. In a sense, by calculating the metrics over a model capturing GUI relevant information instead of over the code, the knowledge gained becomes closer to the type of knowledge obtained from external metrics.

While Thimbleby and Gow manually develop their models from inspections of the running software/devices, an analogous approach can be carried out analysing the models generated by GUISURFER. Indeed, by calculating metrics over the behavioural models produced by GUISURFER, relevant knowledge may be acquired about the dialogue induced by the interface, and, as a consequence, about how users might react to it.

[3] http://www-01.ibm.com/software/awdtools/logiscope/, last accessed May 22, 2011

Throughout this document we will make use of interactive applications as running examples. The first application, named *Agenda*, models an agenda of contacts: it allows users to perform the usual actions of adding, removing and editing contacts. Furthermore, it also allows users to find a contact by giving its name. The application consists of four windows, named *Login*, *MainForm*, *Find* and *ContacEditor*, as shown in Figure 2.

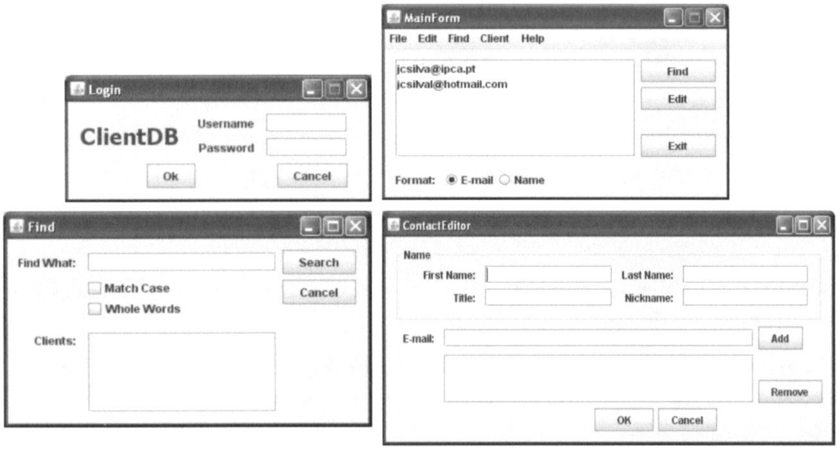

Fig. 2. A GUI application

We will use this example to present our approach to GUI reasoning. Let us discuss it in detail. The initial *Login* window (Figure 2, top left window) is used to control users' access to the agenda. Thus, a login and password have to be introduced by the user. If the user introduces a valid login/password pair and presses the *Ok* button, then the login window closes and the main window of the application is displayed. On the contrary, if the user introduces an invalid login/password pair, then the input fields are cleared, a warning message is produced, and the login window continues to be displayed. By pressing the *Cancel* button in the *Login* window, the user exits the application.

Authorized users, can use the main window (Figure 2, top right window) to find and edit contacts (*Find* and *Edit* buttons). By pressing the *Find* button in the main window, the user opens the *Find* window (Figure 2, bottom left window). This window is used to search and obtain a particular contact's data given its name. By pressing the *Edit* button in the main window, the user opens the *ContactEditor* window (Figure 2, bottom right window). This last window allows the edition of all contact data, such as name, nickname, e-mails, etc. The *Add* and *Remove* buttons enable edition of the list of e-mail addresses of the contact. If there are no e-mails in the list then the *Remove* button is automatically disabled.

4.1 *Graph-Tool*

Graph-Tool is an efficient python module for manipulation and statistical analysis of graphs[4]. It allows for the easy creation and manipulation of both directed or undirected graphs. Arbitrary information can be associated with the vertices, edges or even the graph itself, by means of property maps.

Furthermore, *Graph-Tool* implements all sorts of algorithms, statistics and metrics over graphs, such as shortest distance, isomorphism, connected components, and centrality measures.

[4] see, http://projects.skewed.de/graph-tool/, last accessed 27 July, 2011.

Now, for brevity, the graph described in Figure 3 will be considered. All vertices and edges

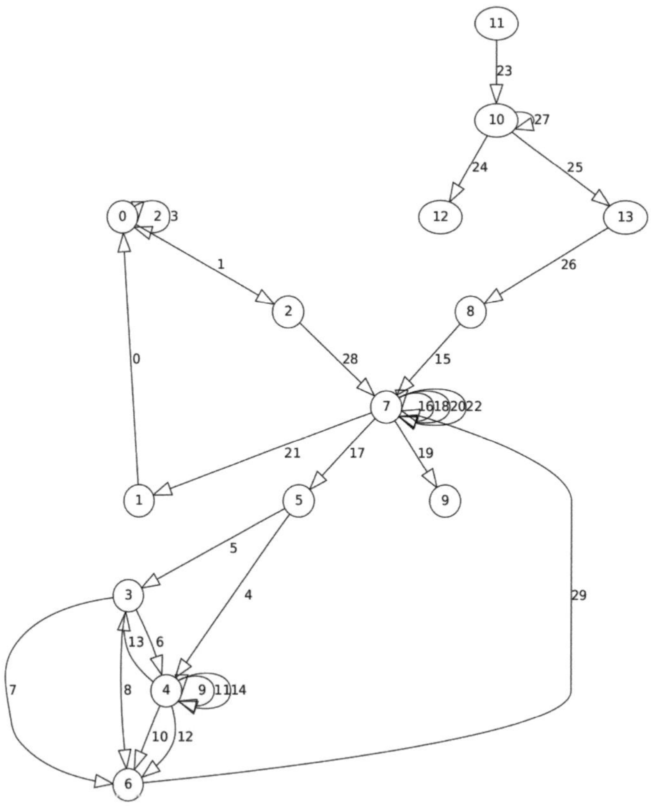

Fig. 3. *Agenda*'s behaviour graph (numbered)

are labeled with unique identifiers.

To illustrate the analysis performed with *Graph-Tool*, three metrics will be considered: Shortest distance between vertices, Pagerank and Betweenness.

4.1.0.1 Shortest Distance

Graph-Tool enables the calculation of the shortest path between two vertices. A path is a sequence of edges in a graph such that the target vertex of each edge is the source vertex of the next edge in the sequence. If there is a path starting at vertex u and ending at vertex v then v is reachable from u.

For example, the following *Python* command calculate the shortest path between vertices 11 and 6 (i.e. between the *Login* window and a particular *ContactEditor* window state), cf. Figure 3.

```
vlist, elist = shortest_path(g, g.vertex(11), g.vertex(6))
print "shortest path vertices", [str(v) for v in vlist]
print "shortest path edges", [str(e) for e in elist]
```

The results for the shortest path between vertices 11 and 6 are:

```
shortest path vertices:
       ['11','10','13','8','7','5','4','6']
shortest path edges:
       ['(11,10)','(10,13)','(13,8)','(8,7)',
        '(7,5)','(5,4)','(4,6)'
       ]
```

Two representations of the path are provided, one focusing on vertices, the another on edges. This is useful to calculate the number of steps a user needs to perform in order a particular task.

Now let us consider another inspection. The next result gives the shortest distance (minimum number of edges) from the *Login* window (vertice 11) to all other vertices. The *Python* command is defined as follows:

```
dist = shortest_distance(g, source=g.vertex(11))
print "shortest_distance from Login"
print dist.get_array()
```

The obtained result is a sequence of values:

```
shortest distance from Login
[6 5 7 6 6 5 7 4 3 5 1 0 2 2]
```

Each value gives the distance from vertice 11 to a particular target vertice. The index of the value in the sequence corresponds to the vertice's identifier. For example the first value is the shortest distance from vertice 11 to vertice 0, which is 6 edges long.

Another similar example makes use of *MainForm* window (vertice 7) as starting point:

```
dist = shortest_distance(g, source=g.vertex(7))
print "shortest_distance from MainForm"
print dist.get_array()
```

The result list may contains negative values: they indicate that there are no paths from Mainform to those vertices.

```
shortest distance from MainForm
[2 1 3 2 2 1 3 0 -1 1 -1 -1 -1 -1]
```

This second kind of metric is useful to analyse the complexity of an interactive application's user interface. Higher values represent complex tasks while lower values express behaviour composed by more simple tasks. This example also shows that its possible to detect parts of the interface that can become unavailable. In this case, there is no way to go back to the login window once the Main window is displayed (the value at indexs 10-13 are equal to -1).

This metric can also be used to calculate the center of a graph. The center of a graph is the set of all vertices where the greatest distance to other vertices is minimal. The vertices in the center are called central points. Thus vertices in the center minimize the maximal distance from other points in the graph.

Finding the center of a graph is useful in GUI applications where the goal is to minimize the steps to execute tasks (i.e. edges between two points). For example, placing the main window of an interactive system at a central point reduces the number of steps a user has to execute to accomplish tasks.

4.1.0.2 Pagerank

Pagerank is a distribution used to represent the probability that a person randomly clicking on links will arrive at any particular page (Berkhin, 2005). That probability is expressed as a numeric value between 0 and 1. A 0.5 probability is commonly expressed as a "50% chance" of something happening.

Pagerank is a link analysis algorithm, used by the Google Internet search engine, that assigns a numerical weighting to each element of a hyperlinked set of documents. The main objective is to measure their relative importance.

This same algorithm can be applied to our GUI's behavioural graphs. Figure 4 provides the *Python* command when applying this algorithm to the *Agenda'* graph model.

```
pr = pagerank(g)
graph_draw(g, size=(70,70),
              layout="dot",
              vsize = pr,
              vcolor="gray",
              ecolor="black",
              output="graphTool-Pagerank.pdf",
              vprops=dict([('label', "")]),
              eprops=dict([('label', ""),
                           ('arrowsize',2.0),
                           ('arrowhead',"empty")]))
```

Fig. 4. *Python* command for Pagerank algorithm

Figure 5 shows the result of the Pagerank algorithm giving the *Agenda*'s model/graph as input. The size of a vertex corresponds to its importance within the overall application behaviour. This metric is useful, for example, to analyse whether complexity is well distributed along the application behaviour. In this case, the Main window is clearly a central point in the interaction to see vertices and edges description).

4.1.0.3 Betweenness

Betweenness is a centrality measure of a vertex or an edge within a graph (Shan & et al., 2009). Vertices that occur on many shortest paths between other vertices have higher betweenness than those that do not. Similar to vertices betweenness centrality, edge betweenness centrality is related to shortest path between two vertices. Edges that occur on many shortest paths between vertices have higher edge betweenness.

Figure 6 provides the *Python* command for applying this algorithm to the *Agenda'* graph model. Figure 7 displays the result. Betweenness values for vertices and edges are expressed visually. Highest betweenness edges values are represented with thicker edges. The Main window has the highest (vertices and edges values) betweenness, meaning it acts as a hub

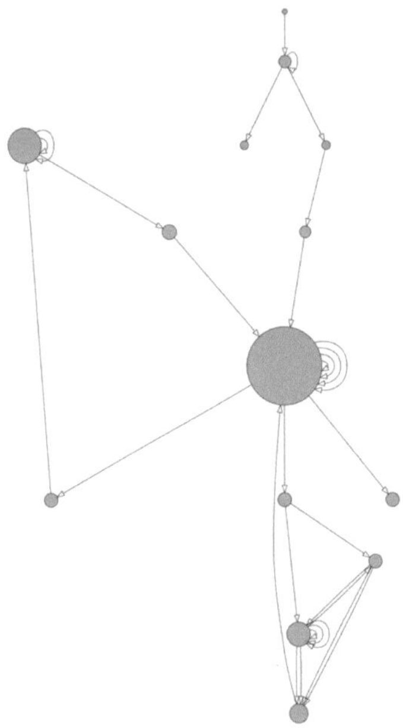

Fig. 5. *Agenda*'s pagerank results

```
bv, be = betweenness(g)
be1 = be
be1.get_array()[:] = be1.get_array()[:]*120+1
graph_draw(g, size=(70,70),
              layout="dot",
              vcolor="white",
              ecolor="gray",
              output="graphTool-Betweenness.pdf",
              vprops=dict([('label', bv)]),
              eprops=dict([('label', be),
                           ('arrowsize',1.2),
                           ('arrowhead',"normal"),
                           ('penwidth',be1)]))
```

Fig. 6. *Python* command for Betweenness algorithm

from where different parts of the interface can be reached. Clearly it will be a central point in the interaction.

4.1.0.4 Cyclomatic complexity

Another important metric is cyclomatic complexity which aims to measures the total number of decision points in an application (Thomas, 1976). It is used to give the number of tests for software and to keep software reliable, testable, and manageable. Cyclomatic complexity is based entirely on the structure of software's control flow graph and is defined as $M = E\text{-}V + 2P$ (considering a single exit statement) where E is the number of edges, V is the number of vertices and P is the number of connected components.

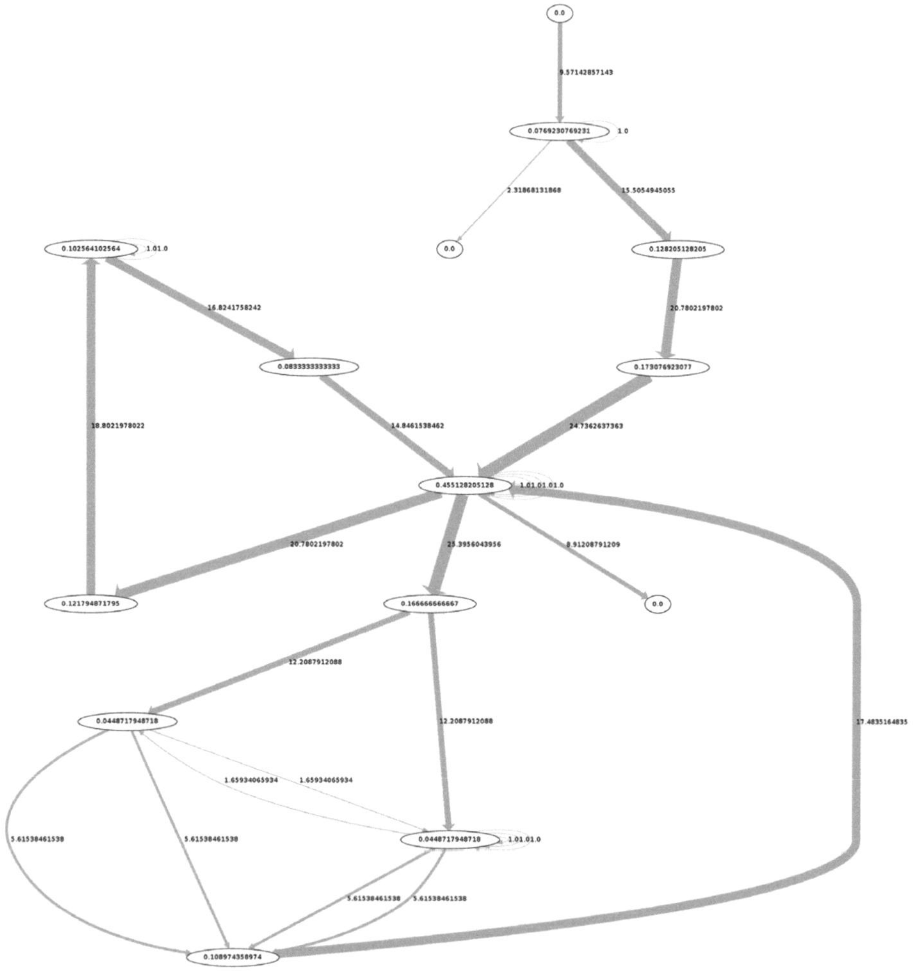

Fig. 7. *Agenda*'s betweenness values (highest betweenness values represented with thicker edges)

Considering Figure 5 where edges represent decision logic in the *Agenda* GUI layer, the GUI's overall cyclomatic complexity is 18 and each *Agenda*'s window has a cyclomatic complexity less or equal than 10. In applications there are many good reasons to limit cyclomatic complexity. Complex structures are more prone to error, are harder to analyse, to test, and to maintain. The same reasons could be applied to user interfaces. McCabe proposed a limit of 10 for functions's code, but limits as high as 15 have been used successfully as well (Thomas, 1976). McCabe suggest limits greater than 10 for projects that have operational advantages over typical projects, for example formal design. User interfaces can apply the same limits of complexity, i.e. each window behaviour complexity could be limited to a particular cyclomatic complexity. Defining appropriate values is an interesting topic for further research, but one that is out of the scope of the present Chapter.

4.2 Summarizing GUI reasoning approach

In this Section a GUISURFER based GUI analysis process has been illustrated. The process uses GUISURFER's reverse engineering capabilities to enable a range of model-based analysis being carried out. Different analysis methodologies are described. The methodologies automate the activities involved in GUI reasoning, such as, test case generation, or verification. GUI behavioural metrics are also described as a way to analyse GUI quality.

5. HMS case study: A larger interactive system

In previous Sections, we have presented the GUISURFER tool and all the different techniques involved in the analysis an the reasoning of interactive applications. We have used a simple examples in order to motivate and explain our approach. In this Section, we present the application of GUISURFER to a complex/large real interactive system: a Healthcare management system available from *Planet-source-code*. The goal of this Section is twofold: Firstly, it is a proof of concept for the GUISURFER. Secondly, we wish to analyse the interactive parts of a real application.

The choosen interactive system is related to a Healthcare Management System (*HMS*), and can be downloaded from *Planet-source-code* website[5]. *Planet-source-code* is one of the largest public source code database on the Internet.

The HMS system is implemented in *Java/Swing* and supports patients, doctors and bills management. The implementation contains 66 classes, 29 windows forms (message box included) and 3588 lines of code. The following Subsections provide a description of the main *HMS* windows and the results generated by the application of GUISURFER to its source code.

5.1 Bills management

This Section presents results obtained when working with the billing form provided in Figure 8. Using this form, users can search bills (by clicking on the *SEARCH* button), clear all widget's assigned values (by clicking on the *CLEAR* button) or go back to the previous form. Figure 9 presents the generated state machine. There is only one way to close the form *Billing*. Users must select the *bback* event, verifying the *cond9* condition (cf. pair *bback/cond9/[1,2]*). This event enables moving to the *close* node, thus closing the *Billing* form, and opening the *startApp* form through action reference 1.

5.2 GUI Reasonning

In this Section, two metrics will be applied in order to illustrate the same kind of analysis: Pagerank and Betweenness.

Figure 10 provides a graph with the overall behaviour of the HMS system. This model can be seen in more detail in the electronic version of this Chapter. Basically, this model aggregates the state machines of all HMS forms. The right top corner node specifies the HMS entry point, i.e. the *mainAppstate0* creation state from the login's state machine

Pagerank is a link analysis algorithm, that assigns a numerical weighting to each node. The main objective is to measure the relative importance of the states. Larger nodes specifies window internal states with higher importance within the overall application behaviour.

[5] http://www.planet-source-code.com/vb/scripts/ShowCode.asp?txtCodeId=6401&lngWId=2, last accessed May 22, 2011

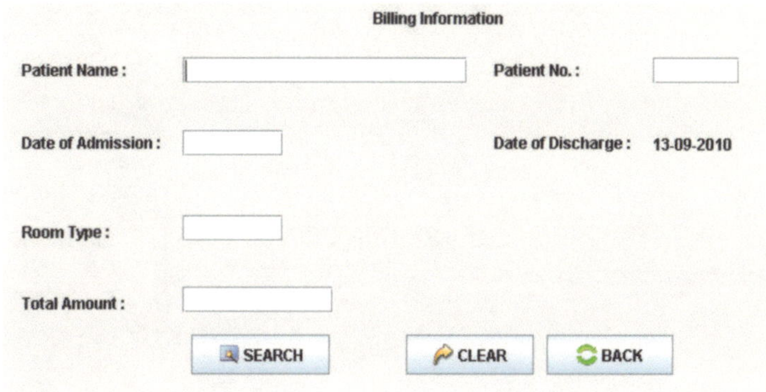

Fig. 8. *HSM*: Billing form

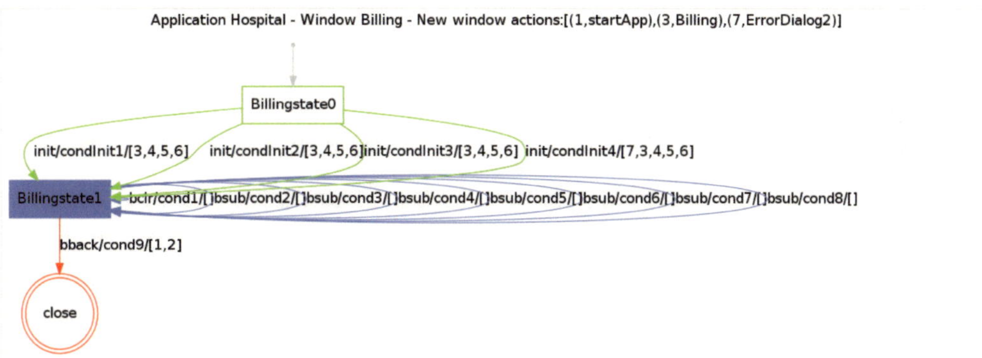

Fig. 9. *HSM*: Billing form behaviour state machine

Figure 11 provides the result obtained when applying the pagerank algorithm to graph of Figure 10. This metric can have several applications, for example, to analyse whether complexity is well distributed along the application behaviour. In this case, there are several points with higher importance. The interaction complexity is well distributed considering the overall application.

Betweenness is a centrality measure of a vertex or an edge within a graph. Vertices that occur on many shortest paths between other vertices have higher betweenness than those that do not. Similar to vertices betweenness centrality, edge betweenness centrality is related to shortest path between two vertices. Edges that occur on many shortest paths between vertices have higher edge betweenness. Figure 12 provides the obtained result when applying the betweenness algorithm. Betweenness values are expressed numerically for each vertices and edges. Highest betweenness edges values are represented by larger edges. Some states and edges have the highest betweenness, meaning they act as a hub from where different parts of the interface can be reached. Clearly they represent a central axis in the interaction between users and the system. In a top down order, this axis traverses the following states *patStartstate0*, *patStartstate1*, *startAppstate0*, *startAppstate1*, *docStartstate0* and *docStartstate1*. States *startAppstate0* and *startAppstate1* are the main states of the *startApp* window's state machine. States *patStartstate0*, *patStartstate1* are the main states of the *patStart* window's state machine. Finally, *docStartstate0* and *docStartstate1* belong to *docStart* window's state machine (*docStart* is the main doctor window).

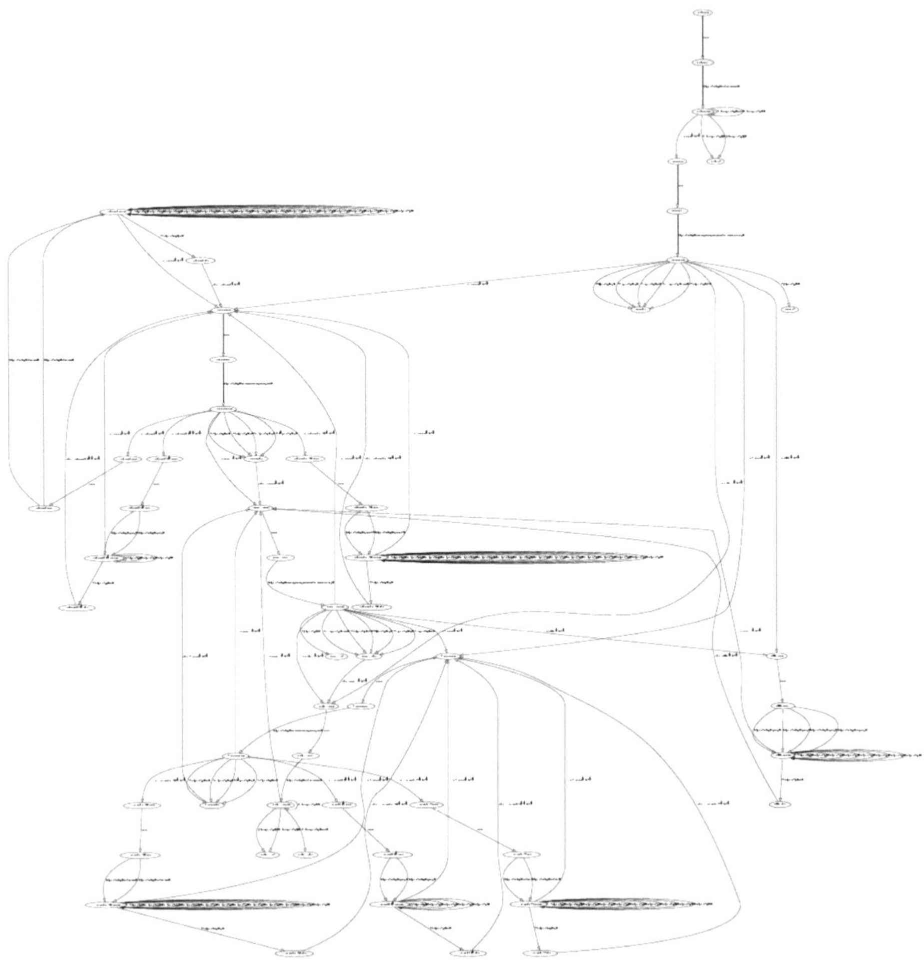

Fig. 10. *HSM*: The overall behaviour

5.3 Summarizing case study

This Section described the results obtained with GUISURFER when applying it to a larger interactive system. The choosen interactive system case study is related to a healthcare management system (*HMS*). The HMS system is implemented in *Java/Swing* programming language and implement operations to allow for patients, doctors and bills management. A description of main *HMS* windows has been provided, and *GUIsurfer* results have been described. The GUISURFER tool enabled the extraction of different behavioural models. Methodologies have been also applied automating the activities involved in GUI model-based reasoning, such as, pagerank and betweenness algorithms. GUI behavioural metrics have been used as a way to analyse GUI quality. This case study demonstrated that GUISURFER enables the analysis of real interactive applications written by third parties.

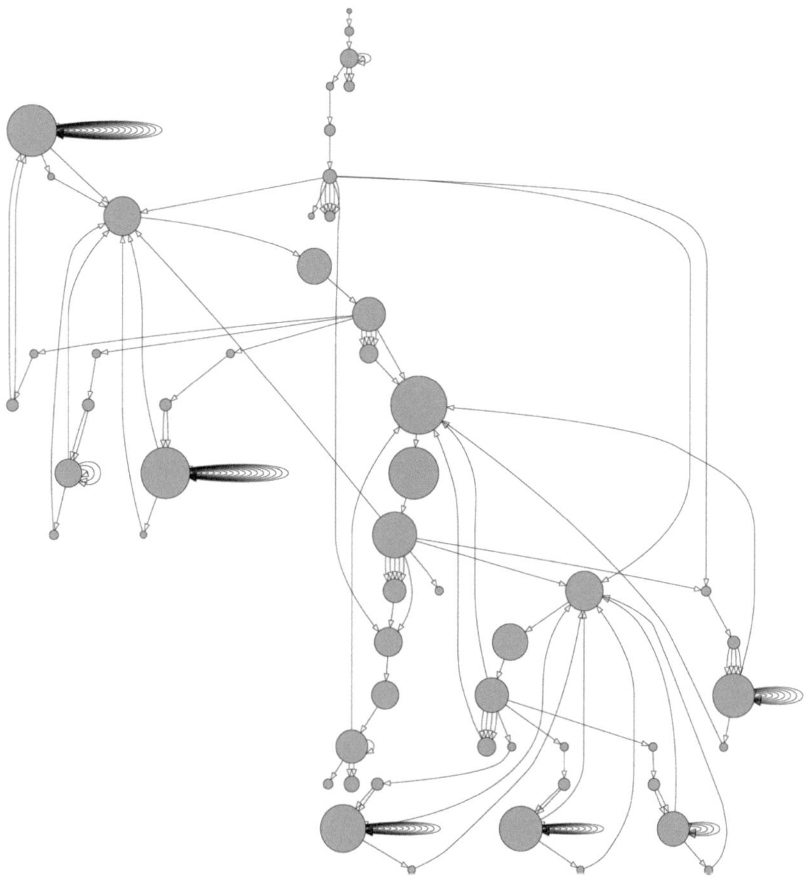

Fig. 11. *HSM*'s pagerank results

6. Conclusions and future work

This Chapter presented an approach to GUI reasoning using reverse engineering techniques. This document concludes with a review of the work developed. The resulting research contributions are presented and directions for future work are suggested.

The first Section describes the contributions of the Chapter. A discussion about GUISURFER limitations is provided in Section 2. Finally, the last Section presents some future work.

6.1 Summary of contributions

The major contribution of this work is the development of the GUISURFER prototype, an approach for improving GUI analysis through reverse engineering. This research has demonstrated how user interface layer can be extracted from different source codes, identifying a set of widgets (graphical objects) that can be modeled, and identifying also a set of user interface actions. Finally this Chapter has presented a methodology to generate behavioural user interface models from the extracted information and to reason about it.

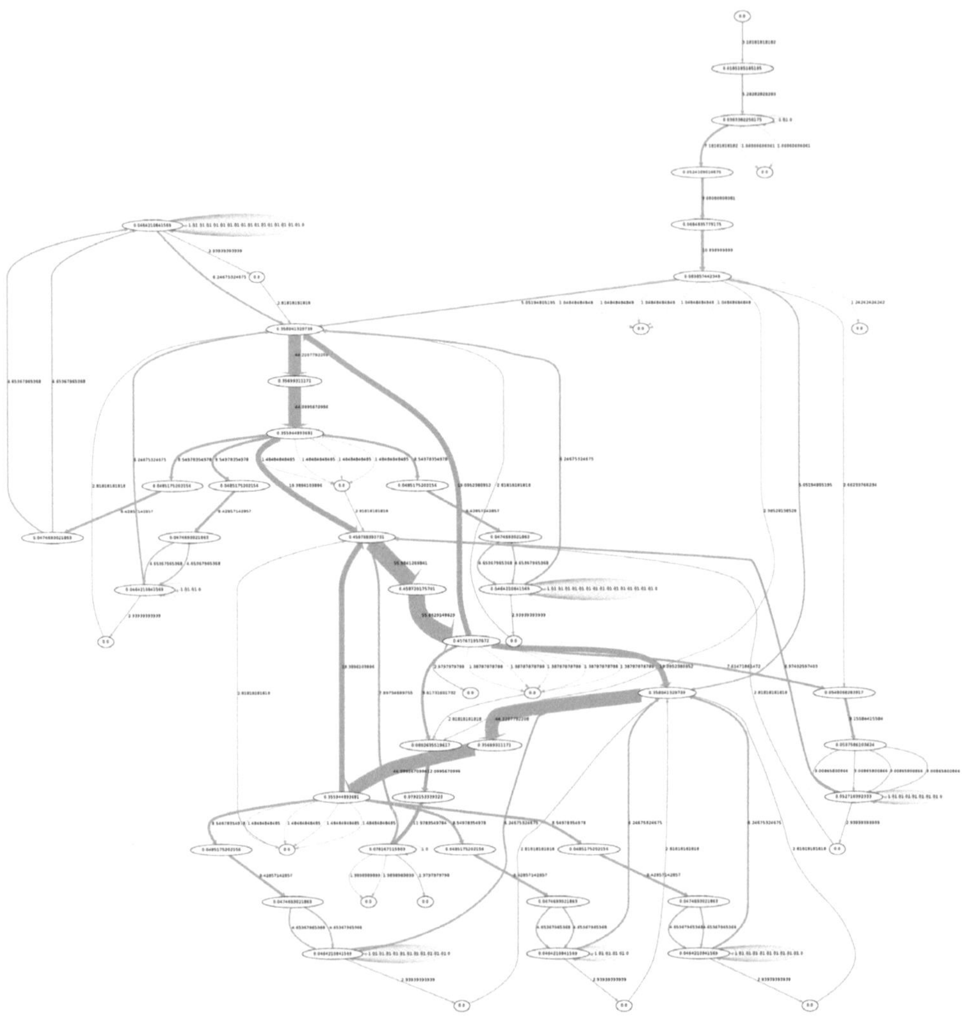

Fig. 12. *HSM*'s betweenness values

The approach is very flexible, indeed the same techniques have been applied to extract similar models from *Java/Swing*, *GWT* and *WxHaskell* interactive applications.

This work is an approach to bridging the gap between users and programmers by allowing the reasoning about GUI models from source code. This Chapter described GUI models extracted automatically from the code, and presented a methodology to reason about the user interface model. A number of metrics over the graphs representing the user interface were investigated. Some initial thoughts on testing the graph against desirable properties of the interface were also put forward. We believe this style of approach can feel a gap between the analysis of code quality via the use of metrics or other techniques, and usability analysis performed on a running system with actual users.

6.2 Discussion

Using GUISURFER, programmers are able to reason about the interaction between users and a given system at a higher level of abstraction than that of code. The generated models are amenable to analysis via model checking (c.f. (Campos & Harrison, 2009)). In this work, alternative lighter weight approaches have been explored .

Considering that the models generated by the reverse engineering process are representations of the interaction between users and system, this research explored how metrics defined over those models can be used to obtain relevant information about the interaction. This means that the approach enable to analyse the quality of the user interface, from the users perspective, without having to resort to external metrics which would imply testing the system with real users, with all the costs that the process carries.

It must be noted that, while the approach enables to analyse aspects of user interface quality without resorting to human test subjects, the goal is not to replace user testing. Ultimately, only user testing will provide factual evidence of the usability of a user interface.

Results show the reverse engineering approach adopted is useful but there are still some limitations. One relates to the focus on event listeners for discrete events. This means the approach is not able to deal with continuous media and synchronization/timing constraints among objects. Another limitation has to due with layout management issues. GUISURFER cannot extract, for example, information about overlapping windows since this must be determined at run time. Thus, it can not be find out in a static way whether important information for the user might be obscured by other parts of the interface. A third issue relates to the fact that generated models reflect what was programmed as opposed to what was designed. Hence, if the source code does the wrong thing, static analysis alone is unlikely to help because it is unable to know what the intended outcome was. For example, if an action is intended to insert a result into a text box, but input is sent to another instead. However, if the design model is available, GUISURFER can be used to extract a model of the implemented system, and a comparison between the two can be carried out.

A number of others issues still needs addressing. In the examples used throughout the Chapter, only one windows could be active at any given time (i.e., windows were modal). When non-modal windows are considered (i.e., when users are able to freely move between open application windows), nodes in the graph come to represents sets of open windows instead of a single active window. This creates problems with the interpretation of metrics that need further consideration. The problem is exacerbated when multiple windows of a given type are allowed (e.g., multiple editing windows).

6.3 Future work

The work developed in this Chapter open a new set of interesting problems that need research. This Section provides some pointers for future work.

6.3.1 GUISURFER extension

In the future, the implementation can be extended to handle more complex widgets. Others programming languages/toolkits can be considered, in order to make the approach as generic as possible.

GUISURFER may be also extended to other kinds of interactive applications. There are categories of user interfaces that cannot be modeled in GUISURFER, for example, system incorporating continuous media or synchronization/timing constraints among objects. Thus, the identification of the problems that GUISURFER may present when modelling these user interfaces would be the first step towards a version of GUISURFER suitable for use with other kinds of interactive applications. Finally, the tool and the approach must be validated externally. Although the approach has already been applied by another researcher, it is fundamental to apply this methodology with designers and programmers.

6.3.2 Patterns for GUI transformation

Patterns may be used to obtain better systems through the re-engineering of GUI source code across paradigms and architectures. The architect Christopher Alexander has introduced design patterns in early 1970. He defines a pattern as a relation between a context, a problem, and a solution. Each pattern describes a recurrent problem, and then describes the solution to that problem. Design patterns gained popularity in computer science, cf. (Gamma et al., 1995). In software engineering, a design pattern is a general reusable solution to a commonly occurring problem in software design. Patterns are used in different areas including software architecture, requirements and analysis. The human computer interaction (HCI) community has also adopted patterns as a user interface design tool. In the HCI community, patterns are used to create solutions which help user interfaces designers to resolve GUI development problems. Patterns have been used in two different contexts: (Stoll et al., 2008) proposes usability supporting software architectural patterns (USAPs) that provide developers with useful guidance for producing a software architecture design that supports usability (called these architectural patterns). Tidwell (Tidwell, 2005) uses patterns from a user interface design perspective, defining solutions to common user interface design problems, without explicit consideration of the software architecture (called these interaction patterns). Harrison makes use of interaction styles to describe design and architectural patterns to characterize the properties of user interfaces (Gilroy & Harrison, 2004). In any case these patterns have typically been used in a forward engineering context.

Application of patterns-based re-engineering techniques could be used to implement the interactive systems adaptation process. One of the most important features of patterns, which justifies its use here, is that they are platform and implementation independent solutions. Pattern-based approach may support user interface plasticity (Coutaz & Calvary, 2008) and generally help the maintenance and migration of GUI code.

7. References

Abowd, G., Bowen, J., Dix, A., Harrison, M. & Took, R. (1989). User interface languages: a survey of existing methods, *Technical report*, Oxford University.

Belli, F. (2001). Finite state testing and analysis of graphical user interfaces, *Proceedings.of the 12th International Symposium on Software Reliability Engineering, ISSRE 2001*, IEEE, pp. 34–42.
URL: *http://ieeexplore.ieee.org/iel5/7759/21326/00989456.pdf?tp=&arnumber=989456&isnumber=21326&arSt=34&ared=43&arAuthor=Belli%2C+F.%3B*

Berard, B. (2001). *Systems and Software Verification*, Springer.

Berkhin, P. (2005). A survey on pagerank computing, *Internet Mathematics* 2: 73–120.

Blandford, A. E. & Young, R. M. (1993). Developing runnable user models: Separating the problem solving techniques from the domain knowledge, *in* J. Alty, D. Diaper

& S. Guest (eds), *People and Computers VIII — Proceedings of HCI'93*, Cambridge University Press, Cambridge, pp. 111–122.

Bumbulis, P. & Alencar, P. C. (1995). A framework for prototyping and mechaniacally verifying a class of user interfaces, *IEEE* .

Campos, J. C. (1999). *Automated Deduction and Usability Reasoning*, PhD thesis, Department of Computer Science, University of York.

Campos, J. C. (2004). The modelling gap between software engineering and human-computer interaction, *in* R. Kazman, L. Bass & B. John (eds), *ICSE 2004 Workshop: Bridging the Gaps II*, The IEE, pp. 54–61.

Campos, J. C. & Harrison, M. D. (2009). Interaction engineering using the IVY tool, *ACM Symposium on Engineering Interactive Computing Systems (EICS 2009)*, ACM, New York, NY, USA, pp. 35–44.

Chen, J. & Subramaniam, S. (2001). A gui environment for testing gui-based applications in Java, *Proceedings of the 34th Hawaii International Conferences on System Sciences* .

Claessen, K. & Hughes, J. (2000). Quickcheck: A lightweight tool for random testing of haskell programs, *Proceedings of International Conference on Functional Programming (ICFP), ACM SIGPLAN, 2000.*

Coutaz, J. & Calvary, G. (2008). HCI and software engineering: Designing for user interface plasticity, *The Human Computer Interaction Handbook*, user design science, chapter 56, pp. 1107–1125.

d'Ausbourg, B., Seguin, C. & Guy Durrieu, P. R. (1998). Helping the automated validation process of user interfaces systems, *IEEE* .

Dix, A., Finlay, J. E., Abowd, G. D. & Beale, R. (2003). *Human-Computer Interaction (3rd Edition)*, Prentice-Hall, Inc., Upper Saddle River, NJ, USA.

Duke, D., Barnard, P., Duce, D. & May, J. (1998). Syndetic modelling, *Human-Computer Interaction* 13(4): 337–393.

Duke, D. J. & Harrison, M. D. (1993). Abstract interaction objects, *Computer Graphics Forum* 12(3): 25–36.

E. Stroulia, M. El-ramly, P. I. & Sorenson, P. (2003). User interface reverse engineering in support of interface migration to the web, *Automated Software Engineering* .

Ellson, J., Gansner, E., Koutsofios, L., North, S. & Woodhull, G. (2001). Graphviz - an open source graph drawing tools, *Lecture Notes in Computer Science*, Springer-Verlag, pp. 483–484.

Gamma, E., Helm, R., Johnson, R. E. & Vlissides, J. (1995). *Design Patterns: Elements of Reusable Object-Oriented Software*, Addison-Wesley, Reading, MA.

Gilroy, S. W. & Harrison, M. D. (2004). Using interaction style to match the ubiquitous user interface to the device-to-hand, *EHCI/DS-VIS*, pp. 325–345.

Hanson, R. & Tacy, A. (2007). *GWT in Action: Easy Ajax with the Google Web Toolkit*, Manning Publications Co., Greenwich, CT, USA.

ISO/IEC (1999). Software products evaluation. DIS 14598-1.

Ivory, M. Y. & Hearst, M. A. (2001). The state of the art in automating usability evaluation of user interfaces, *ACM COMPUTING SURVEYS* 33: 470–516.

Loer, K. & Harrison, M. (2005). Analysing user confusion in context aware mobile applications, *in* M. Constabile & F. Paternò (eds), *PINTERACT 2005*, Vol. 3585 of *Lecture Notes in Computer Science*, Springer, New York, NY, USA, pp. 184–197.

Melody, M. (1996). A survey of representations for recovering user interface specifications for reengineering, *Technical report*, Institute of Technology, Atlanta GA 30332-0280.

Memon, A. M. (2001). *A Comprehensive Framework for Testing Graphical User Interfaces*, PhD thesis, Department of Computer Science, University of PittsBurgh.

Miller, S. P., Tribble, A. C., Whalen, M. W. & Heimdahl, M. P. (2004). Proving the shalls early validation of requirements through formal methods, *Department of Computer Science and Engineering* .

Moore, M. M. (1996). Rule-based detection for reverse engineering user interfaces, *Proceedings of the Third Working Conference on Reverse Engineering, pages 42-8, Monterey, CA* .

Müller, H. A., Jahnke, J. H., Smith, D. B., Storey, M.-A., Tilley, S. R. & Wong, K. (2000). Reverse engineering: a roadmap, *ICSE '00: Proceedings of the Conference on The Future of Software Engineering*, ACM, New York, NY, USA, pp. 47–60.

Myers, B. A. (1991). Separating application code from toolkits: Eliminating the spaghetti of call-backs, *School of Computer Science* .

Nielsen, J. (1993). *Usability Engineering*, Academic Press, San Diego, CA.

Paiva, A. C. R., Faria, J. C. P. & Mendes, P. M. C. (eds) (2007). *Reverse Engineered Formal Models for GUI Testing, 10th International Workshop on Formal Methods for Industrial Critical Systems*. Berlin, Germany.

SC4, I. S.-C. (1994). Draft International ISO DIS 9241-11 Standard, International Organization for Standardization.

Shan, S. Y. & et al. (2009). Fast centrality approximation in modular networks.

Stamelos, I., Angelis, L., Oikonomou, A. & Bleris, G. L. (2002). Code quality analysis in open source software development, *Information Systems Journal* 12: 43–60.

Stoll, P., John, B. E., Bass, L. & Golden, E. (2008). Preparing usability supporting architectural patterns for industrial use. Computer science, Datavetenskap, Malardalen University, School of Innovation, Design and Engineering.

Systa, T. (2001). Dynamic reverse engineering of Java software, *Technical report*, University of Tampere, Finland.

Thimbleby, H. & Gow, J. (2008). Applying graph theory to interaction design, *EIS 2007* pp. 501–519.

Thomas, J. M. (1976). A complexity measure, *Intern. J. Syst. Sci.* 2(4): 308.

Tidwell, J. (2005). *Designing Interfaces: Patterns for Effective Interaction Design*, O' Reilly Media, Inc.

Yoon, Y. S. & Yoon, W. C. (2007). Development of quantitative metrics to support UI designer decision-making in the design process, *Human-Computer Interaction. Interaction Design and Usability*, Springer Berlin / Heidelberg, pp. 316–324.

Young, R. M., Green, T. R. G. & Simon, T. (1989). Programmable user models for predictive evaluation of interface designs, *in* K. Bice & C. Lewis (eds), *CHI'89 Proceedings*, ACM Press, NY, pp. 15–19.

3

MDA-Based Reverse Engineering

Liliana Favre
Universidad Nacional del Centro de la Provincia de Buenos Aires
Comisión de Investigaciones Científicas de la Provincia de Buenos Aires
Argentina

1. Introduction

Nowadays, almost companies are facing the problematic of having to modernize or replace their legacy software systems. These old systems have involved the investment of money, time and other resources through the ages. Many of them are still business-critical and there is a high risk in replacing them. Therefore, reverse engineering is one of the major challenges for software engineering today.

The most known definition of reverse engineering was given by Chikofsky and Cross (1990): "the process of analyzing a subject system to (i) identify the system's components and their interrelationships and (ii) create representations of the system in another form or at a higher-level of abstraction". Reverse engineering is the process of discovering and understanding software artifacts or systems with the objective of extracting information and providing high-level views of them that can be later on manipulated or re-implemented. That is to say, it is the processes of examination, not a process of change such as forward engineering and reengineering. Forward engineering is the traditional process of moving from high-level abstractions and implementation-independent designs to the physical implementation of a system. On the other hand, software reengineering includes a reverse engineering phase in which abstractions of the software artifacts to be reengineered are built, and a forward engineering phase that moves from abstractions to implementations (Sommerville, 2004) (Canfora &Di Penta, 2007).

Reverse Engineering is also related with software evolution and maintenance. Software evolution is the process of initial development of a software artifact, followed by its maintenance. The ANSI/IEEE standard 729-1983 (Ansi/IEEE, 1984) defines software maintenance "as the modification of a software product after delivery to correct faults, to improve performance or other attributes, or to adapt the product to a changed environment". Reverse engineering techniques can be used as a mean to design software systems by evolving existing ones based on new requirements or technologies. It can start from any level of abstraction or at any stage of the life cycle.

Reverse engineering is hardly associated with modernization of legacy systems that include changes not only in software but in hardware, business processes and organizational strategies and politics. Changes are motivated for multiple reasons, for instance the constantly changing IT technology and the constantly changing business world.

Large number of software systems have been developed and successfully used. These systems resume today key knowledge acquired over the life of the underlying organization; however, many of them have been written for technology which is expensive to maintain and which may not be aligned with current organizational politics.

Over the past two decades, reverse engineering techniques focused mainly on recovering high-level architectures or diagrams from procedural code to face up to problems such as comprehending data structures or databases or the Y2K problem. By the year 2000, many different kinds of slicing techniques were developed and several studies were carried out to compare them.

Over time, a growing demand of object-oriented reengineering appeared on the stage. New approaches were developed to identify objects into legacy code (e.g. legacy code in COBOL) and translate this code into an object-oriented language. Object-oriented programs are essentially dynamic and present particular problems linked to polymorphism, late binding, abstract classes and dynamically typed languages. For example, some object-oriented languages introduce concepts such as reflection and the possibility of loading dynamically classes; although these mechanisms are powerful, they affect the effectiveness of reverse engineering techniques. During the time of object-oriented programming, the focus of software analysis moved from static analysis to dynamic analysis, more precisely static analysis was complemented with dynamic analysis (Fanta & Rajlich, 1998) (Systa, 2000).

When the Unified Modeling Language (UML) comes into the world, a new problem was how to extract higher-level views of the system expressed by different kind of UML diagrams (UML, 2010a) (UML, 2010b). Relevant work for extracting UML diagrams (e.g. class diagram, state diagram, sequence diagram, object diagram, activity diagram and package diagram) from source code was developed (Tonella & Potrich, 2005).

1.1 Reverse engineering today

To date there are billions upon billions of lines of legacy code in existence, which must be maintained with a high cost. Instead of building from scratch, software industry has realized the advantages of modernizing existing systems. As the demands for modernized legacy systems rise, so does the need for frameworks for integrating or transforming existing systems. The Object Management Group (OMG) has adopted the Model Driven Architecture (MDA) which is an evolving conceptual architecture that aligns with this demand (OMG, 2011) (MDA, 2005).

MDA raises the level of reasoning to a more abstract level that places change and evolution in the center of software development process. The original inspiration around the definition of MDA had to do with the middleware integration problem in internet. Beyond interoperability reasons, there are other good benefits to use MDA such as to improve the productivity, process quality and maintenance costs.

The outstanding ideas behind MDA are separating the specification of the system functionality from its implementation on specific platforms, managing the software evolution from abstract models to implementations increasing the degree of automation and achieving interoperability with multiple platforms, programming languages and formal languages (MDA, 2005).

The initial diffusion of MDA was focused on its relation with UML as modeling language. However, there are UML users who do not use MDA, and MDA users who use other modeling languages such as some DSL (Domain Specific Language). The essence of MDA is the meta-metamodel MOF (Meta Object Facility) that allows different kinds of artifacts from multiple vendors to be used together in a same project (MOF, 2006). The MOF 2.0 Query, View, Transformation (QVT) metamodel is the standard for expressing transformations (QVT, 2008).

The success of MDA-based reverse engineering depends on the existence of CASE (Computer Aided Software Engineering) tools that make a significant impact on the process automation. Commercial MDA tools have recently begun to emerge. In general, pre-existing UML tools have been extended to support MDA. The current techniques available in these tools provide forward engineering and limited facilities for reverse engineering (CASE MDA, 2011). The Eclipse Modeling Framework (EMF) (Eclipse, 2011) was created for facilitating system modeling and the automatic generation of Java code and several tools aligned with MDA are been developed. Modisco is an official Eclipse project dedicated to Model Driven Reverse Engineering (MDRE) from IT legacy systems and supports reverse engineering of UML class diagrams (Modisco, 2011).

Validation, verification and consistency are crucial activities in the modernization of legacy systems that are critical to safety, security and economic profits. One of the important features for a rigorous development is the combination of tests and proofs. When artifacts at different levels of abstraction are available, a continuous consistency check between them could help to reduce development mistakes, for example checking whether the code is consistent with the design or is in compliance with assertions.

1.2 Outline of the chapter

The progress in the last decade in scalability and incremental verification of basic formal methods could be used as a complement of static and dynamic analysis with tests, assertions and partial formal specification. In this light, this chapter describes MDA reverse engineering of object-oriented code that is based on the integration of traditional compiler techniques such as static and dynamic analysis, metamodeling techniques based on MDA standards and, partial formal specification. We propose to exploit the source code as the most reliable description of both, the behavior of the software and the organization and its business rules. Different principles of reverse engineering are covered, with special emphasis on consistency, testing and verification. We propose a formal metamodeling technique to control the evolution of metamodels that are the essence to achieve interoperability between different software artifacts involved in reverse engineering processes. Rather than requiring that users of transformation tools manipulate formal specification, we want to provide formal semantic to graphical metamodeling notations and develop rigorous tools that permit users to directly manipulate metamodels they have created. As an example, we analyze the reverse engineering of Java code however the bases of our approach can be easily applied to other object-oriented languages.

The following sections include background on MDA and Case tools, foundations of innovative processes based on formal specification and, challenges and strategic directions that can be adopted in the field of MDA reverse engineering.

2. Model driven architecture: An introduction

The architecture of a system is a specification of software components, interrelationships, and rules for component interactions and evolution over time.

In 2001 OMG adopted an architecture standard, the Model Driven Architecture (MDA). With the emergence of internet applications, the interoperability problem moved from the integration of platforms and programming languages on a company intranet to the integration of different middleware on the Internet. In this situation, the middleware is part of the problem itself (MDA, 2005). The original inspiration around the definition of MDA had to do with this internet middleware integration problem. Apart from interoperability reasons, there are other good benefits to use MDA such as to improve the productivity, code and processes quality and, software maintenance costs.

MDA is an architectural framework for improving portability, interoperability and reusability through separation of concerns. It uses models to direct the complete lifecycle of a system; all artifacts such as requirement specifications, architecture descriptions, design descriptions and code, are regarded as models. MDA provides an approach for specifying a system independently of the platforms that it supports, specifying platforms, selecting a particular platform for the system, and transforming the system specification into one implementation for the selected particular platform. It distinguishes Computation Independent Model (CIM), Platform Independent Model (PIM), Platform Specific Model (PSM) and Implementation Specific Model (ISM).

The Unified Modeling Language (UML) (UML,2010a) (UML,2010b) combined with the Object Constraint Language (OCL) (OCL, 2010) is the most widely used way for writing either PIMs or PSMs.

Model Driven Development (MDD) refers to a range of development approaches that are based on the use of software models as first class entities. MDA is the specific realization of MDD proposed by OMG. It is carried out as a sequence of model transformations: the process of converting one model into another one of the same system preserving some kind of equivalence relation between them.

The idea behind MDA is to manage the evolution from CIMs to PIMs and PSMs that can be used to generated executable components and applications. The high-level models that are developed independently of a particular platform are gradually transformed into models and code for specific platforms.

The concept of metamodel, an abstract language for describing different types of models and data, has contributed significantly to some of the core principles of the emerging MDA. The Meta Object Facility (MOF), an adopted OMG standard, (latest revision MOF 2.0) provides a metadata management framework, and a set of metadata services to enable the development and interoperability of model and metadata driven systems (MOF, 2006).

MDA reverse engineering can be used to recover architectural models of legacy systems that will be later used in forward engineering processes to produce new versions of the systems. OMG is involved in a series of standards to successfully modernize existing information systems. Modernization supports, but are not limited to, source to source conversion, platform migration, service oriented architecture migration and model driven architecture migration. Architecture Driven Modernization (ADM) is an OMG initiative related to extending the modeling approach to the existing software systems and to the concept of reverse engineering (ADM, 2010). One of ADM standards is Knowledge Discovery Metamodel (KDM) to facilitate the exchange of existing systems meta-data for various modernization tools (KDM, 2011). The following section presents the concepts of model, metamodel and transformation in more detail.

2.1 Basic MDA concepts

2.1.1 Models

A model is a simplified view of a (part of) system and its environments. Models are expressed in a well-defined modeling language. They are centered in a set of diagrams and textual notations that allow specifying, visualizing and documenting systems.

For instance, a model could be a set of UML diagrams, OCL specifications and text. MDA distinguishes different kinds of models which go from abstract models that specify the system functionality to platform-dependent and concrete models linked to specific platforms, technologies and implementations. MDA distinguishes at least the following ones:

- Computation Independent Model (CIM)
- Platform Independent Model (PIM)
- Platform Specific Model (PSM)
- Implementation Specific Model (ISM)

A CIM describes a system from the computation independent viewpoint that focuses on the environment of and the requirements for the system. It is independent of how the system is implemented. In general, it is called domain model and may be expressed using business models. The CIM helps to bridge the gap between the experts about the domain and the software engineer. A CIM could consist of UML models and other models of requirements.

In the context of MDA, a platform "is a set of subsystems and technologies that provides a coherent set of functionality through interfaces and specified usage patterns, which any application supported by that platform can use without concern for the details of how the functionality provided by the platform is implemented". (MDA, 2005). An application refers to a functionality being developed. A system can be described in terms of one or more applications supported by one or more platforms. MDA is based on platform models expressed in UML, OCL, and stored in a repository aligned with MOF.

A PIM is a view of the system that focuses on the operation of a system from the platform independent viewpoint. Analysis and logical models are typically independent of implementation and specific platforms and can be considered PIMs.

A PIM is defined as a set of components and functionalities, which are defined independently of any specific platforms, and which can be realized in platform specific models. A PIM can be viewed as a system model for a technology-neutral virtual machine that includes parts and services defined independently of any specific platform. It can be viewed as an abstraction of a system that can be realized by different platform-specific ways on which the virtual machine can be implemented.

A PSM describes a system in the terms of the final implementation platform e.g., .NET or J2EE. A PSM is a view of the system from the platform specific viewpoint that combines a PIM with the details specifying how that system uses a particular type of platform. It includes a set of technical concepts representing the different parts and services provided by the platform.

An ISM is a specification which provides all the information needed to construct an executable system.

Although there is a structural gap between CIM and PIM, a CIM should be traceable to PIM. In the same way, a PIM should be traceable to PSMs which in turn should be traceable to ISMs.

2.1.2 Metamodels

Metamodeling is a powerful technique to specify families of models. A metamodel is a model that defines the language for expressing a model, i.e. "a model of models". A metamodel is an explicit model of the constructs and rules needed to build specific models. It is a description of all the concepts that can be used in a model.

A meta-metamodel defines a language to write metamodels. Since a metamodel itself is a model, it can be usually defined using a reflexive definition in a modeling language. A metamodel can be viewed as a model of a modeling language.

Metamodeling has become an essential technique in MDA. In particular, MDA is based on the use of a language to write metamodels called the Meta Object Facility (MOF). MOF uses an object modeling framework that is essentially a subset of the UML 2.2 core. The four main modeling concepts are classes, which model MOF meta-objects; associations, which model binary relations between meta-objects; Data Types, which model other data; and Packages, which modularize the models (MOF, 2006). The UML itself is defined using a metamodeling approach.

The metamodeling framework is based on four meta-layer architectures: meta-metamodel, metamodel, model and object model layers. The primary responsibility of these layers is to define languages that describe metamodels, models, semantic domains and run-time instances of model elements respectively.

Related OMG standard metamodels and meta-metamodels share a common design philosophy. All of them, including MOF, are expressed using MOF that defines a common way for capturing all the diversity of modeling standards and interchange constructs that are used in MDA. Its goal is to define languages in a same way and hence integrate them semantically.

2.1.3 Transformations

Model transformation is the process of converting one model into another model of the same system preserving some kind of equivalence relation between both of these models.

The idea behind MDA is to manage the evolution from CIMs to PIMs and PSMs that can be used to generated executable components and applications. The high-level models that are developed independently of a particular platform are gradually transformed into models and code for specific platforms.

The transformation for one PIM to several PSMs is at the core of MDA. A model-driven forward engineering process is carried out as a sequence of model transformations that includes, at least, the following steps: construct a CIM; transform the CIM into a PIM that provides a computing architecture independent of specific platforms; transform the PIM into one or more PSMs, and derive code directly from the PSMs.

We can distinguish three types of transformations to support model evolution in forward and reverse engineering processes: refinements, code-to-models and refactorings.

A refinement is the process of building a more detailed specification that conforms to another that is more abstract. On the other hand, a code-to-model transformation is the process of extracting from a more detailed specification (or code) another one, more abstract, that is conformed by the more detailed specification. Refactoring means changing a model leaving its behavior unchanged, but enhancing some non-functional quality factors such as simplicity, flexibility, understandability and performance.

Metamodel transformations are contracts between a source metamodel and a target metamodel and describe families of transformations.

Figure 1 partially depicts the different kind of transformations and the relationships between models and metamodels.

The MOF 2.0 Query, View, Transformation (QVT) specification is the OMG standard for model transformations (QVT, 2008). The acronym QVT refers to:

- Query: ad-hoc "query" for selecting and filtering of model elements. In general, a query selects elements of the source model of the transformation.
- View: "views" of MOF metamodels (that are involved in the transformation).
- Transformation: a relation between a source metamodel S and a target metamodel T that is used to generate a target model (that conforms to T) from a source model (that conforms to S).

QVT defines a standard for transforming a source model into a target model. One of the underlying ideas in QVT is that the source and target model must conform to arbitrary MOF metamodels. Another concept is that the transformation is considered itself as a model that conforms to a MOF metamodel.

The QVT specification has a hybrid declarative/imperative nature. The declarative part of this specification is structured in two layers:

- A user-friendly Relations metamodel and language which supports the creation of object template, complex object pattern matching and the creation of traces between model elements involved in a transformation.
- A Core metamodel and language defined using minimal extensions to EMOF and OCL. All trace classes are explicitly defined as MOF models, and trace instance creation and deletion is in the same way as the creation and deletion of any other object. This specification describes three related transformational languages: Relations, Core and Operational Matching.

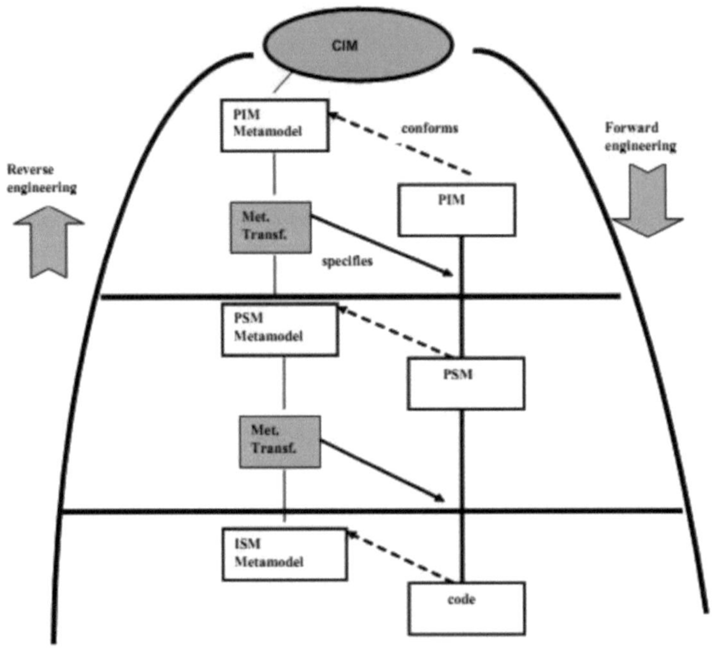

Fig. 1. Model, metamodels and transformations

2.2 MDA case tools

The success of MDA depends on the existence of CASE tools that make a significant impact on software processes such as forward engineering and reverse engineering processes, however all of the MDA tools are partially compliant to MDA features. The main limitations of MDA tools are related to the incipient evolution of metamodeling standards such as QVT or KDM and to the lack of specification (in terms of MDA standards) of various platforms. The article (Stevens, 2008) argues that a considerable amount of basic research is needed before suitable tools will be fully realizable.

The major developments taking place in the framework of the Eclipse project (Eclipse, 2011).

For instance, the Eclipse Modeling Framework (EMF) was created for facilitating system modeling and the automatic generation of Java code. EMF started as an implementation of MOF resulting Ecore, the EMF metamodel comparable to EMOF. EMF has evolved starting from the experience of the Eclipse community to implement a variety of tools and to date is highly related to Model Driven Engineering (MDE). For instance, ATL (Atlas Transformation Language) is a model transformation language in the field of MDE that is developed on top of the Eclipse platform (ATL, 2011).

Commercial tools such as IBM Rational Software Architect, Spark System Enterprise Architect or Together are integrated with Eclipse-EMF (CASE MDA, 2011).

Few MDA-based CASE tools support QVT or at least, any of the QVT languages. As an example, IBM Rational Software Architect and Spark System Enterprise Architect do not implement QVT. Other tools partially support QVT, for instance Together allows defining and modifying transformations model-to-model (M2M) and model-to-text (M2T) that are QVT-Operational compliant. Medini QVT partially implements QVT (Medini, 2011). It is integrated with Eclipse and allows the execution of transformations expressed in the QVT-Relation language. Eclipse M2M, the official tool compatible with of Eclipse 3.5 and EMF 2.5.0, is still under development and implements the specification of QVT-Operational.

Blu Age and Modisco are ADM compliant Case tools and built on Eclipse that allow reverse engineering (Modisco, 2011) (CASE MDA, 2011). Modisco is considered by ADM as the reference provider for real implementations of several of its standards such as KDM and Abstract Syntax Tree Metamodel (ASTM), in particular. MoDisco provides an extensible framework to develop model-driven tools to support use-cases of existing software modernization. It uses EMF to describe and manipulate models, M2M to implement transformation of models into other models, Eclipse M2T to implement generation of text and Eclipse Java Development Tools (JDT). At the moment, Modisco supports reverse engineering of class diagrams. Some interesting challenges are still open in it, for instance, reverse engineering of different UML diagrams and scalability.

Another limitation of the MDA tools has to do with model validation. Reasoning about models of systems is well supported by automated theorem provers and model checkers, however these tools are not integrated into CASE tools environments. Only research tools provide support for formal specification and deductive verification. As an example, we can mention USE 3.0 that is a system for specification of information systems in OCL. USE allows snapshots of running systems can be created and manipulated during an animation, checking OCL constraints to validate the specification against non-formal requirements (Use, 2011) (OCL USE, 2011).

3. Metamodel formalization

The essence of MDA is metamodeling, MOF in particular. OCL is widely used by MOF-based metamodels to constrain and perform evaluations on them. OCL contains many inconsistencies and evolves with MDA standards (Willink, 2011). OCL has a denotational semantics that has been implemented in tools that allow dynamic validation of snapshots. However, it cannot be considered strictly a formal specification language due to a formal language must at least provide syntax, some semantics and an inference system. The syntax defines the structure of the text of a formal specification including properties that are expressed as axioms (formulas of some logic). The semantics describes the models linked to a given specification; in the formal specification context, a model is a mathematical object that defines behavior of the realizations of the specifications. The inference system allows defining deductions that can be made from a formal specification. These deductions allow new formulas to be derived and checked. So, the inference system can help to automate testing, prototyping or verification.

A combination of MOF metamodeling and formal specification can help us to address MDA-based processes such as forward engineering and reverse engineering. In light of this we define a special-purpose language, called NEREUS, to provide extra support for metamodeling. NEREUS takes advantage of existing theoretical background on formal methods, for instance, the notions of refinement, implementation correctness, observable equivalences and behavioral equivalences that play an essential role in model-to-model transformations. Most of the MOF metamodel concepts can be mapped directly to NEREUS. The type system of NEREUS was defined rigorously in the algebraic framework.

The semantics of MOF metamodels (that is specified in OCL) can be enriched and refined by integrating it with NEREUS. This integration facilitates proofs and tests of models and model transformations via the formal specification of metamodels. Some properties can be deduced from the formal specification and could be re-injected into the MOF specification without wasting the advantages of semi-formal languages of being more intuitive and pragmatic for most implementers and practitioners.

Our approach has two main advantages linked to automation and interoperability. On the one hand, we show how to generate automatically formal specifications from MOF metamodels. Due to scalability problems, this is an essential prerequisite. We define a system of transformation rules for translating MOF metamodels specified in OCL into algebraic languages. On the other hand, our approach focuses on interoperability of formal languages. Languages that are defined in terms of NEREUS metamodels can be related to each other because they are defined in the same way through a textual syntax. Any number of source languages such as different DSLs and target languages (different formal language) could be connected without having to define explicit metamodel transformations for each language pair. Such as MOF is a DSL to define semi-formal metamodels, NEREUS can be viewed as a DSL for defining formal metamodels.

In addition to define strictly the type system, NEREUS, like algebraic languages, allows finding instance models that satisfy metamodel specification. Semiformal metamodels such as MOF do not find instance models and only detect constraint violations.

Another advantage of our approach is linked to pragmatic aspects. NEREUS is a formal notation closed to MOF metamodels that allows meta-designers who must manipulate metamodels to understand their formal specification.

NEREUS allows specifying metamodels such as the Ecore metamodel, the specific metamodel for defining models in EMF (Eclipse Modeling Framework) (Eclipse, 2010). Today, we are integrating NEREUS in EMF.

3.1 NEREUS language specification

NEREUS consists of several constructs to express classes, associations and packages and a repertoire of mechanisms for structuring them. Next, we show the syntax of a class in NEREUS:

CLASS className [*<parameterList>*]	**OPERATIONS** *<operationList>*
IMPORTS *<importList>*	**EFFECTIVE**
IS-SUBTYPE-OF *<subtypeList>*	**TYPES** *<sortList>*
INHERITS *<inheritList>*	**OPERATIONS** *<operationList>*
GENERATED-BY *<constructorList>*	**AXIOMS** *<varList>*
DEFERRED	*<axiomList>*
TYPES *<sortList>*	**END-CLASS**

NEREUS distinguishes variable parts in a specification by means of explicit parameterization. The IMPORTS clause expresses client relations. The specification of the new class is based on the imported specifications declared in *<importstList>* and their public operations may be used in the new specification. NEREUS distinguishes inheritance from subtyping. Subtyping is like inheritance of behavior, while inheritance relies on the module viewpoint of classes. Inheritance is expressed in the INHERITS clause, the specification of the class is built from the union of the specifications of the classes appearing in the *<inheritList>*. Subtypings are declared in the IS-SUBTYPE-OF clause. A notion closely related with subtyping is polymorphism, which satisfies the property that each object of a subclass is at the same time an object of its superclasses. NEREUS allows us to define local instances of a class in the IMPORTS and INHERITS clauses.

NEREUS distinguishes deferred and effective parts. The DEFERRED clause declares new types or operations that are incompletely defined. The EFFECTIVE clause either declares new sorts or operations that are completely defined, or completes the definition of some inherited sort or operation. Attributes and operations are declared in ATTRIBUTES and OPERATIONS clauses. NEREUS supports higher-order operations (a function f is higher-order if functional sorts appear in a parameter sort or the result sort of f). In the context of OCL Collection formalization, second-order operations are required. In NEREUS it is possible to specify any of the three levels of visibility for operations: public, protected and private. NEREUS provides the construction LET… IN.. to limit the scope of the declarations of auxiliary symbols by using local definitions.

NEREUS provides a taxonomy of type constructors that classifies associations according to kind (aggregation, composition, association, association class, qualified association), degree (unary, binary), navigability (unidirectional, bidirectional) and connectivity (one-to one, one-to-many, many-to-many). New associations can be defined by the ASSOCIATION construction. The IS clause expresses the instantiation of *<typeConstructorName>* with classes, roles, visibility, and multiplicity. The CONSTRAINED-BY clause allows the specification of static constraints in first order logic. Next, we show the association syntax:

ASSOCIATION <relationName>
IS <typeConstructorName>
[…:class1;…:class2;…:role1;…:role2;…:mult1;…:mult2;…:visibility1;…:visibility2]
CONSTRAINED-BY <constraintList>
END

Associations are defined in a class by means of the ASSOCIATES clause:

CLASS className…
ASSOCIATES <<associationName>>…
END-CLASS

The PACKAGE construct groups classes and associations and controls its visibility. *<importsList>* lists the imported packages; *<inheritList>* lists the inherited packages and *<elements>* are classes, associations and packages. Next, we show the package syntax:

PACKAGE packageName
IMPORTING <importsList>
GENERALIZATION <inheritsList>
NESTING <nestingList>
CLUSTERING <clusteringList>
<elements>
END-PACKAGE

NEREUS is an intermediate notation open to many other formal languages such as algebraic, logic or functional. We define its semantics by giving a precise formal meaning to each of the constructs of the NEREUS language in terms of the CASL language (Bidoit & Mosses, 2004).

3.2 Transforming metamodels into NEREUS

We define a bridge between EMOF- and Ecore- metamodels and NEREUS. The NEREUS specification is completed gradually. First, the signature and some axioms of classes are obtained by instantiating reusable schemes. Associations are transformed by using a reusable component ASSOCIATION. Next, OCL specifications are transformed using a set of transformation rules and a specification that reflects all the information of MOF metamodels is constructed.

The OCL basic types are associated with NEREUS basic types with the same name. NEREUS provides classes for collection type hierarchies. The types Set, Ordered Set, Bag and Sequence are subtypes of Collection.

The transformation process of OCL specifications to NEREUS is supported by a system of transformation rules. By analyzing OCL specifications we can derive axioms that will be included in the NEREUS specifications. Preconditions written in OCL are used to generate preconditions in NEREUS. Postconditions and invariants allow us to generate axioms in NEREUS. We define a system of transformation rules that only considers expressions based on Essential OCL (OCL, 2010). The following metaclasses defined in complete OCL are not part of the EssentialOCL: *MessageType, StateExp, ElementType, AssociationClassCallExp, MessageExp,* and *UnspecifiedValueExp*. Any well-formed rules defined for these classes are consequently not part of the definition of the transformation rule system.

The system includes a small set with around fifty rules. It was built by means of an iterative approach through successive refinements. The set of rules was validated by analyzing the different OCL expression attached to the UML metamodels, MOF and QVT.

As an example we show a few rules of the system. A detailed description of the system may be found at (Favre, 2010). In each rule the shaded text denotes an OCL expression that can be translated by the non-shaded text in NEREUS:

Rule	OCL NEREUS
R1	v. operation(parameters) operation(*Translate*$_{\text{NEREUS}}$(v),*Translate*$_{\text{NEREUS}}$ (parameters))
R2	v->operation (parameters) operation(*Translate*$_{\text{NEREUS}}$(v),*Translate*$_{\text{NEREUS}}$ (parameters))
R3	v.attribute attribute (v)
R4	**context** Assoc object.rolename *Let a:Assoc* get_rolename (a, object)

R5	e.op e: expression op(*Translate*$_{NEREUS}$(e))
R6	exp1 infix-op exp2 *Translate*$_{NEREUS}$(exp1)*Translate*$_{NEREUS}$(infix-op) *Translate*$_{NEREUS}$(exp2) *Translate*$_{NEREUS}$(infix-oper) (*Translate*$_{NEREUS}$(exp1),*Translate*$_{NEREUS}$(exp2))
R7	T-> operationName (v :Type | bool-expr-with-v) OperationName ::= forAll | exists | select | reject T ::= Collection | Set | OrderedSet | Bag operationName (v) (*Translate*$_{NEREUS}$ (T), [*Translate*$_{NEREUS}$ (bool-expr-with-v)])

As an example, we show the formalization in NEREUS of a simplified QVT Core metamodel (Figure 2). The Core language is as powerful as the Relation language and may be used as a reference for the semantics of relations, which are mapped to Core. The complete diagram may be found at (QVT, 2008, pp.15). Figure 2 shows a simplified metamodel including transformation and rules classes.

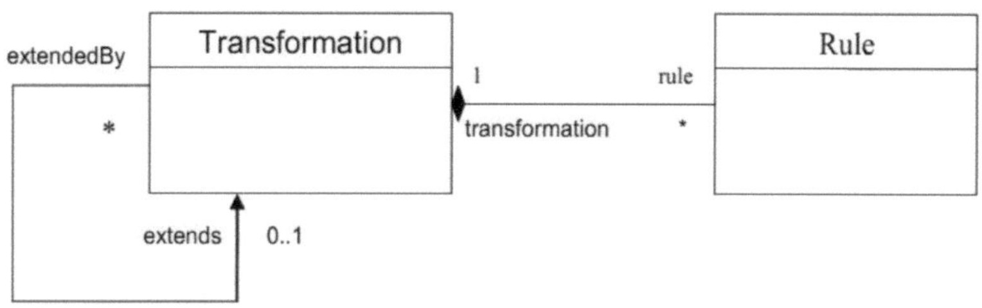

Fig. 2. A simplified metamodel

A transformation defines how one set of models can be transformed into another. It is composed by a set of rules that specify its execution behavior. The following constraints (*extendingRule* and *transitiveRule*) may be attached to Figure 2 specifying that the rules of the extended transformation are included in the extending transformation and the extension is transitive:

extendingRule = Transformation.allInstances ->
forAll (t | t.extends.size = 1 implies t.extends.rule -> include (t.rule))
transitiveRule = Transformation.allInstances ->
forAll (t1, t2, t3 | t1.extends.size = 1 and t2.extends.size = 1 and t3.extends.size = 1
and (t1.extends.rule -> includes (t2.rule) and
t2.extends.rule -> includes (t3.rules)) implies t1.extends.rule -> includes (t3.rule)

The OCL specification, *extendingRule* and *transformationRule* can be translated into the shaded axioms of the following specification:

PACKAGE QVTBase
CLASS Transformation
IMPORTS EMOF::Tag
INHERITS EMOF::MetaClass, EMOF::Package

ASSOCIATES <<Transformation-Tag>> <<Transformation-Transformation>>
<<Transformation-Rule>> <<Transformation-TypeModel>>
AXIOMS ass1: <<Transformation-Transformation>>; ass2: <<Transformation-Rule>> ;
t: Transformation ;...
size (get_extends (ass1, t)) = 1 implies
includes (get_rule (ass2, get_extends (ass1, t)), get_rule (ass1, t))
END-CLASS
CLASS TypedModel
IMPORTS EMOF::Package
IS-SUBTYPE-OF EMOF::NamedElement
ASSOCIATES
<<Transformation-TypeModel>> <<TypeModel-Package>> <<Domain-TypeModel>>
<<TypeModel-TypeModel>>
END-CLASS
CLASS Domain
IS-SUBTYPE-OF EMOF::NamedElement
ASSOCIATES <<Rule-Domain>> <<Domain-TypeModel>>
DEFERRED
ATTRIBUTES
isCheckable: Domain -> Boolean
isEnforceable: Domain -> Boolean
END-CLASS
CLASS Rule
IS-SUBTYPE-OF EMOF::NamedElement
ASSOCIATES
<<Rule-Domain>> <<Rule-Rule>> <<Transformation-Rule>>
END-CLASS
ASSOCIATION Transformation-Transformation
IS Unidirectional-2 [Transformation: class1; Transformation: class2; extendedBy: role1; extends: role2; *: mult1; 0..1: mult2; +: visibility1; + : visibility2]
END-ASSOCIATION
ASSOCIATION Transformation-Rule
IS Composition-2 [Transformation: class1; Rule: class2; transformation: role1; rule: role2; 1: mult1; *: mult2; +: visibility1; +: visibility2]
END-ASSOCIATION...
END-PACKAGE

NEREUS can be integrated with object-oriented languages such as Eiffel. The article (Favre, 2005) describes a forward engineering process from UML static models to object-oriented code. More information related to the NEREUS approach may be found at (Favre, 2010) and (Favre, 2009). However, we would like remark that here NEREUS is used as an intermediate formal notation to communicate the essential of an MDA reverse engineering approach.

4. Reverse engineering of object-oriented code

In this section we analyze traditional reverse engineering techniques based on static and dynamic analysis. We show how to reverse engineering object-oriented code to models, in particular. Static analysis extracts static information that describes the structure of the software reflected in the software documentation (e.g., the text of the source code) while dynamic analysis information describes the structure of the run-behavior. Static information can be extracted by using techniques and tools based on compiler techniques such as parsing and data flow algorithms. On the other hand, dynamic information can be extracted by using debuggers, event recorders and general tracer tools.

Figure 3 shows the different phases. The source code is parsed to obtain an abstract syntax tree (AST) associated with the source programming language grammar. Next, a metamodel extractor extracts a simplified, abstract version of the language that ignores all instructions that do not affect the data flows, for instance all control flows such as conditional and loops.

The information represented according to this metamodel allows building the OFG for a given source code, as well as conducting all other analysis that do not depend on the graph. The idea is to derive statically information by performing a propagation of data. Different kinds of analysis propagate different kinds of information in the data-flow graph, extracting the different kinds of diagrams that are included in a model.

The static analysis is based on classical compiler techniques (Aho, Sethi & Ullman, 1985) and abstract interpretation (Jones & Nielson, 1995). The generic flow propagation algorithms are specializations of classical flow analysis techniques. Because there are many possible executions, it is usually not reasonable to consider all states of the program. Thus, static analysis is based on abstract models of the program state that are easier to manipulate, although lose some information. Abstract interpretation of program state allows obtaining automatically as much information as possible about program executions without having to run the program on all input data and then ensuring computability or tractability.

The static analysis builds a partial model (PIM or PSM) that must be refined by dynamic analysis. Dynamic analysis is based on testing and profiling. Execution tracer tools generate execution model snapshots that allow us to deduce complementary information. Execution models, programs and UML models coexist in this process. An object-oriented execution model has the following components: a set of objects, a set of attributes for each object, a location for each object, each object refers to a value of an object type and, a set of messages that include a name selector and may include one or more arguments. Additionally, types are available for describing types of attributes and parameters of methods or constructors. On the other hand, an object-oriented program model has a set of classes, a set of attributes for each class, a set of operations for each class, and a generalization hierarchy over classes.

The combination of static and dynamic analysis can enrich the reverse engineering process. There are different ways of combination, for instance performing first static analysis and then dynamic analysis or perhaps iterating static and dynamic analysis.

4.1 Static analysis

The concepts and algorithms of data flow analysis described in (Aho, Sethi & Ullman, 1985) are adapted for reverse engineering object-oriented code. Data flow analysis infers information about the behavior of a program by only analyzing the text of the source code. The basic representation of this static analysis is the Object Flow Graph (OFG) that allows tracing information of object interactions from the object creation, through object assignment to variables, attributes or their use in messages (method invocations). OFG is defined as an oriented graph that represents all data flows linking objects.

The static analysis is data flow sensitive, but control flow insensitive. This means that programs with different control flows and the same data flows are associated with the same analysis results. The choice of this program representation is motivated by the computational complexity of the involved algorithms. On the one hand, control flow sensitive analysis is computationally intractable and on the other hand, data flow sensitive analysis is aligned to the "nature" of the object-oriented programs whose execution models impose more constraints on the data flows than on the control flows. For example, the sequence of method invocations may change when moving from an application which uses a class to another one, while the possible ways to copy and propagate object references remains more stable.

A consequence of the control flow insensitivity is that the construction of the OFG can be described with reference to a simplified, abstract version of the object-oriented languages in which instructions related to flow control are ignored. A generic algorithm of flow propagation working on the OFG processes object information. In the following, we describe the three essential components of the common analysis framework: the simplified abstract object-oriented language, the data flow graph and the flow propagation algorithm.

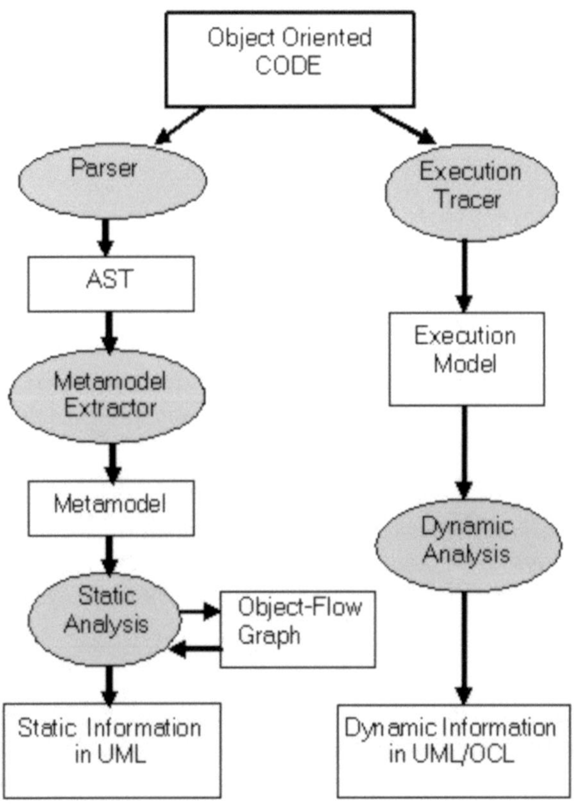

Fig. 3. Static and dynamic analysis

All instructions that refer to data flows are represented in the abstract language, while all control flow instructions such as conditional and different iteration constructs are ignored. To avoid name conflicts all identifiers are given fully scoped names including a list of enclosing packages, classes and methods. The abstract syntax of a simplified language (Tonella & Potrich, 2005) is as follows:

(1)	P	::=	D*S*
(2)	D	::=	a
(3)		|	m (p_1,p_2,…,p_j)
(4)		|	cons (p_1,p_2,…,p_j)
(5)	S	::=	x = new c (a_1,a_2,…a_j)
(6)		|	x = y
(7)		|	[x =] y.m (a_1,a_2,…,a_j)

Some notational conventions are considered: non-terminals are denoted by upper case letters; a is class attribute name; *m* is method name; p_1, p_2,…p_j are formal parameters; a_1,a_2,…a_j are actual parameters and *cons* is class constructor and *c* is class name. *x* and *y* are program locations that are globally data objects, i.e. object with an address into memory such as variables, class attributes and method parameters

A program P consists of zero or more declarations (D*) concatenated with zero or more statements (S*). The order of declarations and statements is irrelevant. The nesting structure of packages, classes and statements is flattened, i.e. statements belonging to different methods are identified by using their fully scope names for their identifiers.

There are three types of declarations: attribute declarations (2), method declarations (3) and constructor declaration (4). An attribute declaration is defined by the scope determined by the list of packages, classes, followed by the attribute identifier. A method declaration consists in its name followed by a list of formal parameter (p_1,p_2,…p_j). Constructors have a similar declaration.

There are three types of statement declarations: allocation statements (5), assignments (6) and method invocation (7). The left hand side and the right hand side of all statements is a program location. The target of a method invocation is also a program location.

The process of transformation of an object-oriented program into a simplified language can be easily automated.

The Object Flow Graph (OFG) is a pair (N, E) where N is a set of nodes and E is a set of edges. A node is added for each program location (i.e. formal parameter or attribute). Edges represent the data flows appearing in the program. They are added to the OFG according to the rules specified in (Tonella & Potrich, 2005, pp. 26). Next, we describe the rules for constructing OFG from Java statements:

(1)	P	::=	D*S*	{}
(2)	D	::=	a	{}
(3)		|	m ($p_1,p_2,\ldots,p_j$)	{}
(4)		|	cons ($p_1,p_2,\ldots,p_j$)	{}
(5)	S	::=	x = new c ($a_1,a_2,\ldots a_j$)	{(a_1,p_1) ∈E,..(a_j,p_j) ∈E, (cons.this,x)∈ E}
(6)		|	x = y	{(y,x) ∈ E}
(7)		|	[x =] y.m ($a_1,a_2,\ldots,a_j$)	{(y, m.this) ∈E, (a_1,p_1) ∈E,..(a_j,p_j)∈E, (m.return,x) ∈E}

When a constructor or method is invoked, edges are built which connect each actual parameter a_i to the respective formal parameter p_i. In case of constructor invocation, the newly created object, referenced by *cons.this* is paired with the left hand side *x* of the related assignment. In case of method invocation, the target object *y* becomes *m.this* inside the called method, generating the edge (*y, m.this*), and the value returned by method *m* (if any) flows to the left hand side *x* (pair (*m.return, x*)).

Some edges in the OFG may be related to object flows that are external to the analyzed code. Examples of external flows are related with the usage of class libraries, dynamic loading (through reflection) or the access to modules written in other programming language. Due to these external flows can be treated in a similar way next, we show how to affect the OFG the usage of class libraries.

Each time a library class introduces a data flow from a variable *x* to a variable *y* an edge *(x,y)* must be included in the OFG. Containers are an example of library classes that introduce external data flows, for instance, any Java class implementing the interface *Collection* or the interface *Map*. Object containers provide two basic operations affecting the OFG: insert and extract for adding an object to a container and accessing an object in a container respectively. In the abstract program representation, insertion and extraction methods are associated with container objects.

Next, we show a pseudo-code of a generic forward propagation algorithm that is a specific instance of the algorithms applied to control flow graph described in (Aho, Sethi & Ullman, 1985):

```
for each node n ∈N
in[n] = {};
out[n]= gen[n] U (in[n] - kill[n])
endfor
while any in[n] or out[n] changes
for each node n ∈N
in[n] = U_{p∈pred(n)} out[p];
out[n] = gen[n] U(in[n] - kill[n])
endfor
endwhile
```

Let *gen[n]* and *kill[n]* be two sets of each basic node n ∈ N. *gen[n]* is the set of flow information entities generated by *n. kill[n]* is the set of definition outside of *n* that define entities that also have definitions within n. There are two sets of equations, called data-flow equations that relate incoming and outgoing flow information inside the sets:

$$in[n] = \cup_{p \in pred(n)} out[p]$$
$$out[n] = gen[n] \cup (in[n] - kill[n])$$

Each node *n* stores the incoming and outgoing flow information inside the sets *in[n]* and *out[n],* which are initially empty. Each node *n* generates the set of flow information entities included in *gen[s]* set, and prevents the elements of *kill[n]* set from being further propagated after node n. In forward propagation *in[n]* is obtained from the predecessors of node n as the union of the respective out sets.

The OFG based on the previous rules is "object insensitive"; this means that it is not possible to distinguish two locations (e.g. two class attributes) when they belongs to different class instances. An object sensitive OFG might improve the analysis results. It can be built by giving all non-static program locations an object scope instead of a class scope and objects can be identified statically by their allocation points. Thus, in an object sensitive OFG, non-static class attributes and methods with their parameters and local variables, are replicated for every statically identified object.

4.2 Dynamic analysis

Dynamic analysis operates by generating execution snapshots to collect life cycle traces of object instances and observing the executions to extract information. Ernst (2003) argues that whereas the chief challenge of static analysis is choosing a good abstract interpretation, the chief challenge of performing good dynamic analysis is selecting a representative set of test cases. A test case can help to detect properties of the program, but it can be difficult to detect whether results of a test are true program properties or properties of a particular execution context. The main limitation of dynamic analysis is related to the quality of the test cases used to produce diagrams.

Integrating dynamic and static analysis seems to be beneficial. The static and dynamic information could be shown as separated views or merged in a single view. In general, the outcome of the dynamic analysis could be visualized as a set of diagrams, each one associated with one execution trace of a test case. Although, the construction of these diagrams can be automated, their analysis requires human intervention in most cases. Dynamic analysis depends on the quality of the test cases.

Maoz and Harel (2010) present a powerful technique for the visualization and exploration of execution traces of models that is different from previous approaches that consider execution traces at the code level. This technique belongs to the domain of model-based dynamic analysis adapting classical visualization paradigms and techniques to specific needs of dynamic analysis. It allows relating the system execution traces and its models in different tasks such as testing whether a system run satisfies model properties. We consider that these results allow us to address reverse engineering challenges in the context of model-driven development.

4.3 An example: Recovering class diagram

In this section we describe how to extract class diagrams from Java code. A class diagram is a representation of the static view that shows a collection of static model elements, such as classes, interfaces, methods, attributes, types as well as their properties (e.g., type and visibility). Besides, the class diagram shows the interrelationships holding among the classes (UML, 2010a; UML, 2010b).

Some relevant work for automatic extraction of UML class diagram is present in the literature (Telea et al, 2009) (Milanova, 2007).

Reverse engineering of UML class diagram annotated in OCL from code is difficult task that cannot be fully automated. Certain elements in the class diagram carry behavioral information that cannot be inferred just from the analysis of the code.

A basic algorithm to extract class diagrams can be based on a purely syntactic analysis of the source code.

Figure 4 shows relationships that can be detected in this way between a Java program and a UML class diagram.

By analyzing the syntax of the source code, internal class features such as attributes and methods and their properties (e.g. the parameters of the methods and visibility) can be recovered. From the source code, associations, generalization, realizations and dependencies may be inferred too.

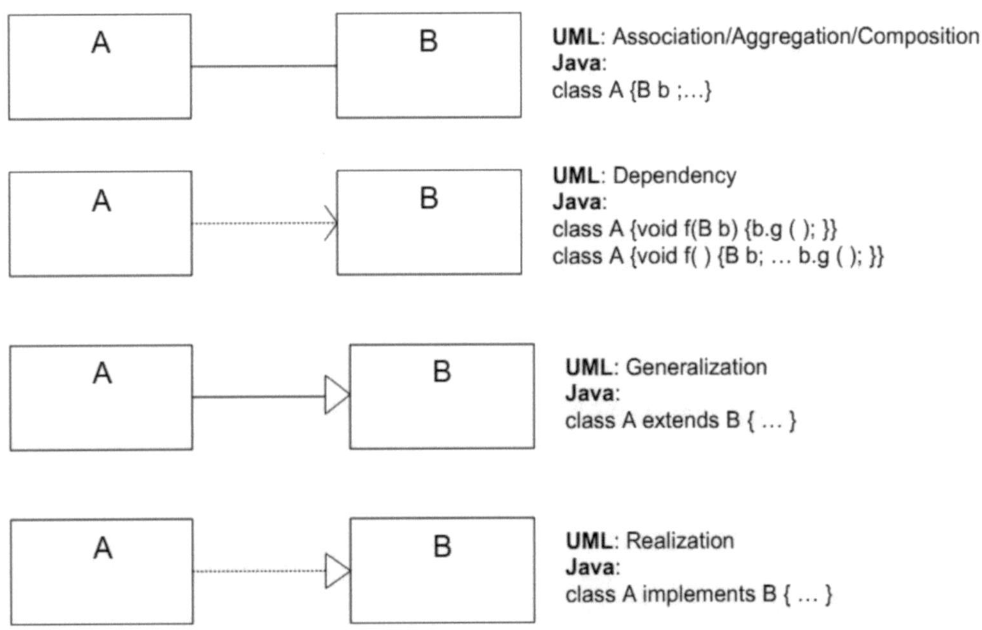

Fig. 4. ISM Java constructs versus PSM Java constructs

The main problems of the basic syntactic analysis are linked to the fact that declared types are an approximation of the classes instantiated due to inheritance and interfaces or, the usage of weakly typed container. Then, associations determined from the types of container declarations in the text do not specify the type of the contained object. A specialization of the generic forward propagation algorithm shown in 4.1 can be defined to solve this problem.

Another problem is how to distinguish between aggregation or composition. For instance, the association between A and B (Figure 4) could be an aggregation or a composition. An aggregation models the situation where an object is made up of several parts. Other properties that characterize the aggregation are the following:

- type-anti-symmetry: the aggregation from a type A (as whole) to a type B (as part), prevents the existence of another aggregation from B (as a whole) to A (as part)
- instance-reflexivity
- instance anti-symmetry

Milanova (2007) proposes an implementation-level ownership and composition model and a static analysis for identifying composition relationships in accordance with the model. In addition, they present an evaluation which shows that the analysis achieves "almost perfect precision, that is, it almost never misses composition relationships".

Another problem is how to infer OCL specifications (e.g. preconditions and postconditions of operations, invariants and association constraints) from code. In these cases, we need to capture system states through dynamic analysis.

Dynamic analysis allows generating execution snapshot to collect life cycle traces of object instances and reason from tests and proofs. Execution tracer tools generate execution model snapshots that allow us to deduce complementary information. The execution traces of different instances of the same class or method, could guide the construction of invariants or pre- and post-conditions respectively.

Dynamic analysis could also help to detect lifetime dependencies in associations scanning dependency configurations between the birth and death of a part object according to those of the whole.

5. Specifying metamodel-based transformations

We specify reverse engineering processes as MOF-based transformations. Metamodel transformations impose relations between a source metamodel and a target metamodel, both represented as MOF-metamodels. The transformations between models are described starting from the metaclass of the elements of the source model and the metaclass of the elements of the target model. The models to be transformed and the target models will be instances of the corresponding metamodel. Transformation semantics is aligned with QVT, in particular with the QVT Core. QVT depends on EssentialOCL (OCL, 2010) and EMOF (MOF, 2006). EMOF is a subset of MOF that allows simple metamodels to be defined using simple concepts. Essential OCL is a package exposing the minimal OCL required to work with EMOF.

A code-to-model transformation is the process of extracting from a more detailed specification (or code) another one, more abstract, that is conformed to the more detailed specification. Next, we describe how to specify code-to-model transformations within the proposed framework.

Figure 5.b shows partially an ISM-Java metamodel that includes constructs for representing classes, fields and operations. It also shows different kind of relationships such as composition and generalization. For example, an instance of JavaClass could be related to another instance of JavaClass that takes the role of *superclass* or, it could be composed by other instances of JavaClass that take the role of *nestedClass*. Figure 5.b shows the metamodel for operations. An operation is a subtype of the metaclass Operation of the UML kernel. There is a generalization between operation, constructor and method and so on.

Figure 5.a shows partially a PSM-Java metamodel that includes constructs for representing classes, fields, operations and association-ends. It also shows different kind of relationships such as composition and generalization. For example, an instance of JavaClass could be related to another instance of JavaClass that takes the role of *superclass* or, it could be composed by other instances of JavaClass that takes the role of *nestedClass*. The main difference between a Java-ISM and a Java-PSM is that the latter includes constructs for associations.

The transformation specification is an OCL contract that consists of a name, a set of parameters, a precondition and postconditions. The precondition states relations between the metaclasses of the source metamodel. The postconditions deal with the state of the models after the transformation. Next, a model-to-code transformation between an ISM-Java and a PSM-Java is partially specified.

Transformation ISM-Java to PSM-Java

parameters

source: ISM-JavaMetamodel::JavaPackage

target: PSM-JavaMetamodel ::Java Package

postconditions

let SetClassSource: Set[ISM-JavaMetamodel::JavaPackage::JavaClass] =

source.ownedMember -> select (oclIsKindOf (JavaPackage).javaClasses

in /*for each Java class in the ISM exists a PSM class with the same name*/

SetClassSource -> forAll (sClass | target.ownedMember ->select (oclIsKindOf (JavaClass))->

exists (tClass | sClass.name = tClass.name) and

/*for each associationEnd of a class in the PSM exists a private attribute of the same name in the ISM*/

sClass.fields->forAll (sField | SetClassSource->

exists (tc1 | tc1.type = sField.type implies tc1.associationEnd -> includes (sField.type)

and /*for each extends relation in Java exists a generalization in the PSM*/

(source.ownedMember -> select(oclIsKindOf (JavaClass).extendingClass ->

includes(sClass)) implies SetClassSource -> exists (t1 | t1.superclass.name = sClass.name)…

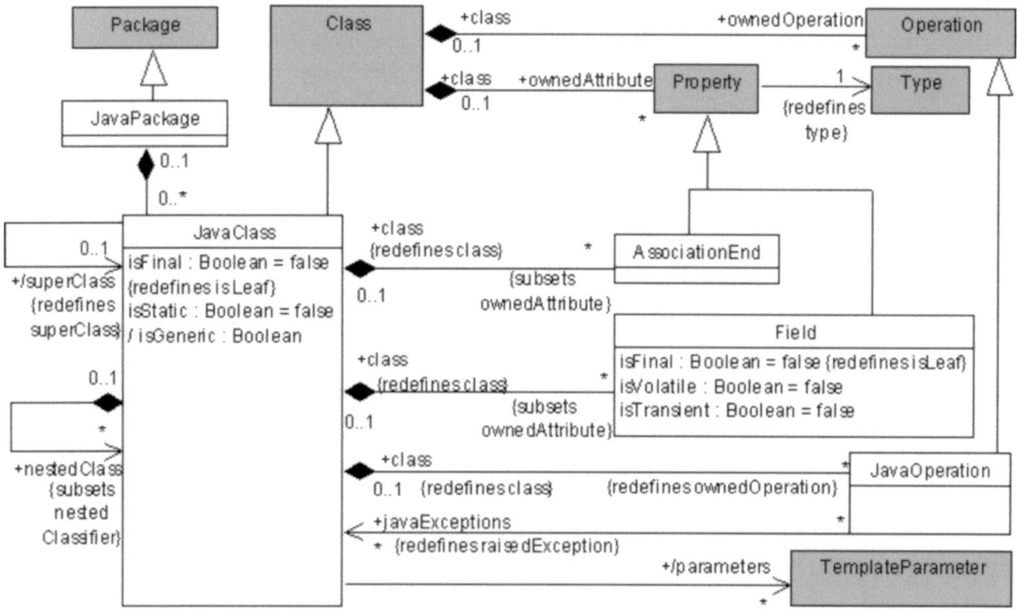

a. Specialized UML Metamodel of PSM Java

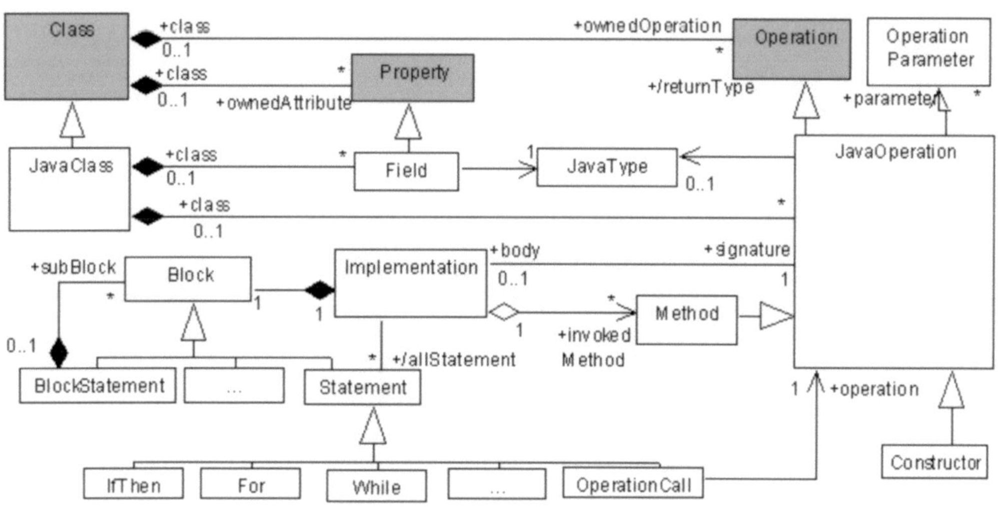

b. Specialized UML Metamodel of ISM Java

Fig. 5. PSM and ISM Java Metamodels

6. Summing up the parts: A framework for reverse engineering

In this section we propose an integration of traditional compiler techniques, metamodeling and formal specification.

Figure 6 shows a framework for reverse engineering that distinguishes three different abstraction levels linked to models, metamodels and formal specifications.

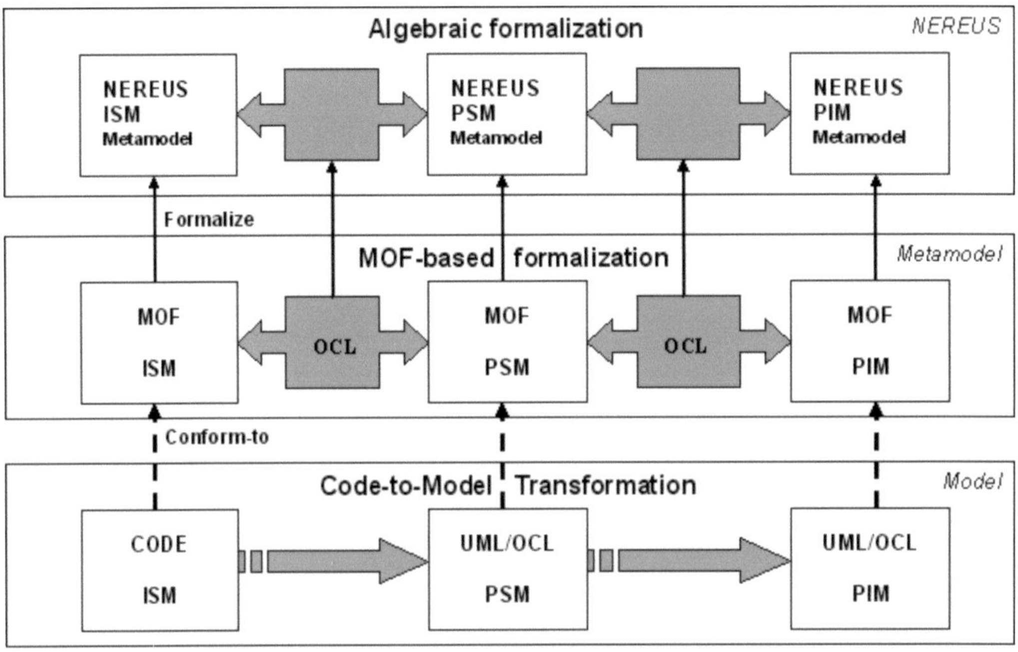

Fig. 6. An MDA-based Reverse Engineering Framework

The model level includes code, PIMs and PSMs. A PIM is a model with a high-level of abstraction that is independent of an implementation technology. A PSM is a tailored model to specify a system in terms of specific platform such J2EE or .NET. PIMs and PSMs are expressed in UML and OCL (UML, 2010a) (UML, 2010b) (OCL, 2010). The subset of UML diagrams that are useful for PSMs includes class diagram, object diagram, state diagram, interaction diagram and package diagram. On the other hand, a PIM can be expressed by means of use case diagrams, activity diagrams, interactions diagrams to model system processes and state diagrams to model lifecycle of the system entities. An ISM is a specification of the system in source code.

At model level, transformations are based on static and dynamic analysis. The metamodel level includes MOF metamodels that describe the transformations at model level. Metamodel transformations are specified as OCL contracts between a source metamodel and a target metamodel. MOF metamodels "control" the consistency of these transformations.

The level of formal specification includes specifications of MOF metamodels and metamodel transformations in the metamodeling language NEREUS that can be used to connect them with different formal and programming languages.

Our framework could be considered as an MDA-based formalization of the process described by Tonella and Potrich (2005). In this chapter we exemplify the bases of our approach with Class Diagram reverse engineering. However, our results include algorithms for extracting different UML diagrams such as interaction diagram, state diagram, use case diagram and activity diagram (Favre, 2010) (Favre, Martinez & Pereira, 2009) (Pereira, Martinez & Favre, 2011) (Martinez, Pereira, & Favre, 2011).

7. Challenges and strategic directions

Nowadays, software and system engineering industry evolves to manage new platform technologies, design techniques and processes. Architectural frameworks for information integration and tool interoperation, such as MDA, had created the need to develop new analysis tools and specific techniques.

A challenge on reverse engineering is the necessity to achieve co-evolution between different types of software artifacts or different representations of them. MDA allows us to develop and relate all different artifacts in a way that ensures their inter-consistency. MDA raises the level of reasoning to a more abstract level and therefore even more appropriate placing change and evolution in the center of software development process. The integration of business models with PIM, PSMs and code is a crucial challenge in MDA.

Existing formal methods provide a poor support for evolving specifications and incremental verification approaches. In particular, with the existing verification tools, simple changes in a system require to verify its complete specification again making the cost of the verification proportional to its size. To use formal methods that place change and evolution in the center of the software development process is another challenge. The progress in the last decade in scalability and incremental verification of formal methods could impact in MDA reverse engineering processes.

OMG is involved in the definition of standards to successfully modernize existing information systems. Concerning ADM, current work involves building standards to facilitate the exchange of existing systems meta-data for various modernization tools. The main limitations of MDA tools are related to the incipient evolution of MDA standards such as QVT or KDM and to the lack of specification in terms of these standards of various platforms and bridges between platforms.

In summary, a lot remains to be done to provide support for MDA-based software evolution: research on formalisms and theories to increase understanding of software evolution processes; development of methods, techniques and heuristics to provide support for software changes; new verification tools that embrace change and evolution as central in software development processes; development of new sophisticated tools to develop industrial size software systems and definition of standards to evaluate the quality of evolved artifacts/systems.

Perhaps, another impediment is the culture change that accompanies this approach. The adoption of reverse engineering techniques in general, should be favored by educating future generations of software engineers, i.e., integrating background on these topics into the computer science curriculum.

8. References

ADM (2010). Standards Roadmap. ADM Task Force. Retrieved October 2011 from adm.omg.org

Aho, A., Sethi, R., & Ullman, J. (1985). *Compilers: Principles, Techniques, and Tools* (2nd ed.). Reading: Addison-Wesley.

ANSI-IEEE. (1984). ANSI/IEEE Software Engineering Standards: Std 729-1983, Std 730-1884, Std 828-1983, 829-1984, 830-1984. Los Alamitos: IEEE/Wiley.

ATL (2011). ATL Documentation. Retrieved October 2011 from *www.eclipse.org/m2m/atl/documentation*

Bidoit, M., & Mosses, P. (2004). *CASL User Manual- Introduction to Using the Common Algebraic Specification Language* (LNCS 2900). Heidelberg: Springer-Verlag.

Canfora, G., & Di Penta, M. (2007). New Frontiers of Reverse Engineering. Future of Software engineering. In *Proceedings of Future of Software Engineering (FOSE 2007)* (pp. 326-341). Los Alamitos:IEEE Press.

CASE MDA (2011). Retrieved October 2011 from www.case-tools.org

Chikofsky, E., & Cross, J. (1990). Reverse engineering and design recovery: A taxonomy. *IEEE Software,* 7(1), 13–17. doi:10.1109/52.43044

Eclipse (2011). The eclipse modeling framework. Retrieved October 2011 from http://www.eclipse.org/emf/

Ernst, M. (2003). Static and Dynamic Analysis: Synergy and duality. In *Proceedings of ICSE Workshop on Dynamic Analysis (WODA 2003)* (pp. 24-27).

Fanta, R., & Rajlich, V. (1998). Reengineering object-oriented code. In *Proceedings of International Conference on Software Maintenance* (pp. 238-246). Los Alamitos: IEEE Computer Society.

Favre, L. (2005) Foundations for MDA-based Forward Engineering. *Journal of Object Technology* (JOT), Vol 4, N° 1, Jan/Feb, 129-153.

Favre, L. (2009). A Formal Foundation for Metamodeling. ADA Europe 2009. *Lecture Notes in Computer Science* (Vol. 5570, pp. 177-191). Heidelberg: Springer-Verlag.

Favre, L., Martinez, L., & Pereira, C. (2009). MDA-based Reverse Engineering of Object-oriented Code. *Lecture Notes in Business Information Processing* (Vol 29, pp. 251-263). Heidelberg: Springer-Verlag.

Favre, L. (2010). *Model Driven Architecture for Reverse Engineering Technologies: Strategic Directions and System Evolution.* Engineering Science Reference, IGI Global, USA.

Jones, N., & Nielson, F. (1995). Abstract interpretation: A semantic based tool for program analysis. In D. Gabbay, S. Abramsky, & T. Maibaum (Eds), *Handbook of Logic in Computer Science* (Vol. 4, pp. 527-636). Oxford: Clarendon Press.

KDM (2011). Knowledge Discovery Meta-Model, Version 1.3-beta 2, March 2011. OMG specification formal 2010-12-12. Retrieved October 2011 from http://www.omg.org/spec/kdm/1.3/beta2/pdf

Maoz, S., & Harel, D. (2010) On Tracing Reactive Systems. *Software & System Modeling*. DOI 10.1007/510270-010-0151-2, Springer-Verlag.

MDA (2005). The Model Driven Architecture. Retrieved October 2011 from www.omg.org/mda.

Martinez, L., Pereira, C., & Favre, L. (2011) Recovering Activity Diagrams from Object-Oriented Code: an MDA-based Approach. In *Proceedings 2011 International Conference on Software Engineering Research and Practice (SERP 2011)*(Vol. I, pp. 58-64), CSREA Press.

Medini (2011). Medini QVT. Retrieved October 2011 from http://projects.ikv.de/qvt

Milanova, A. (2007). Composition Inference for UML Class Diagrams. *Journal Automated Software Engineering*. Vol 14 Issue 2, June.

Modisco (2011). Retrieved October 2011 from http://www.eclipse.org/Modisco

MOF (2006). MOF: Meta Object Facility (MOF ™) 2.0. OMG Specification formal/2006-01-01. Retrieved October 2011 from www.omg.org/mof

OCL (2010). *OCL: Object Constraint Language. Version 2.2*. OMG: formal/2010-02-01.Retrieved October 2011 from www.omg.org

OCL USE (2011). Retrieved October 2011 from http://www.db.informatik.uni-bremen.de/projects/USE

OMG (2011). The Object Management Group Consortium. Retrieved October 2011, from www.omg.org

Pereira, C., Martinez, L., & Favre, L. (2011). Recovering Use Case Diagrams from Object-Oriented Code: an MDA-based Approach. In *Proceedings ITNG 2011, 8th. International Conference on Information Technology: New Generations* (pp. 737-742), Los Alamitos: IEEE Computer Press.

QVT (2008). QVT: MOF 2.0 Query, View, Transformation. Formal/2008-04-03. Retrieved October 2011 from www.omg.org

Stevens, P. (2008) Bidirectional model transformations in QVT: semantic issues and open questions. Software & Systems Modeling. DOI 10.1007/s10270-008-0109-9, Springer-Verlag

Systa, T. (2000). *Static and Dynamic Reverse Engineering Techniques for Java Software Systems*. Ph.D Thesis, University of Tampere, Report A-2000-4.

Sommerville, I. (2004). *Software Engineering* (7th ed.). Reading: Addison Wesley.

Telea, A., Hoogendorp, H., Ersoy, O. & Reniers, D. (2009). Extraction and visualization of call dependencies for large C/C++ code bases. In *Proceedings of VISSOFT 2009* (pp. 19-26) IEEE Computer Press.

Tonella, P., & Potrich, A. (2005). Reverse Engineering of Object-oriented Code. *Monographs in Computer Science*. Heidelberg: Springer-Verlag.

UML (2010a). *Unified Modeling Language: Infrastructure*. Version 2.3. OMG Specification formal/ 2010-05-03. Retrieved October 2011from www.omg.org.

UML (2010b). *UML: Unified Modeling Language: Superstructure*. Version 2.3. OMG Specification: formal/2010-05-05. Retrieved October 2011 from www.omg.org

USE (2011). Use 3.0. Retrieved October 2011 from http://www.db.informatik.uni-bremen.de/projects/USE

Willink, E. (2011). Modeling the OCL Standard Library. *Electronic Communications of the EASST.* Vol. 44. Retrieved October 2011 from http://journal.ub.tu-berlin.de/eceasst/

4

Reverse Engineering Platform Independent Models from Business Software Applications

Rama Akkiraju[1], Tilak Mitra[2] and Usha Thulasiram[2]
[1]IBM T. J. Watson Research Center
[2]IBM Global Business Services
USA

1. Introduction

The reasons for reverse engineering software applications could be many. These include: to understand the design of the software system to improve it for future iterations, to communicate the design to others when prior documentation is either lost or does not exist or is out-dated, to understand competitors' product to replicate the design, to understand the details to discover patent infringements, to derive the meta model which can then be used to possibly translate the business application on to other platforms. Whatever the reasons, reverse engineering business applications is a tedious and complex technical activity. Reverse engineering a business application is not about analyzing code alone. It requires analysis of various aspects of a business application: the platform on which software runs, the underlying features of the platform that the software leverages, the interaction of a software system with other applications external to the software system being analyzed, the libraries and the components of the programming language as well as application development platforms that the business application uses etc. We argue that this context in which a business application runs is critical to analyzing it and understanding it for whatever end-use the analysis may be put to use. Much of the prior work on reverse engineering in software engineering field has focused on code analysis. Not much attention has been given in literature to understanding the context in which a business application runs from various perspectives such as the ones mentioned above. In our work we address this specific aspect of reverse engineering business applications.

Modern-day business applications are seldom developed from scratch. For example, they are often developed on higher-level building blocks such as programming language platforms such as J2EE in case of Java programming language and .Net in case of C# programming language. In addition most companies use even higher level application development platforms offered by vendors such as IBM's Websphere and Rational products [18][19], SAP's NetWeaver [20]and Oracles' Enterprise 2.0 software development platforms for Java J2EE application development [21] and Microsoft's .NET platform for C# programming language [22] etc. These platforms offer many in-built capabilities such as web application load balancing, resource pooling, multi-threading, and support for architectural patterns such as service-oriented architecture (SOA). All of these are part of the context in which a business application operates. Understanding this environment is crucial to reverse engineering any software since the environment significantly influences how code gets written and managed. Reverse engineering models from business applications written on platforms that support higher level programming idioms (such as the ones noted above) is a difficult problem. If the applications developed involve several legacy systems, then reverse engineering is difficult to achieve due to the sheer nature of heterogeneity of systems. The nuances of each system may make reverse engineering difficult even if the code is built using the same programming language (e.g., Java) using the same standards (such as J2EE) on a given platform.

To understand automated reverse engineering, we must first understand model driven development/architecture [2] [3] and the transformation framework. Model driven development and code generation from models (aka *forward engineering*) has been discussed in literature. In a model driven development approach, given two meta-models, i.e., a source meta-model and a target meta-model and the transformation rules that can transform the source meta-model into the target meta-model, any given platform independent model that adheres to the source meta-model can be translated into a platform specific model (PSM) that adheres to the target meta-model. The resulting PSM can then be translated into various implementation artifacts on the target platform. This is called *forward engineering*. By reversing this approach, platform independent models can be extracted from platform specific models and implementation artifacts. Extraction of models from existing artifacts of a business application is termed *reverse engineering*. Figure 1 shows forward engineering transformation approach while Figure 2 shows reverse engineering transformation approach. The gears in the figures represent software transformations that automatically translate artifacts on the left to the artifacts on the right of the arrows they reside.

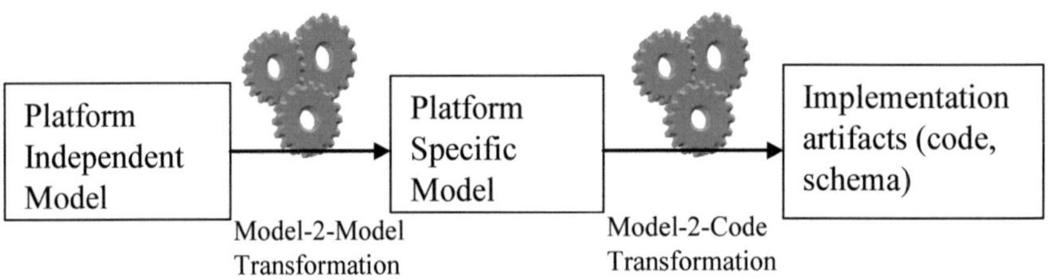

Fig. 1. Model driven transformation approach in forward engineering.

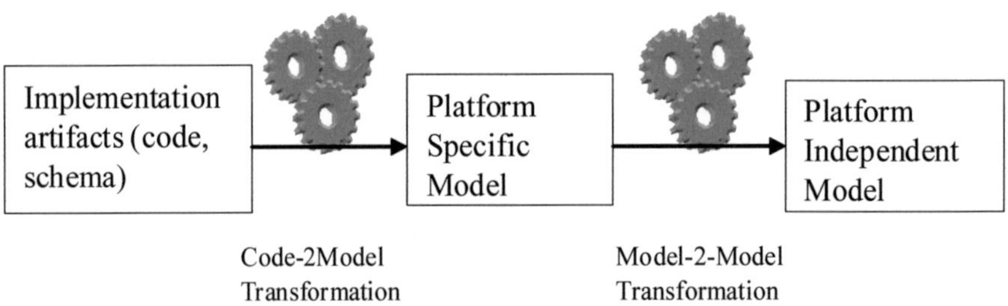

Fig. 2. Model driven transformation approach in reverse engineering.

Prior art [1] [5] [7] [10] [11] [12] and features in vendor tools such as the IBM Rational Software Architect (RSA) offer transformation methods and tools (with several gaps) to extract models. However, most of the reverse engineering work has focused on extracting the structural models (e.g., class models) from implementation artifacts [15] [16] [17]. For example, if a UML model were to be derived from Java code, reverse engineering techniques have looked at deriving structural models such as classes, their data members and interfaces, etc. This approach, although works to a degree, does not provide a high-enough level of abstraction required to interpret the software application at a semantic level. These low level design artifacts lack the semantic context and are hard to reuse. For example, in a service-oriented architecture, modular reusable abstraction is defined at the level of services rather than classes. This distinction is important because abstraction at the level of services enables one to link the business functions offered by services with business objectives. The reusability of the reverse-engineered models with the current state-of-the-art is limited by the lack of proper linkages to higher level business objectives.

In this chapter, we present a method for extracting a platform independent model at *appropriate* levels of abstraction from a business application. The main motivation for reverse engineering in our work is to port a business application developed on one software development platform to a different one. We do this by reverse engineering the design models (we refer to them as platform independent models) from an application that is developed on one software development platform and then apply forward engineering to translate those platform independent models into platform specific models on the target platform. Reverse engineering plays an important role in this porting. While the focus of this book is more on reverse engineering, we feel that it is important to offer context to reverse engineering. Therefore, our work will present reverse engineering mainly from the point-of-view of the need to port business applications from one platform to the other. In the context of our work, a 'platform' refers to a J2EE application development platform such as the ones offered by vendors such as IBM, SAP and Oracle. In this chapter, we present a service-oriented approach to deriving platform independent models from platform specific implementations. We experimentally verify that by focusing on service level components of software design one can simplify the model extraction problem significantly while still achieving up to 40%-50% of model reusability.

The chapter is organized as follows. First, we present our motivation for reverse engineering. Then, we present our approach to reverse engineering followed by the results of our experiment in which we reverse engineer design models from the implementation artifacts of a business application developed and deployed on a specific software development platform.

2. Our motivation for reverse engineering: Cross-platform porting of software solutions

If a software solution is being designed for the first time, our objective is to be able to formally model that software solution and to generate as much of implementation/code from the model on as many software platforms as possible. This will serve our motivation to enable IT services companies to support software solution development on multiple platforms. In cases where a software solution already exists on a platform, our objective is to reuse as much of that software solution as possible in making that solution available on multiple platforms. To investigate this cross-platform portability, we have selected two development platforms namely IBM's WebSphere platform consisting of WebSphere Business Services Fabric [19] and SAP's NetWeaver Developer Studio [20].

One way to achieve, cross-platform portability of software solutions is by reusing code. Much has been talked about code reuse but the promise of code reuse is often hard to realize. This is so because code that is built on one platform may or may not be easily translated into another platform. If the programming language requirements are different for each platform or if the applications to be developed involve integrating with several custom legacy systems, then code reuse is difficult to achieve due to the sheer nature of heterogeneity. The nuances of each platform may make code reuse difficult even if the code is built using the same programming language (eg: Java) using the same standards (such as J2EE) on the source platform as is expected on the target platform. There is a tacit acknowledgement among practitioners that model reuse is more practical than code reuse. Platform independent models (PIMs) of a given set of business solutions either developed manually or extracted through automated tools from existing solutions can provide a valuable starting point for reuse. A platform independent model of a business application is a key asset for any company for future enhancements to their business processes because it gives the company a formal description of what exists. The PIM is also a key asset for IT consulting companies as well if the consulting company intends to develop pre-built solutions. The following technical question is at the heart of our work. *What aspects of the models are most reusable for cross-platform portability?* While we may not be able generalize the results from our effort on two platforms, we believe that our study still gives valuable insights and lessons that can be used for further exploration.

In the remaining portion of this section, we present our approach to cross-platform porting of software solutions.

3. Our approach to reverse engineering

Models are the main artifacts in software development. As discussed earlier, models can be used to represent various things in the software design and development lifecycle. We have discussed platform independent models (PIMs), and platform specific models (PSMs) in Introduction section. These models are at the heart of forward engineering and reverse engineering. In forward engineering, typically platform independent models are developed by humans as part of software design efforts. In reverse engineering, these models are typically derived automatically using model driven transformations. In either case, the elements that constitute a platform independent model have to be understood. Therefore, we begin with details on what constitutes platform independent models and how to build them.

3.1 Creating platform independent models

Object Management Group (OMG) provides some guidance on how to build platform independent models. Many tool vendors support the development of platform independent models. UML is the popular language of choice in the industry for representing platform independent models. In our work, we build on top of OMG's guidance on building platform independent models. We enhance the OMG modeling notions in two ways:

1. *We use a 'service' as first-class modeling construct instead of a 'class' in building the structural models.* A service is a higher level abstraction than a class. In a service-oriented architecture, the modular reusable abstraction is defined at the level of services rather

than classes. This distinction is important because abstraction at the level of services enables one to link the business functions offered by services with business objectives/performance indicators. Establishing and retaining linkages between model elements and their respective business objectives can play a significant role in model reuse. This linkage can serve as the starting point in one's search for reusable models. A service exposes its interface signature, message exchanges and any associated metadata and is often more coarse-granular than a typical class in an object-oriented paradigm. This notion of working with services rather than classes enables us to think of a business application as a composition of services. We believe that this higher level abstraction is useful when deciding which model elements need to be transformed onto the target platforms and how to leverage existing assets in a client environment. This eliminates lower level classes that are part of the detailed design from our consideration set. For code generation purposes we leverage transformations that can transform a high level design to low-level design and code. For reverse engineering purposes, we focus only on deriving higher level service element designs in addition to the class models. This provides the semantic context required to interpret the derived models.

2. *We define the vocabulary to express the user experience modeling elements using the 'service' level abstractions.* Several best practice models have been suggested about user experience modeling but no specific profile is readily available for use in expressing platform independent models. In this work, we have created a profile that defines the language for expressing user experience modeling elements. These include stereotypes for information elements and layout elements. Information elements include screen, input form, and action elements that invoke services on the server side (called service actions) and those that invoke services locally on the client (non-service actions). Layout elements include text, table and chart elements.

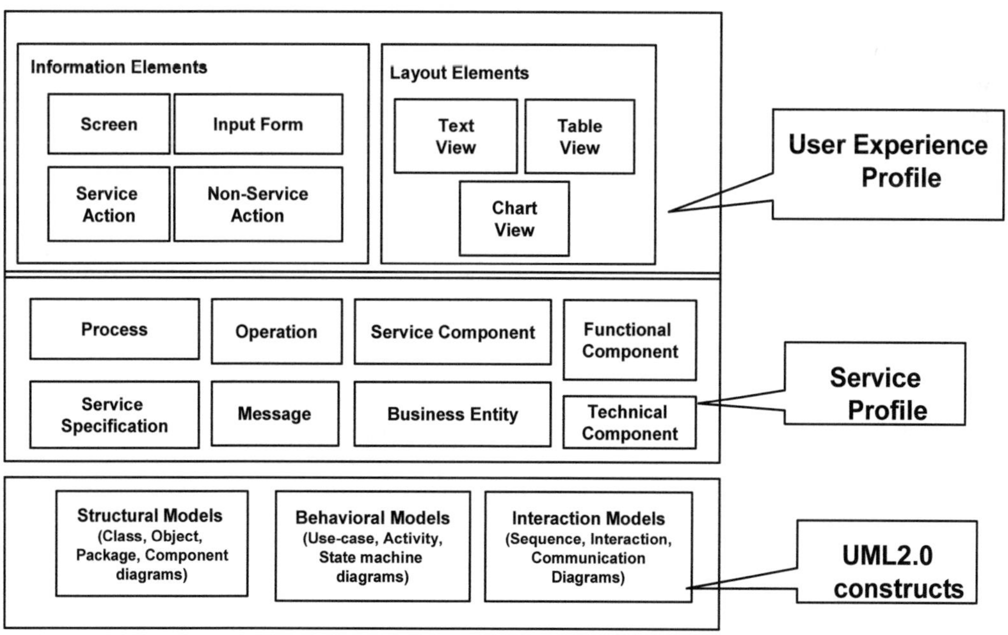

Fig. 3. Platform independent modeling elements: Our point-of-view

Figure 3 above shows the set of modeling elements that we have used to build platform independent models of a given functional specification. The bottom layer in figure 3 contains the traditional UML 2.0 modeling constructs namely the structural, behavioral and interaction models. These models are then elevated to a higher level of abstractions as *services* in a service profile. Finally, the user experience profile that we have developed based on the best practice recommendations gives us the vocabulary required to capture the user interface modules.

So far we have discussed the elements that constitute a platform independent model (PIM). To derive PIM models from implementation artifacts one typically develops model driven transformations. These transformations codify the rules that can be applied on implementation artifacts to derive models in the case of reverse engineering. In the case of forward engineering, the transformation rules codify how to translate the PIM models into implementation artifacts. In the next section, we present transformation authoring framework.

3.2 Transformation authoring

'Transformations create elements in a target model (domain) based on elements from a source model' [6]. A model driven transformation is a set of mapping rules that define how elements in a given source model map to their corresponding elements in a target domain model. These rules are specified between the source and target platform metamodels. Depending on what need to be generated there could be multiple levels of transformations such as model-to-model, model-to-text, model-to-code and code-to-model. Also, depending on the domain and the desired target platform multiple levels of transformations might be required to transform a PIM into implementation artifacts on a target platform in the case of forward engineering and vice versa for reverse engineering. For example, transformations may be required across models of the same type such as a transformation from one PSM to another PSM to add additional levels of refinement or across different levels of abstraction such as from PIM to PSM or from one type of model to another such as from PSM to code or even PIM to code. In our case, we use the traditional PIM-to-PSM and PSM-to-code transformations for forward transformations and code-to-PSM and PSM-to-PIM transformations for model extraction or reverse engineering. Operationally, multiple levels of transformations can be chained so that the intermediate results are invisible to the consumer of the transformations.

Source: Platform Independent Model (PIM) artifacts	Target: SAP NetWeaver artifacts
Operation	Operation
Message	InputOperationMessage, FaultOperationMessage, OutputOperationMessage
ServiceComponent	Service
Entity	BusinessObject
FunctionalComponent	BusinessObject

Table 1. Transformation mappings between the metamodels of our platform independent model and SAP NetWeaver composite application framework module.

Table 1 shows the transformation rules between the metamodels of our PIM and SAP NetWeaver composite application framework (CAF) (PSM) module. Extracting the metamodel of the target platform may not be trivial if that platform is proprietary. One may have to reverse engineer it from exemplars. We reverse engineered models from exemplars in our work. Figure 5 shows how these transformation mapping rules are developed using IBM Rational Software Architect transformation authoring tool. In this work, we developed the transformation rules manually through observation and domain analysis. Automated ways of deriving transformation rules is an active area of research [1].

Transformation Authoring for Forward Engineering: After authoring the model-to-model transformations, the target models need to be converted to implementation artifacts on the target platform. In our work, our objective was to generate Java code and database schema elements for both IBM WebSphere and SAP NetWeaver platforms. For this we have used the Eclipse Modeling Framework (EMF)'s Java Emitter Templates (JET) [6]. Templates can be constructed from fully formed exemplars. Model-to-code transformations can then use these templates to generate the implementation artifacts in the appropriate format.

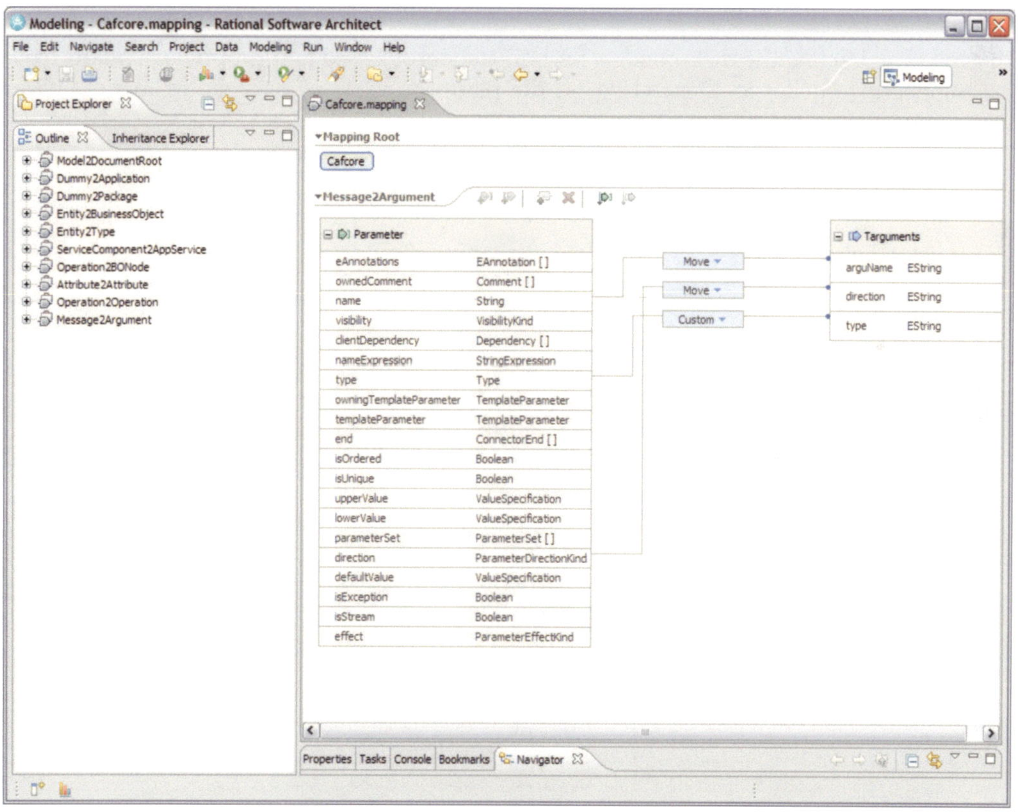

Fig. 5. A visual representation of transformation mapping rules in IBM Rational Software Architect transformation authoring tool.

As mentioned earlier, the model-2-model and model-2-code generation transformations are typically chained so that the two step process is transparent to the user.

The transformations created using mapping rules such as the ones in Table 1 which are codified using a tool such as the one shown in figure 5 can then be run by creating a specific instance of the transformation and by supplying it a specific instance of the source model (eg: A specific industry PIM). The output of this transformation is implementation artifacts on the target platform. The obtained transformations can then be imported into the target platforms and fleshed out further for deployment.

Transformation Authoring for Reverse Engineering: Figure 6 shows our approach for converting platform specific artifacts into a platform independent model. Platform specific code, artifacts, UI elements and schema are processed in a Model Generator Module to generate a platform specific model. The platform specific code, artifacts, UI elements and schema could be present in many forms and formats including code written in programming languages such as Java, or C, or C++ and schema and other artifacts represented as xml files or other files. A Model Generator Module processes the platform specific artifacts in their various formats and extracts a platform specific model from them. In order to do this, it has to know the metamodel of the underlying platform. If one exists, then the implementation artifacts can be mapped to such a platform specific model. But in cases where one does not exist, we use a semi-automated approach to derive metamodels from specific platforms.

In general, extracting the meta-models for non-standards based and proprietary platforms is an engineering challenge. Depending on the platform, varying amounts of manual effort

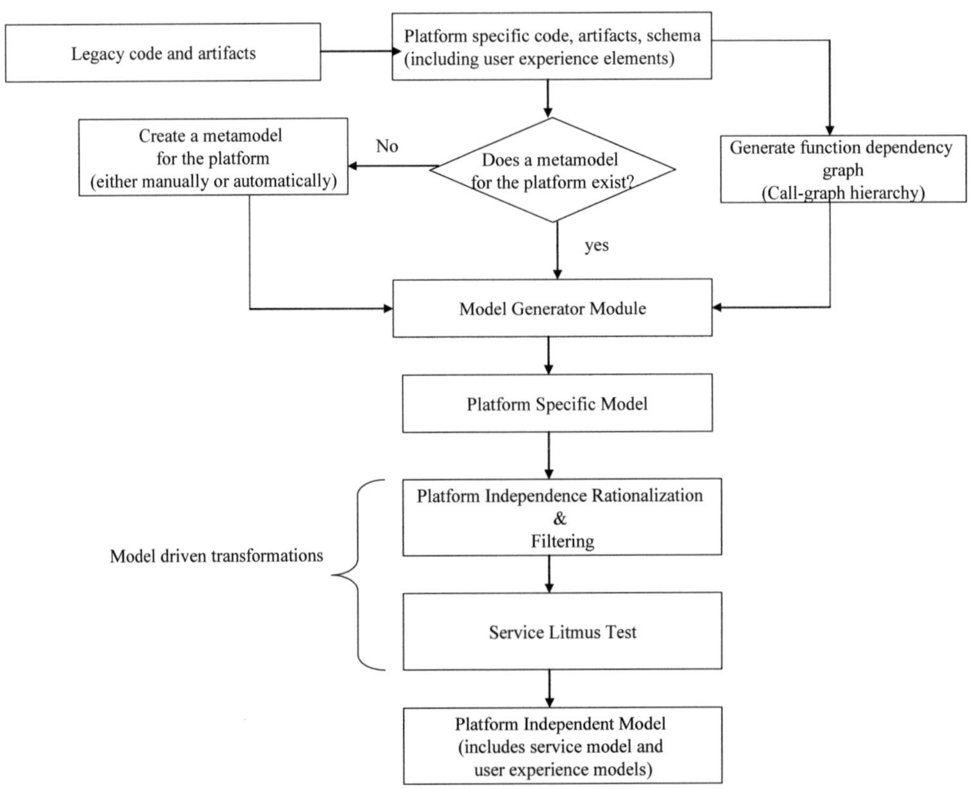

Fig. 6. **Model derivation**: Our approach to deriving platform independent models from implementation artifacts

may be required to extract the meta-modal of the platform. If the meta-models are not published or not accessible, then one may have to resort to manual observation of exemplars to derive the meta-model from the exemplar. This means an exemplar with all possible types of elements needs to be constructed. An exemplar contains the implementation artifacts which include code, schemas, xml files etc. The meta-model extraction may be automated using exemplar analysis tools available in vendor tools such as IBM's Rational Software Architect (RSA). However, an exemplar must be created first to conduct the exemplar analysis. In our work, for the two vendor platforms chosen, we were able to obtain the metamodels for one of the vendor platforms while we had to manually create the other using exemplar creation and exemplar analysis.

This metamodel is then used by the Model Generator Module to generate a platform specific model for specific model instances. Then, filtering is performed to extract only those elements that would be of 'value' at platform independent level in an SOA environment. The rationalization and filtering mechanism can employ predefined rules to perform this. For example, models of artifacts such as factory classes for business objects, and auxiliary data structures and code that setup environment variables and connectivity with legacy systems etc need not be translated onto platform independent models. These types of business objects, data structures, application services, their operations are cleansed and filtered at this stage. Then from the platform specific model, we extract service models and apply a service litmus test as given in IBM's SOMA method [4] to categorize services as process services, information services, security services, infrastructure services etc. SOMA method defines these categories of services. Each service along with its ecosystems of services can be examined in detail to derive this information either automatically or manually. Once done, additional tagging is done on services to note which ones are exposed externally and which ones are internal implementations. The litmus test can be administered manually or can be automated if there is enough semantic information about the code/artifacts to know about the behavior and characteristics. In our work, we used a user-directed mechanism for doing this filtering. A tool has been developed to enable a developer to conduct the filtering. This along with the user experience elements and models are all extracted into a platform independent model via model-driven transformations. In addition one can use code analysis tools to understand the call-graph hierarchy to retrieve an ecosystem of mutually dependent services. Several vendor tools are available for doing this for various programming languages. We use IBM's Rational Software Architect (RSA) [18] tool to do code analysis [6]. This information is captured and reflected in a platform specific model which then gets translated into a platform independent model via model driven transformations. This helps generate a service dependency model at the platform independent model. The service model and the service dependency information together provide static and the dynamic models at the platform independent level.

4. Experimental results

We hypothesize that by focusing on service level components of software design one can simplify the model extraction problem significantly while still achieving up to 40%-50% of model reusability. We have validated our hypotheses experimentally by transforming the derived platform independent model on to a different target software platform in 5 instances of business processes. This in essence is forward engineering the reverse engineered models. We believe that this is a good measure of quality of reverse engineered models. If the reverse engineered models are 'good enough' to be used as inputs to code generation (onto another platform) that means we have made progress toward model reusability. Therefore, for our experiments we chose to put the reverse engineered models to test. The results are consistent with our hypothesis and show 40-50% of savings in development effort. The two platforms investigated are IBM WebSphere and SAP NetWeaver platforms. We tried our approach on 5 different platform independent models - either modeled or derived. On an average, we have noted that by using our transformations we can reduce the develop effort by 40%-50% in a 6 month development project (Table 2).

Phase	Activity	Effort in hours				Model-driven Transformations
		Low	Medium	High	Very High	
Develop & Deploy						
	Develop Back-end Data Objects					No
	Develop Data Dictionary Objects	4	5	7	8	No
	Develop Business Objects					No
	Develop Services					No
	Develop Back-end Services (custom RFCs/BAPIs)					No
	Develop Custom RFC/BAPI(s)	8	16	32	40	No
	Expose RFC/BAPI(s) as Web Services using Web Service Creation Wizard	0.1	0.1	0.1	0.1	No
	Publish Web Services into Service Registry (UDDI Registry)	0.1	0.1	0.1	0.1	No
	Unit Testing of back-end Services	0.25	0.25	0.25	0.25	No
	Develop Entity Services (Local BOs)					
	Development Local (CAF Layer) Business Objects with Attributes, Operations	0.5	0.75	1	1.5	Yes
	Development of Relationship amongst Business Objects	0.1	0.1	0.1	0.1	Yes
	Unit Testing of Local BOs	1	1	2	3	No
	Import External Services					
	Import RFC/BAPI into CAF Core	0.1	0.1	0.1	0.1	Yes
	Import Enterprise Services into CAF Core	0.1	0.1	0.1	0.1	Yes
	Map External Services to Operations of Business Objects	1	1	1	1	No
	Develop Application Services					
	Develop Application Services with Operations	1	2	4	6	Yes
	Map External Services to Operations of Application Services	1	1	2	2	Yes
	Implement Operations with Business Logic	8	16	24	36	No
	Expose Application Services as Web Services	0.1	0.1	0.1	0.1	Yes
	Publish Web Services into Service Registry (UDDI Registry)	0.1	0.1	0.1	0.1	No
	Unit Testing of Application Service Operations	0.5	1	2	4	No
	Deploy Entity Services into Web Application Server (WAS)					No
	Deploy Application Services into Web Application Server (WAS)		0.1			No
	Configure External Services after Deploying into Web Application Server (WAS)	1	1	2	2	No
	Develop User Interfaces					
	Develop Visual Composer(VC) based User Interfaces	4	8	16	32	No
	Implement GP Callable Object Interface	8	12	20	24	No
	Develop WebDynpro (WD) Java based User Interfaces	16	32	48	64	Yes
	Develop Adobe Interactive Form (AIF) based User Interfaces	16	24	32	48	No

SAP NetWeaver (Composite Core + Web DynPro)				
With Model-driven Transformations	18.9	36.15	55.4	73.9
Total	38.6	68.25	106.5	144
Percentage Generated by Model-driven Transformations	**48.96**	**52.97**	**52.02**	**51.32**

Table 2. Catalogs the development phase activities that our transformations help automate and the development effort reductions associated with them on SAP NetWeaver platform.

Our rationale for focusing on service abstractions in models is to keep the reverse transformations simple and practical. This allows developers to develop the forward and reverse transformations relatively quickly for new platforms and programming languages. In addition, one has to consider the capabilities of various vendor software middleware platforms as well in trying to decide how much of the modeling is to be done or to be extracted. For instance, software middleware platforms these days offer the capability to generate low level design using best-practice patterns and the corresponding code given a high-level design. So, trying to extract every aspect of a design from implementation artifacts might not be necessary depending on the target software middleware platform of choice. We believe that this insight backed by the experimental results we have shown is a key contribution of our work.

5. Conclusions

In this paper, we presented our approach to porting software solutions on multiple software middleware platforms. We propose the use of model-driven transformations to achieve cross-platform portability. We propose approaches for two scenarios. First, in cases where no software solution exists on any of the desired target middleware platforms, we advocate developing a platform independent model of the software solution in a formal modeling language such as UML and then applying model-driven transformations to generate implementation artifacts such as code and schemas from the models on the desired target platforms. Second, if a software solution already exists on one specific middleware platform, we propose applying reverse transformations to derive a platform independent model from the implementation artifacts and then applying forward transformations on the derived model to port that software solution on to a different target platform. We advance the traditional model-driven technique by presenting a service-oriented approach to deriving platform independent models from platform specific implementations.

The experiments we have conducted in deriving platform independent models from implementation artifacts have provided useful insights in a number of aspects and pointed us to future research topics in this area. The ability to leverage existing assets in a software environment depends significantly on the granularity of services modeled and exposed. Providing guidance on how granular the services should be for optimal reuse could be a topic for research. Rationalizing services that operate at different levels of granularity is another topic for further research.

6. Acknowledgements

We would like thank many of our colleagues at IBM who have contributed to related work streams which have helped inform some of the ideas presented in this paper. These colleagues include: Pankaj Dhoolia, Nilay Ghosh, Dipankar Saha, Manisha Bhandar, Shankar Kalyana, Ray Harishankar, Soham Chakroborthy, Santhosh Kumaran, Rakesh Mohan, Richard Goodwin, Shiwa Fu and Anil Nigam.

7. References

[1] Andreas Billig, Susanne Busse, Andreas Leicher, and Jörn Guy Süß;. 2004. Platform independent model transformation based on triple. In *Proceedings of the 5th ACM/IFIP/USENIX international conference on Middleware* (Middleware '04). Springer-Verlag New York, Inc., New York, NY, USA, 493-511.

[2] Mellor, S. J., Clark, A. N., and Futagami, T. Model-driven development. IEEE Software 20, 5 (2003), 14–18.

[3] Frankel, David S.: Model Driven Architecture: Applying MDA to Enterprise Computing. OMG Press: 2003. OMG Unified Modeling Language Specification, Object Management Group, 2003,

[4] Arsanjani A.: Service Oriented Modeling and Architecture (SOMA). http://www.ibm.com/developerworks/webservices/library/ws-soa-design1/
[5] Albert, M et al.: Model to Text Transformation in Generating Code from Rich Associations Specifications, In: Advances in Conceptual Modeling - Theory and Practice, LNCS 4231, Springer Berlin:2006.
[6] Java Emitter Templates (JET) http://www.eclipse.org/articles/Article-JET/jet_tutorial1.html
[7] S. Sendall, W. Kozaczynski; "Model Transformation - the Heart and Soul of Model-Driven Software Development". IEEE Software, vol. 20, no. 5, September/October 2003, pp. 42-45.
[8] Sendall S. Kuster J. "*Taming Model Round-Trip Engineering*". In Proceedings of Workshop 'Best Practices for Model-Driven Software Development.
[9] Uwe Aßmann, Automatic Roundtrip Engineering, Electronic Notes in Theoretical Computer Science, Volume 82, Issue 5, April 2003, Pages 33-41, ISSN 1571-0661, 10.1016/S1571-0661(04)80732-1.
[10] Nija Shi; Olsson, R.A.; , "Reverse Engineering of Design Patterns from Java Source Code," *Automated Software Engineering, 2006. ASE '06. 21st IEEE/ACM International Conference on* , vol., no., pp.123-134, 18-22 Sept. 2006.
[11] L. C. Briand, Y. Labiche, and J. Leduc. Toward the reverse engineering of uml sequence diagrams for distributed java software. *IEEE Trans. Software Eng.*, 32(9):642–663, 2006.
[12] G. Canfora, A. Cimitile, and M. Munro. Reverse engineering and reuse re-engineering. *Journal of Software Maintenance and Evolution - Research and Practice*, 6(2):53–72, 1994.
[13] R. Fiutem, P. Tonella, G. Antoniol, and E.Merlo. A clich´e based environment to support architectural reverse engineering. In *Proceedings of the International Conference on Software Maintenance*, pages 319–328. IEEE Computer Society, 1996.
[14] Gerardo CanforaHarman and Massimiliano Di Penta. 2007. New Frontiers of Reverse Engineering. In *2007 Future of Software Engineering* (FOSE '07). IEEE Computer Society, Washington, DC, USA, 326-341. DOI=10.1109/FOSE.2007.15 http://dx.doi.org/10.1109/FOSE.2007.15
[15] Atanas Rountev, Olga Volgin, and Miriam Reddoch. 2005. Static control-flow analysis for reverse engineering of UML sequence diagrams. In *Proceedings of the 6th ACM SIGPLAN-SIGSOFT workshop on Program analysis for software tools and engineering* (PASTE '05), Michael Ernst and Thomas Jensen (Eds.). ACM, New York, NY, USA, 96-102. DOI=10.1145/1108792.1108816 http://doi.acm.org/10.1145/1108792.1108816
[16] Rountev A., Kagan S., and Gibas, M. Static and dynamic analysis of call chains in Java. In International Symposium on Software Testing and Analysis, pages 1.11, July 2004.
[17] L. Briand, Y. Labiche, and Y. Miao. Towards the reverse engineering of UML sequence diagrams. In Working Conference on Reverse Engineering, pages 57.66, 2003.
[18] IBM Rational Software Architect. http://www.ibm.com/developerworks/rational/products/rsa/
[19] IBM WebSphere Services Fabric: http://www-01.ibm.com/software/integration/wbsf/
[20] SAP NetWeaver: Adoptive technology for the networked Fabric. http://www.sap.com/platform/netweaver/index.epx
[21] Oracle Enterprise 2.0 http://www.oracle.com/technetwork/topics/ent20/whatsnew/index.html
[22] Microsoft .Net http://www.microsoft.com/net

5

Reverse Engineering the Peer to Peer Streaming Media System

Chunxi Li[1] and Changjia Chen[2]
[1]*Beijing Jiaotong University*
[2]*Lanzhou Jiaotong University*
China

1. Introduction

Peer to peer (P2P) content distribution network like BitTorrent (BT) is one of most popular Internet applications today. Its success heavily lies on the ability to share the capacity of all the individuals as a whole. As the first deployed prototype on the real Internet, CoolStreaming (Zhang et al., 2005) for the first time manifests what a great application potential and huge business opportunity it can reach if the content is delivered not only in large scale but also on real-time. Along the way to the large-scale Along the way to such as system, people (Vlavianos et al., 2006) find there is no natural connection between the abilities of mass data delivering and real-time distributing in any protocol. This discovery stimulates people to study how to modify protocols like BT to meet the real-time demand. Since 2004, a series of large-scale systems like PPLive and PPStream have been deployed in China and all over the world, and become the world-class popular platforms. Many research reports on them also mark their success.

However, most existing works are descriptive. They tell about how such a system works and how to measure it, but do not pay much effort to explain why. In this chapter, we take a different route. We seek to better understand the operation and dynamics of P2P systems at a deeper level of detail. We split our understanding objective into the following sub-objectives 1) understand the working principle through the communication protocol crack, 2) comprehend the streaming content-delivery principle, 3) locate the measurable parameters which can be used to evaluate the system performance; 4) understand the P2P network through the models of startup process and user behavior, and analyze the engineering design objectives. The requirements for reaching those goals are as follows. 1) the research must be driven by mass measured data of real network. 2) for us, the measuring platform must be suitable to the normal access situation like the home line. 3) datasets must be available in terms of scalability, quality and correctness of information. 4) the process of reversing engineering should be well designed with ease to set up the analysis, ease to interpret the results and ease to draw conclusions from the presented results.

However, the road towards reaching our research goals is full of challenges. On this road, many new findings are reported, many original problems are presented, and many design philosophies are discussed for the first time. Because all P2P streaming systems so far are proprietary without any public technical documentation available, the fundamental "entry point" of the analysis is to crack the system protocol, and then develop measurement platform to access to the system legally; next, based on the mass raw data, we investigate and study the user/peer behaviors, especially the startup behaviors which are believed to involve much more systematic problems rather than stable stage; at last, the system's performance, scalability and stability are discussed and the design models and philosophy are revealed based on the peer behavior models. The research steps outlined previously in this paragraph are detailed in Sections 3 to 5. In addition, Section 2 presents related work.

2. Related works

Since the deployment of CoolStreaming, many measurement based studies are published. Some useful measurable parameters such as *buffer width, playable video* and *peer offset* are defined in (Ali et al., 2006; Hei et al., 2007a, 2007b; Vu et al., 2006), and startup performance is addressed in user perceptive (Zhou et al., 2007). In fact, nearly all the reports assume a small buffer system, which is far from the real one like PPLive that adopts much large buffer to resist network fluctuant. For a system like PPLive, one can no longer simply assume the same situation for both stable and startup peers. Studies on a mixed system of CDN server and peers can help our study. It is shown in (Lou at el., 2007; Small at el.,2006; Tu at el., 2005; Xu at el., 2003) that, there is a *phase-transition point* $C(t)$ at time t in the mixed network, any chunks below $C(t)$ is easy to fetch. The issue like $C(t)$ in P2P steaming media system has never been studied. Besides, data fetching strategies are theoretically discussed in many reports. The algorithms of rarest first and greedy (Zhou at el., 2007) are two extreme strategies arise from BT and a mixed strategy of them is proposed in (Vlavianos at el., 2006; Zhou at el., 2007), while what is the suitable fetch strategy in P2P streaming media system needs to be answered. On VoD system aspect, very few studies (Cheng, 2007; Huang, 2007) based on so-called P2P VoD system were ever seen in 2008, however the target network is far from we discussed at all. The server-based VoD users' behavior is studied in (Yu et al., 2006; Zheng et al., 2005) based on core server's log file, but it is questionable whether P2P user has the same feature. Besides, intuitionally, data-sharing environment and user behavior will influence each other in P2P VoD system unlike in server based VoD system, however no relative research reports that.

3. Signalling crack and network measurement

Reverse-engineering-based protocol crack is the first step. It helps understand the working mechanism in depth, but also makes our large-scale measuring possible by developing network crawler. To the best of our knowledge, the work presented here and in related papers by the same authors and colleagues is the first in the world who succeeded in cracking and measuring all the top popular P2P streaming media systems in large scale.

3.1 Brief description of P2P VoD system

Referring to Fig.1, a typical P2P media streaming system uses few servers to serve large number of audiences (named as *peer*) with both live and VoD programs (Ali et al., 2006; Hei, et al., 2007a; Zhang, et al., 2005). There are significant different design concerns about P2P VoD system and live system: *i)*. VoD peer uses much more storage space to cache nearly the whole video in long term than live peer to cache very few latest contents temporarily. Besides, VoD peer may share all the cached contents even if he is in a different channel. (b) P2P live system is of source-driven such that seeder controls the content feeding rate, while

P2P VoD system is of receiver-driven and each peer controls playback rate by himself. Unlike live peer, VoD user has more flexibility to choose different playback patterns, such as skipping, fast forwards and fast backwards.

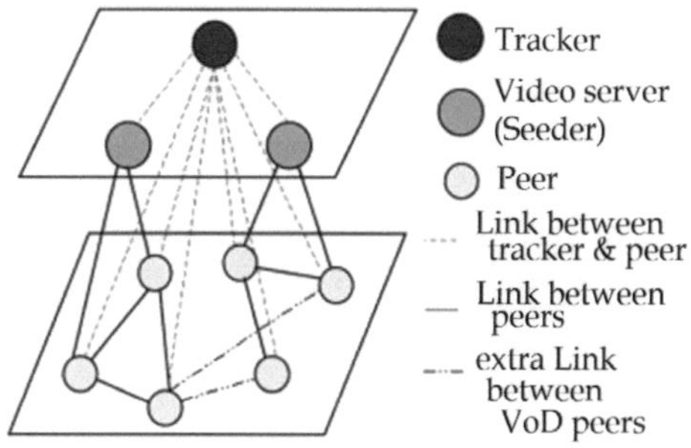

Fig. 1. The system structure

3.2 The communication protocol cracking

In general, the protocol crack is a cycling procedure including following steps:

Network sniffer/measurement: In the first step, performed using a client sniffer, we capture the interactive packets between the local peer and others. We get to know the important protocol messages must be there such as *shake hand* message, buffer map message (*BM*), and peer list message (*peerlist*), based on existing research reports and our experience. By connecting those types of message to the sniffer trace, it is not difficult to distinguish all kinds of message, even though some messages' functions are unknown.

Protocol message guess: Next, we observe each message in different dimensions, including the dimensions of time, channel and peer. For facilitating observation, we use a small software (developed by us) to extract the wanted messages with some query conditions, such as source IP/port, destination IP/port and message type, from the traces. From the extracted records, we can see many regular patterns which help parse the detailed format of each message. Of course, this way doesn't always work well, for the minority of messages can't be explained. So, we don't neglect any available reference information, e.g., we have ever found the fields of total upload/download count and upload/download speed per peer contained in BM based on the information displayed in PPStream client window. In general, we crack more than 80% messages for PPLive, PPStream and UUSee.

Test and Confirmation: In this stage, we analyze and validate the interactive sequences of messages. We guess and try different interactive sequences until the normal peer or tracker gives the right response. At last, nearly all the guesses are confirmed by our successfully and legally access to the real network.

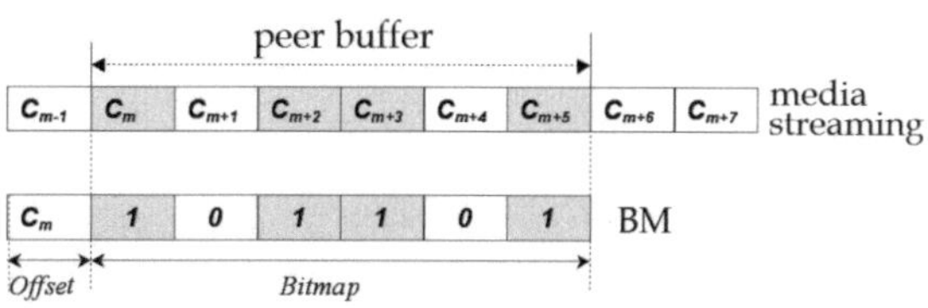

Fig. 2. Buffer and buffer map

Though the crack process, we get to know some principle of the system. In the P2P system, the video streaming is split into many blocks called *chunks*, each of which has a unique ID. In general, *chunk ID* is sequentially assigned in ascending order, i.e. the earlier played chunk has smaller ID as Fig.2 shown. A seeder injects chunks one by one into the network and each peer caches the received chunks in a buffer. Live peer only caches a small fraction of the whole video, while VoD peer caches almost the whole video. A peer buffer is usually partially filled. The downloaded chunks -- the shadow square in Fig.2 are shared, while the empty areas need to be filled by downloading from others. For enabling the key sharing principle between P2P users, a message *BM* is introduced to exchange the buffer information between peers. Referring to Fig.2, for a peer *p*, its BM contains two parts, an offset f_p and a bitmap. The offset f_p is the oldest chunk ID, i.e., the smallest chunk ID in a buffer. The bitmap is a *{0,1}* sequence, which length indicates the buffer width W_p. In the bitmap, a value of 1, respectively 0 at the ith position start from left to right means that the peer has, respectively has not the chunk with $ID_{offset+i-1}$. Since a peer constantly fetches new chunk to fill its buffer and shifts the expired chunk out of the buffer, the chunk IDs at both ends of the buffer will go forward with time, we name the BM *offset* time sequences of as *offset curve* $f_p(t)$ and the largest chunk ID time sequence in the peer's BM as *scope curve* $\xi_p(t)$. Obviously, the difference between them is the peer's *buffer width* $W_p(t)=\xi_p(t)-f_p(t)$. Usually, $W_p(t)$ fluctuates with time. In addition, we get a very useful finding in tracker *peerlist* message: Different from the *peerlist* of a peer, the tracker *peerlist* has two important extra fields, Tk_{OffMin} and Tk_{OffMax}, corresponding to the buffer head (called *seeder offset* f_{tk}) and buffer tail (called *seeder scope* ξ_{tk}) of the seeder, respectively. Obviously, the seeder's buffer width is $W_{tk}=\xi_{tk}-f_{tk}$. The finding can be proved in next section.

3.3 Network measurement and dataset

Using the cracked protocols, we succeeded for the first time to develop crawlers that measure different P2P streaming media systems in a large scale. The crawler first reads a channel's index file. Then it starts to collect BMs and peerlist messages returned by tracker or peers into a log file as the raw trace for our offline studies, meanwhile we insert a local timestamp into each message. The crawler runs on a PC server (512 kbps ADSL home line, window XP, 2.4 GHz CPU, and 1 GB memory). The VoD crawler trace used in this chart is captured from PPLive on October 26, 2007, and lasts for about 90 min. The live crawler trace is also captured from PPLive during the time period from Apr. 2 to Jul. 15, 2007. With the crawlers, nearly all peers in any given channel can be detected, so that much more properties can be found. However, crawler is incapable of detecting a peer within its very beginning stage because the startup peer doesn't emit any signaling messages to a normal peer/crawler. Thus, a live sniffer trace, which is captured on July 3, 11, 12 and 15, 2007 by using a sniffer tool, is used to analyze the startup progress. We call it an experiment for each client sniffing and the trace totally contains about 2500 experiments.

4. Reverse engineering analysis from a peer's viewpoint

Like the BT system, live peer may play roles of *leecher(watcher)* or *seeder*. A seeder has the complete video, while a leecher hasn't. In a P2P live streaming media system, all peers are watchers and a few content servers are seeders. On the other hand, a P2P VoD system also contains two roles. However, they are not classified based on whether a peer has a complete file or not. Although most VoD peers do not own a complete video, he can share it once he is online regardless of the viewing channel. In a channel, we name a peer never downloading from others as a *contributor*, and a peer downloading from others as a *watcher*. VoD *watcher* is just like live watcher in many aspects, while VoD *contributor* may not necessarily have a complete file. As a *contributor*, the VoD peer may upload one movie while watching another. A significant difference of a VoD system from a live system is that *contributors* largely outnumber *watchers*. Our measurement shows that about two-thirds peers are *contributors*.

4.1 Live peer behavior in P2P streaming media system

Nearly all existing studies simply assume a stable playback rate. Thus we start with the problem of video playback rate measurement to launch our analysis. Then, we raised the questions of how a peer reaches its stable playback state, and whether and how a peer can keep in good shape.

4.1.1 Playback rate and service curve

Intuitively, the forward BM offset with time t in peer p, noted as $f_p(t)$, is connected to its playback rate. According to our experience, small rate changes are hidden if we were to visualize $f_p(t)$ directly as a time sequence. Instead, a curve of $rt-f_p(t)$ with proper value of playback rate r can make the changes obviously. However, to check every peer's playback rate is a hard job. In practice, each peer has its own playback rate which roughly equals to the system playback rate, otherwise video continuity cannot be ensured. Thus, a system playback rate should be found as a common reference for observing peer offset progress.

We describe the system playback process by a *service curve* $s(t)$. It is reasonable to use the system maximal chunk ID at any time t as $s(t)$, and then playback rate is $r(t) = ds(t)/dt$. For a channel with playback rate variations, the playback rate vs. time should be a piecewise linear function.

The procedure of finding the rate change is similar to the method in estimating the clock skew in network delay measurements. In (Zhang, 2002), people presented "Convex_Hull_L" algorithm and a segmented algorithm, which are denoted as CHU and SCHU respectively in our research, to calculate the network delay. However, referring to Fig.3, the convex envelope (dash line) calculated by CHU fails to reflect the rate changes in medium time scale in our trace 070502. Through slightly modifying SCHU algorithm, we get a new method called Piecewise Line Envelop Approximation (PLEA) (Li & Chen, 2009). The *rate reset time* $\{t_k\}$ and *reset rate* $\{r_k\}$ is simply the turn point and slope of each segment in the piecewise line calculated by PLEA respectively. The key of PLEA is to take convex hull only in small time scale and follow the rate variation in medium time scale. Thus, a parameter named as *follow-up time* Δ is introduced. An observed point will be kept if the time difference between this point and previously saved point is larger than Δ. Unlike SCHU, our segmentation is automatically adjusted during the calculation procedure without pre-assigned or fixed. The square marked line in Fig.3 shows the result of PLEA with Δ=1500s. It fits the envelope of trace quite well. Comparing PLEA to SCHU in Fig.3, the result of PLEA is much smoother.

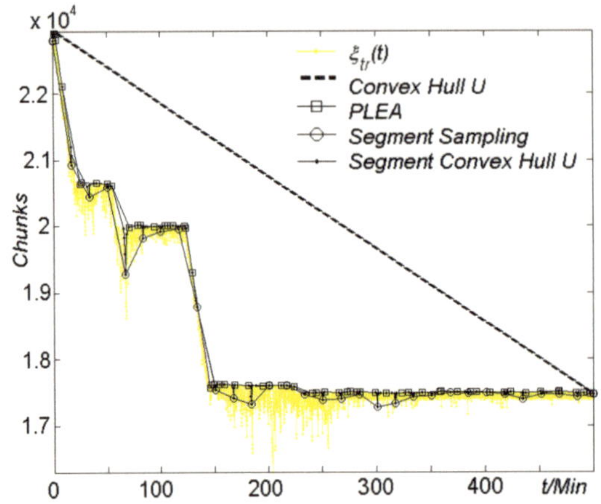

Fig. 3. PLEA v.s. others algorithms

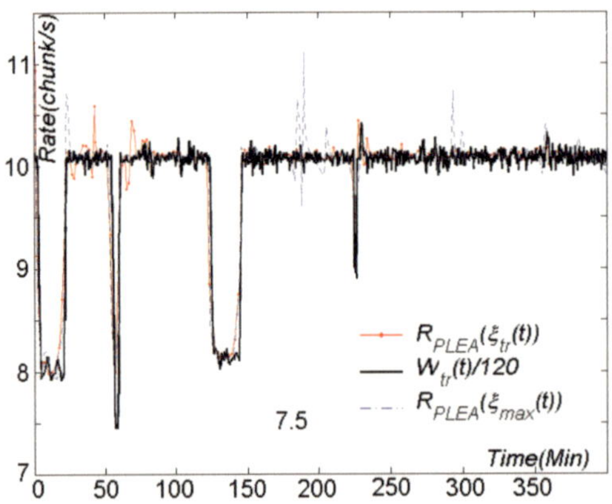

Fig. 4. Comparison of our algorithms

Besides PLEA, we have an occasional but very useful finding during reverse engineering. In PPLive, the seeder's buffer width $W_{tr}(t)$ reported by tracker, which is the difference of seeder's scope minus its offset, is always equals to the product of 120 and current playback rate r, i.e., $W_{tr}(t)$=120$r(t)$. For validation, we draw all the rate curves calculated from PLEA of tracker scope $\xi_{tr}(t)$ and peers max scope $\xi_{max}(t)$, *i.e.*, $R_{PLEA}(\xi_{tr}(t))$ and $R_{PLEA}(\xi_{max}(t))$, as well as $W_{tr}(t)/120$ in the same trace in Fig.4. All rate curves match well except some individual points. Thus we have following observations: For any PPLive channel, the instantaneous rates deduced from both tracker scope and peer maximal scope equal each other, and they are about 1/120 of the seeder's *buffer width*, i.e., $R_{PLEA}(\xi_{tr}(t))=R_{PLEA}(\xi_{max}(t))=W_{tr}(t)/120$.

Then new questions are naturally raised. Whether has the system took the rate variations into account in design? When rate change occurs, can that lead a peer to restart? All such questions involve a primary problem, what is operating mechanism of a peer, especially in its early stage.

4.1.2 The observation of a peer based on key events

By sniffing many single clients, the typical events in peer startup progress are revealed in Fig.5. For simplicity, we call a startup peer as *host*. The first event is the *registration* message a host sends to the tracker after selecting a channel. We take the registration time as the *reference time* 0. After certain *tracker response time* T_{tk} the host gets a peerlist response from the tracker, which contains a list of online peer addresses and the seeder buffer information (Tk_{OffMin} and Tk_{OffMax}). Next, the host connects to the peers known from the peerlist. Shortly after, the host receives its *first BM* at *peer response time* T_p, and the sender of the first BM is correspondingly called the *first neighbor p*. After that, the host chooses an initial chunk as its start point and begins to fetch chunks after that chunk. We denote the time when a host sends its first chunk request as the *chunk request time* T_{chk}. After a while, the host starts periodically advertising its BM to the neighbors. The time when a host sends its first BM is named as the *host advertising time* T_{ad}. This time breaks the whole start process into two phases: the *silent phase* and the *advertising phase.* Only in the advertising phase, a host can be sensed by an outside crawler. We find that, in a short time period after T_{ad}, host reports an invariant BMs' offsets, which indicates a host is busy in building his buffer so that it's not the time to start to play video. At the time called *offset initial time* T_{off} when the host begins to move the BM offset forward, we think the host begins to drain data out from its buffer for playback. By the way, an oftenly-used *offset setup time* τ_s is defined as the time duration between T_p and T_{off}, i.e. $\tau_s = T_{off} - T_p$. Time points of T_{tk}, T_p, and T_{chk} are all in the silent phase and can only be detected by client sniffer. While after T_{ad}, time points of T_{ad} and T_{off} can be collected by either our crawler or a sniffer. We use both two platforms to measure peer's startup process and use T_{ad} as the common reference to connect both platforms.

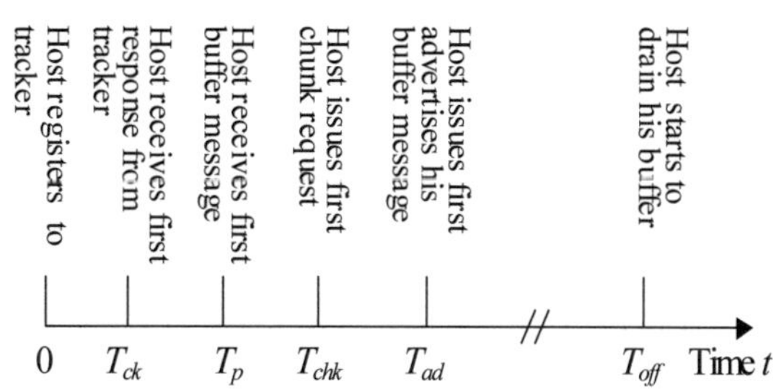

Fig. 5. Events and their occurring time in PPLive

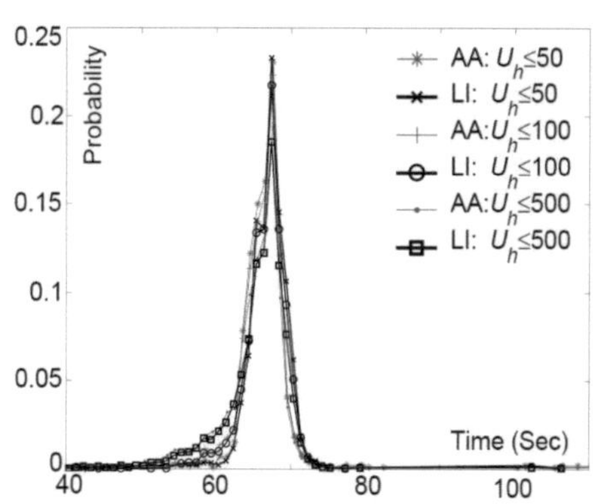

Fig. 6. PDF of τ_s'

Firstly, we measure the events in the silent phase. Statistic based on our 2502 client sniffing experiments shows that the T_{ad} is a multiple of 5s and in most of cases $T_{ad} \approx 5$s. Most trackers return their responses within 0.02 seconds. T_p has an evenly distribution in the time interval [0.9s 2s]. Among T_{tk}, T_p, T_{chk} and T_{ad}, no time points are tightly dependent. The average values of T_{tk}, T_p and T_{chk} are 0.058s, 1.419s and 2.566s respectively.

Secondly, we measure the events in advertising phase. The sniffer method is not used because it can only detect limited hosts which are under our control. With our crawler, nearly all the peers in any given channel can be detected, so that much more properties can be found. For each peer p, we get the offset $f_p(t)$ at each discrete time of $\{t_{p,i}\}$. Not every peer caught by our crawler is a host since many peers have already been there before the crawler inquiries them. A principle is used to extract the hosts from our trace, i.e., a host should have an invariable offset in its early BMs and then increase the offsets later. Two problems are involved in inferring the exact value of T_{off} from BM records. First, T_{ad} is often missed out in BM records. In the most cases, a host has been in progress for uncertain time before our crawler queries him. Second, we can't get the exact time when a host starts to drain data from his buffer because the time span between T_{ad} and T_{off} may last for several tens of seconds. We take following measures. *Buffer fill* $U_h(t)$, which is the number of all downloaded chunks in the buffer, i.e., the number of 1s in a BM at time t for a given host h, is used to solve the first problem. We only choose the peer meeting the condition $U_h(t) \leq$ certain threshold as a host, and take the timestamp of its first BM as its *advertising time* T_{ad}. For checking if the threshold introduces biases, we try different thresholds. For the second problem, we take two different methods to estimate that time when a host changes its offset. Let t_1 and t_2 be the timestamps of the earliest two BMs with different offsets $f(t_1) \neq f(t_2)$. One is the simple arithmetic average (AA) $T_{off} = (t_1+t_2)/2$, and the other is the linear interpolation (LI) $T_{off} = t_2 - (f(t_2) - f(t_1))/r$. The relative offset set time τ_s' for a host is calculated as $\tau_s' = T_{off} - T_{ad}$. The probability distribution functions (PDFs) of τ_s' estimated by AA and LI with different thresholds are plotted in Fig.6. The similarity of the results can validate above methods. Therefore, we get peer's *offset setup time* $\tau_s = \tau_s' + (T_{ad} - T_p) \approx 70$s where the mean value of τ_s' is about 66s and $T_{ad} - T_p$ is about $5 - 1.419 \approx 3.6$s measured in silent phase. Then, what is the root reason for that constant, why not other values? Let's dig it more deeply.

4.1.3 Model-based observation of peer initial offset selection

We name the peer's first wanted chunk as the *initial offset* θ. We reconstruct a peer startup model in Fig.7 to explain the importance of initial offset. Assuming a constant playback rate r, *service curve* $s(t)$ is a global reference. Assuming a constant seeder buffer width W_{tk}, we have the seeder's offset curve $f_{tk}(t) = s(t) - W_{tk}$ below $s(t)$. The host's first neighbor p's *offset curve* and *scope curve* (of its largest chunk ID) are $f_p(t)$ and $\xi_p(t)$ respectively. Since the number of successive chunks in a buffer indicates how long the video can be played continually, we follow (Hei et al., 2007b) to name that as the *buffer's playable video* $V_p(t)$, correspondingly the *peer's playable video* $v_p(t) = f_p(t) + V_p(t)$, which is also drawn in Fig.7. The initial offset is very important for that, once it, saying θ_h, is chosen at certain time t_h, the host's offset lag $L_h = s(t) - f_h(t)$ is totally determined. As shown in Fig.7, $f_h(t)$ begins to increase after the τ_s, meanwhile $s(t)$ has increased $r\tau_s$. Since the host initial offset lag is $L_\theta = s(t_h) - \theta_h$, its *offset lag* at last is $L_h = L_\theta + r\tau_s$. L_h is the playback lag, but also the possible maximum buffer width. It means θ_h can affect the system sharing environment.

For simplicity, we assume the *initial offset* decision is based on the host's *first neighbor p*. Then, host h faces two alternatives -- based on either the tracker or its first neighbor. Seeing Fig.7, at time t_h, host h gets values of $s(t_h)=Tk_{OffMax}$ and $f_{tk}(t_h)= Tk_{OffMin}$ from tracker, and values of $\xi_p(t_h)$, $v_p(t_h)$ and $f_p(t_h)$ from its first neighbor p. Then the host should choice its θ_h between $f_p(t_h)$ and $\xi_p(t_h)$, beyond which scope no chunk is available. For further explanation, the chunk θ_h will shift out of the neighbor p's buffer at time $t_h+(\theta_h-f_p(t_h))/r$. Large θ_h lets host h have more time to fetch this chunk. However, as too large θ_h will lead to a very small *offset lag*, host's *buffer width* maybe not large enough for a good playback performance. So what are the design principles behind the initial offset selection?

We extract the marked points shown in Fig.7 at time t_h from our 2502 experiments, and draw them as a function of sorted experiment sequence in ascending order of W_{tk} and $W_p(t)$ in Fig.8 where we take $f_{tk}(t_h)$ as the horizontal zero reference. The red lines are the seeder's buffer width $\pm W_{tk}=\pm(s(t_h)-f_{tk}(t_h))$. The top one is W_{tk} and the bottom one is $-W_{tk}$. Clearly, PPLive mainly serves two playback rates: 10 chunks/s on the right area and 6 chunks/s on the left area. The *black '.'* and *green 'x'* stand for ξ_p-f_{tk} and f_p-f_{tk} respectively, the distance between which marks in each experiment is peer p's buffer width $W_p=\xi_p-f_p$. Similarly, the vertical distance between top red '-' and *green 'x'* is peer p's offset lag $L_p=s-f_p$. Thus, Fig.8 confirms that PPLive takes certain variable buffer width scheme. Furthermore, seeder has a larger buffer than normal peer. The *blue '*'* is hosts relative initial offset lag θ_h-f_{tk}. Obviously, PPLive doesn't adopt a fixed initial offset lag scheme, or else all *blue '*'* would keep flat. Actually the *blue '*'* and *green 'x'* have a similar shape, which means that *initial offset* may adapt to *first neighbor p's* buffer condition.

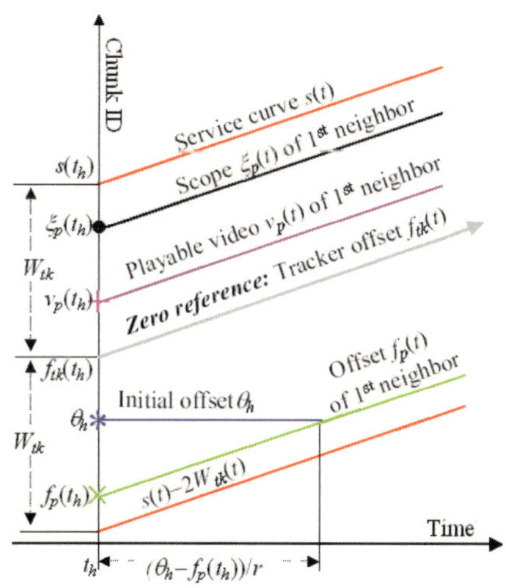

Fig. 7. The startup model

We think certain kind of *Proportional Placement* (PP) strategy (Li & Chen, 2008a) can be introduced to make the decision of *initial offset*. Referring to Fig.8, the distance of the initial offset to its first received BM's offset is somehow proportional to the first neighbor's buffer width $W_p=\xi_p-f_p$ or the first neighbor's offset lag $L_p=s-f_p$. Thus, we guess PPLive chooses the *initial offset* either by $\theta_h=f_p+\alpha_W W_p$ or $\theta_h=f_p+\alpha_L L_p$, where the α_W and α_L are the scale coefficients. Based our measurement, both PDFs of $\alpha_W=(\theta_h-f_p)/W_p$ and

$\alpha_L=(\theta_h-f_p)/L_p$ have the very high peaks at the same coefficient 0.34. The scaled errors of $100(\alpha_W-0.34)$ is shown with the cyan color in Fig.8. It seems that PPLive more likely uses a scheme based on the first neighbor's buffer width since α_W has a more sharp distribution. To check whether the selected *initial offset* θ is easy to download, as well as to evaluate whether PPLive has been designed to make host set its *initial offset* at the most suitable point locally or globally, we have studied the chunk availability. As a result, a host usually receives BMs from 4.69 peers before fetching any chunks. In more than 70% experiments, host can fetch chunks around θ from at least 3 neighbors. It indicates a good initial downloading performance.

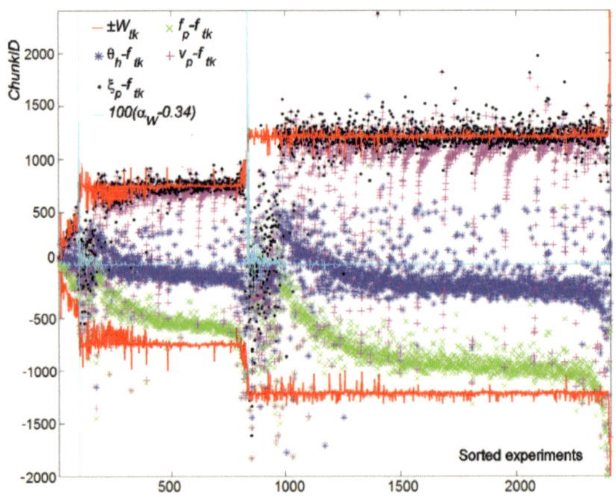

Fig. 8. The measured initial parameters

4.1.4 Model-based peer observation in the startup stage

Once the initial offset is chosen, the host begins to download chunks. We use a simple model to help understand the data fetching process. For any given peer p, the model contains two parts. One is *buffer filling process,* expressed by curves of *buffer width* $W_p(t)$, *playable video in buffer* $V_p(t)$, *and buffer fill* $U_p(t)$ which is the number of all downloaded chunks in the buffer at time t. They reflect a buffer's local conditions, but can't tell the status of peer process in a global sense. The other is *peer evolutionary process* depicted by curves of *offset* $f_p(t)$, scope $\xi_p(t)$, peer *playable video* $v_p(t)$, *download* $u_p(t)=f_p(t)+U_p(t)$ and the reference $s(t)$. Ideally, for a CBR video, all evolutionary process curves should have the same slope equals to the playback rate r. One real progresses of the model can refer to Fig.9. The top line is $s(t)$ as the reference line, the black line at the bottom shows the offset curve $f_p(t)$, and the cyan curve close to $s(t)$ is $u_p(t)$; the solid red curve with mark 'x' is $W_p(t)$, the green curve with mark '*' is $U_p(t)$, and the blue curve with mark '+' is the $V_p(t)$.

Obviously, the downloading procedure contains two kinds of strategies. In Fig.9, both $W_p(t)$ and $V_p(t)$ have a same switch point at ($\tau_{sch}\approx$40s, $C_{sch}\approx$900). We guess, before time τ_{sch}, a peer sequentially fetches chunks from small to large ID, which can be confirmed by the fact of the closeness of $W_p(t)$, $V_p(t)$ and $U_p(t)$ before τ_{sch}. Ideally, the three curves should be the same. However, in real networks, some wanted chunks may not exist in its neighbors or a chunk request maybe rejected by its neighbor. At the switch time point τ_{sch}, the big jump of $W_p(t)$ indicates a fetch strategy change. Therefore, we name τ_{sch} as the *scheduling switch time*. Before and after τ_{sch}, we call the downloading strategies used by a peer as strategy I and strategy II respectively. A peer fetches chunks sequentially in strategy I, while in strategy II it may always fetch the latest chunk first. At the switch point to strategy II, the chunk ID's sudden increase leads to an enlarged buffer width.

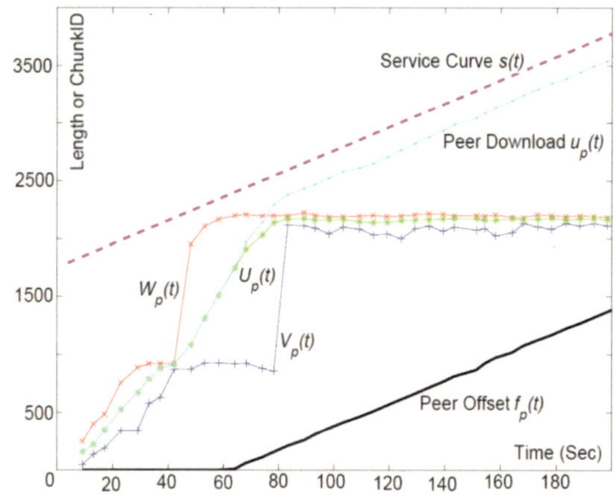

Fig. 9. A PPLive peer's evolution

We believe the downloading strategies switch may be base on certain ratio threshold of buffer filling, and a closer observation can support this guess. As shown Fig.9, BM offset $f_p(t)$ keeps flat in the early 65s. Then, the peer starts to shift the offset forward. Let's see the flat playable video $V_p(t)$ curve duration time [40s, 80s]. We can infer the first flat part in period of [40s, 65s] is for that the peer is downloading the latest chunks according to strategy II. If with the same strategy, the curve of the rest part in period of [65s,80s] should have had sloped downwards. Thus it must have changed the fetch strategy again from strategy II to I, which let peer fetches the most urgent chunks first so as to keep the $V_p(t)$ at certain threshold.

At last, all curves of $W_p(t)$, $V_p(t)$ and $U_p(t)$ converge after a time around 80s, which is named as *convergence time* τ_{cvg}. A sudden big jump in $V_p(t)$ at this time indicates that the last wanted chunk within the buffer are fetched. It proves that the latest chunk is fetched firstly by strategy II in most of the period of [τ_{sch}, τ_{cvg}].

The whole progress can be approximated by a set of piecewise linear functions by a threshold bipolar (TB) protocol, which is very simple in its implementation and design philosophy. For a host, when the current $V_p \leq$ a threshold, the urgent task is to download the most wanted chunks, while if $V_p >$ the threshold, the job is switched to help spread the latest or rarest chunks over the network. We have ever observed some other peers' startup procedures in our trace, and all of them can be interpreted easily by the TB protocol.

By further observation, the piecewise line model involves six structure parameters including video *playback rate* r, peer *initial download rate* r_p, fetching strategy *switch threshold* C_{sch}, *offset setup time* τ_s, the *initial offset* θ_p relative to the first neighbor's offset and the *offset lag* W^*. Among them, r and r_p cannot be designed and the rest four can. Assuming a constant r and a constant r_p, based on the superposition principle at the key points among the piecewise lines, it is not difficult to calculate other key time points, including *scheduling turnover time* τ_{sch} and *convergence time* τ_{cvg}, and then we can draw the piecewise lines. (Li & Chen, 2008b).

We are next interested to better understand the parameters design in PPLive. In order to generalize our discussion we consider all the relative parameters, including C_{sch}, θ_p, W^*, and nearly all buffer progress parameters, to be normalized by playback rate r, and for simplicity, we use the same names for most of the normalized parameters as their originals.

We have known the *offset setup time* $\tau_s\approx$70s in subsection 4.1.2. For C_{sch}, we use *switch threshold factor* $\beta=C_{sch}/r$ instead of C_{sch}. The calculation of C_{sch} is a litter fussy, referring to Fig.9: *i).* let $C_{sch}=W_p(t)$ just before the first jump of $W_p(t)$; *ii).* Let $C_{sch}=V_p(t)$ just after the first big change in $dV_p(t)/dt$; *iii).* let C_{sch} =mean of $V_p(t)$ on its flat part; *iv).* let $C_{sch}=V_p(t)$ just before the jump of $V_p(t)$. The results of all above methods are plotted in Fig.10, and we have β=90s. Next, W^* is deduced from our crawler trace. Based on the statistics over total 15,831 peers lasting for at least 5 minutes since they entered stable state, we get a similar result for both normalized buffer width and offset lag relative to *s(t)*. At last, the *relative initial offset* is figured out from sniffer trace. The distribution of W^* and θ_p are shown in Fig.11. Based on our measurement, we have W^*=210s and θ_p = 70s.

Corresponding to the different sort orders of τ_s, τ_{sch} and τ_{cvg}, i.e. $\tau_s<\tau_{sch}<\tau_{cvg}$, $\tau_{sch}<\tau_s<\tau_{cvg}$ and $\tau_{sch}<\tau_{cvg}<\tau_s$, after computation with these design parameters of PPLive, we get three groups of the buffer process, $\Gamma_0=\{\gamma_p: <\gamma_p\leq 1.286\}$, $\Gamma_1=\{\gamma_p: 1.286<\gamma_p\leq 3\}$ and $\Gamma_2=\{\gamma_p: \gamma_p>3\}$, where γ_p is the *normalized download rate* $\gamma_p=r_p/r$. Peers in group Γ_0 face a very poor startup condition. They take very long time to converge and the convergence time spans from 490s (about 8min) to infinite (γ_p=1, never converge). According to our measured γ_p, less than 10%peers belong to this group, while more than 70% peers belong to group Γ_1. Hence Γ_1 is the normal startup situation, and the convergence time is between 490s and 70s. Peers (more than 20%) in Γ_2 are so fast that they have converged before playing the video.

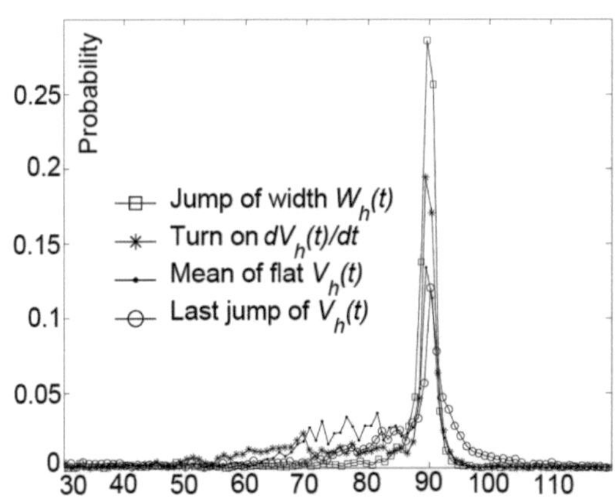

Fig. 10. Probability distribution function of β

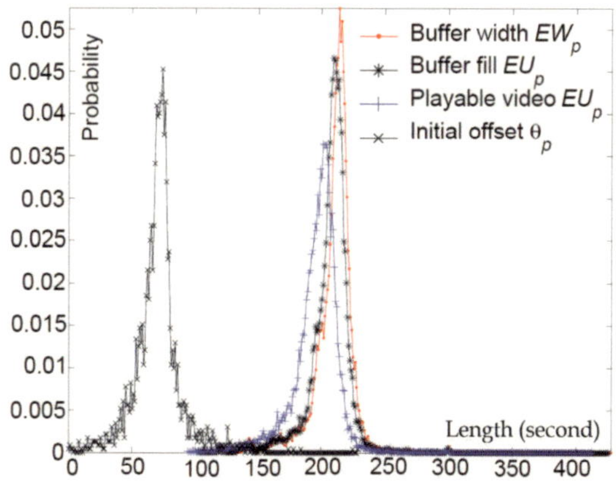

Fig. 11. Probability distribution function of buffer progress (normalized)

In summary, we have described how to approximate peer evolutionary progress based on the six parameters and the so-called design parameters in PPLive. In general, PPLive client has a good startup performance. In next section, we will reveal the systematic concerns behind the parameters design in PPLive.

4.2 VoD user behavior in P2P streaming media systems

In general, A VoD peer can be classified as *contributor* or *watcher* based on whether the number of ones never increases in bitmap of the peer's BM or not during our observation. In our trace, most peers belong to either contributor or watcher. Less than 6% peers even advertised the abnormal all-zero BMs, the bitmap contained nothing. We guess such disordered behavior ascribed to software bugs, e.g. a user deletes his cache file suddenly. We name such those peers as Zpeer. Fig.12 draws the fractions of different peer groups in our measured channel 1. In fact, the rest two measured channel have the similar results. Those curves confirm that contributors always significantly outnumber watchers, and a stationary process can approximate the fractions.

Further, two types of watching modes have been identified. People either watch a movie smoothly until his exit, or see a movie by jumping from one scene to another. We named the former as smooth watching mode and such viewer as smoother, and the latter as the jumping watching mode and that viewer as jumper. Obviously, smoother has continuous 1s in its BM, while jumper has discrete 1s. Table 1 lists the statistics on our trace. We find the majority are smoothers, while the jumpers cannot be ignored. It is different from that "most users always perform some random seeking" (Zheng et al., 2005).

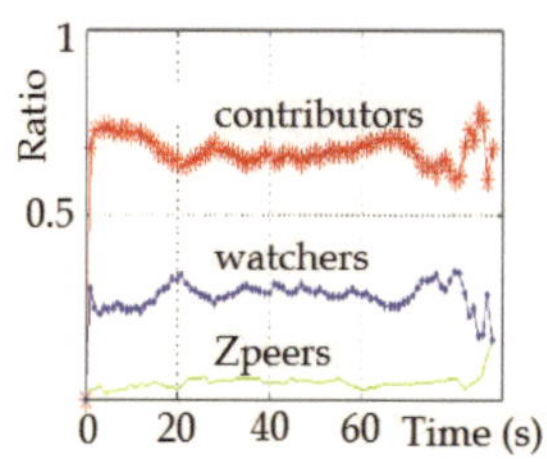

Fig. 12. role ratios in channel 1.

	Contributors				Watchers			
	Smoothers		Jumpers		Smoothers		Jumpers	
	Peers	%	Peers	%	Peers	%	Peers	%
Channel 1	300	70.9	123	29.1	138	87.3	20	12.7
Channel 2	264	86.8	40	13.1	90	90.1	9	9.1
Channel 3	156	73.2	57	26.8	82	78.8	22	21.2

Table 1. Number of smoothers and jumpers

4.2.1 Measureable parameter watching index in user behavior

For quantitative analysis, we introduce *watching index (WI)* to name the position of the last "1" in a BM, which explains how many chunks a smoother has ever watched. Different from definition in (Yu et al., 2006), we use WI to emphasize the aspects of both time and space. As most peers are smoothers, a movie with a larger WI or longer tail in WI distribution in smoothers is usually considered to be more attractive. It means that people watched this movie longer or more people watch the movie. We use probability $p_{WI}(\theta)$ to represent the PDF of WI, which is the fraction of peers whose last "1" in their BMs are at the position θ. Fig.13(a) shows Cumulative Distribution Function (CDF) $F_{WI}(\theta)=\sum_{k\le\theta} p_{WI}(k)$. Obviously, channel 3 and channel 2 were the most and the least attractive respectively. Besides, online time is defined as how long a peer stays in a channel, and Fig.13(b) shows its CDF. Obviously, distributions of WI over all channels are significantly different but their online times are very similar. It indicates that WI is strongly related to the video content, while the contributor's online time is nearly independent of what he is currently contributing.

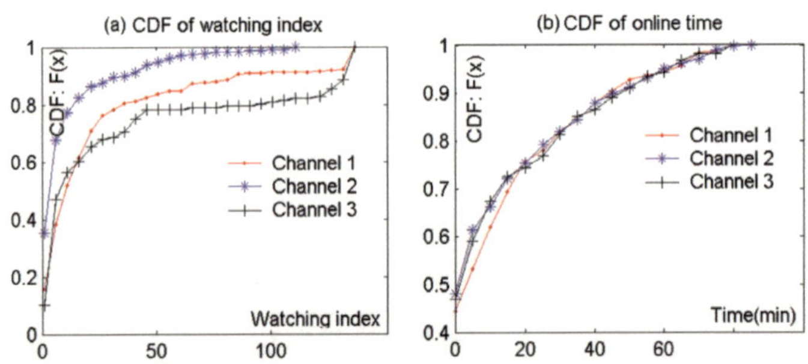

Fig. 13. CDF of WI and online time of contributors

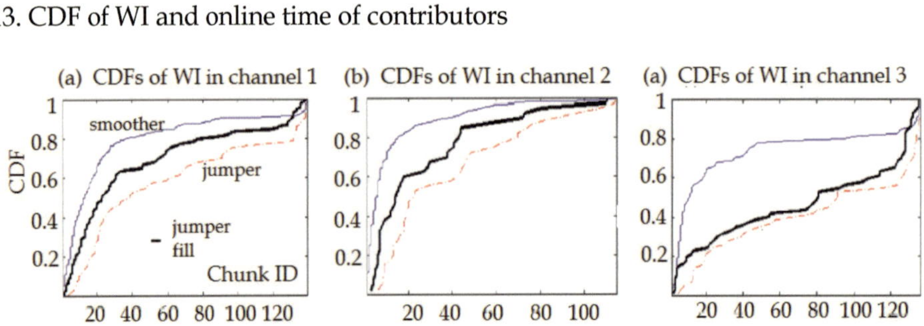

Fig. 14. BM occupancies of contributors

4.2.2 User behavior understanding in terms of watching index

WI help us in better understanding user behavior. Fig.14 shows the CDF of WI for smoothers and jumpers in contributors. The x-axis of each subfigure is the chunk ID or bit positions in the BM. The y-axis is the fraction of the peers. The top curve and bottom curve are of smoother and jumper respectively. The middle curve is the fraction of jumper who has value 1s in its BM at a given bit position. As a peer frequently advertise its BM to others, those subfigures can also be interpreted as the sharing map among VoD peers. Based on this interpretation, we can draw the following conclusions: *i).* although most users are smoother, it may not be good for file-sharing. As lots of people only watch a few chunks, it may lead to overprovision around the initial chunks while under provision for the rest chunks; *ii).* Jumper promotes file-sharing. In each subfigure, the middle curve is significantly below the top curve line. It indicates a jumper contributes more chunks than a smoother. Furthermore, the bottom curve indicates jumpers contribute those chunks with large IDs which smoothers are incapable of sharing; *iii).* Even if jumpers contribute fewer chunks as a whole, their existence is still valuable, as the unbalanced provision resulted from smoothers can be compensated to certain degree by jumpers.

5. Model-based analysis of PPLive at system level

In the section we try to discuss the systematic problems and design concerns on performance, scalability and stability. Based on the live peer's startup models, we will analyze PPLive's design goals, and how PPLive tends to reach the goals; VoD network sharing environment will be analyzed and the inherent connection with user behavior will be revealed.

5.1 System stability based on different initial offset placement schemes

We next introduce two initial offset placement schemes either based on the first neighbor's offset lag or based on its buffer width. We will show how different system design goals can be reached under different schemes, and explain why good peer selection mechanism is critical to make the schemes stable.

5.1.1 Initial offset placement based on offset lag

The first model of initial offset placement makes a new peer (called host as before) decide its *initial offset* based on its *first neighbor*'s offset lag (Li & Chen, 2008a). Assume host h chooses a chunk ID θ as the *initial offset* and begins to fetch chunks at time t_0. After a time interval τ_s, the host starts to drain chunks out of buffer to playback. Then, the offset lag of the host is, $L_h=s(t)-f_h(t)=s(t_0)+r(t-t_0)-r(t-t_0-\tau_s)-\theta=s(t_0)+r\tau_s-\theta$.

As a system designer, for minimizing the workload of tracker server, a person hopes that the wanted chunks are fetched as much as possible from other peers instead of tracker. Thus, the initial offset θ should be chosen when at least one BM has been received for a peer p and θ should be appropriate larger than peer p's offset $f_p(t_0)$. On the other hand, too much diversity among offset lags is not good for sharing environment, so a system designer would wish to control the offset lag, i.e., $L_h-L_p=f_p(t_0)+r\tau_s-\theta$.

It seems a good criterion to let the $L_h-L_p=0$. We call such scheme as *fixed padding* (FP) because of $\theta=f_p(t_0)+r\tau_s$ where $r\tau_s$ is a constant padding. However, FP has no design space.

One can easily find that all peers in such a system will have the same *offset lag* $L \leq W_{tk}$. Buffer width is an important design parameter involving playback performance. Larger buffer can improve playback continuity, but does no good to a tracker for consuming more memories. Thus, FP can't fulfill two design goals at same time: large buffer of peer but small buffer of tracker.

Let's consider a more practical scheme named as *proportional placement* (PP) *based on offset lag*, i.e., $\theta = f_p(t_0) + \alpha L_p$, where α is constant placement coefficient less than 1, and L_p is the first neighbor's offset lag. Since the first neighbor must have been a new peer when it entered the system, we can refer to a very familiar formula $x_{n+1} = bx_n + c$, which is a contraction mapping when the Lipschitz condition satisfies $b<1$. One can easily concludes that such a system has a stable point $L^* = r\tau_s / \alpha$, which is independent of any specific initial offset.

Self-stabilizing is the most attractive property of *proportional placement* scheme. However, in certain extreme conditions, it may lead to a poor performance. For example, the first neighbor has an offset lag of $L_p=1000$ but only contains 50 chunks in his buffer. With a placement coefficient $\alpha=0.3$, the host's $\theta_h = f_p(t_0)+300$, and the host doesn't have any available chunk for download.

5.1.2 Initial offset placement based on buffer width

Instead of offset lag, a host can use $W_p(t)$ for its initial offset placement, where peer p is its first neighbor. We name such a placement scheme as the PP scheme based on buffer width, i.e., $\theta = f_p(t_0) + \alpha W_p(t_0)$. The advantage of this scheme is that, the initial chunk is always available in its neighbor peer. However, the system under this scheme may be not always stable, i.e., this scheme can't guarantee a bounded *offset lag* $L_n = s(t) - f_n(t)$ as $n \to \infty$. In theory, lemmas 1,2 and 3 in (Li & Chen, 2008a) give the offset lag's variant boundaries under certain assumed conditions in line with real situation. According to the lemmas, the measured $E(W)/r=208.3$, and the measured *placement coefficient* $\alpha=0.34$, then we can deduce the *offset setup time* $\tau_s=70.82$s. The deduced τ_s is very close our measurement result. Hence, the placement scheme used in PPLive is stable.

5.2 The system design concerns based on the TB piecewise line model

Recall the normalized piecewise line design model (Li & Chen, 2008b) of peer startup progress in PPLive. Assuming each stable peer has a offset curve $f(t)=t$ and scope curve $\xi(t)=s(t)=t+W^*$,when peer p arrives at time 0, he has to choose an *initial offset* θ_p relative to a *neighbor's offset* equals as $\theta_p = \tau_s$, which has been confirmed in previous sections as both of them equal 70s. Besides, because the stable peer's buffer width W^* is 210s, thus we see that θ_p is just equal to $W^*/3$.

Offset setup time τ_s is roughly the startup latency and the buffer width W^* is the playback lag to the seeder. Usually, people would like to use large buffers to ensure playback continuity. In our model, θ_p is totally decided by τ_s. So why do not people choose a smaller τ_s for shorter startup latency? Smaller τ_s leads to smaller θ_p. A starting peer must ensure to download θ_p within time τ_s, otherwise, it will miss out it. Thus smaller τ_s means larger download rate γ_p requirement. In fact, for a given τ_s, the minimal γ_p required for fetching all initial B chunks (chunks ID from θ_p to θ_p+B-1) is about $r_{min}=B/(\tau_s+B)$ since no one chunk can survivor after τ_s+B seconds. if one wants to decrease the τ_s from 70s to 35s, the peer needs a faster r_{min} , which will impact the startup performance.

There is a physical explanation for the turnover threshold $c_{sch}(t)$ in PPLive. We have $c_{sch}(t)=t+\beta$ *for* $t\geq\tau_s$, which happens to be *the seeder offset* $f_{tk}(t)$ (reported by tracker) since $f_{tk}(t)=t+W^*-120=t+90=t+\beta$. Intuitionally, chunks below $f_{tk}(t)$ may can only be buffered by peers, but those above $f_{tk}(t)$ are cached by both seeder and peers. Designers would like to see a system where peer caches as many as useful chunks while seeder doesn't, and make use of stable peers' resources to help startup peers. Thus β has a lower limit as $\beta\geq 90$.

On the other side, let $v_q(t)=V_q(t)+t$ be the playable video of a neighbor peer q. All chunks below $v_q(t)$ are already fetched by peer q at time t, but chunk $v_q(t)+1$ definitely is not. If we set $c_{sch}(t)>v_q(t)$ and assume q is the only neighbor for host p, then after peer p gets chunk $v_q(t)$, he has to idly wait for peer q to fetch chunk $v_q(t)+1$ according to the TB protocol. If we design $c_{sch}(t)<v_q(t)$, peer p will not waste its time. Substituting model parameters into it, we have $\beta<V_q(t)+t-\tau_s$, for $0\leq t<\tau_s$. If any possible download rates are considered, the right side of the inequality has a minimal value $V_q(t)-\tau_s$. If further assuming $V_q(t)$ for any peer q has the same distribution with a mean V^* and stand deviation σ_V, then we deduced another design rule (Li & Chen, 2010) for the upper limit of β as $\beta<V^*-\alpha\sigma_V-\tau_s$ for $0\leq t<\tau_s$, where coefficient α is introduced to guarantee the switch threshold is below the playable video of his neighbor with larger probability. Based on our measurement in PPLive, V^* is about 196 and σ_V is about 18. For a threshold of 90, α is 2. Through the discussion of system design considerations, we hope to support the claim that PPLive is a well-engineered system.

5.3 VoD network sharing environment

In P2P-based file sharing systems, the number of copies is an important indication to the availability of data blocks. We define the number of copies of chunk θ in the network at a given time t as *availability* $N(\theta,t)$, which equals the number of online peers having this chunk at this time. Our statistics shows that chunks with larger IDs have less availability. Moreover, if we normalize $N(\theta,t)$ by the total number of online peers $N(t)$, or the total number of copies $C(t)=\Sigma_\theta N(\theta,t)$ at time t, then both the results of $\eta(\theta,t)=N(\theta,t)/N(t)\approx\eta(\theta)$ and $\xi(\theta,t)=N(\theta,t)/C(t)\approx\xi(\theta)$, can be observed independent of time t. We named these normalized availabilities as the *sharing profile* (SP) $\eta(\theta)$, and *sharing distribution* (SD) $\xi(\theta)$. $\xi(\theta)$ is a probability distribution as $\sum_\theta \xi(\theta)=1$, while $\eta(\theta)$ is not. Both SP and SD are shown in Fig.15. In each subfigure there are 86 curves in light color, which correspond to$\eta(\theta,t)$ or $\xi(\theta,t)$ calculated at 1, 2, . . . ,86 minutes of our trace time. Clearly, all the light color curves in each subfigure are very similar. This indicates that the SP and SD are well defined in a practical P2P VoD system.

The user watching behavior will affect the network sharing environment, and an inherent connection does exist between user behavior and VoD network sharing, i.e. the SP and SD can be analytically deduced from the distribution of WI. The theorems 1 and 2 in (Li & Chen, 2010) further verify the time-invariant property of SP and SD. yIn Fig.15, the thick black curve is the result theorem 1 in (Li & Chen, 2010). Clearly, the thick curves match the measured light color curves quite well in all subfigures. Equation 3 in theorem 1 says that the average number of copies is related to the second moment of WI. It indicates that the diversity in users' behaviors can promote network sharing, and this provides twofold insights: *i).* the system design should facilitate any kinds of viewing habits, such as watching from the middle, watching by skipping and even watching backward. *ii).* a movie should be designed to lure its viewers to present different behaviors, e.g., guiding viewers go to different sections by properly designed previews. In addition, the network sharing research based on the jumpers' WI has a similar result. In short, a good VoD system should be well-designed on both protocols and contents to accommodate any kind of audience.

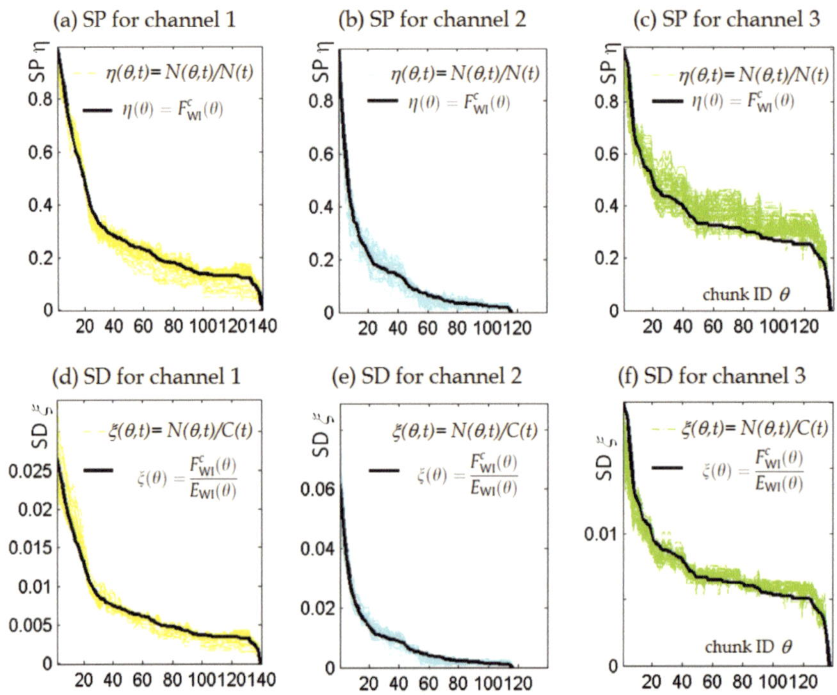

Fig. 15. Sharing profiles (SP) and sharing distributions (SD) in three channels

6. Conclusion

In this chapter, we presented the study of a P2P streaming media system at different levels of detail. The aim of the study is to illustrate different types of analyses and measurements which can be correlated to reverse-engineer, and further give guidelines to optimizing the behavior of such a system in practice. On signaling message level, we tell about our system crack procedure and reveal the protocol flow and message format. Following that, large-scale measurements are carried out with our network crawlers and mass raw data is captured. On peer behavior level, the startup process of live peer is analyzed in two aspects including initial offset placement and chunk fetch strategies. We discover that the initial offset is the only decision factor to a peer's offset lag (playback delay), and the initial offset selection follows certain proportional placement models based on first neighbor's buffer width or offset lag in PPLive. Once the initial offset is determined, a peer downloads wanted chunks following a TB protocol, which can be depicted by a model of a bunch of piecewise lines. Our measurement proofs that in PPLive most live peers (more than 90%) have seemingly good performance. Moreover, VoD peer's behavior is discussed in user (person) behavior. With the help of measurable parameter of WI, we reveal that although majority peers are smoothers, jumpers tend to be the real valuable file-sharing contributor. On system level, the systematic problems and design concerns on performance, scalability and stability are discussed. Based on the live peer's startup models (PP models and piecewise line model of TB protocol) driven by our trace, we analyze P2P live system's design goals such as the large buffer in peer/small buffer in seeder and self-stability on offset lags, and confirm PPLive tends to really reach those goals. VoD network sharing environment is analyzed in terms of network sharing profile and sharing distribution, and we find the sharing environment is heavily affected by user viewing behavior.

In addition, we will further our study on following issues. We believe live peer chooses its initial offset base on good neighbour, but the evaluation principle of good peer is not answered; The playback rate change has been found in a system designed for CBR video. It needs to be analyzed whether the system can keep in good health when playing a VBR video and how to improve the performance. Besides, we will continue to study what have changed in the continually updated systems.

7. References

Ali, S.; Mathur, A. & Zhang, H. (2006). Measurement of commercial peer-to-peer live video streaming, *In Proceedings of ICST Workshop on Recent Advances in Peer-to-Peer Streaming (2006),* Aug. 2006.

Cheng, B.; Liu, X.Z.; Zhang, Z.Y. & Jin, H. (2007). A measurement study of a peer-to-peer video-on-demand system, *Proceedings of the 6th International Workshop on Peer-to-Peer Systems (IPTPS'07),* Washington, USA, Feb. 26-27, 2007

Hei, X.; Liang, C.; Liang,J.; Liu Y. & Ross ,K.W. (2007a). A measurement study of a large-scale P2P IPTV system, *Journal of IEEE Transactions on Multimedia,* Oct. 2007, Volume 9, Issue 8, (Dec. 2007), pp. 1672-1687, ISSN 1520-9210

Hei, X.J.; Liu, Y. & Ross, K. (2007b). Inferring Network-Wide Quality in P2P Live Streaming Systems, *IEEE Journal on Selected Areas in Communications,* Vol. 25, No. 10, (Dec. 2007), pp. 1640-1654, ISSN : 0733-8716

Huang, C.; Li, J. & Ross, K.W. (2007). Can internet video-on-demand be profitable? *Proceedings of ACM Sigcomm 2007.* pp. 133-144, ISBN 978-1-59593-713-1, Kyoto, Japan, 27-31 Aug., 2007

Li, C.X. & Chen C.J. (2008b). Fetching Strategy in the Startup Stage of P2P Live Streaming Available from http://arxiv.org/ftp/arxiv/papers/0810/0810.2134.pdf

Li, C.X. & Chen C.J. (2008a). Initial Offset Placement in P2P Live Streaming Systems http://arxiv.org/ftp/arxiv/papers/0810/0810.2063.pdf

Li, C.X. & Chen C.J. (2009). Inferring Playback Rate and Rate Resets of P2P Video Streaming Transmissions by Piecewise Line Envelope Approximation. *Journal of China Univ. of Post and Telecom.,* Vol.16, Issue 2, (April 2009), pp. 58-61, ISSN 1005-8885

Li, C.X. & Chen C.J. (2010). Measurement-based study on the relation between users' watching behavior and network sharing in P2P VoD systems. *Journal of Computer Networks,* Vol.54, Issue 1, (Jan. 2010), pp. 13-27, ISSN 1389-1286

Lou, D.F.; Mao, Y.Y. & Yeap T.H. (2007). The production of peer-to-peer video-streaming networks, *Proceedings of the 2007 workshop on Peer-to-peer streaming and IP-TV,* pp. 346-351,ISBN 978-1-59593-789-6, Kyoto, Japan, 31 Aug. 2007

Small, T.; Liang, B. & Li, B. (2006). Scaling laws and tradeoffs of peer-to-peer live multimedia streaming. Proceedings of ACM Multimedia 2006, pp.539-548, ISBN 1595934472, Santa Barbara, CA, USA, 23-27 Oct. 2006

Tu, Y.C.; Sun, J.Z.; Hefeeda, M. & Prabhakar, S. (2005). An analytical study of peer-to-peer media streaming systems, *Journal of ACM Transactions on Multimedia Computing, Communications, and Applications,* Vol.1, Issue 4, (Nov. 2005), ISSN 1551-6857

Vlavianos,A.; Iliofotou,M.; Faloutsos,M. & Faloutsos, M. (2006). BiToS: Enhancing BitTorrent for Supporting Streaming Applications, *Proceedings of INFOCOM 2006*, pp.1-6, ISSN 0743-166X, Barcelona, 23-29 April 2006

Vu, L.; Gupta, I.; Liang, J. & Nahrstedt, K. (2006). Mapping the PPLive Network: Studying the Impacts of Media Streaming on P2P Overlays, *UIUC Tech report*, August 2006

Xu, D.Y.; Chai, H.K.; Rosenberg, C. & Kulkarni, S. (2003). Analysis of a Hybrid Architecture for Cost-Effective Streaming Media Distribution, *Proceedings SPIE/ACM Conf. on Multimedia Computing and Networking (MMCN'03)*, San Jose, CA, Jan. 2003.

Yu, H.L.; Zheng, D.D.; Zhao, B.Y. & Zheng, W.M. (2006). Understanding user behavior in large-scale video-on-demand systems, *Proceedings of the 1st ACM SIGOPS/EuroSys European Conference on Computer Systems 2006 (Eurosys'06)*, pp. 333-344, ISBN 1-59593-322-0 Leuven,Belgium, April 18-21, 2006.

Zhang, L.; Liu, Z. & Xia, C.H. (2002). Clock Synchronization Algorithms for Network Measurements, *Proceedings of the IEEE INFOCOM 2002*, Vol.1, pp. 160-169, ISBN 0-7803-7477-0, New York, USA, June 23-27, 2002,

Zhang, X.;Liu, J.;Li, B. & Yum, T.-S.P. (2005). Coolstreaming/donet: A data-driven overlay network for Peer-to-Peer live media streaming,. *Proceedings of INFOCOM 2005*, vol. 3, pp.2102-2111, ISBN 0743-166X, Miami, FL, USA, 13-17 March 2005

Zheng, C.X.; Shen, G.B. & Li, S.P. (2005). Distributed pre-fetching scheme for random seek support in peer-to-peer streaming applications, *Proceedings of the ACM Workshop on Advances in Peer-to-Peer Multimedia Streaming (P2PMMS'05)*, pp. 29-38, ISBN 1-59593-248-8, Singapore, Nov. 11, 2005

Zhou,Y.P.; Chiu, D.M. & Lui, J.C.S. (2007). A Simple Model for Analyzing P2P Streaming Protocols, *Proceedings of international conference on network procotols 2007*,pp.226–235, ISBN 978-1-4244-1588-5, Beijing, China,5 Nov. 2007

Part 2

Reverse Engineering Shapes

6

Surface Reconstruction from Unorganized 3D Point Clouds

Patric Keller[1], Martin Hering-Bertram[2] and Hans Hagen[3]
[1]*University of Kaiserslautern*
[2]*University of Applied Sciences Bremen*
[3]*University of Kaiserslautern*
Germany

1. Introduction

Computer-based surface models are indispensable in several fields of science and engineering. For example, the design and manufacturing of vehicles, such as cars and aircrafts, would not be possible without sophisticated CAD and simulation tools predicting the behavior of the product. On the other hand, designers often do not like working on virtual models, though sophisticated tools, like immersive VR-environments are available. Hence, a designer may produce a physical prototype made from materials of his choice that can be easily assembled and shaped like clay models. Reverse engineering is the process of reconstructing digital representations from physical models. The overall reverse-engineering framework mainly is composed of four steps (see Figure 1): data acquisition, pre-processing, surface reconstruction, and post-processing;

The point cloud acquisition generally is performed by stationary scanning devices, like laser-range or computer-tomography scanners. In the case of a 3D laser scanner, the surface is sampled by one or more laser beams. The distance to the surface is typically measured by the time delay or by the reflection angle of the beam. After taking multiple scans from various sides or by rotating the object, the sampled points are combined into a single point cloud, from which the surface needs to be reconstructed.

Pre-processing of the data may be necessary, due to sampling errors, varying sampling density, and registration errors. Regions covered by multiple scans, for example, may result in noisy surfaces since tangential distances between nearest samples may be much smaller than the sampling error orthogonal to the surface. In this case, it is necessary to remove redundant points introduced by combining different points from multiple scans. In other regions, the density may be lower due to cavities and highly non-orthogonal scanning. If additional information, like a parametrization originating from each scan is available, interpolation can be used to fill these gaps.

In the present chapter, a powerful algorithm for multi-resolution surface extraction and -fairing, based on hybrid-meshes Guskov et al. (2002), from unorganized 3D point clouds is proposed (cf. Keller et al. (2005) and Keller et al. (2007)). The method uses an octree-based voxel hierarchy computed from the original points in an initial *hierarchical space partitioning* (HSP) process. At each octree level, the *hybrid mesh wrapping* (HMW) extracts the outer

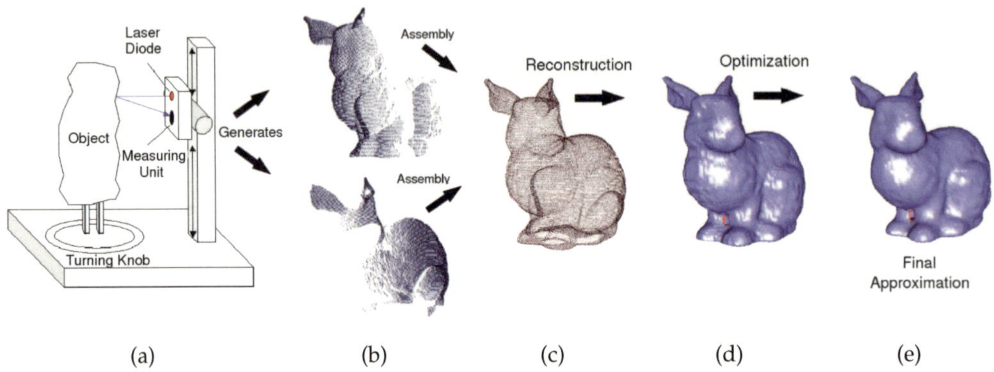

Fig. 1. Principle steps of reverse engineering: (a) point cloud acquisition by 3D object scanner, mostly laser range scan devices; (b) slices scanned from different views, (c) combined point cloud, (d) reconstructed mesh, (e) result after post-processing.

boundary of the voxel complex, taking into account the shape on the next coarser level. The resulting meshes both are linked into a structure with subdivision connectivity, where local topological modifications guarantee the resulting meshes are two-manifold. Subsequently, a *vertex mapping* (VM) procedure is proposed to project the mesh vertices onto locally fitted tangent planes. A final post-processing step aims on improving the quality of the generated mesh. This is achieved by applying a mesh relaxation step based on the constricted repositioning of mesh vertices tangential to the approximated surface.

The remainder of the chapter is structured as followed. In Section 2 a short overview about related reconstruction techniques is provided. Section 3 discusses the individual steps of our approach in detail. Section 4 presents some results and discusses the advantages and disadvantages of the proposed method in terms of performance, quality and robustness. In addition section 5 presents some experimental results in the context of surface reconstruction from environmental point clouds. The conclusion is part of section 6.

2. Related work

A possible approach to obtain surfaces from unorganized point clouds is to fit surfaces to the input points Goshtasby & O'Neill (1993), such as fitting polynomial Lei et al. (1996) or algebraic surfaces Pratt (1987). To be able to fit surfaces to a set of unorganized points it is necessary to have information about the topology of the point cloud inherent surfaces or to have some form of parametrization in advance. For example, Eck and Hoppe Eck & Hoppe (1996) generate a first parametrization using their approach presented in Hoppe et al. (1992) and fit a network of B-Spline patches to the initial surface. This allows to reconstruct surfaces of arbitrary topology. A competing spline-based method is provided by Guo Guo (1997). Another form of surface reconstruction algorithm applying high-level model recognition is presented in Ramamoorthi & Arvo (1999).

Alexa et al. Alexa et al. (2001) introduced an approach for reconstructing point set surfaces from point clouds based on Levin's MLS projection operator. Further approaches following the idea of locally fitting polynomial surface patches to confined point neighborhoods are proposed in Alexa et al. (2003) Nealen (2004.) Fleishman et al. (2005) Dey & Sun (2005). In

Mederos et al. (2003) the authors introduce a MLS reconstruction scheme which takes into account local curvature approximations to enhance the quality of the generated surfaces. One of the main problems associated with the MLS-based techniques is that, in general, they have to adapt to meet the underlying topological conditions. Depending on the type of input data this can be rather challenging. Another drawback is, that the MLS-technique in general is not capable of constructing surfaces having sharp features. One attempt for solving this problem was proposed by Fleishman et al. Fleishman et al. (2005).

Whenever accuracy matters, adaptive methods are sought, capable of providing multiple levels of resolution, subdivision surfaces, for example, can be used together with wavelets Stollnitz et al. (1996) to represent highly detailed objects of arbitrary topology. In addition, such level-of-detail representations are well suited for further applications, like view-dependent rendering, multi-resolution editing, compression, and progressive transmission. In addition to adaptive polyhedral representations, subdivision surfaces provide smooth or piecewise smooth limit surfaces similar to spline surfaces. In Hoppe et al. (1994) Hoppe et al. introduce a method for fitting subdivision surfaces to a set of unorganized 3D points. Another class of reconstruction algorithms are computational geometry approaches. These algorithms usually extract the surface from previously computed Delaunay- or dual complexes. The reconstruction is based on mathematical guarantees but relies on clean data e.g., noisy, and non-regularly sampled points perturb the reconstruction process and may cause the algorithms to fail.

An early work concerning a Delaunay-based surface reconstruction scheme was provided by Boissonnat (1984). Following this idea, methods like the crust algorithm introduced by Amenta, Bern & Kamvysselis (1998) have been developed exploiting the structure of the Voronoi diagrams of the input data. Other works Funke & Ramos (2002) Amenta et al. (2001) Mederos et al. (2005) aimed at improving the original crust algorithm regarding efficiency and accuracy. The cocone algorithm Amenta et al. (2000) evolved from the crust algorithm provides further enhancements. Based on this work Dey et. al. Dey & Goswami. (2003) introduced the tight cocone. Other Delaunay/Voronoi-based reconstruction algorithms are presented by Kolluri et al. (2004), Dey & Goswami (2004).

One challenge concerns the separation of proximal sheets of a surface Amenta, Bernd & Kolluri (1998). When considering local surface components, it may be helpful to construct a surface parametrization, i.e. a one-to-one mapping from a proper domain onto the surface. Having a surface of arbitrary topology split into a set of graph surfaces, for example by recursive clustering Heckel et al. (1997), one can reduce the reconstruction problem to scattered-data approximation in the plane Bertram et al. (2003). A very powerful meshless parametrization method for reverse engineering is described by Floater and Reimers Floater & Reimers (2001).

A completely different approach is the construction of α-shapes described by Edelsbrunner and Mücke Edelsbrunner & Mücke (1994). Depending on a single radius α, their method collects all simplices (e.g. points, lines, triangles, tetrahedra, etc.) fitting into an α-sphere. The method efficiently provides a data structure valid for all choices of α, such that a user may interactively adapt α to obtain a proper outer boundary of a point cloud. Out-of-core methods like ball-pivoting Bernardini et al. (1999) employ the same principle, rolling a ball of sufficiently large radius around the point cloud filling in all visited triangles. Other methods e.g., Azernikov et al. (2003) and Wang et al. (2005), exploit octree-based grid structures to guide surface reconstruction.

3. Reconstruction approach

3.1 Overview

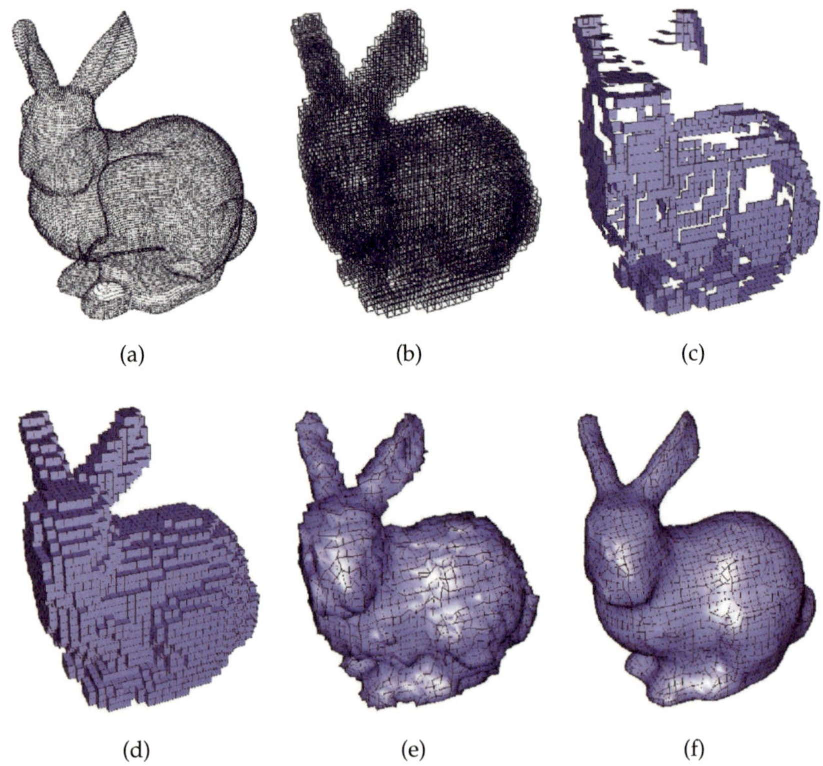

Fig. 2. (a)-(f) principle steps of the proposed multi-resolution surface reconstruction approach. (a) input point cloud of the Stanford bunny data set, consisting of 35,947 points, (b) voxel grid after 4 subdivision steps, (c) and (d) extracted voxel hull before and after application of the HMW operation, (e) surface mesh after vertex projection, (f) final surface after mesh relaxation.

This work aims at finding an efficient way to extract a connected quadrilateral two-manifold mesh out of a given 3D point cloud in a way that the underlying "unknown" surface is approximated as accurately as possible. The resulting adaptive reconstruction method is based upon the repetitive application of the following steps:

- Starting from an initial bounding voxel enclosing the original point cloud (see Figure 2(a)), the hierarchical space partitioning creates a voxel set by recursively subdividing each individual voxel into eight subvoxels. Empty subvoxel are not subject to subdivision and are deleted. Figure 2(b) presents an example of a generated voxel grid.
- The outer boundary of the generated voxel complex is extracted by the HMW operation. This exploits the voxel-subvoxel connectivity between the current and the next coarser

voxel grid. The resulting mesh is obtained by subdividing the coarser mesh (cf. Figure 2(c)) and adapting its topology at locations where voxels have been removed (see Figure 2(d)).

- The final vertex mapping locally constrains the mesh toward the point cloud (cf. Figure 2(e)). All vertices are projected onto local tangent planes defined by the points of the individual voxels. The resulting mesh is relaxed toward its final position by applying additional post-processing (see Figure 2(f)).

3.2 Hierarchical spatial partitioning

The HSP presumes an already existing voxel set V^j defining the voxel complex at level j. At the coarsest level this set V^0 consists of the bounding voxel enclosing the entire point cloud. To obtain V^{j+1} the following steps are performed:

1 Subdivide every voxel $v \in V^j$ into 8 subvoxels.

2 Assign the points of v to the corresponding subvoxel and delete empty subvoxels.

The task of managing and maintaining the originated non-empty set V^{j+1} is accomplished by the usage of an octree data structure. As required by the succeeding HM wrapping operation we need certain connectivity information facilitating the localization of proximate voxel neighborhoods. The algorithm applied uses an efficient octree-based navigation scheme related to the approach of Bhattacharya Bhattacharya (2001).

3.3 Hybrid mesh wrapping

The most difficult part of this work concerns the extraction of a two-manifold mesh from the generated voxel complex V^{j+1}. For the following let M^j denote the set of faces representing the existing mesh corresponding to the voxel complex V^j, where the term face abstracts the quadrilateral sidepart of a voxel. M^0 defines the face patches of V^0 forming the hull of the bounding voxel. Starting from the existing mesh M^j, we obtain the next finer mesh representation M^{j+1} by performing regular and irregular refinement operations. This includes the subdivision of M^j and the introduction of new faces at M^{j+1} inducing local changes in the mesh topology. These operations require M^j to meet the following conditions:

- Each face $f \in M^j$ is associated with exactly one voxel $v \in V^j$ (no two voxel can be associated with the same face). Thus the maximum number of faces associated with a voxel is restricted to six.
- The mesh represented by M^j is a two-manifold mesh.
- A face is linked to each of its proximate neighbor face. n is called a neighbor of (or adjacent to) the face f, if both share a common voxel edge. With limitation of one neighbor per edge the number of possible neighbor faces of f is four.

3.4 Regular mesh refinement

To accomplish the acquisition of the boundary hull associated with V^{j+1} the first step concerns the regular refinement of M^j. The refinement is achieved by subdividing each face $f \in M^j$ into four subfaces. To guarantee the resulting mesh fulfills the conditions outlined above, we assign the subfaces of f to voxel of V^{j+1}. For the following let $v \in V^j$ be the voxel

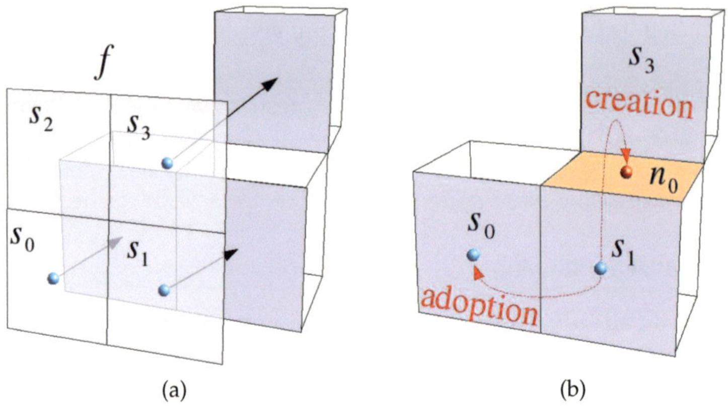

Fig. 3. (a) regular refinement: Principles of the subface projection operation; (b) irregular mesh refinement: Principles of face creation and adoption;

assigned to $f \in M^j$ and s be a subface of f. The assignment procedure projects s onto the corresponding subvoxel of v as illustrated in Figure 3(a). f is restricted only to be projected onto the immediate subvoxel of v. Since we only address the extraction of the outer hull of V^j, additional rules have to be defined preventing faces of M^j to capture parts of the interior hull of the voxel complex e.g., in cases the surface is not closed. Thus, the subface s can not be assigned to a subvoxel of v if this subvoxel already is associated with an face on the opposite. Subfaces that can not be assigned because no corresponding subvoxel exist they could be projected onto, are removed. The resulting refinement operator $\mathcal{R}$ defines the set $N^{j+1} := \mathcal{R}(M^j)$, with $N^0 = M^0$ representing the collection of the created and projected subfaces (cf. Figure 2(c)). So far N^{j+1}, consisting of unconnected faces, represents the base for the subsequent *irregular mesh refinement*, in which the final mesh connectivity is recovered.

3.5 Irregular mesh refinement

The *irregular mesh refinement* recovers the mesh connectivity i.g., it reconnects the faces of N^{j+1} and closes resulting breaks in the mesh structure induced by the regular mesh refinement. This procedure is based on the propagation of faces or the adoption of existing proximate neighbor faces (see Figure 3(b)). More precisely: Assume f to be a face of N^{j+1}, the irregular refinement detects existing neighbor faces in N^{j+1} sharing a common voxel edge or creates new faces in case no neighbor is found. Considering the configuration of the principle voxel neighborhoods there are three possible cases a neighbor face of f can be adapted/created. Figure 4 depicts these cases. For the following considerations let $n \in N^{j+1}$ specifying the "missing" neighbor face of f, $v \in V^{j+1}$ the voxel associated with f, and $w \in V^{j+1}$ the voxel associated with n. Exploiting the voxel neighborhood relations, the propagation/adoption of n is performed according the summarized rules below:

1. In case that v and w are identical the creation/adoption of n is admitted if f does not already share an edge with a face on the opposite of v (see Figure 4(a)).
2. The faces n and f share a common edge, the corresponding voxel w and v adjoin a common face (see Figure 4(b)). The creation/adoption of n is allowed if no other face is associated with w, vis-a-vis from n (additional *cavity rule*).

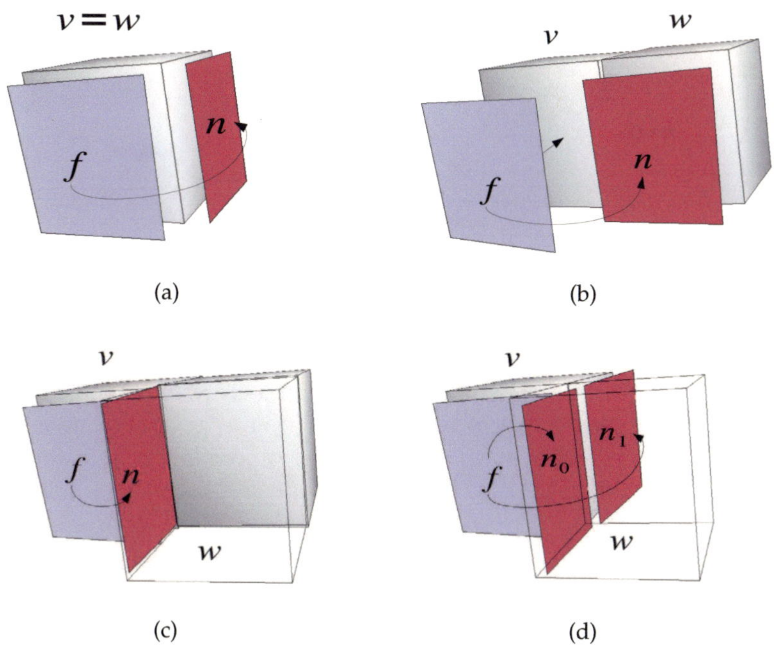

Fig. 4. Graphical interpretation of the face-propagation rules concerning the possible cases.

3. The voxel v and w adjoin a common edge. In this case we have to differentiate between two cases: a) an additional voxel adjoins v (see Figure 4(c)). In this case the creation/adoption of n is permitted. b) only v and w adjoin a common edge (see Figure 4(d)). This case requires to detect the underlying topological conditions. If the underlying surface passes v and w, we adopt/create n_0, otherwise, if the points within v and w represent a break of the underlying surface we adopt/create n_1. The right case is filtered out by comparing the principal orientation of the points within v and w.

The irregular refinement procedure is performed as followed: Given two initial sets $A^0 = N^{j+1}$ and $B^0 = \emptyset$, once a new neighbor face n is created/adopted, it is added to $A^{i+1} = A^i \cup \{n\}$. Simultaneously, every $n \in A^i$ which is fully connected to all of its existing neighbor faces is removed $A^{i+1} = A^i \setminus \{n\}$ and attached to $B^{j+1} = B^j \cup \{n\}$. This procedure is repeated until $A^i = \emptyset$ or $A^{j+1} = A^j$.

Applying the irregular mesh refinement operator $\mathcal{I}$ on N^{j+1} results in $M^{j+1} = \mathcal{I}(N^{j+1})$, where $M^{j+1} = A^i \cup B^j$ represents the final mesh at level $j+1$. Figure 3(b) illustrates the propagation procedure, where one neighbor is created and another adopted.

To force M^{j+1} to maintain the two-manifold condition each case at which the propagation of a face leads to a non-manifold mesh structure e.g., more than two faces share an edge, is identified and the mesh connectivity is resolved by applying vertex- and edge-splits. Figure 5(a) and Figure 5(b) illustrate the principles according to these the non-manifold mesh structures are resolved. In the depicted cases the connectivity of the vertices v and v_1, v_2 cause the mesh to be non-manifold. We avoid this by simply splitting the corresponding vertices and edges (see right part of Figure 5(a) and Figure 5(b)).

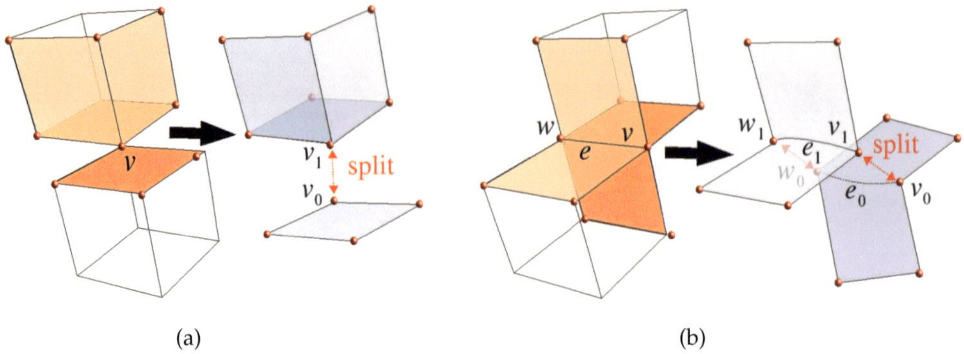

Fig. 5. (a) example in which a non-manifold mesh structure is resolved by a vertex-split, (b) resolving non-manifold mesh structure by first applying an edge-split followed by two vertex-splits.

3.6 Vertex-mapping

The next step concerns moving the mesh toward the "unknown" surface by projecting the mesh vertices onto the local tangent planes defined by the set of proximate sample points. This is accomplished for each vertex v of the mesh M by first identifying the voxel set W directly adjoining v and collecting the enclosed points P_v. Next, we fit a plane to the points P_v by computing the centroid $\vec{c}$ and the plane normal $\vec{n}$ obtained from the covariance matrix C of P_v. In order to improve the accuracy of the fitting the points of P_v can be filtered according their distance to v yielding $P_v' = \{p \in P_v |\, 2\|p - v\| < l\}$, with l representing the edge length of the voxel complex W. The normal $\vec{n}$ is defined by the eigenvector associated with the smallest eigenvalue of C. Together with the former position of the vertex $\vec{v}$ we are able to compute the new coordinates of $\vec{v}_n$ by

$$\vec{v_n} = \vec{v} - ((\vec{v} - \vec{c}) \cdot \vec{n})\vec{n}\,. \tag{1}$$

To be able to perform this projection the number of points of P_v has to be $|P_v| \geq 3$. Otherwise, points from adjacent voxels need to be added from surrounding voxels. By extending W to

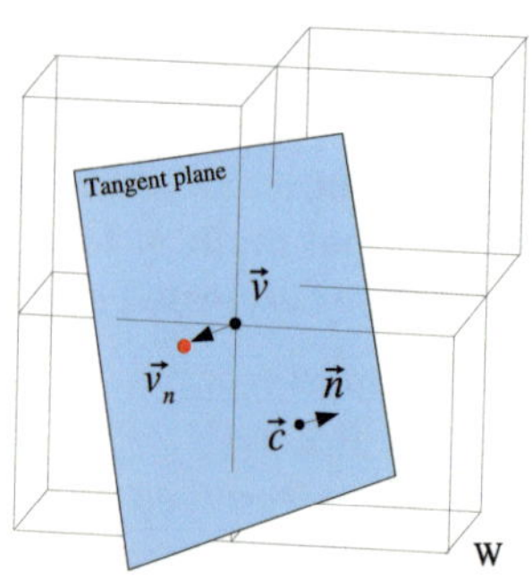

Fig. 6. Vertex projected onto the tangent plane defined by the points P_v of the adjacent voxel set W.

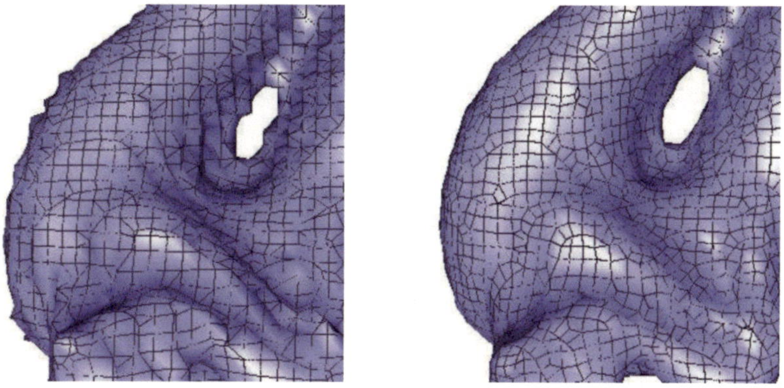

(a) (b)

Fig. 7. (a) part of the reconstructed surface mesh from the dragon data set before smoothing was applied, (b) corresponding mesh after few relaxation steps.

$W' = W \cup \{v \in V \setminus W | v$ is directly adjacent [1] to at least one $w \in W\}$ the number of points in P_v can be increased.

3.6.1 Post-processing

To improve the quality of the generated mesh we perform an additional mesh optimization step. Based on the principles of Laplacian smoothing, the vertices of the mesh are repositioned by first computing the centroid of the directly connected neighbor vertices. In a subsequent step these centroids are again projected onto the tangent planes of the corresponding point sets according to equation (1). Generally, mesh-optimization is a repetitive process, applied several times to obtain the most possible gain in surface quality, see Figure 7(a) and Figure 7(b).

4. Results

4.1 Performance

To find the overall time complexity we have to look at every step of the algorithm separately. We begin discussing the spatial decomposition analysis: In order to distribute the points contained by a voxel set V^{k-1} to their respective subvoxel we need to determine the subvoxel affiliation of every point. This leads to an computational complexity of $O(|P|)$ in every refinement step. Considering the HM wrapping we have to differentiate between the regular $\mathcal{R}$ and the irregular $\mathcal{I}$ operation but keep in mind that both are interdependent. Due to the fact that $\mathcal{R}$ basically depends linearly on the number of faces of $|M^{k-1}|$ and hence on $|V^{k-1}|$ we obtain a complexity of $O(|V^{k-1}|)$. Since it is difficult to estimate the number of attempts needed to find M^k we cannot reveal accurate statements concerning the computation time for $\mathcal{I}$. Based on empirical observations, an average time complexity of $O(k \cdot |V^k|)$ holds.

Assuming that $|V^k| \ll |P|$ with constant k (say $0 < k \leq 10$) the combined results of the particular sub-processes leads to an overall complexity of $O(|P|)$, concerning one single

[1] Two distinct voxels are directly adjacent if they share a common vertex, edge or face.

refinement step. The complexity to completely generate a mesh representing the unknown surface at refinement level k averages $O(k \cdot |P|)$.

The following time tables confirm the above discussed propositions. Table 1 shows the measured computation times for several data sets (*Stanford Scan Repository* (2009)) performed on an Intel Pentium 4 system with 1.6 GHz and 256 MB main memory. Table 2 presents more detailed results for the individual reconstruction steps for the Stanford dragon point data set.

Object	points	faces	ref. level	time[sec] reconstr.	time[sec] opt.
Rabbit	8171	25234	6	1.058	0.244
Dragon	437645	72955	7	5.345	0.714
Buddha	543652	56292	7	5.170	0.573

Table 1. Computation time table regarding several input models whereas the VM and the mesh-optimization (4 passes) are performed after the last reconstruction step.

Ref.-Level	Spatial-Partitioning [sec]	HM-Extraction $\mathcal{R}$ [sec]	HM-Extraction $\mathcal{I}$ [sec]	Vertex-Mapping [sec]	Opt. [sec]	Complete [sec]
1	0.240	< 0.001	< 0.001	0.019	< 0.001	0.262
2	0.330	< 0.001	< 0.001	0.068	< 0.001	0.401
3	0.388	< 0.001	0.002	0.241	0.002	0.634
4	0.401	< 0.001	0.014	0.676	0.008	1.100
5	0.278	0.002	0.056	0.787	0.050	1.173
6	0.362	0.008	0.170	0.928	0.180	1.648
7	0.662	0.039	0.717	1.683	0.725	3.826

Table 2. Time values for each reconstruction step of the Stanford dragon.

4.2 Robustness and quality

As shown by the examples our reconstruction method delivers meshes of good quality, as long as the resolution of the voxel complex does not exceed a point density induced threshold. Topological features, such as holes and cavities were always detected correctly after a proper number of refinements, see figure 8(a). The HM wrapping rules prevent the underlying object from caving by simultaneously covering the real surface completely. Table 3 shows the measured L_2-errors obtained by processing point clouds of different models for several refinement levels.

ref. level	1	2	3	4	5	6	7
L_2-error Bunny	25,86	9.47	3.60	1.13	0.41	0.14	-
L_2-error Buddha	-	51.92	18.80	7.61	3.47	1.58	0.66

Table 3. L_2-error values of the Bunny and Buddha reconstruction for each ref. level (measured in lengths of diagonal of the Bounding Box).

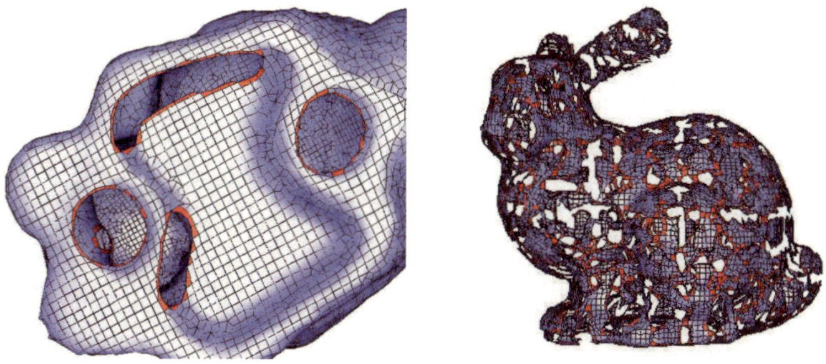

(a) (b)

Fig. 8. (a) correctly detected holes in the bunny model, (b) fragmentation of the mesh due to lacking density of point cloud.

In case the voxel refinement level exceeds a specific bound imposed by sampling density, the resulting mesh may be incomplete in some areas, due to empty voxels, see figure 8(b). If a very fine mesh is desired, one can fix the topology at a coarser level and apply subdivision and vertex mapping in consecutive steps.

5. Experimental reconstruction of environmental point data

The exploration of point data sets, like environmental LiDaR data, is a challenging problem of current interest. In contrast to the point clouds obtained from stationary scanning devices, data complexity is increased by e.g., noise, occlusion, alternating sample density and overlapping samples. Despite of the high scanning resolution, additional undersampling may occur at small and fractured artifacts like fences and leaves of trees. These are only some problems immanent to the reconstruction of surfaces from unorganized environmental point clouds.

We have applied our method to environmental point clouds in order to analyse the effects of the aforementioned influence factors on our proposed reconstruction approach. In this context we have performed some experiments on environmental input data generated by tripod mounted LiDaR scanners. Figure 10(a) shows a point cloud of a water tower located at the UC Davis, CA, USA. It consists of about 4.3 million points and features complex environmental structures like buildings and trees. Figure 10(b) shows the corresponding reconstruction after 10 steps. The generated mesh exhibiting about 300 thousand faces took 23 seconds on an Intel Core2 Duo system with 4GB RAM to finish. Another example is presented in figure 11. It shows the final surface representation (215 thousand faces) of a slope with parts of a building and some vegetation. The underlying point cloud has 3.8 million points. The reconstruction finished at level 9 after 24 second. The reconstructed mesh features holes and cracks at those areas at which the resolution lacks in density.

Environmental point clouds by nature are large (consisting of up to several million points) and feature high complexity. The experiments showed that our reconstruction approach is capable of producing reliable representations even in cases in which the point clouds are not optimally conditioned. However, the reconstruction lacks at some regions in which the point density does not exhibit the required/satisfied resolution. Despite of this fact the introduced method

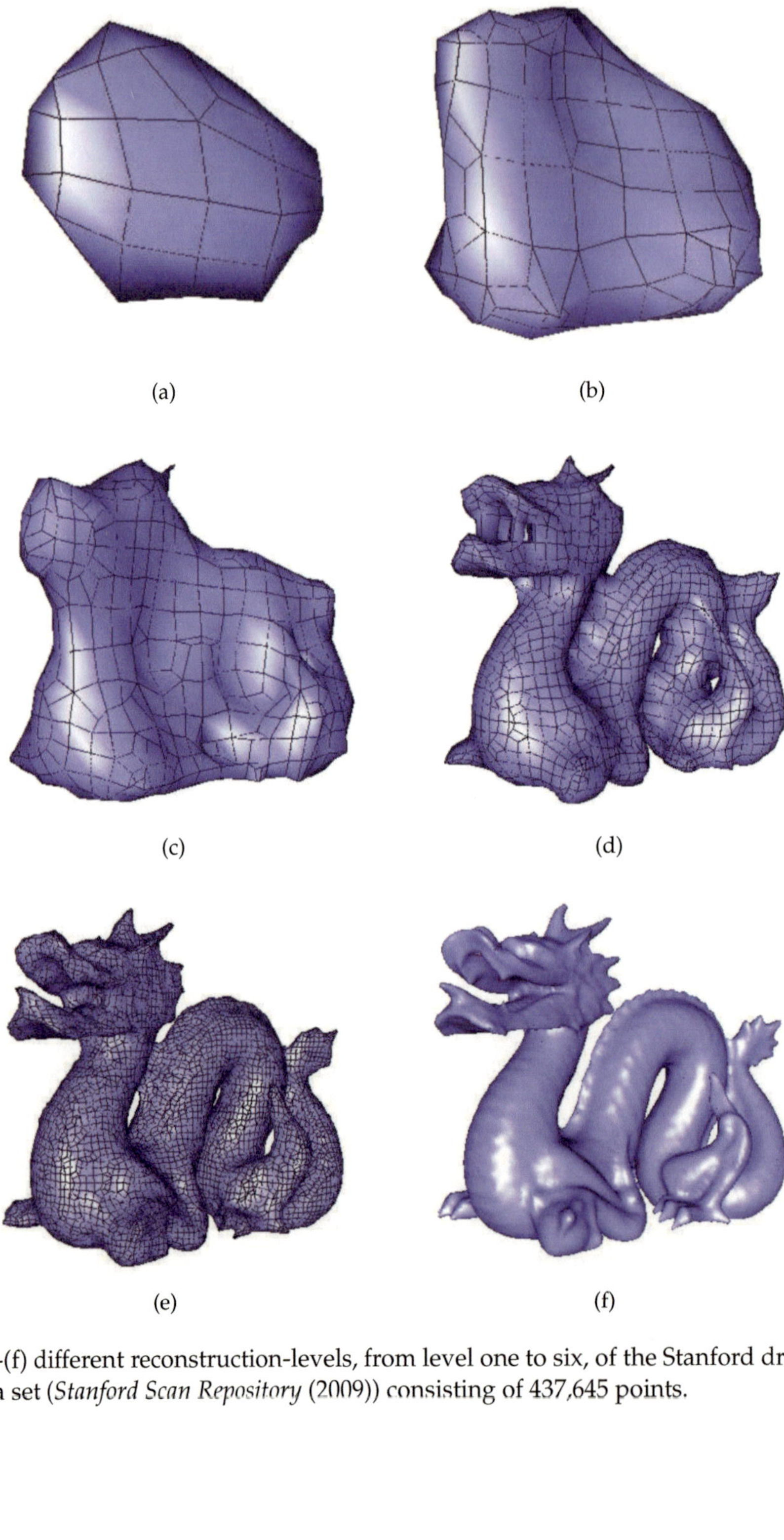

Fig. 9. (a)-(f) different reconstruction-levels, from level one to six, of the Stanford dragon point data set (*Stanford Scan Repository* (2009)) consisting of 437,645 points.

(a) (b)

Fig. 10. Water tower scan at the campus of UC Davis. (a) Raw point cloud having 4.3 mio. points, (b) reconstruction having 300k faces (10 subdivision steps) (total reconstruction time of about 23 seconds performed with an Intel Core2 Duo).

Fig. 11. Reconstruction of environmental point cloud (3.8 mio. points, 215k faces, 9 steps, 24 seconds).

is well suited for providing a fast preview of complex environmental scenes and serves as basis for providing initial reconstructions with respect to further mesh processing.

6. Conclusion

We provided a novel multi-resolution approach to surface reconstruction from point clouds. Our method automatically adapts to the underlying surface topology and provides a fully-connected hybrid-mesh representation. In the context of reverse engineering it is able to provide accurate reconstructions assumed that the input data shows a sufficient point density. However, in case the point distribution is not continuous the generated reconstruction may exhibit cracks and holes. One possible direction for future work would be the improvement of the stability of the approach regarding such unwanted effects. This could be achieved e.g., by adapting the reconstruction in order to become more sensitive to irregular point distributions.

7. Acknowledgements

This work was supported by the German Research Foundation (DFG) through the International Research Training Group (IRTG) 1131, and the Computer Graphics Research Group at the University of Kaiserslautern. It was also supported in parts by the W.M. Keck Foundation that provided support for the UC Davis Center for Active Visualization in the Earth Sciences (KeckCAVES). We also thank the members of the Computer Graphics Research Group at the Institute for Data Analysis and Visualization (IDAV) at UC Davis, the UC Davis Center for Active Visualization in the Earth Sciences (KeckCAVES) as well as the Department of Geology at UC Davis for their support and for providing us the data sets.

8. References

Alexa, M., Behr, J., Cohen-Or, D., Fleishman, S., Levin, D. & Silva, C. (2003). Computing and rendering point set surfaces, *IEEE Transactions on Visualization and Computer Graphics* 9(1): 3–âĂŞ15.

Alexa, M., Behr, J., Cohen-Or, D., Fleishman, S., Levin, D. & Silva, C. T. (2001). Point set surfaces, *Conference on Visualization*, IEEE Computer Society, pp. 21–28.

Amenta, N., Bern, M. & Kamvysselis, M. (1998). A new vornonoi-based surface reconstruction algorithm, *ACM Siggraph '98*, pp. 415–421.

Amenta, N., Bernd, M. & Kolluri, D. E. (1998). The crust and the beta-skeleton: combinatorial curve reconstruction, *Graphical Models and Image Processing, 60*, pp. 125–135.

Amenta, N., Choi, S., Dey, T. K. & Leekha, N. (2000). A simple algorithm for homeomorphic surface reconstruction, *SCG '00: Proceedings of the sixteenth annual symposium on Computational geometry*, pp. 213–222.

Amenta, N., Choi, S. & Kolluri, R. K. (2001). The power crust, *6th ACM symposium on Solid Modeling and Applications*, ACM Press, pp. 249–266.

Azernikov, S., Miropolsky, A. & Fischer, A. (2003). Surface reconstruction of freeform objects based on multiresolution volumetric method, *ACM Solid Modeling and Applications*, pp. 115–126.

Bernardini, F., Mittleman, J., Rushmeier, H., Silva, C. & Taubin, G. (1999). The ball-pivoting algorith for surface reconstruction, *IEEE Transactions on Visualization and Computer Graphics (TVCG)* 5(4): 349–359.

Bertram, M., Tricoche, X. & Hagen, H. (2003). Adaptive smooth scattered-data approximation for large-scale terrain visualization, *Joint EUROGRAPHICS - IEEE TCVG Symposium on Visualization*, pp. 177–184.

Bhattacharya, P. (2001). Efficient neighbor finding algorithms in quadtree and octree.

Boissonnat, J.-D. (1984). Geometric structures for three-dimensional shape representation, *ACM Trans. Graph.* 3(4): 266–286.

Dey, T. K. & Goswami., S. (2003). Tight cocone: A water tight surface reconstructor, *Proc. 8th ACM Sympos. Solid Modeling Appl.*, pp. 127–134.

Dey, T. K. & Goswami, S. (2004). Provable surface reconstruction from noisy samples, *20th Annual Symposium on Computational Geometry*, ACM Press, pp. 330–339.

Dey, T. K. & Sun, J. (2005). An adaptive mls surface for reconstruction with guarantees, *3rd Eurographics Symposium on Geometry Processing*, pp. 43–52.

Eck, M. & Hoppe, H. (1996). Automatic reconstruction of b-spline surfaces of arbitrary topological type, *ACM Siggraph*, pp. 325–334.

Edelsbrunner, H. & Mücke, E. P. (1994). Three-dimensional alpha shapes, *ACM Transactions on Graphics* 13(1): 43–72.

Fleishman, S., Cohen-Or, D. & Silva, C. (2005). Robust moving least-squares fitting with sharp features, *ACM Siggraph*, pp. 544–552.

Floater, M. & Reimers, M. (2001). Meshless parameterization and surface reconstruction, 18(2): 77–92.

Funke, S. & Ramos, E. A. (2002). Smooth-surface reconstruction in near-linear time, *SODA '02: Proceedings of the thirteenth annual ACM-SIAM symposium on Discrete algorithms*, pp. 781–790.

Goshtasby, A. & O'Neill, W. D. (1993). Surface fitting to scattered data by a sum of gaussians, *Comput. Aided Geom. Des.* 10(2): 143–156.

Guo, B. (1997). Surface reconstruction: from points to splines, 29(4): 269–277.

Guskov, I., Khodakovsky, A., Schroeder, P. & Sweldens, W. (2002). Hybrid meshes: Multiresolution using regular and irregular refinement, *ACM Symposium on Geometric Modeling (SoCG)*, pp. 264–272.

Heckel, B., Uva, A. & Hamann, B. (1997). Cluster-based generation of hierarchical surface models, *Scientific Visualization, Dagstuhl*, pp. 113–222.

Hoppe, H., DeRose, T., Duchamp, T., Halstead, M., Jin, H., McDonald, J., Schweitzer, J. & Stuetzle, W. (1994). Piecewise smooth surface reconstruction, *ACM SIGGRAPH 1994 Conference Proceedings*, pp. 295–302.

Hoppe, H., DeRose, T., Duchamp, T., McDonald, J. & Stuetzle, W. (1992). Surface reconstruction from unorganized points, *ACM SIGGRAPH '92 Conference Proceedings*, pp. 71–78.

Keller, P., Bertram, M. & Hagen, H. (2005). Multiresolution surface reconstruction from scattered data based on hybrid meshes, *IASTED VIIP*, pp. 616–621.

Keller, P., Bertram, M. & Hagen, H. (2007). Reverse engineering with subdivision surfaces, *Computing 2007*, pp. 127–134.

Kolluri, R., Shewchuk, J. R. & O'Brien, J. F. (2004). Spectral surface reconstruction from noisy point clouds, *SGP '04: Proceedings of the 2004 Eurographics/ACM SIGGRAPH symposium on Geometry processing*, pp. 11–21.

Lei, Z., Blane, M. M. & Cooper, D. B. (1996). 3l fitting of higher degree implicit polynomials, 2(4): 148–153.

Mederos, B., Velho, L. & de Figueiredo, L. H. (2003). Moving least squares multiresolution surface approximation, *Sibgraphi*.

Mederos, L. V. B., Amenta, N., Velho, L. & de Figueiredo, L. (2005). Surface reconstruction from noisy point clouds, *Eurographics Symposium on Geometry Processing*.

Nealen, A. (2004.). An as-short-as-possible introduction to the least squares, weighted least squares and moving least squares methods for scattered data approximation and interpolation, *Technical Report, TU Darmstadt*.

Pratt, V. (1987). Direct least-squares fitting of algebraic surfaces, *SIGGRAPH Comput. Graph.* 21(4): 145–152.

Ramamoorthi, R. & Arvo, J. (1999). Creating generative models from range images, *SIGGRAPH '99: Proceedings of the 26th annual conference on Computer graphics and interactive techniques*, pp. 195–204.

Stanford Scan Repository (2009).
URL: *http://graphics.stanford.edu/data/3Dscanrep/*

Stollnitz, E., DeRose, T. & Salesin, D. (1996). *Wavelets for Computer Graphics–Theory and Applications*, Morgan Kaufmann.

Wang, J., Oliveira, M. & Kaufman, A. (2005). Reconstructing manifold and non-manifold surfaces from point clouds, *IEEE Visualization*, pp. 415–422.

7

A Systematic Approach for Geometrical and Dimensional Tolerancing in Reverse Engineering

George J. Kaisarlis
Rapid Prototyping & Tooling – Reverse Engineering Laboratory
Mechanical Design & Control Systems Section,
School of Mechanical Engineering,
National Technical University of Athens (NTUA)
Greece

1. Introduction

In the fields of mechanical engineering and industrial manufacturing the term Reverse Engineering (RE) refers to the process of creating engineering design data from existing parts and/or assemblies. While conventional engineering transforms engineering concepts and models into real parts, in the *reverse engineering* approach real parts are transformed into engineering models and concepts (Várady et al., 1997). However, apart from its application in mechanical components, RE is a very common practice in a broad range of diverse fields such as software engineering, animation/entertainment industry, microchips, chemicals, electronics, and pharmaceutical products. Despite this diversity, the reasons for using RE appear to be common in all these application fields, e.g. the original design data and documentation of a product are either not updated, not accessible, do not exist or even have never existed. Focusing on the mechanical engineering domain, through the application of RE techniques an existing part is recreated by acquiring its' surface and/ or geometrical features' data using contact or non contact scanning or measuring devices (Wego, 2011). The creation of an RE component computer model takes advantage of the extensive use of CAD/CAM/CAE systems and apparently provides enormous gains in improving the quality and efficiency of RE design, manufacture and analysis. Therefore, RE is now considered one of the technologies that provide substantial business benefits in shortening the product development cycle (Raja & Fernandes, 2008).

Tolerance assignment is fundamental for successful mechanical assembly, conformance with functional requirements and component interchangeability, since manufacturing with perfect geometry is virtually unrealistic. In engineering drawings Geometric Dimensioning and Tolerancing (GD&T) correlates size, form, orientation and location of the geometric elements of the design model with the design intent, therefore it has a profound impact on the manufacturability, ease of assembly, performance and ultimate cost of the component. High geometrical and dimensional accuracy leads to high quality; however, tight tolerances lead to an exponential increase of the manufacturing cost. Though the importance of tolerance design is well understood in the engineering community it still remains an engineering task that largely depends on experimental data, industrial databases and guidelines, past experience and individual expertise, (Kaisarlis et al., 2008). Geometrical and dimensional tolerances are of particular importance, on the other hand, not only in industrial production but also in product development, equipment upgrading and maintenance. The last three activities include, inevitably, RE tasks which go along with the reconstruction of an object CAD model from measured data and have to do with the assignment of dimensional and geometrical manufacturing tolerances to this object. In that context, tolerancing of RE components address a wide range of industrial applications and real-world manufacturing problems such as tolerance allocation in terms of the actual functionality of a prototype assembly, mapping of component experimental design modifications, spare part tolerancing for machines that are out of production or need improvements and no drawings are available, damage repair, engineering maintenance etc.

The objective of remanufacturing a needed mechanical component which has to fit and well perform in an existing assembly and, moreover, has to observe the originally assigned functional characteristics of the product is rather delicate. The objective in such applications is the designation of geometric and dimensional tolerances that match, as closely as possible, to the original *(yet unknown)* dimensional and geometrical accuracy specifications that reveal the original design intend. RE tolerancing becomes even more sophisticated in case that Coordinate Measuring Machines' (CMM) data of a few or just only one of the original components to be reversibly engineered are within reach. Moreover, if operational use has led to considerable wear/ damage or one of the mating parts is missing, then the complexity of the problem increases considerably. The RE tolerancing problem has not been sufficiently and systematically addressed to this date. Currently, in such industrial problems where typically relevant engineering information does not exist, the conventional trial and error approach for the allocation of RE tolerances is applied. This approach apparently requires much effort and time and offers no guarantee for the generation of the best of results.

This research work provides a novel, modern and integrated methodology for tolerancing in RE. The problem is addressed in a systematic, time and cost efficient way, compatible with the current industrial practice. The rest of the chapter is organized as follows: after the review of relevant technical literature in Section 2, the theoretical analysis of RE dimensional and geometrical tolerancing is presented *(Sections 3 and 4 respectively)*. The application of Tolerance Elements (TE) method for cost-effective, competent tolerance designation in RE is then introduced in Section 5. Certain application examples that illustrate the effectiveness of the methodology are further presented and discussed in Section 6. Main conclusions and future work orientation are included in the final Section 7 of the chapter.

2. Literature review

The purpose and the main application areas of RE along with current methodologies and practical solutions for reverse engineering problems in industrial manufacturing are identified and discussed in several reference publications, e.g (Ingle, 1994; Raja & Fernandes, 2008; Wego, 2011). Moreover, the application of RE techniques and their implementation on modern industrial engineering practice is the subject of a numerous research works, e.g. (Abella et al., 1994; Bagci, 2009; Dan & Lancheng, 2006; Endo, 2005; Zhang, 2003). In that context, RE methodologies are applied for the reconstruction of mechanical components and assemblies that have been inevitably modified during several stages of their life cycle, e.g. surface modifications of automotive components during prototype functionality testing (Chant et al., 1998; Yau, 1997), mapping of sheet metal forming deviations on free form surface parts (Yuan et al., 2001), monitoring on the geometrical stability during test runs of mock-up turbine blades used in nuclear power generators (Chen & Lin, 2000), repair time compression by efficient RE modeling of the broken area and subsequent rapid spare part manufacturing (Zheng et al., 2004), recording of die distortions due to thermal effects for the design optimization of fan blades used in aero engines (Mavromihales et al., 2003).

The principles and applications of tolerancing in modern industrial engineering can also be found in several reference publications, e.g. (Drake, 1999; Fischer, 2004). An extensive and systematic review of the conducted research and the state of the art in the field of dimensioning and tolerancing techniques is provided by several recent review papers, e.g. (Singh et al. 2009a, 2009b) and need not be reiterated here. In the large number of research articles on various tolerancing issues in design for manufacturing that have been published over the last years, the designation of geometrical tolerances has been adequately studied under various aspects including tolerance analysis and synthesis, composite positional tolerancing, geometric tolerance propagation, datum establishment, virtual manufacturing, inspection and verification methods for GD&T specifications, e.g. (Anselmetti and Louati, 2005; Diplaris & Sfantsikopoulos, 2006; Martin et al., 2011).

Although RE-tolerancing is a very important and frequently met industrial problem, the need for the development of a systematic approach to extract appropriate design specifications that concern the geometric accuracy of a reconstructed component has been only recently pointed out, (Borja et al., 2001; Thompson et al., 1999; VREPI, 2003). In one of the earliest research works that systematically addresses the RE-tolerancing problem (Kaisarlis et al., 2000), presents the preliminary concept of a knowledge-based system that aims to the allocation of standard tolerances as per ISO-286. The issue of datum identification in RE geometric tolerancing is approached in a systematic way by (Kaisarlis et al, 2004) in a later publication. Recently, (Kaisarlis et al, 2007, 2008) have further extend the research on this area by focusing on the RE assignment of position tolerances in the case of fixed and floating fasteners respectively. The methodology that is presented in this Chapter further develops the approach that is proposed on these last two publications. The novel contribution reported here deals with *(i)* the systematic assignment of *both* geometrical and dimensional tolerances in RE and their possible interrelation through the application of material modifiers on *both* the RE features and datums and *(ii)* the consideration of cost-effective, competent tolerance designation in RE in a systematic way.

3. Dimensional tolerancing in reverse engineering

Reconstructed components must obviously mate with the other components of the mechanical assembly that they belong to, in *(at least)* the same way as their originals, in order the original assembly clearances to be observed, i.e. they must have appropriate manufacturing tolerances. As pointed out in Section 1, this is quite different and much more difficult to be achieved in RE than when designing from scratch where, through normal tolerance analysis/synthesis techniques and given clearances, critical tolerances are assigned, right from the beginning, to all the assembly components. Integration of geometric accuracy constrains aimed at the reconstruction of 3D models of RE-conventional engineering objects from range data has been studied adequately, (Raja & Fernandes, 2008; Várady et al., 1997). These studies deal, however, with the mathematical accuracy of the reconstructed CAD model by fitting curves and surfaces to 3D measured data. Feature-based RE (Thompson et al., 1999; VREPI, 2003) does not address, on the other hand, until now issues related with the manufacturing tolerances which have to be assigned on the CAD drawings in order the particular object to be possible to be made as required. A methodology for the problem treatment is proposed in the following sections.

Engineering objects are here classified according to their shape either as *free-form objects* or as *conventional engineering objects* that typically have simple geometric surfaces *(planes, cylinders, cones, spheres and tori)* which meet in sharp edges or smooth blends. In the following, Feature–Based RE for mechanical assembly components of the latter category is mainly considered. Among features of size (ASME, 2009), *cylindrical features* such as holes in conjunction with pegs, pins or (screw) shafts are the most frequently used for critical functions as are the alignment of mating surfaces or the fastening of mating components in a mechanical assembly. As a result, their role is fundamental in mechanical engineering and, consequently, they should be assigned with appropriate dimensional and geometrical tolerances. In addition, the stochastic nature of the manufacturing deviations makes crucial, for the final RE outcome, the quantity of the available (same) components that serve as reference for the measurements. The more of them are available the more reliable will be the results. For the majority of the RE cases, however, their number is extremely limited and usually ranges from less than ten to only one available item. Mating parts can also be inaccessible for measurements and there is usually an apparent lack of adequate original design and/or manufacturing information. In the scope of this research work, the developed algorithms address the full range of possible scenarios, from "only one original component - no mating component available" to "two or more original pairs of components available", focusing on parts for which either an ISO 286-1 clearance fit (of either hole or shaft basis system) or ISO 2768 (general tolerances) were originally designated.

Assignment of RE dimensional tolerances is accomplished by the present method in five sequential steps. In the primary step (a) the analysis is appropriately directed to ISO fits or general tolerances. In the following steps, the candidate *(Step b)*, suggested *(Step c)* and preferred *(Step d)* sets of RE-tolerances are produced. For the final RE tolerance selection *(Step e)* the cost-effective tolerancing approach, introduced in Section 5, is taken into consideration. For the economy of the chapter, the analysis is only presented for the "*two or more original pairs of components available*" case, focused on ISO 286 fits, as it is considered the most representative.

3.1 Direction of the analysis on ISO fits and/or general tolerances

Let $\boldsymbol{Rd}_{M\_h}$, $\boldsymbol{RF}_h$, $\boldsymbol{RRa}_h$, $\boldsymbol{U}_h$ and $\boldsymbol{Rd}_{M\_s}$, $\boldsymbol{RF}_s$, $\boldsymbol{RRa}_s$, $\boldsymbol{U}_s$ be the sets of the measured diameters, form deviations, surface roughness, and the uncertainty of CMM measurements for the RE-*hole* and the RE-*shaft* features respectively. The Δ_{max}, Δ_{h_max}, Δ_{s_max} limits are calculated by,

$$\Delta_{\max}= \max\{(\max\boldsymbol{Rd}_{M\_h} - \min\boldsymbol{Rd}_{M\_h}), (\max\boldsymbol{Rd}_{M\_s} - \min\boldsymbol{Rd}_{M\_s}), \max\boldsymbol{RF}_h, \max\boldsymbol{RF}_s, (60\cdot\text{mean}\boldsymbol{RRa}_h), (60\cdot\text{mean}\boldsymbol{RRa}_s), \boldsymbol{U}_h, \boldsymbol{U}_s\},$$

$$\Delta_{h\_max} = \max\{(\max\boldsymbol{Rd}_{M\_h} - \min\boldsymbol{Rd}_{M\_h}),\ \max\boldsymbol{RF}_h,\ (60\cdot\text{mean}\boldsymbol{RRa}_h),\ \boldsymbol{U}_h\},$$

$$\Delta_{s\_max} = \max\{(\max\boldsymbol{Rd}_{M\_s} - \min\boldsymbol{Rd}_{M\_s}),\ \max\boldsymbol{RF}_s,\ (60\cdot\text{mean}\boldsymbol{RRa}_s),\ \boldsymbol{U}_s\}$$

In this step, the analysis is directed on the assignment of either ISO 286-1 clearance fits or ISO 2768 general tolerances through the validation of the condition,

$$\Delta_{h\_max} + \Delta_{s\_max} + |a| \geq \max\boldsymbol{Rd}_{M\_h} - \min\boldsymbol{Rd}_{M\_s} \tag{1}$$

where $|a|$ is the absolute value of the maximum ISO 286 clearance Fundamental Deviation (FD) for the relevant nominal sizes range *(the latter is approximated by the mean value of* $\boldsymbol{Rd}_{M\_h}$, $\boldsymbol{Rd}_{M\_s}$ *sets)*. If the above condition is *not* satisfied the analysis is exclusively directed on ISO 2768 general tolerances. Otherwise, the following two cases are distinguished, *(i)* $\Delta_{max} \leq$ IT 11 and *(ii)* IT 11< $\Delta_{max} \leq$ IT 18. In the first case the analysis aims only on ISO 286 fits, whereas in the second case, *both* ISO 286 and ISO 2768 RE tolerances are pursued.

3.2 Sets of candidate IT grades, fundamental deviations and nominal sizes

The starting point for the *Step (b)* of the analysis is the production of the Candidate tolerance grades sets, $\boldsymbol{IT}_{CAN\_h}$, $\boldsymbol{IT}_{CAN\_s}$, for the hole and shaft features respectively. It is achieved by filtering the *initial Candidate IT grades* set, $\boldsymbol{IT}_{CAN\_INIT}$, which includes all standardized IT grades from IT01 to IT18, by the following conditions *(applied for <u>both</u> the h and s indexes)*,

$$\begin{array}{ll} IT_{CAN} \geq \max\boldsymbol{RF}, & IT_{CAN} \geq \max\boldsymbol{Rd}_M - \min\boldsymbol{Rd}_M \\ IT_{CAN} \leq 60\cdot\text{mean}\boldsymbol{RRa}, & IT_{CAN} \geq \boldsymbol{U} \end{array} \tag{2}$$

Moreover, in case when estimated maximum and minimum functional clearance limits are available (maxCL, minCL), candidate IT grades are qualified by the validation of,

$$\begin{array}{c} IT_{CAN} < \text{maxCL} \\ IT_{CAN} < \text{maxCL} - \text{minCL} \end{array} \tag{3}$$

The above constraints are applied separately for the hole and shaft and qualify the members of the $\boldsymbol{IT}_{CAN\_h}$, $\boldsymbol{IT}_{CAN\_s}$ sets. Likewise, the set of *initial* Candidate Fundamental Deviations, $\boldsymbol{FD}_{CAN\_INIT}$, that contains all the FDs applicable to clearance fits i.e. $\boldsymbol{FD}_{CAN\_INIT}$ = {a, b, c, cd, d, e, f, fg, g, h}, is filtered by the constraints,

$$FD_{CAN} \leq \min\boldsymbol{Rd}_{M\_h} - \max\boldsymbol{Rd}_{M\_s} \tag{4}$$

$$\begin{array}{c} FD_{CAN} \geq \text{minCL} \\ FD_{CAN} < \text{maxCL} - (\min\boldsymbol{IT}_{CAN\_h} + \min\boldsymbol{IT}_{CAN\_s}) \end{array} \tag{5}$$

The latter constraints, (5), apparently only apply in case of maxCL and/or minCL availability. All qualified FDs are included in the common set of Candidate Fundamental Deviations, $\boldsymbol{FD}_{CAN}$. In the final stage of this step, the Candidate Nominal Sizes Sets, $\boldsymbol{NS}_{CAN\_h}$, $\boldsymbol{NS}_{CAN\_s}$, are initially formulated for the *hole* and *shaft* respectively. Their first members are obtained from the integral part of the following equations,

$$\begin{array}{l} NS_{CAN\_h\_1} = \text{int}\,[\min\boldsymbol{Rd}_{M\_h} - \max FD_{CAN} - \max IT_{CAN\_h}] \\ NS_{CAN\_s\_1} = \text{int}\,[\max\boldsymbol{Rd}_{M\_s} + \max FD_{CAN} + \max IT_{CAN\_s}] \end{array} \tag{6}$$

Following members of the sets are then calculated by an incremental increase, δ, of $NS_{CAN\_h\_1}$ and $NS_{CAN\_s\_1}$,

$$\begin{aligned} NS_{CAN\_h\_2} &= NS_{CAN\_h\_1} + \delta \\ NS_{CAN\_h\_3} &= NS_{CAN\_h\_2} + \delta \\ &\ldots\ldots \\ NS_{CAN\_h\_v} &= NS_{CAN\_h\_v-1} + \delta \end{aligned} \qquad \begin{aligned} NS_{CAN\_s\_2} &= NS_{CAN\_s\_1} - \delta \\ NS_{CAN\_s\_3} &= NS_{CAN\_s\_2} - \delta \\ &\ldots\ldots \\ NS_{CAN\_s\_\mu} &= NS_{CAN\_s\_\mu-1} - \delta \end{aligned} \tag{7}$$

bounded by,

$$\begin{aligned} NS_{CAN\_h\_v} &\leq \min \boldsymbol{Rd}_{M\_h} \\ NS_{CAN\_s\_\mu} &\geq \max \boldsymbol{Rd}_{M\_s} \end{aligned} \tag{8}$$

with the populations v, μ not necessarily equal. In the relevant application example of section 6, δ is taken $\delta = 0.05mm$. Other δ-values can be, obviously, used depending on the case. Since both hole and shaft have a common nominal size in ISO-286 fits, the Candidate Nominal Sizes Set, $\boldsymbol{NS}_{CAN}$, is then produced by the common members of $\boldsymbol{NS}_{CAN\_h}$, $\boldsymbol{NS}_{CAN\_s}$,

$$\boldsymbol{NS}_{CAN} = \boldsymbol{NS}_{CAN\_h} \cap \boldsymbol{NS}_{CAN\_s} \tag{9}$$

3.3 Sets of suggested fits

In Step (c) of the analysis, a combined qualification for the members of the $\boldsymbol{IT}_{CAN\_h}$, $\boldsymbol{IT}_{CAN\_s}$, $\boldsymbol{FD}_{CAN}$ and $\boldsymbol{NS}_{CAN}$ sets is performed in order to produce the two sets of *suggested* Basic Hole, $\boldsymbol{BH}_{SG}$, and Basic Shaft $\boldsymbol{BS}_{SG}$ fits. The members of $\boldsymbol{IT}_{CAN\_h}$ and $\boldsymbol{IT}_{CAN\_s}$ sets are sorted in ascending order. For the production of the $\boldsymbol{BH}_{SG}$ set, every candidate nominal size of the $\boldsymbol{NS}_{CAN}$ set is initially validated against all members of the $\boldsymbol{IT}_{CAN\_h}$ set, Figure 1(a),

$$NS_{CAN\_n} + IT_{CAN\_h\_\kappa} \geq \max \boldsymbol{Rd}_{M\_h} \quad \forall \; NS_{CAN\_n} \in \boldsymbol{NS}_{CAN} \tag{10}$$

$\kappa = 1, 2, \ldots, i \quad 1 \leq i \leq 20$

In case no member of the $\boldsymbol{IT}_{CAN\_h}$ set satisfies the condition (10) for a particular NS_{CAN_n}, the latter is excluded from the $\boldsymbol{BH}_{SG}$ set. In order to qualify for the $\boldsymbol{BH}_{SG}$ set, candidate nominal sizes that validate the condition (10) are further confirmed against all members of the $\boldsymbol{FD}_{CAN}$ set, the candidate IT grades of the $\boldsymbol{IT}_{CAN\_s}$ set and, as well as, the measured RE-shaft data, through the constraints, Figure 1(b),

$$NS_{CAN\_n} - FD_{CAN\_q} \geq \max \boldsymbol{Rd}_{M\_s} \quad \forall \; FD_{CAN\_q} \in \boldsymbol{FD}_{CAN} \tag{11}$$

$\zeta = 1, 2, \ldots, j \qquad 1 \leq j \leq 20$

$$\min \boldsymbol{Rd}_{M\_s} \geq NS_{CAN\_n} - FD_{CAN\_q} - IT_{CAN\_s\_\zeta} \quad \forall \; FD_{CAN\_q} \in \boldsymbol{FD}_{CAN} \tag{12}$$

In case no member of the $\boldsymbol{FD}_{CAN}$ set satisfies the condition (11) for a particular NS_{CAN_n}, the latter is excluded from the $\boldsymbol{BH}_{SG}$ set. Moreover, in case no member of the $\boldsymbol{IT}_{CAN\_s}$ set satisfies the condition (12) for a particular pair of FD_{CAN_q} and NS_{CAN_n}, validated by (11), they are both excluded from the $\boldsymbol{BH}_{SG}$ set. In a similar manner, the production of the suggested Basic Shaft fits set is achieved by the following set of conditions,

$$\min \boldsymbol{Rd}_{M\_s} \geq NS_{CAN\_n} - IT_{CAN\_s\_\zeta} \quad \forall \; NS_{CAN\_n} \in \boldsymbol{NS}_{CAN} \tag{13}$$

$\zeta=1, 2, \ldots, j \quad 1 \leq j \leq 20$

$$\min \boldsymbol{Rd}_{M\_h} \geq NS_{CAN\_n} + FD_{CAN\_q} \ \forall \ FD_{CAN\_q} \in \boldsymbol{FD}_{CAN} \tag{14}$$

$$NS_{CAN\_n} + FD_{CAN\_q} + IT_{CAN\_h\_\kappa} \geq \max \boldsymbol{Rd}_{M\_h} \ \forall \ FD_{CAN\_q} \in \boldsymbol{FD}_{CAN} \tag{15}$$

$\kappa=1, 2, \ldots, i \quad 1 \leq i \leq 20$

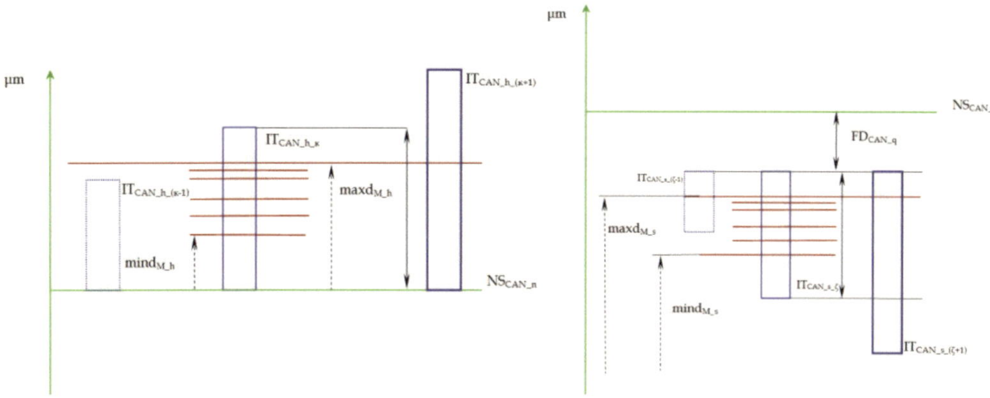

(a) (b)

Fig. 1. Suggested Basic Hole fits qualification

3.4 Sets of preferred fits

A limited number of *Preferred Fits* out of the *Suggested* ones is proposed in Step (d) through the consideration of ISO proposed fits. Moreover, the implementation of manufacturing guidelines, such as the fact that it is useful to allocate a slightly larger tolerance to the hole than the shaft, preference of Basic Hole fits over Basic Shaft ones, preference of nominal sizes that are expressed in integers or with minimum possible decimal places etc, are additionally used to "filter" the final range of the preferred fits. The final selection, Step (e), out of the limited set of preferred fits and the method end result is reached by the consideration of the machine shop capabilities and expertise in conjunction with the application of the cost - effective RE tolerancing approach, presented in Section 5 of the chapter.

4. Geometrical tolerancing in reverse engineering

In order to observe interchangeability, *geometrical* as well as dimensional accuracy specifications of an RE component must comply with those of the mating part(-s). GD&T in RE must ensure that a reconstructed component will fit and perform well without affecting the function of the specific assembly. The methodology that is presented in this section focuses on the RE assignment of the main type of geometrical tolerance that is used in industry, due to its versatility and economic advantages, the True Position tolerance. However, the approach can be easily adapted for RE assignment of other location geometrical tolerances types, such as coaxiality or symmetry and, as well as, for run-out or profile tolerances.

Position tolerancing is standardized in current GD&T international and national standards, such as (ISO, 1998; ISO 1101, 2004; ASME, 2009). Although the ISO and the ASME tolerancing systems are not fully compatible, they both define position geometrical tolerance as the total permissible variation in the location of a feature about its exact true position. For cylindrical features such as holes or bosses the position tolerance zone is usually the diameter of the cylinder within which the axis of the feature must lie, the center of the tolerance zone being at the exact true position, Figure 2, whereas for size features such as slots or tabs, it is the total width of the tolerance zone within which the center plane of the feature must lie, the center plane of the zone being at the exact true position. The position tolerance of a feature is denoted with the size of the diameter of the cylindrical tolerance zone (or the distance between the parallel planes of the tolerance zone) in conjunction with the theoretically exact dimensions that determine the true position and their relevant datums, Figure 2. Datums are, consequently, fundamental building blocks of a positional tolerance frame in positional tolerancing. Datum features are chosen to position the toleranced feature in relation to a Cartesian system of three mutually perpendicular planes, jointly called Datum Reference Frame (DRF), and restrict its motion in relation to it. Positional tolerances often require a three plane datum system, named as primary, secondary and tertiary datum planes. The required number of datums (1, 2 or 3) is derived by considering the degrees of freedom of the toleranced feature that need to be restricted. Change of the datums and/or their order of precedence in the DRF results to different geometrical accuracies, (Kaisarlis et al., 2008).

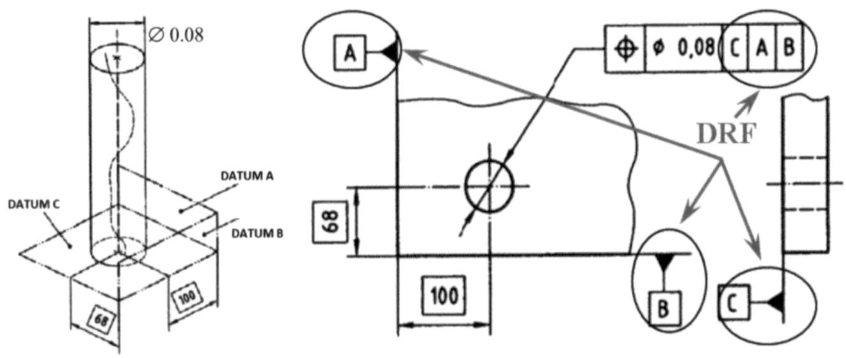

Fig. 2. Cylindrical tolerance zone and geometric true position tolerancing for a cylindrical feature according to ISO 1101 (Kaisarlis et al, 2008)

The versatility and economic benefits of true position tolerances are particularly enhanced when they are assigned at the Maximum Material Condition (MMC). At MMC, an increase in position tolerance is allowed, equal to the departure of the feature from the maximum material condition size, (ISO, 1988; ASME, 2009). As a consequence, a feature with size beyond maximum material but within the dimensional tolerance zone and its axis lying inside the enlarged MMC cylinder is acceptable. The accuracy required by a position tolerance is thus relaxed through the MMC assignment and the reject rate reduced. Moreover, according to the current ISO and ASME standards, datum features of size that are included in the DRF of position tolerances can also apply on either MMC, Regardless of Feature Size (RFS) or Least Material Condition (LMC) basis.

Position tolerances mainly concern clearance fits. They achieve the intended function of a clearance fit by means of the relative positioning and orientation of the axis of the true geometric counterpart of the mating features with reference to one, two or three Cartesian datums. The relationship between mating features in such a clearance fit may be classified either as a fixed or a floating fastener type, (ASME, 2009; Drake, 1999), Figure 3. Floating fastener situation exists where two or more parts are assembled with fasteners such as bolts and nuts, and all parts have clearance holes for the bolts. In a fixed fastener situation one or more of the parts to be assembled have clearance holes and the mating part has restrained fasteners, such as screws in threaded holes or studs. The approach that is here presented deals with *both* the floating and fixed fastener cases by integrating the individual case methodologies published by (Kaisarlis et al. 2007; 2008).

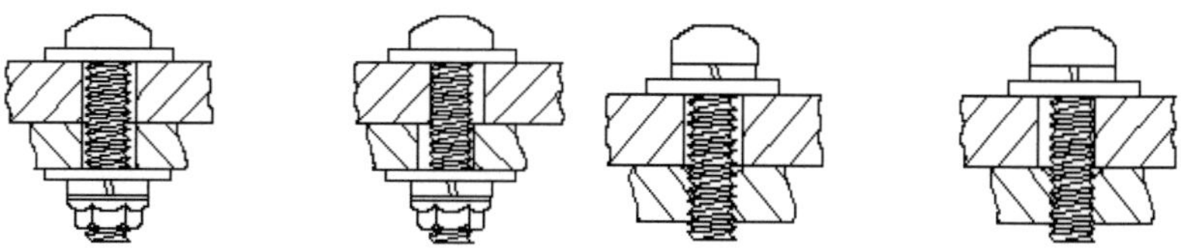

Fig. 3. Typical floating and fixed fasteners and worst case assembly conditions (Drake, 1999)

Basic issues of the assignment of a Position Tolerance in RE are included in Table 1. Limited number of reference components that does not allow for statistical analysis, availability or not of the mating parts and the presence of wear may affect the reliability of the RE results. Moreover, datum selection and the size of the position tolerance itself should ensure, obviously, a stress-free mechanical mating. The analytic approach presented in this section deals with the full range of these issues in order to produce a reliable solution within realistic time.

i.	*The number of available RE components that will be measured. The more RE parts are measured, the more reliable will be the extracted results. Typically, the number of available RE components is extremely limited, usually ranging from less than ten to a single one article.*
ii.	*Off the shelf, worn or damaged RE components. Off the shelf RE components are obviously ideal for the job, given that the extent of wear or damage is for the majority of cases difficult to be quantified or compensated.*
iii.	*Accessibility of the mating part (-s).*
iv.	*Existence of repetitive features in the RE component that may have the same function (group or pattern of features).*
v.	*Type of assembly (e.g. floating or fixed fasteners).*
vi.	*The size and the form (cylindrical, circular, square, other) of the geometrical tolerance zone.*
vii.	*Candidate datums and datum reference frames. Depending on the case more possible DRFs may be considered.*
viii.	*Precedence of datum features in DRFs.*
ix.	*Theoretical (basic) dimensions involved.*
x.	*Assignment of Maximum Material and Least Material Conditions to both the RE-feature and RE datum features.*
xi.	*Measurement instrumentation capabilities in terms of final uncertainty of the measurements results. Measurements methods and software.*

Table 1. Issues of Geometrical Tolerance Assignment in RE

Assignment of RE-position tolerance for both the fixed and the floating fastener case is accomplished by the present method in five sequential steps. The analysis is performed individually for each feature that has to be toleranced in the RE-component. At least two RE reference components, intact or with negligible wear, need to be available in order to minimize the risk of measuring a possibly defective or wrongly referenced RE component and, as it is later explained in this section, to improve the method efficiency. This does not certainly mean that the method cannot be used even when only one component is available. Mating part availability is desirable as it makes easier the datum(s) recognition. Minimum assembly clearance and, as well as, the dimensional tolerance of the RE-feature *(hole, peg, pin or screw shaft)* and RE-Datums *(for features of size)* are taken as results from the RE dimensional tolerance analysis presented in the previous section of the chapter in conjunction with those quoted in relevant application- specific standards.

The primary step (a) of the analysis concerns the recognition of the critical features on the RE component that need to be toleranced and, as well as, their fastening situation. This step is performed interactively and further directs the analysis on either the fixed or the floating fastener option. In step (b) mathematical relationships that represent the geometric constraints of the problem are formulated. They are used for the establishment of an initial *set of candidate position tolerances.* The next step (c) qualifies *suggested sets* out of the group (b) that have to be in conformance with the measured data of the particular RE-feature. The step (d) of the analysis produces then a set of *preferred position tolerances* by filtering out the output of step (c) by means of knowledge-based rules and/or guidelines. The capabilities and expertise of the particular machine shop, where the new components will be produced, and the cost-tolerance relationship, are taken into consideration in the last step (e) of the analysis, where the required position tolerance is finally obtained. For every *datum feature* that can be considered for the position tolerance assignment of an *RE-feature,* the input for the analysis consists of *(i)* the measured form deviation of the datum feature (e.g. flatness), *(ii)* its measured size, in case that the datum is a feature of size (e.g. diameter of a hole) and *(iii)* the orientation deviation (e.g. perpendicularity) of the RE-feature axis of symmetry with respect to that datum. The orientation deviations of the latter with respect to the two other datums of the same DRF have also to be included (perpendicularity, parallelism, angularity). Input data relevant with the RE-feature itself include its measured size (e.g. diameter) and coordinates, e.g. X, Y measured dimensions by a CMM, that locate its axis of symmetry. Uncertainty of the measured data should conform to the pursued accuracy level. In that context the instrumentation used for the measured input data, e.g. ISO 10360-2 accuracy threshold for CMMs, is considered appropriate for the analysis only if its uncertainty is at six times less than the minimum assembly clearance.

4.1 Sets of candidate position tolerance sizes

The size of the total position tolerance zone is determined by the minimum clearance, min*CL*, of the (hole, screw-shaft) assembly. It ensures that mating features will assemble even at worst case scenario, i.e. when both parts are at MMC and located at the extreme ends of the position tolerance zone (ASME, 2009). The equations (16 -i) and (16-ii) apply for the fixed and floating fastener case respectively,

$$\begin{aligned} &(i)\ T_{POS} = \text{minCL} = T_{POS\_s} + T_{POS\_h} = MMC_h - MMC_s \\ &(ii)\ T_{POS} = \text{minCL} = T_{POS\_h} \end{aligned} \tag{16}$$

For the fixed fasteners case, in industrial practice the *total position tolerance* T_{POS} of equation (16-i) is distributed between shaft and hole according to the ease of manufacturing, production restrictions and other factors that influence the manufacturing cost of the mating parts. In conformance with that practice a set of 9 candidate sizes for the position tolerance of the RE-shaft, $\boldsymbol{R}_{CAN\_s}$ and/ or the RE-hole, $\boldsymbol{R}_{CAN\_h}$, is created by the method with a (T_{POS} /10) step, which includes the 50% -50% case,

$$\begin{aligned} &\boldsymbol{R}_{CAN\_h} = \boldsymbol{R}_{CAN\_s} = \{T_{POS1}, T_{POS2}, \ldots, T_{POSi}, \ldots, T_{POS9}\} \\ &\text{where,}\quad T_{POSi} = i \cdot T_{POS}/10, \qquad i=1, 2, \ldots, 9 \end{aligned} \tag{17}$$

For the floating fasteners case the *total position tolerance* T_{POS} of equation (16-ii) actually concerns only RE-features of the Hole type. Therefore, the $\boldsymbol{R}_{CAN\_h}$ set only contains the T_{POS} element. The above tolerances attain, apparently, their maximum values when the RE feature own dimensional tolerance zone is added,

$$\begin{aligned} T_{POSi\_MAX} &= T_{POSi} + LMC_h - MMC_h \quad \text{(RE-feature / Hole)} \\ T_{POSi\_MAX} &= T_{POSi} + MMC_s - LMC_s \quad \text{(RE- feature / Shaft)} \end{aligned} \tag{18}$$

4.2 Sets of candidate DRFs and theoretical dimensions

To ensure proper RE-part interfacing and safeguard repeatability, datum features of the original part and those of the RE-part should, ideally, coincide. In order to observe this principle the original datum features and their order of precedence have to be determined. Initial recognition of datum features among the features of the RE-part is performed interactively following long established design criteria for locating or functional surfaces and the same, and taking into consideration the mating parts function. Out of all candidate recognized datums an initial set of candidate DRFs, $\boldsymbol{D}_{CAN\_INIT}$, is produced by taking all combinations in couples and in triads between them. A valid DRF should conform with the constraints that have to do with the arrangement and the geometrical deviations of its datums. Only DRFs that arrest all degrees of freedom of the particular RE-feature and consequently have three or at least two datums are considered. DRF qualification for geometric feasibility is verified by reference to the list of the valid geometrical relationships between datums as given in (ASME, 1994). The geometric relationship for instance, for the usual case of three datum planes that construct a candidate DRF is in this way validated, i.e. the primary datum not to be parallel to the secondary and the plane used as tertiary datum not to be parallel to the line constructed by the intersection of the primary and secondary datum planes. Planar or axial datum features are only considered by the method as primary when the axis of the RE-feature is perpendicular in the first case or parallel, in the second one, to them.

The following analysis applies for both the hole and the shaft and is common for the fixed and floating fasteners case. Consequently, the indexes "*h*" or "*s*" are not used hereafter. It is here also noted that the index "*i*" only concerns the fixed fastener case. For the floating fastener case the index "*i*" has a constant value of 1. Let $\boldsymbol{RF}_{DF}$ be the set of the measured form deviations of a candidate datum feature and $\boldsymbol{RO}$ the orientation deviations of the RE feature axis of symmetry with respect to that datum. Fitness of the members of the initial DRF set, $\boldsymbol{D}_{CAN\_INIT}$, against the members of the $\boldsymbol{R}_{CAN}$ set of candidate position tolerance sizes is confirmed regarding the primary datum through the following constraints,

$$\max(\boldsymbol{RF}_{DF}) \leq T_{POSi} \tag{19}$$

$$\max(\boldsymbol{RO}) \leq T_{POSi} \tag{20}$$

Mutual orientation deviations of the secondary and/or tertiary datums, $\boldsymbol{RO}_{DF}$, in a valid DRF should also conform with the position tolerance of equation (16),

$$\begin{array}{ll} \max(\boldsymbol{RF}_{DF}) \leq k \cdot T_{POSi}, & \max(\boldsymbol{RO}) \leq k \cdot T_{POSi} \\ \max(\boldsymbol{RO}_{DF}) \leq k \cdot T_{POSi}, & k \geq 1 \end{array} \tag{21}$$

where k is a weight coefficient depending on the accuracy level of the case. A set of *Candidate* DRFs is thus created, $\boldsymbol{D}_{CAN}{}^{(i)}$, that is addressed to each i member (i=1,…9) of the $\boldsymbol{R}_{CAN}$ set.

Sets of *Candidate Theoretical Dimensions*, $[(\boldsymbol{C}_{CAN}{}^{(ij)}X,\ \boldsymbol{C}_{CAN}{}^{(ij)}Y),\ i=1,2,\ldots 9,\ j=1,2,\ldots,n]$, which locate the RE feature axis of symmetry with reference to every one of the n candidate $\mathrm{DRF}^{(i)}{}_j$ of the $\boldsymbol{D}_{CAN}{}^{(i)}$ set are generated at the next stage of the analysis. Measured, from all the available RE reference parts, *axis location coordinates* are at first integrated into sets, $[\boldsymbol{C}_{CAN}{}^{(ij)}X_M,\ \boldsymbol{C}_{CAN}{}^{(ij)}Y_M]$. Sets of Candidate Theoretical Dimensions are then produced in successive steps starting from those calculated from the integral part of the difference between the minimum measured coordinates and the size of the position tolerance, T_{POSi},

$$X^{(ij)}{}_1 = \mathrm{int}[\min(\boldsymbol{C}_{CAN}{}^{(ij)}X_M) - T_{POSi}],\ Y^{(ij)}{}_1 = \mathrm{int}[\min(\boldsymbol{C}_{CAN}{}^{(ij)}Y_M) - T_{POSi}] \tag{22}$$

Following members of the $\boldsymbol{C}_{CAN}{}^{(ij)}X$, $\boldsymbol{C}_{CAN}{}^{(ij)}Y$ sets are calculated by an incremental increase δ of the theoretical dimensions $X^{(ij)}{}_1$, $Y^{(ij)}{}_1$,

$$\begin{array}{ll} X^{(ij)}{}_2 = X^{(ij)}{}_1 + \delta, & Y^{(ij)}{}_2 = Y^{(ij)}{}_1 + \delta \\ X^{(ij)}{}_3 = X^{(ij)}{}_2 + \delta, & Y^{(ij)}{}_3 = Y^{(ij)}{}_2 + \delta \\ \ldots\ldots\ldots\ldots\ldots & \ldots\ldots\ldots\ldots\ldots \\ X^{(ij)}{}_p = X^{(ij)}{}_{(p-1)} + \delta, & Y^{(ij)}{}_q = Y^{(ij)}{}_{(q-1)} + \delta \end{array} \tag{23}$$

where as upper limit is taken that of the maximum measured $X^{(ij)}{}_M$, $Y^{(ij)}{}_M$ coordinates plus the position tolerance T_{POSi},

$$X^{(ij)}{}_p \leq \max(\boldsymbol{C}_P{}^{(ij)}X_M) + T_{POSi},\quad Y^{(ij)}{}_q \leq \max(\boldsymbol{C}_P{}^{(ij)}Y_M) + T_{POSi} \tag{24}$$

with the populations p, q of the produced $\boldsymbol{C}_{CAN}{}^{(ij)}X$ *and* $\boldsymbol{C}_{CAN}{}^{(ij)}Y$ sets of candidate theoretical dimensions not necessarily equal. In the case study that is presented δ=0.05mm. Other δ-values can be used as well.

4.3 Sets of suggested position tolerances

Sets of *Suggested DFR*s that are produced in step (b), $\boldsymbol{D}_{SG}{}^{(i)}$, are qualified as subgroups of the sets of *Candidate DFR*s, $\boldsymbol{D}_{CAN}{}^{(i)}$, in accordance with their conformance with the measured location coordinates and the application or not of the Maximum or Least Material Conditions to the RE-feature size or to the RE-Datum size. In conjunction with equation (16), qualification criterion for the Suggested DFR's, $\mathrm{DRF}^{(i)}{}_j$ j=1,2,…, n, is, Figure 4(a),

$$\max\{\Delta X^{(ij)}{}_M,\ \Delta Y^{(ij)}{}_M\} \leq T_{POSi} \tag{25}$$

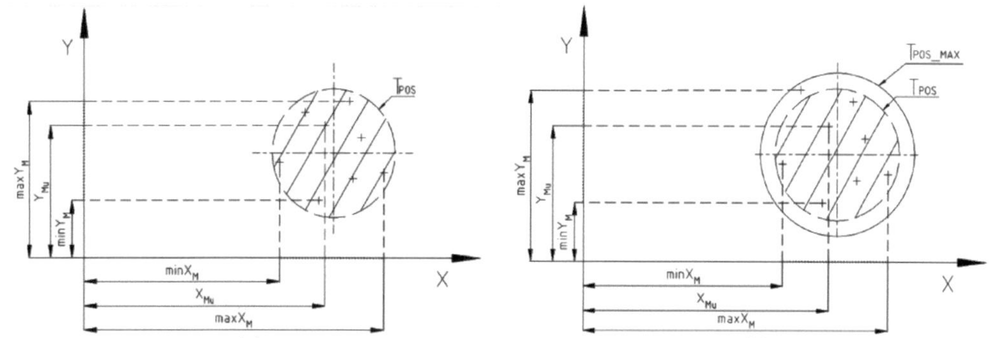

(a) (b)

Fig. 4. Qualification conditions for suggested DRFs (Kaisarlis et al., 2007)

where,

$$\begin{aligned} \Delta X^{(ij)}{}_M &= \max(\boldsymbol{C}_{CAN}{}^{(ij)}X_M) - \min(\boldsymbol{C}_{CAN}{}^{(ij)}X_M) \\ \Delta Y^{(ij)}{}_M &= \max(\boldsymbol{C}_{CAN}{}^{(ij)}Y_M) - \min(\boldsymbol{C}_{CAN}{}^{(ij)}Y_M) \end{aligned} \tag{26}$$

In case constraint (25) is not satisfied, a $DRF^{(i)}{}_j$ can only be further considered, when Maximum or Least Material Conditions are applied to RE-feature size, Figure 4(b),

$$\max\{\Delta X^{(ij)}{}_M, \Delta Y^{(ij)}{}_M\} \le T_{POSi\_MAX} \tag{27}$$

In case no member of a $\boldsymbol{D}_{CAN}{}^{(i)}$ (i=1,2,…9) set satisfies either constraint (25) or constraint (27) the relevant T_{POSi} is excluded from the set of Suggested Position Tolerance Sizes, $\boldsymbol{R}_{SG}$.

Let r be the number of the available RE-parts. Sets of *Suggested Theoretical Dimensions*, $[\boldsymbol{C}_{SG}{}^{(ij)}X, \boldsymbol{C}_{SG}{}^{(ij)}Y]$, can now be filtered out of the Candidate Theoretical Dimensions through the application of the relationships,

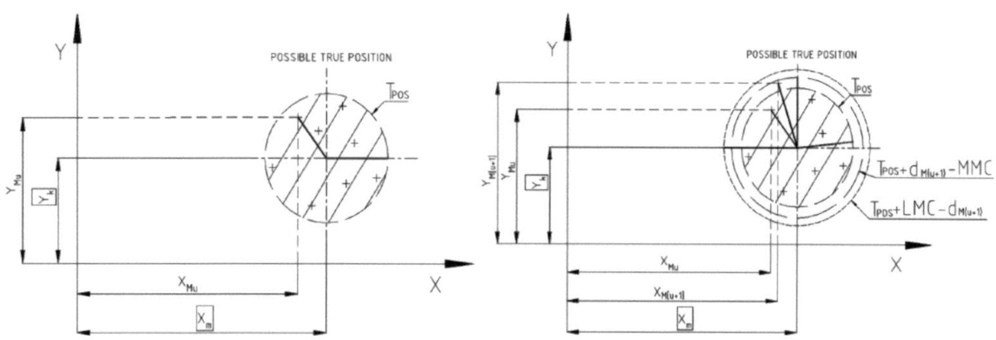

(a) (b)

Fig. 5. Qualification conditions for suggested theoretical dimensions (Kaisarlis et al., 2007)

$$|\ X^{(ij)}{}_m - X^{(ij)}{}_{Mu}\ | \le \frac{T_{POSi\_MAX}}{2}, \quad |\ Y^{(ij)}{}_k - Y^{(ij)}{}_{Mu}\ | \le \frac{T_{POSi\_MAX}}{2} \tag{28}$$

m=1,2, …,p ; k=1,2,…,q ; u=1,2,…,r

and the constraint imposed by the geometry of a position tolerance, Figure 5(a),

$$(X^{(ij)}_m - X^{(ij)}_{Mu})^2 + (Y^{(ij)}_k - Y^{(ij)}_{Mu})^2 \le (\frac{T_{POSi}}{2})^2 \quad (29)$$

m=1,2, …,p ; k=1,2,…,q ; u=1,2,…,r

Candidate Theoretical Dimensions that satisfy the constraints (28) but not the constraint (29) can apparently be further considered in conjunction with constraint (27) when Maximum or Least Material Conditions are used. In these cases they are respectively qualified by the conditions, e.g. for the case of RE-feature /Hole, Figure 5(b),

$$(X^{(ij)}_m - X^{(ij)}_{Mu})^2 + (Y^{(ij)}_k - Y^{(ij)}_{Mu})^2 \le (\frac{T_{POSi} + d_{Mu} - MMC}{2})^2 \quad (30)$$

$$(X^{(ij)}_m - X^{(ij)}_{Mu})^2 + (Y^{(ij)}_k - Y^{(ij)}_{Mu})^2 \le (\frac{T_{POSi} + LMC - d_{Mu}}{2})^2 \quad (31)$$

m=1,2, …,p ; k=1,2,…,q ; u=1,2,…,r

When applicable, the case of MMC or LMC on a RE-Datum feature of size may be also investigated. For that purpose, the size tolerance of the datum, T_{S_DF}, must be added on the right part of the relationships (27) and (28). In that context, the constraints (30) and (31), e.g. for the case of RE-feature /Hole - RE-Datum /Hole on MMC, are then formulated as,

$$(X^{(ij)}_m - X^{(ij)}_{Mu})^2 + (Y^{(ij)}_k - Y^{(ij)}_{Mu})^2 \le (\frac{T_{POSi} + d_{Mu} - MMC + d_{Mu\_DF} - MMC_{DF}}{2})^2 \quad (32)$$

$$(X^{(ij)}_m - X^{(ij)}_{Mu})^2 + (Y^{(ij)}_k - Y^{(ij)}_{Mu})^2 \le (\frac{T_{POSi} + LMC - d_{Mu} + d_{Mu\_DF} - MMC_{DF}}{2})^2 \quad (33)$$

m=1,2, …,p ; k=1,2,…,q ; u=1,2,…,r

where d_{Mu_DF} is the measured diameter of the datum on the *u-th* RE-part and MMC_{DF} the MMC size of the RE-Datum.

4.4 Sets of preferred position tolerances

The next step of the analysis provides for three tolerance selection options and the implementation of manufacturing guidelines for datum designation in order the method to propose a limited number of *Preferred Position Tolerance Sets* out of the *Suggested* ones and hence lead the final decision to a rational end result. The first tolerance selection option is only applicable in the fixed fasteners case and focuses for a maximum tolerance size of a $T_{POS}/2$. The total position tolerance T_{POS}, whose distribution between the mating parts is unknown, will be unlikely to be exceeded in this way and therefore, even in the most unfavourable assembly conditions interference will not occur. The second selection option gives its preference to Position Tolerance Sets that are qualified regardless of the application of the Maximum or Least Material Conditions to the RE-feature size and/ or the RE- datum feature size i.e. through their conformance only with the constraint (29) and not the constraints (30) to (33). Moreover, guidelines for datums which are used in the above context are, (ASME 2009; Fischer, 2004):

- A datum feature should be: *(i)* visible and easily accessible, *(ii)* large enough to permit location/ processing operations and *(iii)* geometrically accurate and offer repeatability to prevent tolerances from stacking up excessively

- Physical surfaces are preferable datum features over derived and/ or virtual ones.
- External datums are preferred over internal ones.
- For the fixed fastener case, a preferred primary datum of the mating parts is their respective planar contact surface.
- Theoretical dimensions and tolerances expressed in integers or with minimum possible decimal places are preferable.

5. Cost - effective RE-tolerance assignment

To assign cost optimal tolerances to the new RE-components, that have to be re-manufactured, the Tolerance Element (TE) method is introduced. Accuracy cost constitutes a vital issue in production, as tight tolerances always impose additional effort and therefore higher manufacturing costs. Within the frame of further development of the CAD tools, emphasis is recently given on techniques that assign mechanical tolerances in terms not only of quality and functionality but also of minimum manufacturing cost. Cost-tolerance functions, however, are difficult to be adopted in the tolerance optimization process because their coefficients and exponents are case-driven, experimentally obtained, and they may well not be representative of the manufacturing environment where the production will take place. The TE method (Dimitrellou et al., 2007a; 2007c, 2008) overcomes the mentioned inefficiencies as it automatically creates and makes use of appropriate cost-tolerance functions for the assembly chain members under consideration. The latter is accomplished through the introduction of the concept of Tolerance Elements (Dimitrellou et al., 2007b) that are geometric entities with attributes associated with the accuracy cost of the specific machining environment where the components will be manufactured.

The accuracy cost of a part dimension depends on the process and resources required for the production of this dimension within its tolerance limits. Given the workpiece material and the tolerances, the part geometrical characteristics such as shape, size, internal surfaces, feature details and/or position are taken into consideration for planning the machining operations, programming the machine tools, providing for fixtures, etc. These characteristics have thus a direct impact on the machining cost of the required accuracy and determine, indirectly, its magnitude. A Tolerance Element (TE) is defined either as a 3D form feature of particular shape, size and tolerance, or as a 3D form feature of particular position and tolerance (Dimitrellou et al., 2007a). It incorporates attributes associated with the feature shape, size, position, details and the size ratio of the principal dimensions of the part to which it belongs. For a given manufacturing environment (machine tools, inspection equipment, supporting facilities, available expertise) to each TE belongs one directly related with this environment cost-tolerance function.

TEs are classified through a five-class hierarch system, Figure 6. Class level attributes are all machining process related, generic and straightforwardly identifiable in conformance with the existing industrial understanding. In first level, TEs are classified according to the basic geometry of the part to which they belong, i.e. rotational TEs and prismatic TEs. Rotational TEs belong to rotational parts manufactured mainly by turning and boring, while prismatic TEs belong to prismatic parts mainly manufactured by milling. The contribution of the geometrical configuration of the part to the accuracy cost of a TE, is taken into account in the second level through the size ratio of the principal dimensions of the part. In this way TEs are classified as short [$L/D \leq 3$] and long [$L/D > 3$] TEs, following a typical way of classification. In third level TEs are classified to external and internal ones as the achievement of internal tolerances usually results to higher accuracy costs. The fourth TE classification level distinguishes between plain and complex TEs depending on the absence or presence of additional feature details (grooves, wedges, ribs, threads etc). They do not change the principal TE geometry but they indirectly contribute to the increase of the accuracy cost. In the final fifth level, the involvement of the TE size to the accuracy cost is considered. TEs are classified, to the nominal size of the chain dimension, into six groups by integrating two sequential ISO 286-1 size ranges.

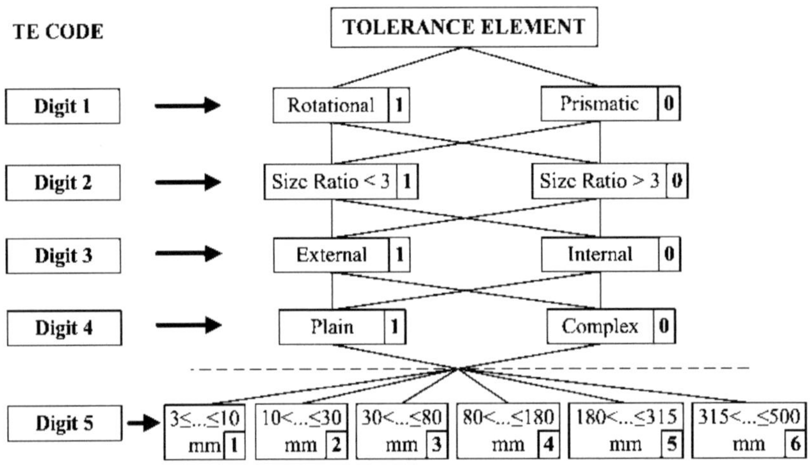

Fig. 6. Tolerance Elements five-class hierarch system (Dimitrellou et al., 2007a)

Based on the TE-method the actual machining accuracy capabilities and the relative cost per TE-class of a particular machine shop are recorded through an appropriately developed Database Feedback Form (DFF). The latter includes the accuracy cost for all the 96 TE-classes in the size range 3-500 mm and tolerances range IT6-IT10. DFF is filled once, at the system commissioning stage, by the expert engineers of the machine shop where the assembly components will be manufactured and can then be updated each time changes occur in the shop machines, facilities and/or expertise. The DFF data is then processed by the system through the least-square approximation and the system constructs and stores a cost-tolerance relationship of the power function type, per TE-class.

5.1 Tolerance chain constrains

In a n-member dimensional chain the tolerances of the individual dimensions $D_1, D_2, \ldots, D_n$, control the variation of a critical end-dimension D_0, according to the chain,

$$D_0 = f(D_1, D_2, \ldots, D_n) \tag{34}$$

where f(D) can be either a linear or nonlinear function. To ensure that the end-dimension will be kept within its specified tolerance zone, the worst-case constrain that provides for 100% interchangeability has to be satisfied,

$$f\left(D_{i\max} + D_{j\min}\right) \leq D_0 + t_0 \tag{35}$$

$$D_0 - t_0 \le f\left(D_{i\min} + D_{j\max}\right) \tag{36}$$

where t_0 is the tolerance of the end-dimension D_0. For an (i+j)-member dimensional chain dimensions D_i constitute the positive members of the chain while dimensions D_j constitute its negative members. In RE tolerancing, preferred alternatives for nominal sizes and dimensional tolerances that are generated from the analysis of Section 3, for each dimension involved in the chain are further filtered out by taking into consideration the above tolerance chain constraints.

5.2 Minimum machining cost

A second sorting out is applied by taking into account the accuracy cost for each combination of alternatives that obtained in the previous stage. Cost-tolerance functions are provided by the machine shop DFF and the total accuracy cost is thus formulated as,

$$C_{total} = \sum_{i=1}^{n} C(t_i) = \sum_{i=1}^{n} \left[A_i + B_i / t_i^{k_i} \right] \rightarrow \min \tag{37}$$

where C(t) is the relative cost for the production of the machining tolerance ±t and A, B, k are constants. The combination of alternatives that corresponds to the minimum cost is finally selected as the optimum one.

6. Application examples and case studies

In order to illustrate the effectiveness of the proposed method three individual industrial case studies are presented in this section. All necessary input data measurements were performed by means of a direct computer controlled CMM (*Mistral*, Brown & Sharpe-DEA) with ISO 10360-2 max. permissible error 3.5μm and PC-DMIS measurement software. A Renishaw PH10M head with TP200 probe and a 10mm length tip with diameter of 2mm were used. The number and distribution of sampling points conformed with the recommendations of BS7172:1989, (Flack, 2001), (9 points for planes and 15 for cylinders).

6.1 Application example of RE dimensional tolerancing

For a reverse engineered component of a working assembly (Part 2, Figure 7) assignment of dimensional tolerances was carried out using the developed methodology. The case study assembly of Figure 7 is incorporated in an optical sensor alignment system. Its' location, orientation and dynamic balance is considered of paramount importance for the proper function of the sensor. The critical assembly requirements that are here examined are the clearance gaps between the highlighted features (D1, D2, D3) of Part 1 – Shaft and Part 2- Hole in Figure 8. Four intact pairs of components were available for measurements. The analysis of section 3 was performed for all three critical features of Figure 8 individually. However, for the economy of the chapter, input data and method results are only presented for the D2 RE-feature, in Tables 2 and 3 respectively. The selected ISO 286 fits, Figure 9, produced in 12min *(10min CMM-measurements + 2min Computer aided implementation)* were experimentally verified and well approved by fitting reconstructed components in existing and in use assemblies.

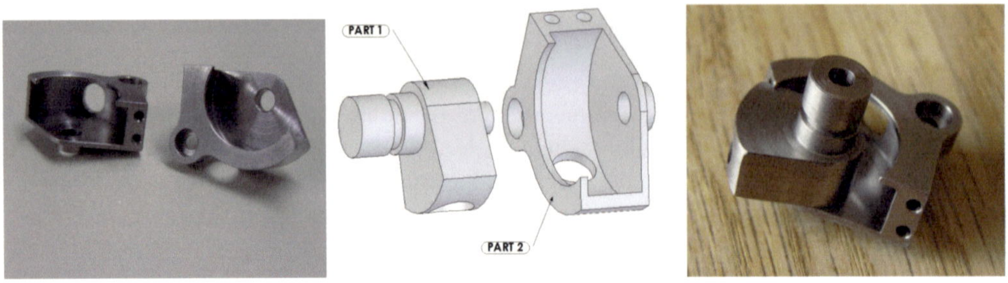

Fig. 7. RE dimensional tolerancing case study parts and assembly

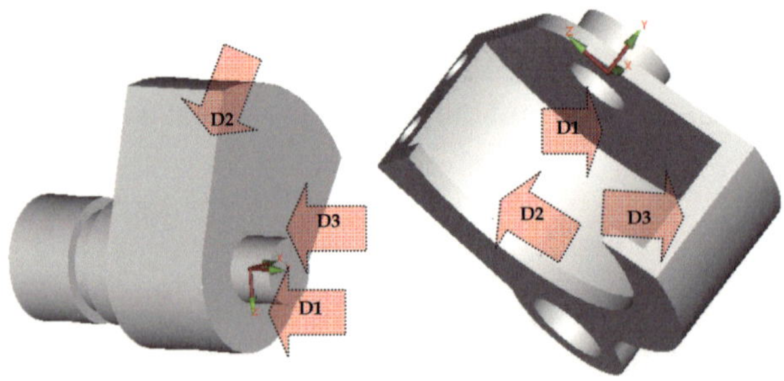

Fig. 8. Critical RE-features of the RE dimensional tolerancing case study parts

Hole	d_{M_h} (mm)	F_h (mm)	R_{a_h}
h #1	22.136	0.008	3.8
h #2	22.128	0.008	
h #3	22.091	0.003	
h #4	22.078	0.004	
U_h = 0.009mm			
Shaft	**d_{M_s} (mm)**	**F_s (mm)**	**R_{a_s}**
s #1	21.998	0.003	2.4
s #2	21.984	0.005	
s #3	21.979	0.006	
s #4	21.972	0.005	
U_s = 0.012mm			

Table 2. Input data related to case study RE-features

Suggested Fits	
∅ 22.000 H12 / g7, H12 / g8, H12 / g9, H12 / g10, H12 / g11, H12 / h8, H12 / h9, H12 / h10, H12 / h11 ∅ 22.050 H11 / e9, H11 / e10, H11 / e11, H11 / f10,	*∅22.000* D10 / h8, D11 / h8, D12 / h8, E11/ h8, E12/ h8, F11 / h8, F12 / h8, G11 / h8, G12 / h8, H12 / h8 D10 / h9, D11 / h9, D12 / h9, E11/ h8, E12/ h9, F11 / h9, F12 / h9, G11 / h9, G12 / h9, H12 / h9 D10 / h10, D11 / h10, D12 / h10, E11/ h10, E12/ h10, F11 / h10, F12 / h10, G11 / h10, G12 / h10, H12 / h10 D10 / h11, D11 / h11, D12 / h11, E11/ h11, E12/ h11, F11 / h11, F12 / h11, G11 / h11, G12 / h11, H12 / h11

H11 / f11, H11 / g7, H11 / g8, H11 / g9, H11 / g10, H11 / g11, H11 / h8, H11 / h9, H11 / h10, H11 / h11, H12 / e9, H12 / e10, H12 / e11, H12 / f10, H12 / f11, H12 / g7, H12 / g8, H12 / g9, H12 / g10, H12 / g11 H12 / h8, H12 / h9, H12 / h10, H12 / h11	*Ø22.050* F10 / h10, F11 / h10, F12 / h10, G10 / h10, G11 / h10, G12 / h10, H11 / h10, H12 / h10 F10 / h11, F11 / h11, F12 / h11, G10 / h11, G11 / h11, G12 / h11, H11 / h11, H12 / h11
Preferred Fits	
Ø 22.050 H11 / e9, H11 / h8, H11 / h9, H11 / h11	Ø 22.000 D10 / h9, D11 / h9, D10 / h8, D11 / h8, D10 / h11, D11 / h11
Ø 22.000 D10 / h9, D11 / h9, D10 / h8, D11 / h8	

Table 3. Sets of Suggested and Preferred fits for the case study

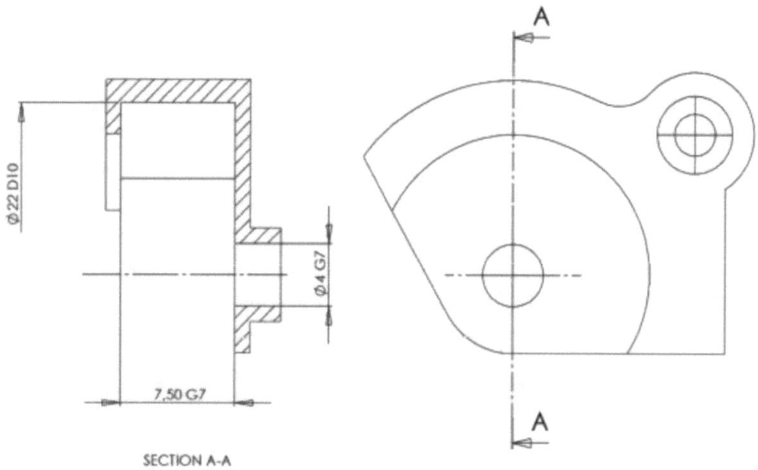

Fig. 9. Selected ISO 286 fits applied on the case study mechanical drawing

6.2 Application example of RE geometrical tolerancing

A new optical sensor made necessary the redesign of an existing bracket that had to be fastened on the old system through the original group of 4 x M5 threaded bolts, Figure 10. The accuracy of the location and orientation of the sensor bracket was considered critical for the sensor proper function. Bracket redesign had to be based on two available old and not used reference components. In the following, the method application is focused only on the allocation of position tolerances for the four bracket mounting holes. The problem represents, apparently, a typical fixed fastener case. For the chapter economy the input data and the produced results for the allocation of the position tolerance for the through hole H1, Figure 11, are only here presented and discussed. Standard diameter of the holes is 5.3mm ± 0.1mm and minimum clearance between hole and M5 screw 0.2mm.The weight coefficient in the relationships (21) was taken k=1.

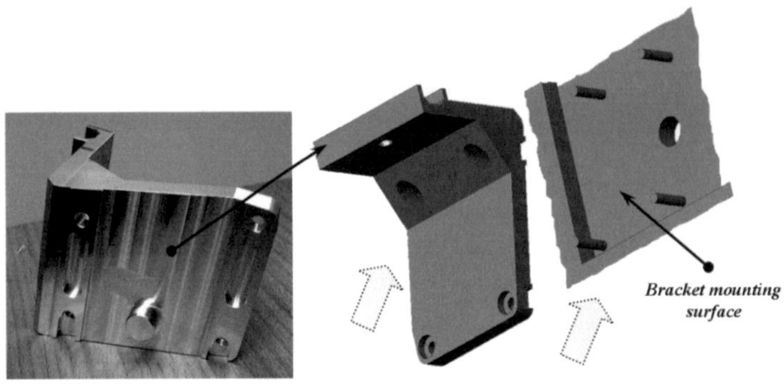

Fig. 10. Reference RE part and mating parts assembly

The CAD model of the redesigned new bracket was created in Solidworks taking into account the measured data of the reference components and, as well as, the new sensor mounting requirements. Datum and feature *(hole H1)* related input data are given in Table 4. Four candidate datum features A, B, C and D were considered, Figure 11. In step (a) 10 candidate DRFs (|A|B|C|, |A|C|B|, |A|B|D|, |A|D|B|, |A|C|D|, |A|D|C|, |D|A|C|, |D|A|B|, |D|B|A|, |D|C|A|) were produced by the algorithm for 7 position tolerance sizes, 0.06-0.18mm and consequently 10 sets of candidate theoretical dimensions, [$(C_P^{(ij)}X$, $C_P^{(ij)}Y)$, i=3,…9, j=1,…,10]. Negligible form and orientation deviations of datums A and D reduced the DRFs to the first six of them as |D|A|C|≡|A|D|C|≡|D|C|A| and |D|A|B|≡|A|D|B|≡|D|B|A|, having thus provided for 751 suggested tolerances in the following step (b). A representative sample of these tolerances is shown in Table 5. Although computational time difference is not significant, it is noticed that the quantity of the suggested results is strongly influenced by the number of the initially recognized possible datum features, weight coefficient k of the constraints (21), parameter δ of the equations (23) and the number of the available reference components.

d_M (mm)			A|B|C	A|C|B	A|B|D	A|C|D	A|D|B	A|D|C
Part1	5.291	X_{M1}	7.023	7.031	7.025	31.014	31.007	31.011
		Y_{M1}	5.972	5.961	50.981	5.964	50.980	50.978
Part2	5.244	X_{M2}	6.988	7.004	6.987	30.973	30.962	30.971
		Y_{M2}	6.036	6.019	51.028	6.017	51.026	51.012

Datum	*RF_{DF} (mm)*		*RO (mm)*		*RO_{DF} (mm)*	
	Part 1	*Part 2*	*Part 1*	*Part 2*	*Part 1*	*Part 2*
A	0.008	0.011	0.005	0.006	B-0.024 /C-0.021 /D-0.008	B-0.027/C-0.019 /D-0.007
B	0.026	0.023	0.012	0.010	A-0.041 /C-0.039 /D-0.035	A-0.046/C-0.043 /D-0.042
C	0.016	0.021	0.016	0.011	A-0.042 /B-0.034 /D-0.041	A-0.038/B-0.036 /D-0.033
D	0.005	0.008	0.003	0.007	A-0.010 /B-0.022 /C-0.020	A-0.009/ B-0.025 /C-0.017

Table 4. Input data related to case study feature and datum

T_{POS}	*DRF*	*X*	*Y*	*Material Modifier*	T_{POS}	*DRF*	*X*	*Y*	*Material Modifier*
∅ 0.060	|A|B|C|	7.000	6.000	MMC	∅ 0.120	|A|D|C|	30.950	50.950	MMC
∅ 0.060	|A|C|B|	6.950	5.950	LMC	∅ 0.120	|A|D|C|	30.900	51.000	LMC
∅ 0.060	|A|C|B|	7.100	6.000	LMC	....				
∅ 0.060	|A|B|D|	7.050	51.000	LMC	∅ 0.140	|A|B|C|	7.050	6.000	MMC
∅ 0.060	|A|C|D|	30.950	6.000	MMC	∅ 0.140	|A|C|B|	7.000	5.950	-
∅ 0.060	|A|D|B|	31.000	51.000	MMC	∅ 0.140	|A|C|B|	7.050	6.000	-
∅ 0.060	|A|D|B|	31.050	51.050	LMC	∅ 0.140	|A|B|D|	7.000	51.100	LMC
∅ 0.060	|A|D|C|	30.950	51.000	MMC	∅ 0.140	|A|C|D|	31.050	6.000	MMC
∅ 0.060	|A|D|C|	31.050	50.950	LMC	∅ 0.140	|A|C|D|	31.100	6.000	LMC
....					∅ 0.140	|A|C|D|	31.100	6.050	LMC
∅ 0.080	|A|B|C|	7.000	6.000	-	∅ 0.140	|A|D|B|	30.950	51.000	-
∅ 0.080	|A|B|C|	7.100	6.000	LMC	∅ 0.140	|A|D|B|	30.900	51.000	MMC
∅ 0.080	|A|C|B|	7.050	6.000	MMC	∅ 0.140	|A|D|C|	30.950	50.950	-
∅ 0.080	|A|B|D|	7.000	51.000	-	∅ 0.140	|A|D|C|	30.950	51.000	-
∅ 0.080	|A|B|D|	7.100	51.000	LMC	∅ 0.140	|A|D|C|	30.900	51.000	MMC
∅ 0.080	|A|C|D|	31.000	6.000	-	....				
∅ 0.080	|A|D|B|	31.000	51.000	MMC	∅ 0.160	|A|B|C|	6.950	5.950	-
∅ 0.080	|A|D|B|	30.950	51.000	LMC	∅ 0.160	|A|B|C|	6.950	6.000	-
∅ 0.080	|A|D|C|	31.000	6.000	-	∅ 0.160	|A|C|B|	7.000	5.950	-
∅ 0.080	|A|D|C|	30.095	51.050	MMC	∅ 0.160	|A|C|B|	7.150	6.000	LMC
∅ 0.080	|A|D|C|	31.050	51.050	LMC	∅ 0.160	|A|B|D|	7.000	51.100	MMC
....					∅ 0.160	|A|B|D|	7.100	51.000	LMC
∅ 0.100	|A|B|C|	7.000	6.000	-	∅ 0.160	|A|C|D|	30.950	6.000	-
∅ 0.100	|A|C|B|	7.000	6.000	-	∅ 0.160	|A|C|D|	30.900	5.900	LMC
∅ 0.100	|A|C|B|	7.050	6.000	-	∅ 0.160	|A|D|B|	31.000	51.050	-
∅ 0.100	|A|B|D|	7.000	51.000	-	∅ 0.160	|A|D|C|	31.050	51.000	-
∅ 0.100	|A|B|D|	6.950	51.000	LMC	∅ 0.160	|A|D|C|	30.900	51.000	MMC
∅ 0.100	|A|C|D|	31.000	6.000	-	∅ 0.160	|A|D|C|	30.950	50.900	LMC
∅ 0.100	|A|C|D|	30.950	5.950	MMC	....				
∅ 0.100	|A|D|B|	31.000	51.050	MMC	∅ 0.180	|A|B|C|	7.050	6.000	-
∅ 0.100	|A|D|B|	30.950	50.900	LMC	∅ 0.180	|A|B|C|	7.150	6.000	LMC
∅ 0.100	|A|D|C|	30.950	51.000	LMC	∅ 0.180	|A|C|B|	6.950	5.950	-
∅ 0.100	|A|D|C|	31.050	50.950	LMC	∅ 0.180	|A|C|B|	6.900	6.000	LMC
....					∅ 0.180	|A|B|D|	6.900	51.000	MMC
∅ 0.120	|A|B|C|	7.050	6.050	MMC	∅ 0.180	|A|B|D|	6.900	51.050	MMC
∅ 0.120	|A|B|C|	7.100	6.000	LMC	∅ 0.180	|A|C|D|	31.050	6.000	-
∅ 0.120	|A|C|B|	7.050	5.900	LMC	∅ 0.180	|A|C|D|	31.100	6.100	LMC
∅ 0.120	|A|C|B|	7.100	5.950	LMC	∅ 0.180	|A|D|B|	30.900	51.050	MMC
∅ 0.120	|A|B|D|	7.000	50.900	LMC	∅ 0.180	|A|D|B|	31.050	51.000	MMC
∅ 0.120	|A|C|D|	31.050	6.000	MMC	∅ 0.180	|A|D|B|	31.100	51.000	LMC
∅ 0.120	|A|C|D|	31.050	6.000	LMC	∅ 0.180	|A|D|C|	30.950	51.000	-
∅ 0.120	|A|D|B|	31.000	51.050	MMC	∅ 0.180	|A|D|C|	31.050	50.950	MMC
∅ 0.120	|A|D|B|	30.900	50.950	LMC	∅ 0.180	|A|D|C|	30.900	50.900	LMC

Table 5. Representative sample of application example suggested position tolerances

T_{POS}	DRF	X	Y	Material Modifier	T_{POS}	DRF	X	Y	Material Modifier
∅ 0.080	|A|B|C|	7.000	6.000	-	∅ 0.100	|A|C|B|	7.000	6.000	-
∅ 0.800	|A|B|D|	7.000	51.000	-	∅ 0.100	|A|C|B|	7.050	6.000	-
∅ 0.080	|A|C|D|	31.000	6.000	-	∅ 0.100	|A|B|D|	7.000	51.000	-
∅0.080	|A|D|C|	31.000	51.000	-	∅ 0.100	|A|C|D|	31.000	6.000	-
∅ 0.100	|A|B|C|	7.000	6.000	-	∅ 0.100	|A|D|B|	31.000	51.000	-
					∅ 0.100	|A|D|C|	31.000	51.000	-

Table 6. Set of preferred position tolerances for the application example

The preferred 11 out of 751 position tolerances of the Table 6 were obtained applying the selection options and guidelines of the section 4.4. Parallel results were obtained for the other three holes. As it came out, all of them belong to a group of holes with common DRF. The position tolerance size ∅ 0.100mm and the DRF |A|B|C|were finally chosen by the machine shop. Theoretical hole location dimensions are shown in Figure 11. The results were experimentally verified and approved. Time needed for the entire task was 12min (CMM) + 6min (Analysis) =18min. The usual trial-and-error way would, apparently, require considerably longer time and produce doubtful results. Reliability of the results can certainly be affected by failing to recognize initial datum features. In machine shop practice however, risk for something like that is essentially negligible.

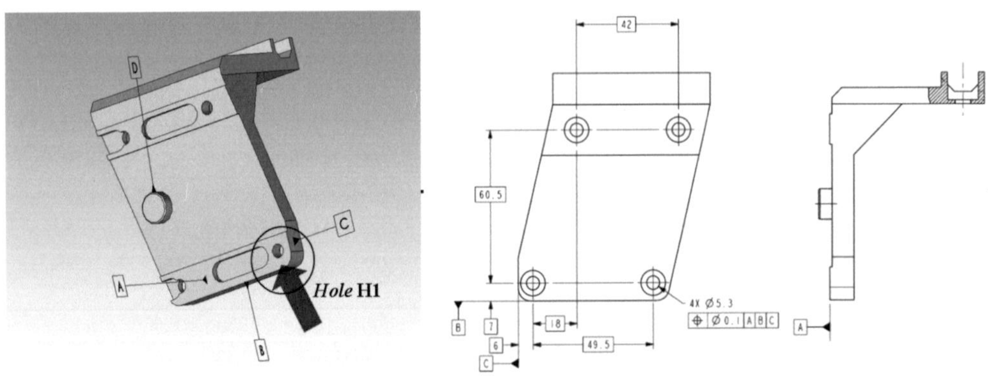

(a) (b)

Fig. 11. Case study datums (a) and the selected position tolerance of the case study (b)

6.3 Application example of cost-effective RE tolerancing

In the assembly of components A-B-C of Figure 12 the dimension D4 = 74.95 ± 0.25mm is controlled through the dimensional chain,

$$D_4 = \sin D_3 \left(D_1 + D_2 + D_7 + D_{10} - D_{11} - D_5 - D_6 + D_9 \right)$$

with D_1 = 190mm, D_2 = 15mm, D_3 = 45°, D_5 = 14mm, D_6 = 95mm, D_7 = 20mm, D_9 = 75mm, D_{10} = 12mm, D_{11} = 97mm. Component B is reverse engineered and needs to be remanufactured with main intention to fit and perform well in the existing assembly. All of the original component design and manufacturing information is, however, not available and the dimensional accuracy specifications for component B reconstruction have to be reestablished.

The machine shop where the part will be manufactured has an IT6 best capability and its DFF processed and the results stored. Alternatives for parts A, C and B, provided by the RE dimensional analysis of Section 3, are shown in Table 7(a) and (b) respectively. The 64 possible combinations of the part B alternatives are filtered out according to the tolerance chain constrains and, as a result, 24 combinations occur for the dimensions and tolerances $D_5 \pm t_5$, $D_6 \pm t_6$, $D_7 \pm t_7$ as shown in Table 8. The optimum combination that corresponds to the minimum accuracy cost is the combination 64.

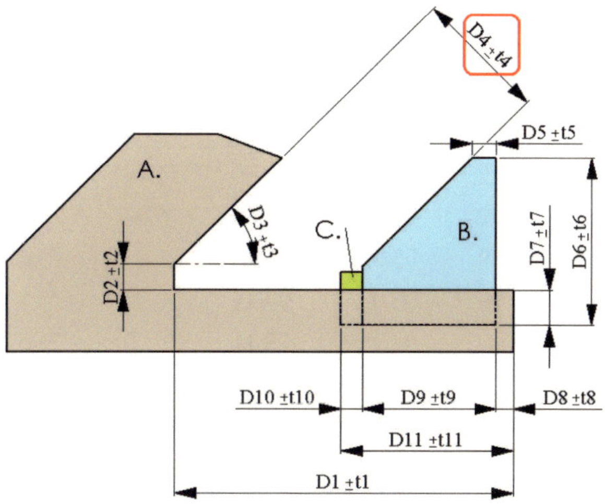

Fig. 12. Application example of Cost-Effective RE tolerancing

	Alternative 1		*Alternative 2*	
	D_{min}	D_{max}	D_{min}	D_{max}
D_1	190.01	190.04	189.97	190.00
D_2	14.99	15.02	14.98	15.00
D_3	45.01	45.02	44.98	45.00
D_7	20.00	20.01	19.99	20.005
D_{10}	12.01	12.025	11.98	12.00
D_{11}	97.00	97.02	96.98	97.025

a/a	D_5		D_6		D_9	
	D_{min}	D_{max}	D_{min}	D_{max}	D_{min}	D_{max}
1	14.00	14.12	95.03	95.15	74.67	75.23
2	13.89	14.30	94.98	95.11	75.00	75.01
3	13.98	13.99	94.86	94.99	74.77	74.99
4	13.89	14.01	94.95	95.14	74.98	75.10

Table 7. Dimensional alternatives for parts A, C and B

Combination	D_5		D_6		D_9		Accuracy Cost
	D_{min}	D_{max}	D_{min}	D_{max}	D_{max}	D_{min}	
2	14.00	14.12	95.03	95.15	75.00	75.01	3.3540
4	14.00	14.12	95.03	95.15	74.98	75.10	0.9035
6	14.00	14.12	94.98	95.11	75.00	75.01	3.3190
8	14.00	14.12	94.98	95.11	74.98	75.10	0.8684
10	14.00	14.12	94.86	94.99	75.00	75.01	3.3190
12	14.00	14.12	94.86	94.99	74.98	75.10	0.8684
14	14.00	14.12	94.95	95.14	75.00	75.01	3.1836
34	13.98	13.99	95.03	95.15	75.00	75.01	4.6426
36	13.98	13.99	95.03	95.15	74.98	75.10	2.1920
38	13.98	13.99	94.98	95.11	75.00	75.01	4.6075
40	13.98	13.99	94.98	95.11	74.98	75.10	2.1569
42	13.98	13.99	94.86	94.99	75.00	75.01	4.6075
43	13.98	13.99	94.86	94.99	74.77	74.99	2.0459
44	13.98	13.99	94.86	94.99	74.98	75.10	2.1569
46	13.98	13.99	94.95	95.14	75.00	75.01	4.4721
48	13.98	13.99	94.95	95.14	74.98	75.10	2.0216
50	13.89	14.01	95.03	95.15	75.00	75.01	3.3540
52	13.89	14.01	95.03	95.15	74.98	75.10	0.9035
54	13.89	14.01	94.98	95.11	75.00	75.01	3.3190
56	13.89	14.01	94.98	95.11	74.98	75.10	0.8684
58	13.89	14.01	94.86	94.99	75.00	75.01	3.3190
59	13.89	14.01	94.86	94.99	74.77	74.99	0.7574
62	13.89	14.01	94.95	95.14	75.00	75.01	3.1836
64	13.89	14.01	94.95	95.14	74.98	75.10	0.7330

Table 8. Filtered out combinations

7. Conclusion

In industrial manufacturing, tolerance assignment is one of the key activities in the product creation process. However, tolerancing is much more difficult to be successfully handled in RE. In this case all or almost all of the original component design and manufacturing information is not available and the dimensional and geometric accuracy specifications for component reconstruction have to be re-established, one way or the other, practically from scratch. RE-tolerancing includes a wide range of frequently met industrial manufacturing problems and is a task that requires increased effort, cost and time, whereas the results, usually obtained by trial-and-error, may well be not the best. The proposed methodology offers a systematic solution for this problem in reasonable computing time and provides realistic and industry approved results. This research work further extends the published research on this area by focusing on type of tolerances that are widely used in industry and almost always present in reverse engineering applications. The approach, to the extent of the author's knowledge, is the first of the kind for this type of RE problems that can be directly implemented within a CAD environment. It can also be considered as a pilot for further research and development in the area of RE tolerancing. Future work is oriented towards the computational implementation of the methodology in 3D-CAD environment, the RE *composite* position tolerancing that concerns patterns of repetitive features, the methodology application on the whole range of GD&T types and the integration of function oriented wear simulation models in order to evaluate input data that come from RE parts that bear considerable amount of wear.

8. References

Abella, R.J.; Dashbach, J.M. &, McNichols, R.J. (1994). Reverse Engineering Industrial Applications, *Computers & Industrial Engineering*, Vol.26, No. 2, pp. 381-385, ISSN: 0360-8352

Anselmetti, B. & Louati, H. (2005). Generation of manufacturing tolerancing with ISO standards, *International Journal of Machine Tools & Manufacture,* Vol. 45, pp. 1124–1131, ISSN: 0890-6955

ASME Standard. (1994). *Y14.5.1M-1994: Mathematical Definition of Dimensioning and Tolerancing Principles,* The American Society of Mechanical Engineers, New York, USA

ASME Standard. (2009). *Y14.5M–2009: Dimensioning and Tolerancing,* The American Society of Mechanical Engineers, New York, USA

Bagci, E. (2009). Reverse engineering applications for recovery of broken or worn parts and re-manufacturing: Three case studies, *Advances in Engineering Software,* Vol. 40, pp. 407–418, ISSN: 0965-9978

Borja, V., Harding, J.A. & Bell, B. (2001). A conceptual view on data-model driven reverse engineering, *Int. J. Prod. Res.,* Vol.39, No 4, pp. 667-687

Chant, A.; Wilcock, D. & Costello, D. (1998). The Determination of IC engine inlet port geometries by Reverse Engineering, *International Journal of Advanced Manufacturing Technology,* Vol.14, pp. 65–69, ISSN: 0268-3768

Chen, L.C. & Lin G.C.I. (2000). Reverse engineering in the design of turbine blades: a case study in applying the MAMDP, *Robotics and Computer Integrated Manufacturing*, Vol.16, pp. 161-167, ISSN: 0736-5845

Dan, J. & Lancheng, W. (2006). Direct generation of die surfaces from measured data points based on springback compensation, *International Journal of Advanced Manufacturing Technology*, Vol.31, pp. 574–579, ISSN: 0268-3768

Dimitrellou S.; Kaisarlis J. G.; Diplaris C. S. & Sfantsikopoulos M. M. (2009). A Cost Optimal Tolerance Synthesis Methodology for Design and Manufacturing Integration, *Proceedings of 11th CIRP Conference on Computer Aided Tolerancing*, Annecy, France March 26 – 27, 2009

Dimitrellou, S.; Diplaris, S.C. & Sfantsikopoulos, M.M. (2007b). A Systematic Approach for Cost Optimal Tolerance Design, *Proceedings of the International Conference On Engineering Design - ICED'07*, IBSN: 1-904670-02-4, Paris, France, August 28 – 31, 2007

Dimitrellou, S.; Diplaris, S.C. & Sfantsikopoulos, M.M. (2007a). Cost-competent Tolerancing in CAD, *International Journal of Advanced Manufacturing Technology*, Vol. 35, Nos. 5-6, pp. 519-526, ISSN: 0268-3768

Dimitrellou, S.; Diplaris, S.C. & Sfantsikopoulos, M.M. (2008). Tolerance Elements. An Alternative Approach for Cost Optimum Tolerance Transfer, *Journal of Engineering Design, Special Issue: Cost Engineering*, Vol. 19, No. 2, pp. 173-184, ISSN: 0954-4828

Dimitrellou, S.; Kaisarlis, G.J.; Diplaris, S.C. & Sfantsikopoulos, M.M. (2007c). A systematic approach for functional and cost optimal dimensional tolerancing in reverse engineering, *Proceedings of XVII Metrology and Metrology Assurance (MMA 2007) Conference*, ISBN: 9789543340613, pp. 193 – 197, Sozopol, Bulgaria, September 10 - 14, 2007

Diplaris, S. & Sfantsikopoulos, M.M. (2006). Maximum material condition in process planning, *Production Planning & Control*, Vol. 17, No. 3, pp. 293-300, ISSN: 0953-7287

Drake, P.J. (1999). *Dimensioning and Tolerancing Handbook*, ISBN 0-07-018131-4, McGraw – Hill, New York, USA

Endo, M. (2005). Reverse Engineering and CAE, *JSME International Journal, Series:C*, Vol.48, No. 2, pp. 218-223

Fischer, B.R. (2004). *Mechanical Tolerance Stackup and Analysis*. Marcel Dekker, ISBN: 0824753798, New York, USA

Flack, D. (2001). *CMM Measurement Strategies NPL Measurement Good Practice Guide No. 41*. NPL - Crown, ISSN 1368-6550, Teddington, UK.

Ingle, K.A. (1994). *Reverse engineering*, McGraw Hill, New York, USA.

ISO Standard, (2004). *ISO-1101: Geometrical Product Specifications (GPS) - Geometrical tolerancing - Tolerances of form, orientation, location and run-out*, The International Organization for Standardization, Geneva, Switzerland

ISO Standard, (1998). *ISO 5458: Geometrical Product Specifications (GPS) - Geometrical Tolerance - Position Tolerancing*, The International Organization for Standardization, Geneva, Switzerland

ISO Standard, (1988). *ISO 2692: Technical drawings - geometrical tolerancing - maximum material principle*, The International Organization for Standardization, Geneva, Switzerland

Kaisarlis, G.J.; Diplaris, S.C. & Sfantsikopoulos, M.M. (2000). A Knowledge-Based System for Tolerance Allocation in Reverse Engineering, *Proceedings of 33rd MATADOR Conference*, D.R. Hayhurst (Ed), pp. 527 - 532, Manchester, UK, July 13-14, 2000, Springer Verlag, IBSN: 1852333235, London, UK

Kaisarlis, G.J.; Diplaris, S.C. & Sfantsikopoulos, M.M. (2004). Datum Identification in Reverse Engineering, *Proceedings of IFAC Conference on Manufacturing, Modelling, Management and Control*, G. Chryssolouris, D. Mourtzis (Ed), pp. 179 – 183, Athens, Greece, October 21-22, 2004, Elsevier Science Ltd, , ISBN: 0080445624, Amsterdam, The Netherlands

Kaisarlis, G.J.; Diplaris, S.C. & Sfantsikopoulos, M.M. (2007). Position Tolerancing in Reverse Engineering: The Fixed Fastener Case, *Journal of Engineering Manufacture, Proceedings of the Institution of Mechanical Engineers, Part B,* Vol. 221, pp. 457 - 465, ISSN: 0954-4054

Kaisarlis, G.J.; Diplaris, S.C. & Sfantsikopoulos, M.M. (2008). Geometrical position tolerance assignment in reverse engineering, *International Journal of Computer Integrated Manufacturing*, Vol. 21, No 1, pp. 89 - 96, ISSN: 0951-192X

Martin, P.; Dantan, J.Y. & D'Acunto, A. (2011). Virtual manufacturing: prediction of work piece geometric quality by considering machine and set-up accuracy, *International Journal of Computer Integrated Manufacturing,* Vol.24, No. 7, pp. 610-626, ISSN: 0951-192X

Mavromihales, M.; Mason, J. & Weston, W. (2003). A case of Reverse Engineering for the manufacture of wide chord fan blades (WCFB) in Rolls Royce aero engines, *Journal of Materials Processing Technology*, Vol.134, pp. 279-286, ISSN: 0924-0136

Raja, V. & Fernandes, K. (2008). *Reverse Engineering : an industrial perspective*, Springer Series in Advanced Manufacturing, Springer-Verlag, ISBN 978-1-84628-855-5, London, UK

Singh, P.K.; Jain, P.K.; & Jain, S.C. (2009a). Important issues in tolerance design of mechanical assemblies. Part 2: Tolerance Synthesis. *Proc. IMechE, Part B: J. Engineering Manufacture,* Vol.223, pp. 1225-1247, ISSN: 0954-4054

Singh, P.K.; Jain, P.K.; & Jain, S.C. (2009b). Important issues in tolerance design of mechanical assemblies. Part 2: Tolerance Analysis. *Proc. IMechE, Part B: J. Engineering Manufacture*, Vol.223, pp. 1249-1287, ISSN: 0954-4054

Thompson, W.B.; Owen, J.C.; de St. Germain, H.J.; Stark Jr, S.R. & Henderson, T.C. (1999). Feature based reverse engineering of mechanical parts, *IEEE Transactions on Robotics and Automation*, Vol.15, pp. 56-66, ISSN: 1042-296X

Várady, T.; Martin, R. & Cox, J. (1997). Reverse engineering of geometric models—an introduction, *Computer-Aided Design*, Vol. 29, No 4, pp. 255-268, ISSN: 0010-4485

VPERI. (2003). *Army research office virtual parts engineering research initiative,* 20.09.2011, Available from: <http://www.cs.utah.edu/gdc/Viper/Collaborations/VPERI-Final-Report.pdf>

Wego, W. (2011). *Reverse engineering: Technology of Reinvention,* CRC Press - Taylor & Francis, ISBN 978-1-4398-0631-9, Florida, USA

Yau, H.T. (1997). Reverse engineering of engine intake ports by digitization and surface approximation, *Int. Journal of Machine Tools & Manufacturing*, Vol.37, No. 6, pp. 855-871, ISSN: 0890-6955

Yuan, X.; Zhenrong, X. & Haibin, W. (2001). Research on integrated RE technology for forming sheet metal with a free form surface, *Journal of Materials Processing Technology*, Vol.112, pp. 153–156, ISSN: 0924-0136

Zhang, W. (2003) Research into the engineering application of Reverse Engineering technology, *Journal of Materials Processing Technology*, Vol. 139, pp. 472-475, ISSN: 0924-0136

Zheng, J.; Li, Z. & Chen, X. (2004). Broken area modeling for repair automation, *Journal of Advanced Manufacturing Systems*, Vol. 3, No. 2, pp. 129-140, ISSN: 0219-6867

8

A Review on Shape Engineering and Design Parameterization in Reverse Engineering

Kuang-Hua Chang
The University of Oklahoma
Norman, OK
USA

1. Introduction

3D scanning technology has made enormous progress in the past 25 years (Blais, 2004); especially, the non-contact optical surface digitizers. These scanners or digitizers become more portable, affordable; and yet capturing points faster and more accurately. A hand-held laser scanner captures tens of thousands points per second with a level of accuracy around 40 μm, and can cost as low as fifty thousand dollars, such as *ZScanner 800* (ZCorp). Such technical advancement makes the scanners become largely accepted and widely used in industry and academia for a broad range of engineering assignments. As a result, demand on geometric modeling technology and software tools that support efficiently processing large amount of data points (scattered points acquired from a 3D scanning, also called point cloud) and converting them into useful forms, such as NURB (non-uniform rational B-spline) surfaces, become increasingly higher.

Auto surfacing technology that automatically converts point clouds into NURB surface models has been developed and implemented into commercial tools, such as *Geomagic* (Geomagic), *Rapidform* (INUS Technology, Inc.), *PolyWorks* (innovMetric), *SolidWorks/Scan to 3D* (SolidWorks, Inc.), among many others. These software tools have been routinely employed to create NURB surface models with excellent accuracy, saving significant time and effort. The NURB surface models are furnished with geometric information that is sufficient to support certain types of engineering assignments in maintenance, repair, and overhaul (MRO) industry, such as part inspection and fixture calibration. The surface models support 3D modeling for bioengineering and medical applications, such as (Chang et al., 2003; Sun et al., 2002; Liu et al., 2010; Lv et al., 2009). They also support automotive industry and aerospace design (Raja & Fernades 2008). NURB surface models converted from point clouds have made tremendous contributions to wide range of engineering applications. However, these models contain only surface patches without the additional semantics and topology inherent in feature-based parametric representation. Therefore, they are not suitable for design changes, feature-based NC toolpath generations, and technical data package preparation. Part re-engineering that involves design changes also requires parametric solid models.

On the other hand, shape engineering and design parameterization aims at creating fully parametric solid models from scanned data points and exporting them into mainstream

CAD packages that support part re-engineering, feature-based NC toolpath generations, and technical data package preparation. Although, converting data points into NURB surface models has been automated, creating parametric solid models from data points cannot and will not be fully automated. This is because that, despite technical challenges in implementation, the original design intent embedded in the data points must be recovered and realized in the parametric solid model. Modeling decisions have to be made by the designer in order to recover the original design intents. However, designers must be relieved from dealing with tedious point data manipulations and primitive geometric entity constructions. Therefore, the ideal scenario is having software tools that take care of labor intensive tasks, such as managing point cloud, triangulation, etc., in an automated fashion; and offer adequate capabilities to allow designers to interactively recover design intents. Such an ideal scenario has been investigated for many years. After these many years, what can be done with the technology and tools developed at this point? Many technical articles already address auto surfacing. In this chapter, in addition to auto surfacing, we will focus on solid modeling and design parameterization.

We will present a brief review and technical advancement in 3D shape engineering and design parameterization for reverse engineering, in which discrete point clouds are converted into feature-based parametric solid models. Numerous efforts have been devoted to developing technology that automatically creates NURB surface models from point clouds. Only very recently, the development was extended to support parametric solid modeling that allows significant expansion on the scope of engineering assignments. In this chapter, underlying technology that enables such advancement in 3D shape engineering and design parameterization is presented. Major commercial software that offers such capabilities is evaluated using practical examples. Observations are presented to conclude this study. Next, we will present a more precise discussion on design parameterization to set the tone for later discussion in this chapter.

2. Design parameterization

One of the common approaches for searching for design alternatives is to vary the part size or shape of the mechanical system. In order to vary part size or shape for exploring better design alternatives, the parts and assembly must be adequately parameterized to capture design intents.

At the parts level, design parameterization implies creating solid features and relating dimensions so that when a dimension value is changed the part can be rebuilt properly and the rebuilt part revealed design intents. At the assembly level, design parameterization involves defining assembly mates and relating dimensions across parts. When an assembly is fully parameterized, a change in dimension value can be automatically propagated to all parts affected. Parts affected must be rebuilt successfully; and at the same time, they will have to maintain proper position and orientation with respect to one another without violating any assembly mates or revealing part penetration or excessive gaps. For example, in a single-piston engine shown in Fig. 1 (Silva & Chang, 2002), a change in the bore diameter of the engine case will alter not only the geometry of the case itself, but also all other parts affected, such as piston, piston sleeve, and even crankshaft. Moreover, they all have to be rebuilt properly and the entire assembly must stay intact through assembly mates, and faithfully reveal design intents.

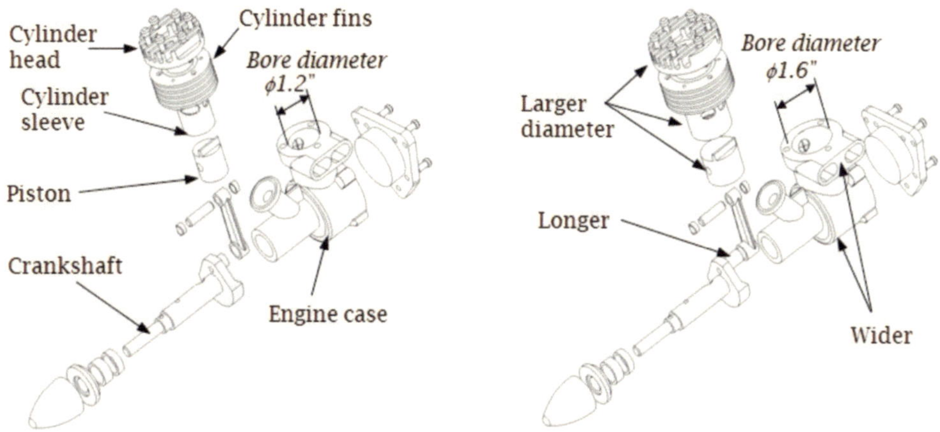

Fig. 1. A single-piston engine—exploded view, (a) bore diameter 1.2", and (b) bore diameter 1.6"

3. Shape engineering

The overall process of shape engineering and parametric solid modeling is shown in Fig. 2, in which four main phases are involved. They are (1) triangulation that converts data points to a polygon mesh, (2) mesh segmentation that separates a polygon mesh into regions based on the characteristics of the surface geometry they respectively represent, (3) solid modeling that converts segmented regions into parametric solid models, and (4) model translation that exports solid models constructed to mainstream CAD systems. Note that it is desired to have the entire process fully automated; except for Phase 3. This is because that, as stated earlier, Phase 3 requires designer's interaction mainly to recover original design intents. These four phases are briefly discussed in the following subsections.

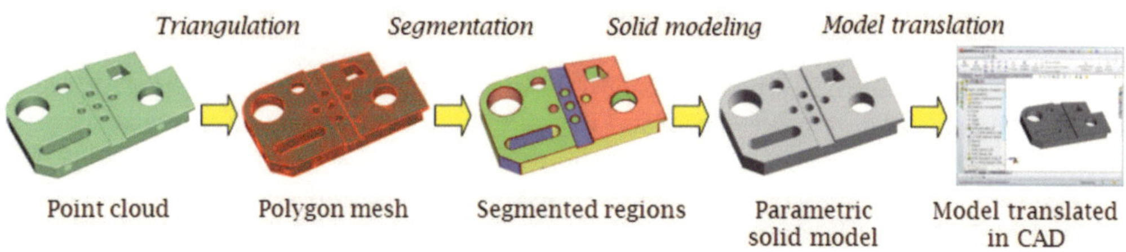

Fig. 2. General process of shape engineering and parametric solid model construction

3.1 Triangulation

The mathematic theory and computational algorithms for triangulation have been well developed in the past few decades. A polygon mesh can be automatically and efficiently created for a given set of data points. The fundamental concept in triangulation is Delaunay triangulation. In addition to Delaunay triangulation, there are several well-known mathematic algorithms for triangulation, including marching cubes (Lorensen et al., 1987), alpha shapes (Edelsbrunner et al., 1983), ball pivoting algorithm (BPA) (Bernardini et al., 1999), Poisson surface reconstruction (Kazhdan et al., 2006), moving least squares (Cuccuru et al., 2009), etc. A few high profile projects yield very good results, such as sections of Michelangelo's Florentine

Pietà composed of 14M triangle mesh generated from more than 700 scans (Bernardini et al., 1999), reconstruction of "Pisa Cathedral" (Pisa, Italy) from laser scans with over 154M samples (Cuccuru et al., 2009), and head and cerebral structures (hidden) extracted from 150 MRI slices using the marching cubes algorithm (about 150,000 triangles), as shown in Fig. 3.

Fig. 3. Sample projects of scanning and triangulation, (a) Michelangelo's Florentine Pietà, (b) Pisa Cathedral, and (c) head and cerebral structures

Although many triangulation algorithms exist, they are not all fool-proof. They tend to generate meshes with a high triangle count. In addition, these algorithms implicitly assume topology of the shape to be reconstructed from triangulation, and the parameter settings often influences results and stability. A few mesh postprocessing algorithms, such as decimation (for examples, Schroeder, 1997; Hoppe et al., 1993), and mesh smoothness (e.g., Hansen et al., 2005; Li et al., 2009), are worthwhile mentioning for interested readers.

3.2 Segmentation

One of the most important steps in shape engineering is mesh segmentation. Segmentation groups the original data points or mesh into subsets each of which logically belongs to a single primitive surface.

In general, segmentation is a complex process. Often iterative region growing techniques are applied (Besl & Jain, 1988; Alrashdan et al., 2000; Huang & Meng, 2001). Some use non-iterative methods, called direct segmentation (Várady et al., 1998), that are more efficient. In general, the segmentation process, such as (Vanco & Brunnett, 2004) involves a fast algorithm for *k*-nearest neighbors search and an estimate of first- and second-order surface properties. The first-order segmentation, which is based on normal vectors, provides an initial subdivision of the surface and detects sharp edges as well as flat or highly curved areas. The second-order segmentation subdivides the surface according to principal curvatures and provides a sufficient foundation for the classification of simple algebraic surfaces. The result of the mesh segmentation is subject to several important parameters, such as the *k* value (number of neighboring points chosen for estimating surface properties), and prescribed differences in the normal vectors and curvatures (also called sensitivity thresholds) that group the data points or mesh. As an example shown in Fig. 4a, a high sensitive threshold leads to scattered regions of small sizes, and a lower sensitive threshold tends to generate segmented regions that closely resemble the topology of the object, as illustrated in Fig. 4b.

Most of the segmentation algorithms come with surface fitting, which fits a best primitive surface of appropriate type to each segmented region. It is important to specify a hierarchy of surface types in the order of geometric complexity, similar to that of Fig. 5 (Várady et al., 1997). In general, objects are bounded by relatively large primary (or functional) surfaces.

The primary surfaces may meet each other along sharp edges or there may be secondary or blending surfaces which may provide smooth transitions between them.

Fig. 4. Example of mesh segmentation, (a) an object segmented into many small regions due to a high sensitivity threshold, and (b) regions determined with a low sensitivity threshold

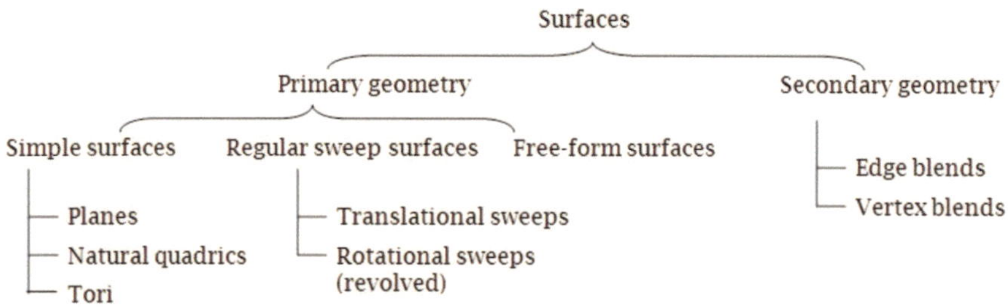

Fig. 5. A hierarchy of surfaces

As discussed above, feature-based segmentation provides a sufficient foundation for the classification of simple algebraic surfaces. Algebraic surfaces, such as planes, natural quadrics (such as sphere, cylinders, and cones), and tori, are readily to be fitted to such regions. Several methods, including (Marshall et al., 2004), have been proposed to support such fitting, using least square fitting.

In addition to primitive algebraic surfaces, more general surfaces with a simple kinematic generation, such as sweep surfaces, revolved surfaces (rotation sweep), extrusion surfaces (translation sweep), pipe surfaces, are directly compatible to CAD models. Fitting those surfaces to segmented data points or mesh is critical to the reconstruction of surface models and support of parameterization (Lukács et al., 1998).

In some applications, not all segmented regions can be fitted with primitives or CAD-compatible surfaces within prescribed error margin. Those remaining regions are classified as freeform surfaces, where no geometric or topological regularity can be recognized. These can be a collection of patches or possibly trimmed patches. They are often fitted with NURB surfaces. Many algorithms and methods have been proposed to support NURB surface fitting, such as (Tsai et al., 2009).

3.3 Solid modeling

Solid modeling is probably the least developed in the shape engineering process in support of reverse engineering. Boundary representation (B-rep) and feature-based are the two basic representations for solid models. There have been some methods, such as (Várady et al., 1998), proposed to automatically construct B-rep models from point clouds or triangular mesh. Some focused on manufacturing feature recognition for process planning purpose, such as (Thompson, 1999). One promising development in recent years was the geometric feature recognition (*GFR*), which automatically recognizes solid features embedded in the B-rep models. However, none of the method is able to fully automate the construction process and generate fully parametric solid models. Some level of manual work is expected.

3.3.1 Boundary representation

Based on segmented regions (with fitted surfaces), a region adjacent graph is built. This graph reflects the complete topology and serves as the basis for building the final B-rep model, also called stitched models, where the individual bounded surfaces are glued together along their common edges to form an air-tight surface model.

In general, there are three steps involved in constructing B-rep models, flattening, edges and vertices calculations, and stitching (Várady et al., 1998). In flattening step, regions are extended outwards until all triangles have been classified. Note that this step is necessary to remove all gaps between regions. Sharp edges can be calculated using surface-surface intersection routines, and vertices where three surfaces meet are also determined. During the process, a complete B-rep topology tree is also constructed. A B-rep model can then be created by stitching together the faces, edges, and vertices. This operation is commonly supported by most solid modeling kernels.

3.3.2 Solid feature recognition

B-rep models are not feature-based. In order to convert a B-rep model into a feature-based solid model, the embedded solid features must be recognized, and a feature tree that describes the sequence of feature creation must be created.

One of the most successful algorithms for geometric feature recognition has been proposed by (Venkataraman et al., 2001). The algorithm uses a simple four step process, (1) simplify imported faces, (2) analyze faces for specific feature geometry, (3) remove recognized feature and update model; and (4) return to Step 2 until all features are recognized. The process is illustrated in Fig. 6. Once all possible features are recognized, they are mapped to a new solid model of the part (Fig. 6d) that is parametric with a feature tree. This feature tree defines the feature regeneration (or model rebuild) sequence.

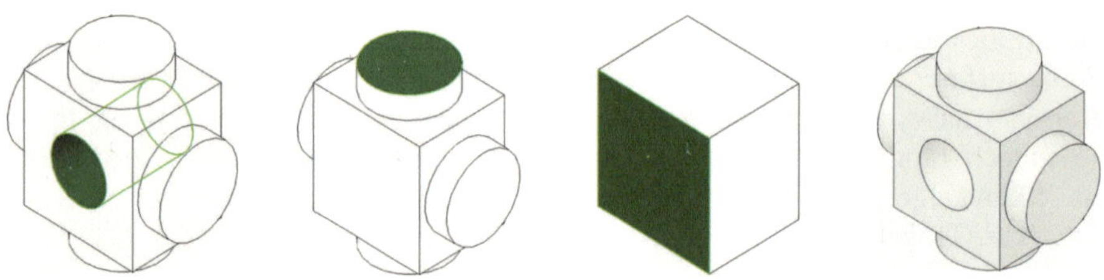

Fig. 6. Illustration of *GFR* algorithm, (a) imported surface model with hole surface selected, (b) hole recognized and removed, extruded face of cylinder selected, (c) cylindrical extrusions recognized, base block extrusion face selected, and (d) all features recognized and mapped to solid model

Venkataraman's method was recently commercialized by Geometric Software Solutions, Ltd. (GSSL), and implemented in a number of CAD packages, including *SolidWorks* and

CATIA, capable of recognizing basic features, such as extrude, revolve, and more recently, sweep. This capability has been applied primarily for support of solid model interchanges between CAD packages with some success, in which not only geometric entities (as has been done by IGES—Initial Graphics Exchange Standards) but also parametric features are translated.

One of the major issues revealed in commercial *GFR* software is design intent recovery. For example, the flange of an airplane tubing would be recognized as a single revolve feature, where a profile sketch is revolved about an axis (Fig. 7a). However, current *GFR* implementations are not flexible. As shown in Fig. 7b, without adequate user interaction, the single sketch flange may be recognized as four or more separate features. While the final solid parts are physically the same, their defining parameters are not. Such a batch mode implementation may not be desirable in recovering meaningful design intents.

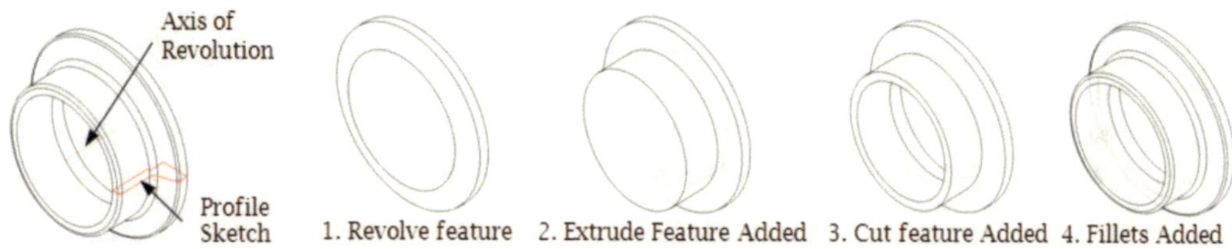

Fig. 7. Feature recognition for airplane tubing flange, (a) single revolved feature, and (b) four features: revolve, extrude, cut, and fillet

3.3.3 Design parameterization

A feature-based parametric solid model consists of two key elements: a feature tree, and fully parameterized sketches employed for protruding solid features. A fully parameterized sketch implies that the sketch profile is fully constrained and dimensioned, so that a change in dimension value yields a rebuilt in accordance with design intents as anticipated. To the author's knowledge, there is no such method proposed or offered that fully automates the process. Some capabilities are offered by commercial tools, such as *Rapidform*, that support designers to interactively create fully parameterized sketches, which accurately conform to the data points and greatly facilitates the solid modeling effort.

3.4 Solid model export

Since most of the promising shape engineering capabilities are not offered in CAD packages (more details in the next section), the solid models constructed in reverse engineering software will have to be exported to mainstream CAD packages in order to support common engineering assignments. The conventional solid model exchanges via standards, such IGES or STEP AP (application protocols), are inadequate since parametric information, including solid features, feature tree, sketch constraints and dimensions, are completely lost through the exchanges. Although feature recognition capability offers some relief in recognizing geometric features embedded in B-rep models, it is still an additional step that is often labor intensive. Direct solid model export has been offered in some software, such as *liveTransfer*™ module of *Rapidform XOR3* as well as third party software, such as *TransMagic*. More will be discussed for *liveTransfer*™.

4. Engineering software evaluations

The key criteria for the software evaluations are the capabilities of supporting automatic surface construction from point clouds and parametric solid modeling. We did the first screening on nine leading software tools that are commercially available. This screening was carried out based on the information provided in product brochure, technical reports (for example, Siddique, 2002; Chang et al., 2006), thesis (for examle, Gibson, 2004), company web sites, on-line software demo, case study reports, etc. After the screening, we acquired four tools and conducted hands-on evaluations, using five industrial examples. With this, we are able to identify pros and cons in each software tool, make a few observations, and conclude the study.

4.1 Software screening

After extensive research and development in the past decade, software tools for reverse engineering have made impressive advancement. In general, these tools can be categorized into two groups, feature-based and RE-based. The feature-based CAD packages, such as *Pro/ENGINEER*, *SolidWorks*, and *CATIA*, emphasize recovering the original design intents of the parts. Following standard CAD capabilities, such as sketching, extrusion, and Boolean operations, designers are able to create parts with design intents recovered. On the contrary, RE-based packages; such as *Geomagic*, *Rapidform*, and *Paraform*, focus on reconstructing the geometry of the objects from scanned data, usually in the form of NURB surfaces. RE-based packages offer excellent capabilities in editing points, creating meshes, and generating NURB surfaces. In addition, the display performance of mass data offered by the RE-based package is far better than the feature-based CAD software; that is, in the context of reverse engineering.

In this study, we looked for two key engineering capabilities; i.e., surface construction and parametric solid modeling from a point cloud or a polygon mesh. All feature-based and RE-based software tools offer some capabilities for surface constructions. However, manually constructing curves and surfaces from point clouds or polygon meshes are tedious and extremely time consuming. It is critical that a serious RE software must offer auto surfacing; i.e., allowing for creating air-tight, high accuracy, and high quality surface models with only a few button clicks. On the other hand, constructing solid models has to be carried out in an interactive manner, allowing designers to recover original design intents. Software must offer adequate capabilities to assist designers to sketch section profiles and create solid features efficiently, without directly dealing with point clouds or polygon meshes. Certainly, the software will have to be stable and capable of handling massive data. Millions of point data need huge computer resources to process. Zoom, pan or rotate the object, for example, on the screen may take time for software to respond. Speed is the key for modern RE-based software. We are essentially searching for software that offers auto surfacing and parametric modeling capabilities with fast and stable performance.

In addition, several software related criteria are defined, as listed in Table 1. These criteria are categorized into four groups, (1) general capabilities, such as speed; (2) generation of NURB models, including auto surfacing and geometric entity editing capabilities; (3) generation of solid models, including section profiling and parametric capabilities; and (4) usability.

From Table 1, we observe that most surveyed software offers basic capabilities for editing and manipulating points, polygon meshes and NURB curves and surfaces. Particularly, we found both *Geomagic* and *Rapidform* support auto surfacing. Solid modeling using scanned data can be commonly achieved by creating section sketches from polygon meshes and following feature creating steps similar to CAD packages. Based on the survey, *Rapidform* is found the only software that supports parametric solid modeling. For hands-on evaluations, we selected *Geomagic* and *Rapidform,* in addition to a few CAD packages.

G=good, F=fair, P=poor, U=unknown, N=Not available	Geomagic Studio	Rapidform XOR3	SolidWorks	Wildfire	CATIA	Paraform	ICEM	Imageware	CopyCAD
General capabilities:									
Speed: How quickly can surface fitting be done?	G	G	P	P	F	G	F	G	G
Data/file size that the software can process	G	G	P	P	G	G	G	G	G
Screen refresh resolution	G	G	P	P	G	G	G	G	G
Output file format: transferred to other software	G	G	G	G	G	G	G	G	G
Recognition of geometry types (such as circles)	G	G	P	N	F	P	G	G	F
Generation of NURB models									
Auto Surfacing	G	G	P	N	N	N	N	N	N
Modification of points	G	G	P	P	G	G	G	G	G
Hole filling	G	G	G	P	G	G	G	G	G
Modification of spline curves	G	G	P	P	G	G	G	G	G
NURB surfaces deviation analysis	G	G	G	G	G	G	G	G	G
How complicated shapes can be generated?	G	G	F	P	G	G	G	G	G
Surface smoothness	G	G	F	F	G	G	G	G	G
Generation of solid models									
Parametric: Can parametric solid models be generated?	P	G	F	P	F	N	P	F	U
Section sketch	F	G	P	N	P	N	P	G	U
Dimensions and geometric constraints on sketch	P	F	P	N	U	N	U	U	U
Level of human interaction with the geometry required	F	G	P	P	P	N	U	F	U
Is the generated solid model easy to modify?	P	G	P	P	P	N	U	F	U
Parametric model export	P	G	P	P	P	N	U	U	U

Table 1. A summary of commercial software tools surveyed

4.2 Examples for hands-on evaluations

For hands-on evaluations, we carried out two rounds of study; round 1 focuses on auto surfacing, and round 2 is for parametric solid modeling. After surveying most advanced software as discussed in Section 4.1, we selected four candidate software tools for hands-on evaluations. They are RE-based software *Geomagic Studio v.11* and *Rapidform XOR3*; and feature-based CAD software *Pro/ENGINEER Wildfire v.4* and *SolidWorks 2009*. As shown in Table 2, all tools support surface and solid model construction, except for *Wildfire*, which does not support parametric solid modeling using scanned data.

	Surface Reconstruction	Parametric Modeling
Geomagic Studio v. 11	Shape Phase	Fashion Phase
Rapidform XOR3	Auto Surfacing	Solid/ Surface Primitives
SolidWorks 2009	Scan to 3D	Scan to 3D
Wildfire v. 4	Facet + Restyle	Not Available

Table 2. Software selected for hands-on evaluations

For round 1 evaluations, we focus on auto surfacing and the software stability. In round 2, we focus on parametric solid modeling, we look for primitive feature recognition (such as cylinder, cone, etc.), parametric modeling, and model exporting to CAD packages.

We selected five examples for hands-on evaluation, as listed in Table 3. Among the five examples, two are given as polygon meshes and the other three are point clouds. These five parts represent a broad range of applications. Parts like the *block*, *tubing*, and *door lock* are more traditional mechanical parts with regular solid features. In contrast, *sheetmetal* part (Model 3) is a formed part with large curvature, and the *blade* is basically a free-form object.

	Model 1 *Block*	Model 2 *Tubing*	Model 3 *Sheetmetal*	Model 4 *Blade*	Model 5 *Door Lock*
Model Pictures					
Scanned data	634,957 points	589,693 polygons	134,089 polygons	252,895 points	207,282 points
Dimensions	5×3×0.5 (inch)	125×93×17 (mm)	16×10×9 (inch)	2×3×4 (inch)	7×3×2 (inch)

Table 3. Examples selected for hands-on evaluations

4.3 Round 1: Auto surfacing

In round 1 evaluation, we are interested in investigating if software tools evaluated are able to support auto surfacing; i.e., automatically constructing air-tight, accurate, and high quality surface models from scanned data. We look for the level of automation, software stability, and capabilities for editing geometric entities (such as points, meshes, and NURB patches).

Based on the evaluations, we found that all software tools evaluated are able to support surface modeling either fully automatically or close to fully automation. Table 4 summarizes the test results. The results show that *Geomagic* is the only software that is able to create surface models for all five examples automatically, without any user interventions. *Rapidform* comes close second. *Rapidform* is able to construct surface models for two out of the five examples fully automatically. For the remaining three examples, only minor interventions or editing from the user are required. However, *SolidWorks* and *Wildfire* are able to support only some of the examples even after spending long hours. It took extremely long time using *SolidWorks* or *Wildfire* to process some of the examples, and yet without achieving meaningful results. Software crashed without giving warning message while conducting triangulation or surface fitting. The size of the scanned data also presents problems for *SolidWorks* and *Wildfire*. They are able to support only up to about 300,000 data points. The software becomes unstable or even crashes while handling more data points.

	Model 1 *Block*	Model 2 *Tubing*	Model 3 *Sheetmetal*	Model 4 *Blade*	Model 5 *Door Lock*
Geomagic Studio v.11	Completed (Automated) 	Completed (Automated) 	Completed (Automated) 	Completed (Automated) 	Completed (Automated) 
Rapidform XOR3	Completed (Automated) 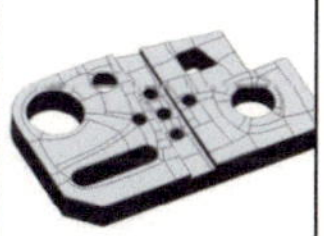	Completed (Partial-auto) 	Completed (Partial-auto) 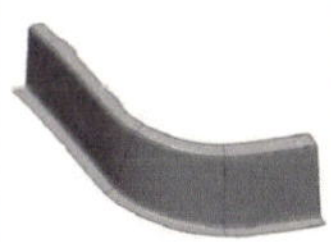	Completed (Partial-auto) 	Completed (Automated) 
SolidWorks 2009	Fail (Gaps remained, shown in red) 	Software crashed	Fail (Gaps remained, shown in red) 	Completed (Automated) 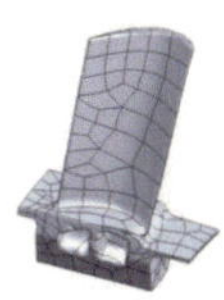	Software crashed
Wildfire v.4	Software Crashed	Software crashed	Completed (Automated) 	Completed (Automated) 	Software crashed

Table 4. Results of Round 1 evaluations

One important finding worth noting is that the mesh segmentation capability is only available in *Geomagic* and *Rapidform*. This capability allows users to adjust a sensitivity index to vary the size of segmented regions so that the regions match closely to the distinct surfaces of the object. Such segmentation is critical since the properly segmented regions facilitate surface fitting and primitive feature recognition.

Based on the findings, we exclude further discussion on *SolidWorks* and *Wildfire* due to their poor performance in the first evaluation round. In the following we discuss results of *Geomagic* and *Rapidform* for selected examples to consolidate our conclusions.

4.3.1 *Geomagic Studio v.11*

Geomagic demonstrates an excellent surface construction capability with a high level of automation. Based on our evaluations, excellent NURB surface models can be created for all five examples from their respective scanned data in less than 30 minutes. In addition, *Geomagic* offers interactive capabilities that allow users to manually edit or create geometric entities. For examples, *Point Phase* of *Geomagic* supports users to edit points, reduce data noise, and adjust sampling to reduce number of point data. After point editing operations, polygon meshes are created by using *Wrap*. In *Mesh Phase*, self-intersecting, highly creased edges (edge with sharp angle between the normal vectors of the two neighboring polygonal faces), spikes and small clusters of polygons (a group of small isolated polygon meshes) can be detected and repaired automatically by *Mesh Doctor*. Mesh editing tools; such as smooth polygon mesh, define sharp edges, defeature and fill holes; are also provided to support users to create quality polygon meshes conveniently. Once a quality mesh is generated, *Shape Phase* is employed to create NURB surfaces best fit to the polygon mesh.

Auto Surface consists of a set of steps that automatically construct surface models. The steps include *Detect Contour*, *Construct Patches*, *Construct Grids* and *Fit Surfaces*. Before using *Auto Surface*, users only have to consider the quality of the surface model (for example, specifying required tolerance) and the method (for example, with or without mesh segmentation). For the *block* example, we set *surface tolerance* to 0.01 inch and construct NURB surface model with *Detect Contours* option (which performs mesh segmentation) using *Auto Surface*. A complete NURB surface model was created in 5 minutes (Fig. 8). Average deviation of the NURB model is 0.0 inch and the standard deviation is 0.0003 inch. The deviation is defined as the shortest distance (a signed distance) between the polygon mesh and the NURB surfaces. Note that in Figure 8d, green area indicates deviation close to 0 and red spot indicates the max deviation, which is about 0.017 inch in this case.

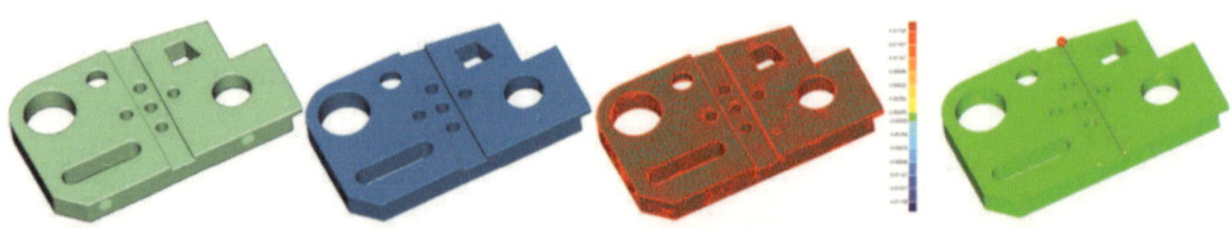

Fig. 8. Results of the *block* example tested using *Geomagic*, (a) point cloud model (634,957 points), (b) polygon mesh (1,271,924 triangles), (c) NURB surface model, and (d) deviation analysis

Two more examples, *tubing* and *sheetmetal*, are processed following the same steps. Results are shown in Figs. 9 and 10, respectively. These examples demonstrate that *Auto surface* of *Geomagic* offers reliable, viable and extremely efficient capability for automated surface reconstruction.

Fig. 9. Results of the *tubing* example tested using *Geomagic*, (a) polygon mesh (589,693 triangles), (b) NURB model (1,107 patches), and (c) deviation analysis

Fig. 10. Results of the sheet metal example tested using *Geomagic*, (a) polygon mesh (126,492 triangles), (b) NURB model (91 patches), and (c) deviation analysis

4.3.2 *Rapidform XOR3*

Like *Geomagic*, *Rapidform* offers excellent capabilities for point data editing and polygon mesh generation, including data sampling, noise reduction, wrap, mesh repair, defeature, and fill holes. *Auto Surfacing* for NURB surface construction in *Rapidform* contains two methods, (1) *Feature Following Network* (with mesh segmentation), and (2) *Evenly Distribution Network* (without mesh segmentation).

Feature Following Network is a very good option for surface reconstruction in *XOR3*. Segmentation was introduced into *Auto Surfacing* to overcome problems of surface transition across sharp edges, especially dealing with mechanical parts with regular features. Using *Feature Following Network* sharp edges can be detected and retained in the surface model. *Feature Following Network* is usually more successful in surface construction. For example, in Fig. 11a, several gaps (circled in red) are found in the *block* example, mostly along narrow and high curvature transition regions, while using *Evenly Distribution Network* option for constructing surfaces. Using *Feature Following Network* option the surface model constructed is air-tight with sharp edges well preserved, as shown in Fig. 11b. Note that large size NURB surfaces (therefore, less number of NURB surfaces) shown in Fig. 11b tend to be created due to incorporation of mesh segmentation.

The NURB surface model of the *block* example (Fig. 12a) was successfully created using *Feature Following Network* option in just about 5 minutes (Fig. 12b). The accuracy measures; i.e., the deviation between the surface model and the polygon mesh, are 0.00 inch and 0.0006 inch in average and standard deviation, respectively, as shown in Fig. 12c.

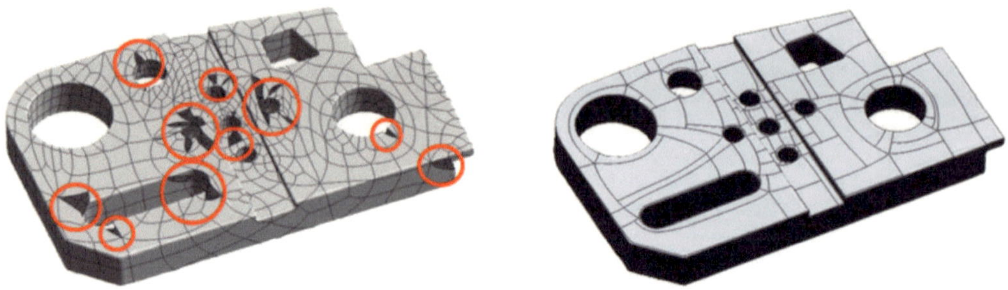

Fig. 11. NURB surface models generated using two different options in *Rapidform*, (a) *Evenly Distribution Network* option , and (b) *Feature Following Network* option

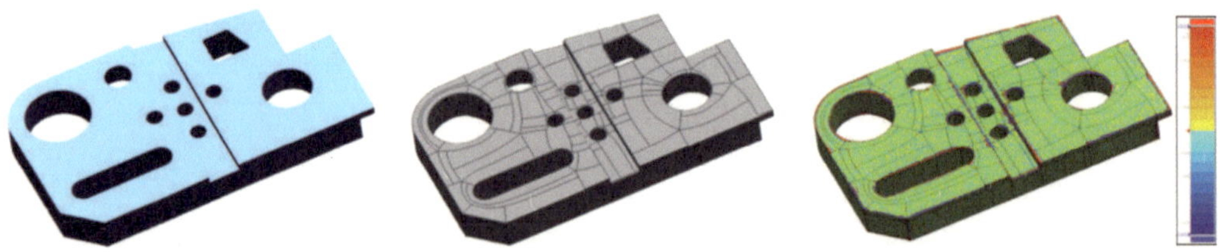

Fig. 12. Results of the *block* example tested using *Rapidform*, (a) polygon mesh (1,062,236 triangles), (b) NURB surface model (273 patches), and (c) deviation analysis

While evaluating *Rapidform* for surface construction, some issues were encountered and worth noting. First, as discussed earlier, *Rapidform* tends to create large size NURB patches that sometimes leave unfilled gaps in the surface model, especially in a long narrow region of high curvature. This happened even with *Feature Following Network* option. As shown in Fig. 13, almost half of the small branch of the *tubing* is missing after auto surfacing with *Feature Following Network* option. When such a problem appears, *Rapidform* highlights boundary curves of the gaps that are not able to be filled. In general, users can choose to reduce the gap size, for example, by adding NURB curves to split the narrow regions, until NURB patches of adequate size can be created to fill the gaps with required accuracy.

For the *tubing* example, the repair process took about 45 minutes to finish. The final surface model was created with some manual work. The average and standard deviation between the surface model and the polygon mesh are -0.0003 mm and 0.0189 mm, respectively, as shown in Fig. 14.

The sheet metal example shown in Fig. 15 also presents minor issues with *Rapidform*. The boundary edge of the part is not smooth, as common to all scanned data. *Rapidform* created a NURB curve along the boundary, and then another smoother curve very close to the boundary edge. As a result, a very long and narrow region was created between these two curves, which present problems in auto surfacing. Similar steps as to the *tubing* example were taken to split the narrow region by adding NURB curves. The final model was split in four main regions and several smaller regions shown in Fig. 16, which allows NURB surfaces to be generated with excellent accuracy (average: 0.0 in, standard deviation: 0.0002 in).

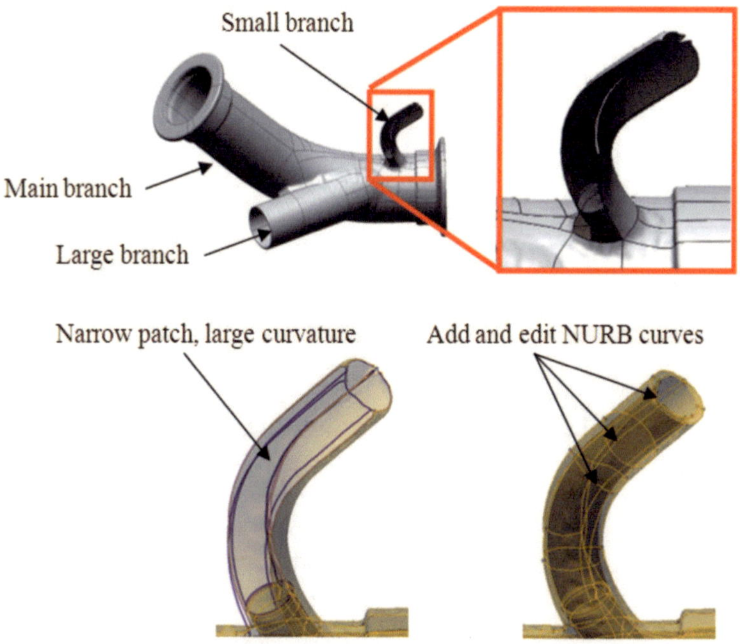

Fig. 13. Incomplete NURB surface model created by *Rapidform*

Fig. 14. Results of the *tubing* example tested using *Rapidform*, (a) polygon mesh (589,693 triangles), (b) NURB surface model (185 patches), and (c) deviation analysis

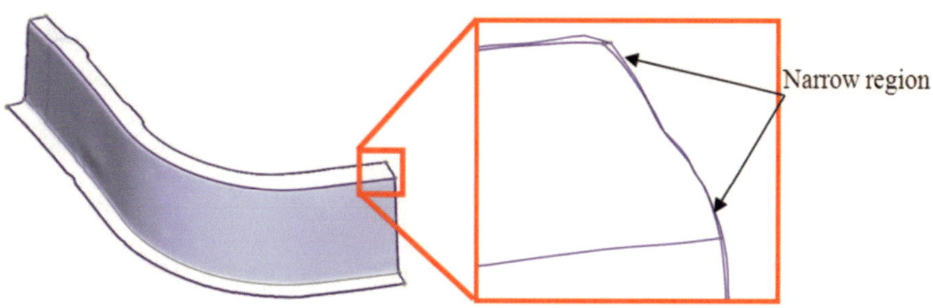

Fig. 15. Narrow regions failed for auto surfacing using *Rapidform*

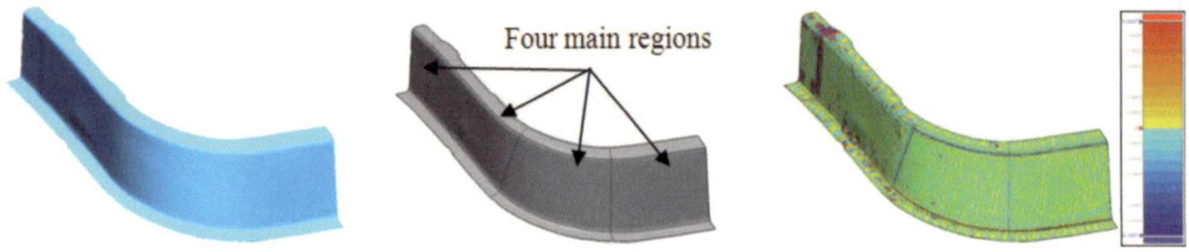

Fig. 16. Results of the sheet metal example tested using *Rapidform*, (a) polygon mesh (126,492 triangles), (b) NURB surface model (43 patches), and (c) deviation analysis

4.3.3 *Summary of round one evaluations*

Based on the software evaluated and examples tested, we concluded that *Geomagic* and *Rapidform* are the only viable software tools for automated surface constructions. Between these two, *Geomagic* offers more flexible and easier to use capabilities in editing NURB curves and surfaces, as well as smoothing NURB surfaces. On the other hand, *Rapidform* offers more quality measurement functions, such as continuity and surface reflection, on the constructed surface model. In addition, *Rapidform* provides feature tree that allows users to roll back and edit geometric entities created previously, which is extremely helpful in dealing with complex models. However, *Rapidform* tends to create larger NURB surfaces that could sometimes lead to problems. Overall, either tool would do a very good job for surface constructions; *Geomagic* has a slight edge in support of editing geometric entities.

4.4 Round 2: Parametric solid modeling

Although NURB surface models represent the part geometry accurately, they are not parametric. There are no CAD-like geometric features, no section profiles, and no dimensions; therefore, design change is impractical with the NURB surface models. In some applications, geometry of the parts must be modified in order to achieve better product performance, among other possible scenarios.

In round 2, we focus on evaluating parametric modeling capabilities in four software tools, including *Geomagic*, *Rapidform*, *SolidWorks*, and *Wildfire*. More specifically, we are looking for answers to the following three questions:

1. Can geometric primitives, such as cones, spheres, etc., be automatically recognized from segmented regions? How many such primitives can be recognized?
2. Whether a section sketch of a geometric feature can be created from a polygon mesh or point cloud (or segmented regions)? This is mainly for generating solid models interactively.
3. Whether a section sketch generated in (2) can be fully parameterized? Can dimensions and geometric constraints, such as concentric, equal radii, etc., be added to the section profile conveniently?

Solid modeling capabilities in the context of reverse engineering for the four selected software are listed in Table 5, based on the first glance. Among these four, *Geomagic*, *Rapidform*, and *SolidWorks* are able to recognize basic primitives, such as plane, cylinder, sphere, etc., from segmented regions. *Wildfire* dose not offer any of the modeling capabilities we are looking for; therefore, is excluded from the evaluation. Although some primitives can be recognized automatically, they often result in a partially recognized or misrecognized solid model. It takes a good amount of effort to interactively recover the remaining primitives or correct misrecognized primitives. Overall, it often requires less effort yet yielding a much better solid model by interactively recovering solid features embedded in the segmented regions. The interactive approach mainly involves creating or extracting section profiles or guide curves from a polygon mesh, and following CAD-like steps to create solid features, for example, sweep a section profile along a guide curve for a sweep solid feature.

	Q1: Recognition of geometric primitives	Recognized primitives	Q2: Section sketch	Q3: Adding dimensions and constraints
Geomagic Studio v.11	Yes (Solid + Surface)	Plane, Cylinder, Cone, Sphere, Free form, Extrusion, Revolve	Yes (Poor)	Yes (Poor)
Rapidform XOR3	Yes (Solid + Surface)	Plane, Cylinder, Cone, Sphere, Torus, Box	Yes (Excellent)	Yes (Fair)
SolidWorks 2009	Yes (Surface only)	Plane, Cylinder, Cone, Sphere, Torus, Free form, Extrusion, Revolve	Yes (Poor)	Yes (Poor)
Wildfire v.4	No	No	No	No

Table 5. Feature primitive recognition capabilities of selected software

Among the remaining three, *SolidWorks* is most difficult to use; especially in selecting misrecognized or unrecognized regions to manually assign a correct primitive type. The system responds very slowly and only supports surface primitive recognition. Therefore, *SolidWorks* is also excluded in this round of evaluations.

4.4.1 *Geomagic Studio v.11*

Geomagic automatically recognizes primitive surfaces from segmented regions. If a primitive surface is misrecognized or unrecognizable, users are able to interactively choose the segmented region and assign a correct primitive type. Often, this interactive approach leads to a solid model with all bounding surfaces recognized. Unfortunately, there is no feature tree, and no CAD-like capabilities in *Geomagic*. Users are not able to see any sketch or dimensions in *Geomagic Studio* v.11. Therefore, users will not be able to edit or add any dimensions or constraints to parameterize the sketch profiles. Section sketches only become available to the users after exporting the solid model to a selected CAD package supported by *Geomagic*.

The *block* example (3in.×5in.×0.5in.) of 634,957 points shown in Fig. 4 is employed to illustrate the capabilities offered in *Geomagic*. As shown in Fig. 17a, primitive surfaces in most regions are recognized correctly. However, there are some regions incorrectly recognized; for example, the hole in the middle of the *block* was recognized as a free-form primitive, instead of a cylinder. There are also regions remained unrecognized; e.g., the middle slot surface.

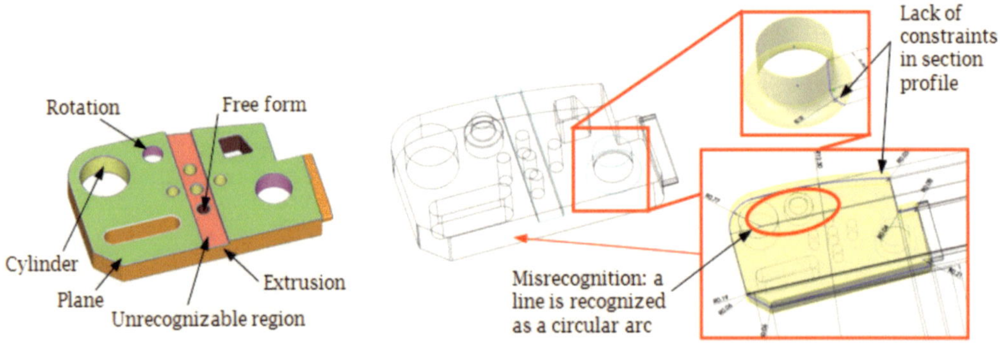

Fig. 17. Primitive surfaces recognized in *Geomagic*, (a) recognized regions, and (b) extracted primitive surfaces in *SolidWorks*

Although most primitives are recognized in *Geomagic*, there are still issues to address. One of them is misrepresented profile. One example is that a straight line in a sketch profile may be recognized as a circular arc with a very large radius, as shown in Fig. 17b (this was found only after exporting the solid model to *SolidWorks*). The sketch profile will have to be carefully inspected to make necessary corrections, as well as adding dimensions and constraints to parameterize the profile. Unfortunately, such inspections cannot be carried out unless the solid model is exported to supported CAD systems. Lack of CAD-like capability severely restricts the usability of the solid models in *Geomagic*, let alone the insufficient ability for primitive surface recognition.

4.4.2 *Rapidform XOR3*

Rapidform offers much better capabilities than *Geomagic* for parametric solid modeling. Very good CAD-like capabilities, including feature tree, are available to the users. These capabilities allow users to create solid models and make design changes directly in *Rapidform*. For example, users will be able to create a sketch profile by intersecting a plane with the polygon mesh, and extrude the sketch profile to match the bounding polygon mesh for a solid feature. On the other hand, with the feature tree users can always roll back to previous entities and edit dimensions or redefine section profiles. These capabilities make *Rapidform* particularly suitable for parametric solid modeling. *Rapidform* offers two methods for solid modeling, *Sketch*, and *Wizard*, supporting fast and easy primitive recognition from segmented mesh. The major drawback of the *Wizard* is that some guide curves and profile sketch generated are non-planar spline curves that cannot be parameterized. Users can use either or both methods to generate solid features for a single part.

Method 1: Sketch

In general, there are six steps employed in using the sketch method, (1) creating reference sketch plane, (2) extracting sketch profile by intersecting the sketch plane with the polygon mesh, (3) converting extracted geometric entities (usually as planar spline curves) into regular line entities, such as arcs and straight lines, (4) parameterizing the sketch by adding dimensions and constraints, (5) extruding, revolving, or lofting the sketches to create solid features; and (6) employing Boolean operations to union, subtract, or intersect features if necessary.

Rapidform provides *Auto Sketch* capability that automatically converts extracted spline curves into lines, circles, arcs, and rectangles, with some constraints added. Most constraints and dimensions will have to be added interactively to fully parameterize the sketch profile. Steps 4 to 6 are similar to conventional CAD operations. With capabilities offered by *Rapidform*, fully constrained parametric solid models can be created efficiently.

For the *block* example, a plane that is parallel to the top (or bottom) face of the base block was created first (by simply clicking more than three points on the surface). The plane is offset vertically to ensure a proper intersection between the sketch plane and the polygon mesh. The geometric entities obtained from the intersection are planar spline curves. The *Auto Sketch* capability of *Rapidform* can be used to extract a set of regular CAD-like line entities that best fit the spline curves. These standard line entities can be joined and parameterized by manually adding dimensions and constraints for a fully parameterized section profile, as shown in Fig. 18a.

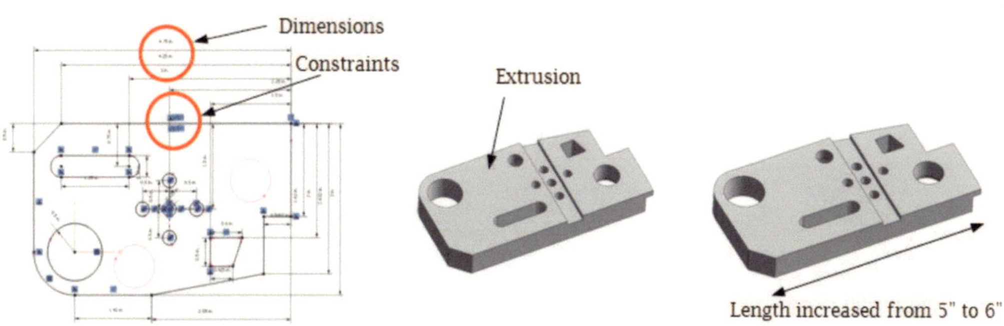

Fig. 18. A parametric solid model of the *block* example created using *Rapidform*, (a) fully parameterized section sketch, (b) extrusion for the base block, and (c) design change

Once the sketch profile is parameterized, it can be extruded to generate an extrusion feature for the base block (Fig. 18b). The same steps can be followed to create more solid features, and Boolean operations can be employed to union, subtract, or intersect solid features for a fully parameterized solid model. The final solid model is analyzed by using *Accuracy*

Analyzer. The solid model generated is extremely accurate, where geometric error measured in average and standard deviation is 0.0002 and 0.0017 in., respectively (between the solid model and point cloud). Since the model is fully parameterized, it can be modified by simply changing the dimension values. For example, the length of the base block can be increased for an extended model, as shown in Fig. 18c.

Method 2: Wizard

Wizard, or *Modeling Wizard*, of *Rapidform* automatically extracts *Wizard* features such as extrude, revolve, pipe, and loft, etc., to create solid models from segmented regions. Note that a *Wizard* feature can be a surface (such as pipe) or a solid feature. There are five *Wizard* features provided: *extrusion*, *revolution* for extracting solid features; and *sweep*, *loft*, and *pipe* for surface features. There are three general steps to extract features using *Wizard*, (1) select mesh segments to generate individual features using *Wizard*, (2) modify the dimensions or add constraints to the sketches extracted in order to parameterize the sketches, and (3) use Boolean operations to union, subtract, or intersect individual features for a final model if needed.

The same *tubing* example shown in Fig. 19 is employed to illustrate the capabilities offered in *Wizard*. We start with a polygon mesh that has been segmented, as shown in Fig. 19a. First, we select the exterior region of the main branch and choose *Pipe Wizard*. *Rapidform* uses a best fit pipe surface to fit the main branch automatically, as shown in Fig. 19b. Note that the *Pipe Wizard* generates section profile and guide curve as spatial (non-planar) spline curves, which cannot be parameterized. Also, wall thickness has to be added to the pipe to complete the solid feature. Next, we choose *Revolution Wizard* to create revolved features for the top and bottom flanges, as shown in Fig. 19c. Note that each individual features are extracted separately. They are not associated. Boolean operations must be applied to these decoupled features for a final solid model.

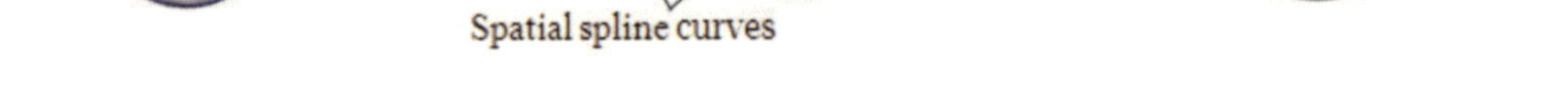

Fig. 19. Feature extraction for the *tubing* example using *Wizard*, (a) selected main branch region, (b) surface created using *Pipe Wizard*, and (c) flange created using *Revolution Wizard*

Although *Wizard* offers a fast and convenient approach for solid modeling, the solid models generated are often problematic. The solid models have to be closely examined for validation. For example, in this *tubing* model, there are gap and interference between features, as indicated in Fig. 20. This is not a valid solid model. It is inflexible to edit and make changes to the *Wizard* features since the sketch profile is represented in spatial spline curves that cannot be constrained or dimensioned.

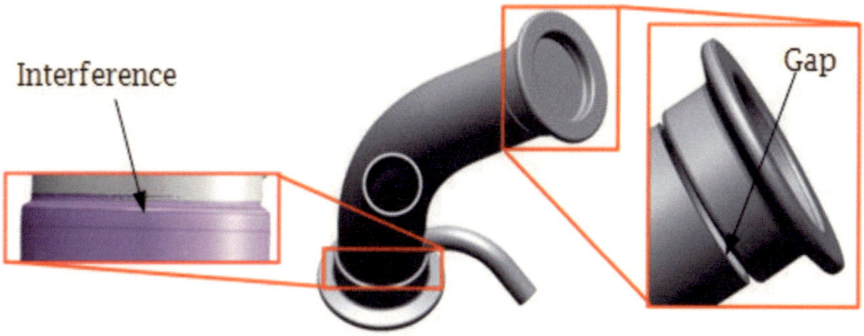

Fig. 20. Gap and interference between solid features in the *tubing* model

In summary, *Rapidform* is the only reverse engineering software that supports for creating parametric solid models from scanned data. *Rapidform* offers CAD-like capabilities that allow users to add dimensions and constraints to sketches and solid features for a fully parametric solid model. In addition, *Rapidform* provides two modeling methods, *Sketch* and *Wizard*. Design intent and model accuracy can be achieved using the *Sketch* method, which is in general a much better option for creating parametric solid models.

4.5 Solid model export

The solid models created in specialized software, such as *Rapidform* and *Geomagic*, have to be exported to mainstream CAD systems in order to support engineering applications. Both *Rapidform* and *Geomagic* offer capabilities that export solid models to numerous CAD systems.

4.5.1 *Parametric Exchange* of *Geomagic*

The solid model of the *block* example created in *Geomagic* was exported to *SolidWorks* and *Wildfire* using *Parametric Exchange* of *Geomagic*. For *SolidWorks*, all seventeen features recognized in *Geomagic* (see Fig. 21a) were exported as individual features, as shown in Fig. 21b. Note that since there are no Boolean operations offered in *Geomagic Studio v.11*, these features are not associated. There is no relation established between them. As a result, they are just "piled up" in the solid model shown in Fig. 21c. Subtraction features, such as holes and slots, simply overlap with the base block. Similar results appear in *Wildfire*, except that one extrusion feature was not exported properly, as shown in Fig. 21d and 21e.

4.5.2 *liveTransfer*™ module of *Rapidform XOR3*

The *liveTransfer*™ module of *Rapidform XOR3* exports parametric models, directly into major CAD systems, including *SolidWorks* 2006+, Siemens NX 4+, *Pro/ENGINEER Wildfire* 3.0+, *CATIA* V4 and V5 and *AutoCAD*.

The *block* example that was fully parameterized in *Rapidform* was first exported to *SolidWorks*. All the solid features were seamlessly exported to *SolidWorks*, except for some datum entities, such as datum points. Since entities such as polygon meshes and segmented regions are not included in *SolidWorks* database, they cannot be exported. As a result, geometric datum features associated with these entities are not exported properly. The dimensions and constraints added to the sketches and solid features in *Rapidform* are exported well, except again for those referenced to entities that are not available in *SolidWorks*. Fortunately, it only requires users to make a few minor changes (such as adding or modifying dimensions or constraints) to bring back a fully parametric solid model in *SolidWorks*. As shown in Fig. 22, the length of the base block was increased and the solid model is rebuilt in *SolidWorks* (Fig. 22b). Similar results were observed in *NX*. However,

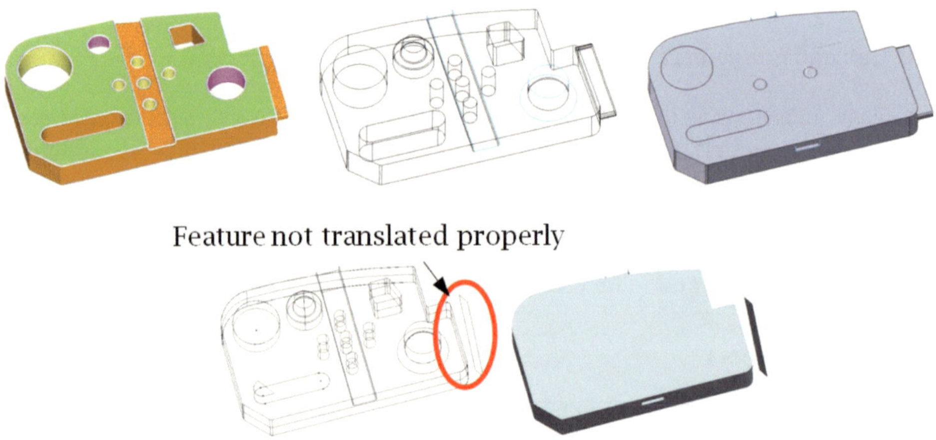

Fig. 21. The *block* model explored to *SolidWorks* and *Wildfire*, (a) seventeen features recognized in *Geomagic*, (b) features exported to *SolidWorks* (wireframe), (c) features "piled up" in *SolidWorks*, (d) features exported to *Wildfire* (wireframe), and (e) features "piled up" in *Wildfire*

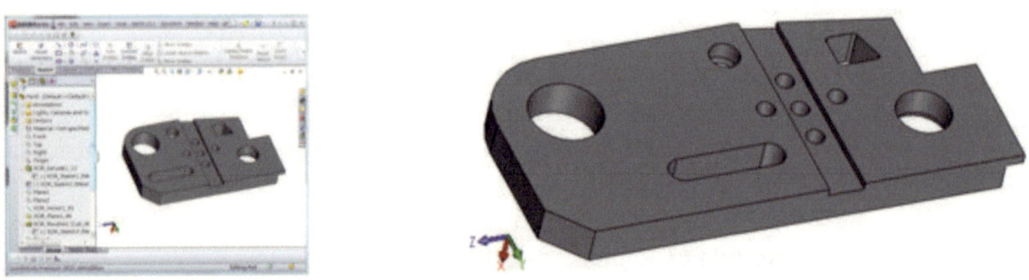

Fig. 22. *Block* exported from *Rapidform* to *SolidWorks*, (a) solid model exported to *SolidWorks*, and (b) design change made in *SolidWorks*

model exported to *Wildfire* 4.0 is problematic, in which numerous issues, such as missing and misinterpretation portion of the section profile, are encountered. In general, parametric solid models created in *Rapidform* can be exported well to *SolidWorks* and *NX*. The export is almost seamless. Although, there were minor issues encountered, such as missing references for some datum points, those issues can be fixed very easily.

5. Discussion

The most useful and advanced shape engineering capabilities are offered in specialized, non-CAD software, such as *Geomagic*, *Rapidform*, etc., that are intended to support reverse engineering. Some CAD packages, such as *SolidWorks*, *Pro/ENGINEER Wildfire*, and *CATIA*, offer limited capabilities for shape engineering. In general, capabilities offered in CAD are labor intensive and inferior to specialized codes while dealing with shape engineering.

After intensive review and survey (Chang & Chen, 2010), to the authors' knowledge, the best software on the market for reverse engineering is *Geomagic Studio* v.11 and *Rapidform XOR3*. This was determined after a thorough and intensive study, following a set of prescribed criteria including auto surfacing, parametric solid modeling, and software usability. Between the two, *Geomagic* has a slight edge in geometric entity editing, which is critical for auto surfacing. In terms of solid modeling, *Geomagic* stops short at only offering primitive surfaces, such as plane, cylinder, sphere, etc., from segmented regions.

Rapidform is superior in support of solid modeling (in addition to excellent auto surfacing) that goes beyond primitive surface fitting. *Rapidform* offers convenient sketching capabilities that support feature-based modeling. As a result, it often requires less effort yet yielding a much better solid model by interactively recovering solid features embedded in the segmented regions. The interactive approach mainly involves creating or extracting section profiles or guide curves from the polygon mesh, and following CAD-like steps to create solid features.

6. Conclusions

In this chapter, technology that enables 3D shape engineering and design parameterization for reverse engineering was reviewed. Software that offers such capabilities was also evaluated and tested using practical examples. Based on the evaluations, we observed that *Rapidform* is the only viable choice for parametric solid modeling in support of 3D shape engineering and design parameterization. *Rapidform* offers CAD-like capabilities for creating solid features, feature tree for allowing roll back for feature editing, and very good sketching functions. In addition, the *liveTransfer*™ module offers model exporting to mainstream CAD systems almost seamlessly.

After research and development in decades, technology that supports 3D shape engineering and design parameterization is matured enough to support general engineering applications. The ideal scenario can now be realized by using software such as *Rapidform* for shape engineering and parameterization, where labor intensive tasks, such as managing point cloud, triangulation, etc., is taken care of in an automated fashion; and design intents can be recovered interactively as desired. One area that might require more work is to incorporate more CAD packages for model export. Major CAD packages, such as *SolidWorks* and *NX*, have been well supported. However, software such as *CATIA* is yet to be included and software like *Wildfire* needs to be streamlined.

7. References

Alrashdan, A.; Motavalli, S.; Fallahi, B.: Automatic Segmentation of Digitized Data for Reverse Engineering Applications, IIE Transactions, 32(1), 2000, 59-69. DOI: 10.1023/A:1007655430826

Bernardini, F.; Mittleman, J.; Rushmeier, H.; Silva, C.; Taubin, G.: The Ball-Pivoting Algorithm for Surface Reconstruction, Visualization and Computer Graphics, 5(4), 1999, 349-359. DOI:10.1109/2945.817351

Besl, P.J.; Jain, R.C.: Segmentation Through Variable-Order Surface Fitting, IEEE Transactions on Pattern Analysis and Machine Intelligence, 10(2), 1988, 167-192. DOI: 10.1109/34.3881

Blais, F.: Review of 20 Years of Range Sensor Development, Journal of Electronic Imaging, 13(1), 2004, 231–240. DOI:10.1117/1.1631921

Chang, K.H.; Magdum, S.; Khera, S.; Goel, V.K.: An Advanced Computer Modeling and Prototyping Method for Human Tooth Mechanics Study, Annals of Biomedical Engineering, 31(5), 2003, 621-631. DOI:10.114/1.1568117

Chang, K.H. and Chen, C., Research and Recommendation of Advanced Reverse Engineering Tools, Final Technical Report, Reference SOW # QIB09-008, September 2010.

Chang, K.H. and Siddique, Z., "Re-Engineering and Fast Manufacturing for Impact-Induced Fatigue and Fracture Problems in Aging Aircrafts," Final Report, AFOSR Grant F49620-02-1-0336, January 31, 2006.

Cuccuru, G.; Gobbetti, E.; Marton, F.; Pajarola, R.; Pintus, R.: Fast Low-Memory Streaming MLS Reconstruction of Point-Sampled Surfaces, Graphics Interface. 2009, 15-22.

Edelsbrunner, H.; Kirkpatrick, D.G.; Seidel, R.: On the Shape of A Set of Points In The Plane, IEEE Transactions on Information Theory, 29(4), 1983, 551-559. DOI:10.1109/TIT.1983.1056714

Geomagic, www.geomagic.com

Gibson, D., Parametric feature recognition and surface construction from digital point cloud scans of mechanical parts, MS Thesis, The University of Oklahoma, December 2004

Hansen, G.A.; Douglass, R.W; and Zardecki, Andrew: *Mesh enhancement*. Imperial College Press, 2005, ISBN-13: 978-1860944871

Hoppe, H.; DeRose, T.; Duchamp, T.; McDonals, J., and Stuetzle, W.: Mesh Optimization, SIGGRAPH '93 Proceedings of the 20th annual conference on Computer graphics and interactive techniques, ACM New York, ISBN:0-89791-601-8

Huang, J.; Menq, C.-H.: Automatic Data Segmentation for Geometric Feature Extraction From Unorganized 3-D Coordinate Points, IIE Transactions on Robotics and Automation, 17(3), 2001, 268-279. DOI:10.1109/70.938384

InnovMetric, www.innovmetric.com

Kazhdan, M.; Bolitho, M.; Hoppe, H.: Poisson Surface Reconstruction, The Fourth Eurographics Symposium on Geometry Processing, 2006.

Li, Z.; Ma, L.; Jin, X.; and Zheng, Z.: A new feature-preserving mesh-smoothing algorithm, The visual computer 2009, vol. 25, nº2, pp. 139-148

Liu, Y.; Dong, X.; Peng, W.: Study on Digital Data Processing Techniques for 3D Medical Model, Bioinformatics and Biomedical Engineering, 4, 2010, 1-4. DOI:10.1109/ICBBE.2010.5518168

Lorensen, W.E.; Cline, H.E.: Marching Cubes: A High Resolution 3D Surface Construction Algorithm, Computer Graphics, 21(4), 1987. DOI:10.1145/37402.37422

Lukács, G.; Martin, R.; Marshall, D.: Faithful Least-Squares Fitting of Spheres, Cylinders, Cones and Tori for Reliable Segmentation, Lecture Notes in Computer Science, 1406, 1998, 671-686. DOI:10.1007/BFb0055697

Lv, Y.; Yi, J.; Liu, Y.; Zhao, L.; Zhang, Y.; Chen, J.: Research on Reverse Engineering for Plastic Operation, Information Technology and Applications, 2009, 389-391. DOI: 10.1109/IFITA.2009.123

Marshall, D.; Lukacs, G.; Martin, Ralph.: Robust Segmentation of Primitives from Range Data in the Presence of Geometric Degeneracy, IEEE Transaction on Pattern Analysis and Machine Intelligence, 23(3), 2001,304-314. DOI:10.1109/34.910883

Raja, V.; Fernandes, K.J.: Reverse Engineering: An industrial Perspective, Springer-Verlag, London, 2008. DOI:10.1007/978-1-84628-856-2

Rapidform, INUS Technology, Inc., www.rapidform.com

Schroeder, W.J.: A topology modifying progressive decimation algorithm, Eighth IEEE Visualization 1997 (VIS '97), Phoenix, AZ, October 19-October 24, ISBN: 0-8186-8262-0

Siddique, Z.: Recommended Tool Kit for Reverse Engineering, CASI Summer Research Program 2002, OC-ALC, August 28, 2002

Silva, J.S.; Chang, K.H.: Design Parameterization for Concurrent Design and Manufacturing of Mechanical Systems, Concurrent Engineering Research and Applications (CERA) Journal, 2002, 10(1), 3-14. DOI:10.1177/1063293X02010001048

SolidWorks, Inc., www.solidworks.com

Sun, Q.; Chang, K.H.; Dormer, K.; Dyer, R.; Gan, R.Z.: An Advanced Computer-Aided Geometric Modeling and Fabrication Method for Human Middle Ear, Medical Engineering and Physics, 24(9), 2002, 595-606. DOI:10.1016/S1350-4533(02)00045-0

Thompson, W.B.; Owen, J.C.; de St. Germain, H.J.; Stark, S.R., Jr.; Henderson, T.C.: Featured-Based Reverse Engineering of Mechanical Parts, IEEE Transactions on Robotics and Automation, 15(1), 1999, 57-66. DOI:10.1109/70.744602

Tsai, Y.C.; Huang, C.Y.; Lin, K.Y.; Lai, J.Y.; Ueng, W.D.: Development of Automatic Surface Reconstruction Technique in Reverse Engineering, The International Journal of Advanced Manufacturing Technology, 42(1–2), 2009, 152–167. DOI:10.1007/S00170-008-1586-2

Vanco, M.; Brunnett, G.: Direct Segmentation of Algebraic Models for Reverse Engineering, Computing, 72(1-2), 2004, 207-220. DOI:10.1007/S00607-003-0058-7

Várady, T.; Benkö, P.; Kós, G.: Reverse Engineering Regular Objects: Simple Segmentation and Surface Fitting Procedures, International Journal of Shape Modeling, 4(3-4), 1998, 127–141. DOI:10.1142/S0218654398000106

Várady, T.; Martin, R.R.; Cox, J.: Reverse Engineering of Geometric Models - An Introduction, Computer-Aided Design, 29(4), 1997, 255–268. DOI:10.1016/S0010-4485(96)00054-1

Venkataraman, S.; Sohoni, M.; Kulkarni, V.: A Graph-Based Framework for Feature Recognition, Sixth ACM Symposium on Solid Modeling and Applications, 2001, 194-205. DOI:10.1145/376957.376980

ZCorp, www.zcorp.com

9

Integrating Reverse Engineering and Design for Manufacturing and Assembly in Products Redesigns: Results of Two Action Research Studies in Brazil

Carlos Henrique Pereira Mello, Carlos Eduardo Sanches da Silva, José Hamilton Chaves Gorgulho Junior, Fabrício Oliveira de Toledo, Filipe Natividade Guedes, Dóris Akemi Akagi and Amanda Fernandes Xavier
Federal University of Itajubá (UNIFEI), Center of Optimization of Manufacturing and Technology Innovation (NOMATI)
Brazil

1. Introduction

Due to increased market pressure, product specifications are required to be developed and updated on a rapid and continual basis. Companies know that to compete in the market they must learn to analyze and address the actual arithmetic increase, but to do so at an exponential pace.

Improving a product involves offering new features, new technology and attractive ways to enhance the quality for market launch. Companies are employing and reaping the benefits of market analysis techniques to assist in predicting what the market is postulating, now and in the future.

Customers anxiously await the release of new products, frequently and expeditiously. Many of these customers expect and anticipate that their favorite brand will launch a new product. In fact, frequency of product updates or the potential of model renewal and variety of versions has become another aspect in redefining the concept of a favorite brand.

The rapid pace of consumer demand compels companies to keep their products on the edge of technology and competitive in market place; therefore, their development process can be no less aggressive. To achieve optimum results, the products must be continuously improved, based on customer need.

Dufour (1996) is emphatic that many new products, even if unintended, are in most cases redesigns, based on an existing product. This activity, however, cannot be held solely in intuitive order, depending only on empiricism.

The redesign needs to be done through a systematic process that guides the work of the designer and the product development team from identification of the problem until the final design of the product, offering a greater chance of success.

Silva (2001) considers that for small and medium companies to be regarded as pioneers in product development, it is not a critical success factor. So, additional scrutiny is applied to the study of manufacture and assembly, the structured assessments of conditions and the productive resources, internally and externally available, as a means of reducing costs and optimizing deadlines for product launching.

As a consequence, the redesign of products, supported by a Reverse Engineering (RE) approach, and integrated Design for Manufacturing and Assembly (DFMA) is a way these companies manage to launch new products with minimal investment and risk. A survey in the main scientific databases (Emerald, Science Direct and SciELO) revealed that this issue has generated 178 publications in journals during the period from 1980 to 2009, as shown in Figure 1.

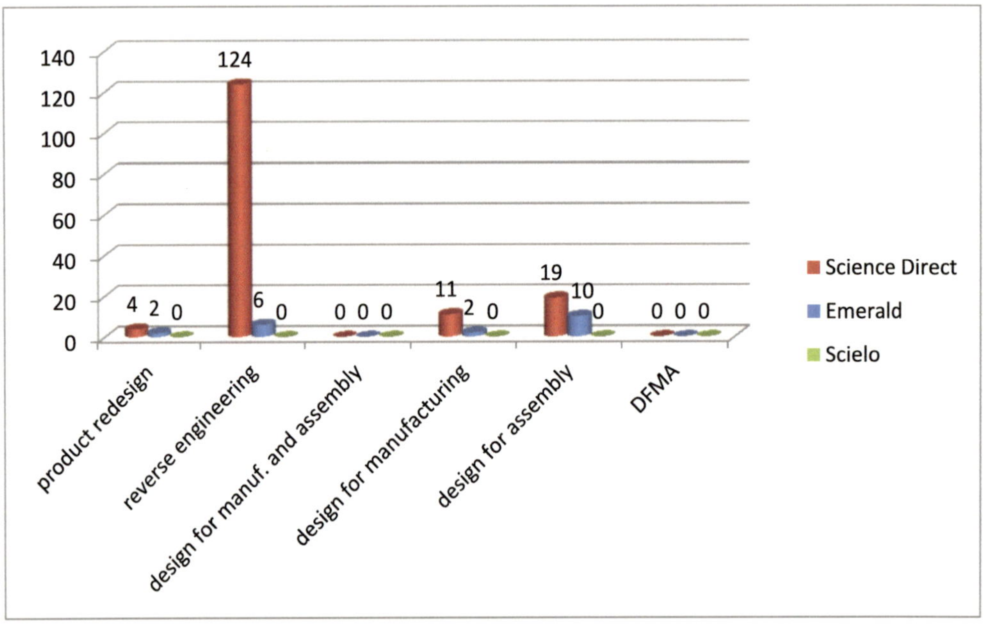

Fig. 1. Publications by keywords in major databases

Figure 2 shows the distribution of these publications within this period, as they are contained in the article title, for the keywords: product redesign; Reverse Engineering; Design for Manufacturing and Assembly; design for manufacturing; design for assembly, and DFMA.

Of note in the analysis is that none of these publications dealt with the integration of RE with DFMA regarding the redesign of products, only with rapid prototyping; thus, this chapter aims to contribute to the knowledge base by filling the gap identified in the literature.

Therefore, the main objective of this study is to analyze the application of a model for the integrated use of the design for manufacturing and the rapid prototyping in a reverse engineering approach in the process of products redesign.

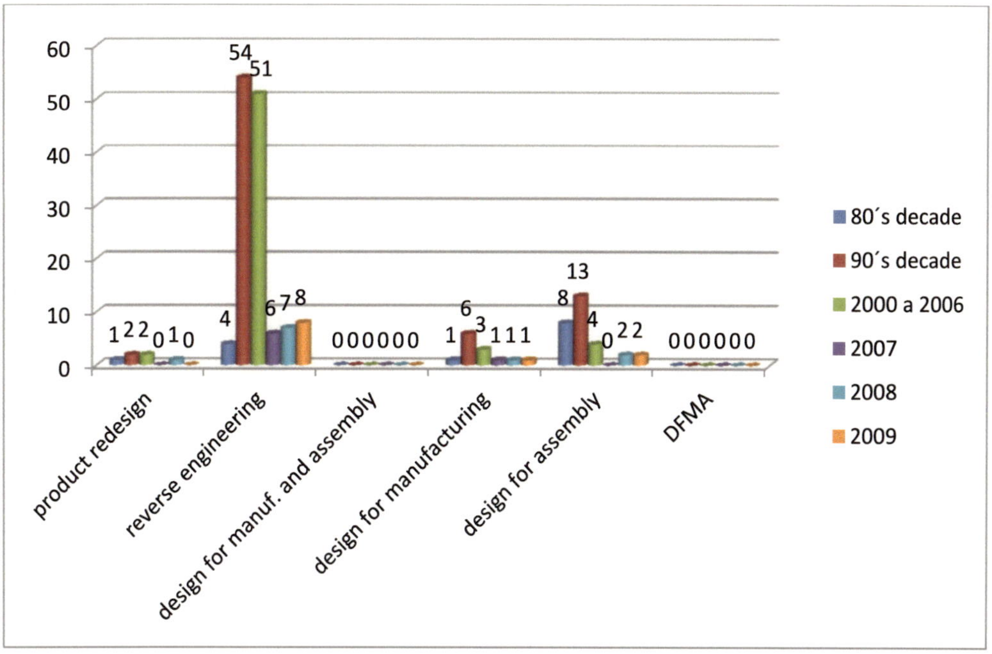

Fig. 2. Publications by keywords between 1980 and 2009

From this main objective on, it is established a secondary objective, to analyze the results from the application of the cited model to reduce production/assembling time, as well as the manufacturing/assembling costs on the redesign of products from the reverse engineering.

The employed research method was the action-research. According to Thiollent (2007) an action-research is a kind of an empirically social research, designed and carried out in close association with an action or with solving a collective problem, in which the researches and participants, representatives of the situation or the problem are involved in a cooperative and participatory way.

This chapter is structured as follows: section 2 presents initially a theoretical framework on the subject studied, followed by section 3 which describes the research method employed. Section 4 analyzes and discusses the results and, finally, section 5 presents the conclusions of the research.

2. Literature review

2.1 Product development process

According to Toledo *et al.* (2008), the product development process (PDP) is considered, increasingly, a critical process to the competitiveness of companies, with a view to a general need for frequent renewal of product lines, costs and development schedules, a more responsive product development to market needs and to companies participating in supplying chain of components and systems, training strategies to participate in joint development (co-design) with customers.

To Rozenfeld *et al.* (2006), develop products consists of a set of activities through which we seek as of market needs and technological possibilities and constraints, and considering the competitive strategies and the company´s products, to reach the design specifications of a product and its production process for the manufacture is able to produce it.

Innovation is the key to societal development, rejuvenation and business growth; critical for the long-term survival of a company if it is to operate in the business world. It is also recognized that innovation is more than the invention of new products, but a complete multidimensional concept, which must be viewed from different perspectives in their specific context (Hüsing and Kohn, 2009).

Many products are made of a variety of components which, taken separately, have no influence on the final consumer; for example, in the automotive industry, some components, such as the engine, brake and suspension systems, are used to produce various car systems, provided the relevant interfaces are standardized. That is why different companies (which may or may not be competitors) often agree to cooperate in developing components (Bourreau and Dogan, 2009).

On product development models, Ogliari (1999) mentions that various available types can be found in the following literature: Back (1983), Rosenthal (1992), Vincent (1989), Wheelwright and Clark (1992), Cooper and Edgett (1999), Pahl *et al.* (2005); Rozenfeld *et al.* (2006) and Backet *et al.* (2008), where the primary difference between them are denominations of their phases, but with their sequences and concepts remaining almost constant.

Pahl *et al.* (2005) mentions a product development model (see Figure 3) which highlights the important aspects for the implementation of concurrent engineering; basically considering the anticipation and intersection of the beginning phases to reduce the necessary time for the development of a new product as well as tracking costs. Figure 3 highlighted the use of DFMA.

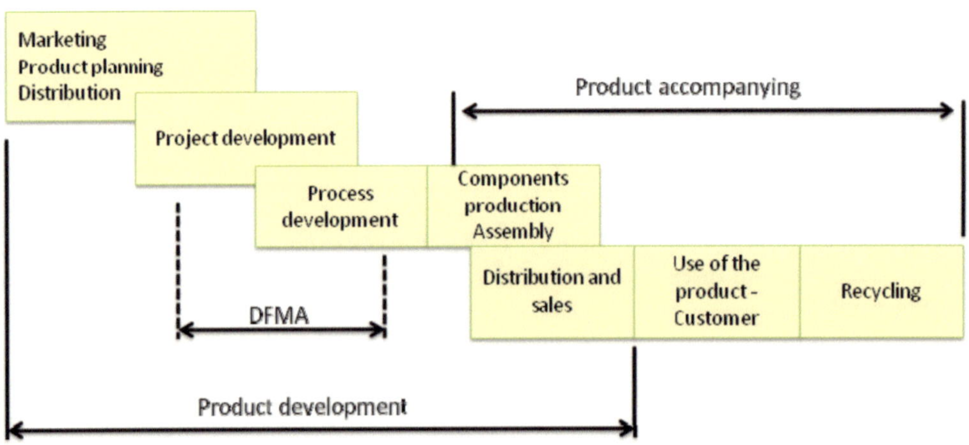

Source: adapted from Pahl *et al.* (2005)

Fig. 3. Reference model for PDP

While creating a product from the perspective of concurrent engineering, the activities of each department of the company are, largely, synchronized. The product is also permanently monitored until the end of its life cycle.

Pahl *et al.* (2005) emphasizes the importance that the development team be composed not only of people directly responsible for the design, but also of others in sectors involved with product development (such as sales, production, marketing, purchasing, engineering), so that the process aspect can be dealt with in order to break out departmental paradigms.

Since, in general, the condition of small and medium enterprise (SME) is not necessarily aggressive (Silva, 2001), due to the need for large investments in research and developing technology, often this understanding and a review of the strategies are the key to reducing costs and is possibly the only way of developing new products in a structured manner and with the greatest chance of success; thus, the Reverse Engineering (RE) approach to the process of product development becomes a plausible method toward achieving innovation within these companies.

2.2 Reverse Engineering (RE)

Reverse Engineering is a very important tool and this technique has been widely recognized as an important step toward developing improved products as well as reducing time and costs in order to achieve profitable production of the new product.

In contrast to the traditional sequence of product development, RE starts typically with the measurement of a reference product, deducing a solid model in order to take advantage of existing technology. The model is later used for manufacturing or rapid prototyping (Bagci, 2009).

According to Kim and Nelson (2005), countries with recent industrialization have used, mainly in the 1960´s and 1970´s, reverse engineering. Zhu, Liang and Xu (2005) argue that the Chinese process of technology acquisition follows the following line: lines of purchasing and manufacturing techniques from developed countries, modifications and identification of parts and components to achieve product development through RE and, finally, optimize the products.

The innovative process in South Korea is through RE, awaiting for the developed countries to generate new technologies and marked, and then indeed develop their own products (Hobday, Rush and Bessant, 2004).

The RE is useful to guide in understanding the system of interest and allows comparison to be made with similar design models, to see what can actually be used from the technology (Kang, Park and Wu, 2007). Ingle (1994) defines the RE as a process of gathering information in a reference product through its disassembly, in order to determine how it was developed, from its separate components till the final product. His approach clearly supports the application of RE in order to produce as similar as possible to the original, with a level of investment that can guarantee the generation of profits to the enterprise.

The main application of RE is the redesign and improvement of existing parts, wherever improvements are desired, such as reducing costs or even adding new features to the product. In addition, an RE project allows, through the construction of replacements parts, off-line or inaccessible, keep up obsolete equipment in operation (Mury, 2000).

Although widely cited in the literature, Ingle´s model (1994) doesn´t include the design integration for manufacturing and assembly with rapid prototyping in a reverse engineering approach to the product redesign. This is a scientific contribution that this work seeks to offer.

Another approach that, integrated with RE, can help analyze the redesign of products, is the design for manufacturing and assembly (DFMA).

2.3 Design for manufacturing and assembly

Among the methods to support the design of products that can help to consider the manufacture and assembly during the conception phase, DFMA is used as a support to improve the product concept, or an existing design. After all, the focus of DFMA is to help generate a design considering the company´s capacity, to facilitate the final product assembly (Estorilio and Simião, 2006).

The DFMA aims the project and production planning to occur, simultaneously, from a set of principles. Already in the DFMA redesign helps bring the product the best characteristics of production and assembly, seeking to improve quality and reduce manufacturing and assembly time (Dufour, 1996).

According to Stephenson and Wallace (1995) and Boothroyd, Dewhurst and Knight (2002), the requirements of the original design should be reviewed to establish the new DFMA quality requirements, always considering the following basic principles of design for manufacturing (DFM) and design for assembly (DFA): simplicity (reducing the parts number, shorter manufacturing sequence etc.); materials and components standardized; tolerances release (avoid too tight tolerances, which imply high costs); use of more processing materials; reduce secondary operations; use of process special features (to take advantage of the special capabilities of manufacturing processes, eliminating costly and unnecessary operations); avoid limitations in the process.

2.4 Rapid prototyping

Rapid Prototyping (RP) is an innovative technology developed within the last two decades. It aims to produce prototypes relatively quickly to visual inspection, ergonomic evaluation, analysis of shape and dimension and, as a standard for the production of master tools, to help reduce process time for product development (Choi and Chan, 2004).

RP allows designers to quickly create tangible prototypes from their projects, rather than bi-dimensional figures, providing an excellent visual aid during preliminary discussions of the project with colleagues or clients.

Currently on the market there is available a multitude of existing rapid prototyping technologies: Stereolithography (SLA), Laminated Object Manufacturing (LOM), Fused Deposition Modeling (FDM) and Three-Dimensional Printing (3D Printing) (Chen, 2000).

This research focused on the technology of Fused Deposition Modeling (FDM), because it offers lower equipment cost (Kochan, 2000); and as such, it is within reach of small and medium enterprises and research institutions.

The basis of FDM is the deposition of layers on a platform from heated filament, and softening of the material for the creation of the plastic model; simultaneously, other softened wires are forming a support for the free surfaces of the suspended model, providing the structure upon which the model can be finished.

The wires for the model are normally made from ABS (Acrylonitrile Butadiene Styrene), while the brackets are a mixture of ABS and lime. From the generated prototype, the team can: review the adopted product as a reference; test its specifications; test manufacturing or assembly scenarios; propose dimensional or constructive amendments; and establish possible improvements to be made in the end product to be developed.

2.5 Integration of RE with DFMA

In the process of creating a product, from the perspective of concurrent engineering, the activities of each department of the company go, largely, in parallel. There is also a permanent monitoring of the product by the end of its life cycle.

Based on the model analyzed by Pahl *et al.* (2005) (see Figure 1), Souza (2007) proposed a modification on the model in order to include considerations by Ingle (1994), so as to contemplate the development of products using the Reverse Engineering method.

After implementing the Reverse Engineering process, it is necessary to allow the phases to unfold logically within the model. When analyzing Ingle´s proposed work (1994), it can be noted there is a major deficiency when considering the need of manufacturing and assembly; thus, Souza´s proposed model (2007) contends that the fundamentals of DFMA, when included in the analysis of Reverse Engineering, complements the proposal by Ingle (1994).

For the analysis of these need, Souza (2007) generated an eight steps model, as illustrated in Figure 4.

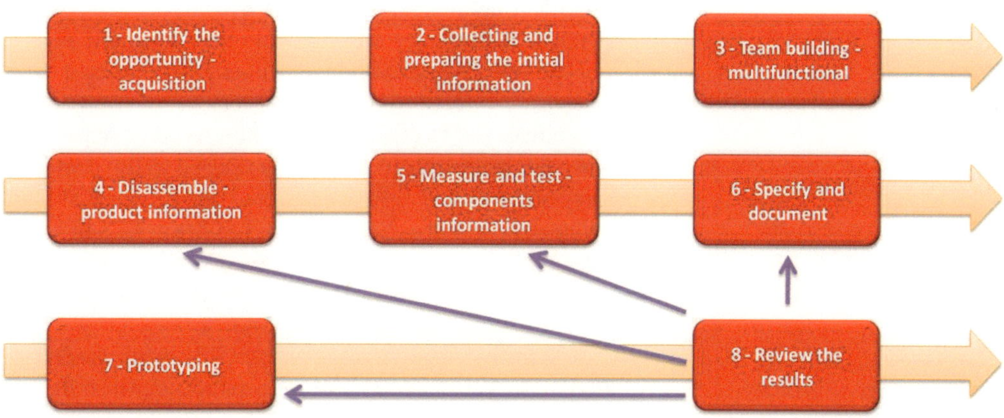

Source: Souza (2007)

Fig. 4. Model proposed for the development of products with DFMA in the Reverse Engineering process

This model does not seek to replace all the phases originally proposed by Pahl *et al.* (2005), but the specific phases of the design development and the process, i.e., the adaptation seeks to optimize the technical process of developing a product, in order to be applied to the existing models, including the redesign of a product, with the expectation of achieving the same final results.

Table 1 provides a brief breakdown of each phase of this model.

Stage	Meaning
Identify the opportunity - acquistion	Identify and recognize the company's marketing position and its operations; and identify the product to be considered as a reference.
Collecting and preparing the initial information	Get an initial survey of the market not only of the reference product, but also for any information that can contribute to a thorough understanding of the product class that is being analyzed. Collect and digest all information that can contribute to the application of Reverse Engineering (RE) and its integration with the principles of Design for Manufacturing and Assembly (DFMA).
Team building - multifunctional	The developing multidisciplinary team needs to have elements that can unite theoretical knowledge with practical and pragmatic details and characteristics of the product manufactured by the company. Everyone on the team ought to be cross-trained in such knowledge, so that no opportunity passes unnoticed.
Disassembled - product information	Systematically analyze the technology and functions of each component and subsystem of the subject product(s) in order to extract information that will be examined in more detail in the next phase. Of cardinal concern is the interaction between the components, with a highly focused view toward all technical details (tolerances, attachments, settings etc.).
Measure and test - components information	Actions taken at this stage are related to measurement and testing of the reference product components, attempting to answer questions related to the product technologies and the processes employed to create the unit and its components.
Specify and document	Documenting the technical information gathered in the previous phase and specifying new information that has been left at this stage by people more directly linked to the details of components and the production process. At this stage the principles of DFMA are used to improve aspects of manufacture and assembly of the product.
Prototyping	Using the prototypes (rapid), within the environment of reverse engineering, to aid as a source of information input in the analysis of DFMA.
Review Results	Conduct a managerial review on all previous phases and how the process is moving forward in relation to time and costs. This phase is conducted by the researchers and project coordinator and should be regarded as the informational hub. After analysis of the prototype, DFMA principles are once again used to optimize the solution for the product redesign.

Source: adapted from Souza (2007)

Table 1. Stages of the model proposed for the development of products with DFMA in the Reverse Engineering process

3. Research method

3.1 Research method definition

The main objective of the research presented in this chapter is to analyze the application of a model for the integrated use of the design for manufacturing and the rapid prototyping in a reverse engineering approach in a product redesign.

From this main objective on, it is established a secondary objective, to analyze the results from the application of the cited model to reduce production/assembling time, as well as the manufacturing/assembling costs on the redesign of products from the reverse engineering.

As to meet these two goals is necessary the intervention of the researcher in the study object, the research method selected was action research. According to Thiollent (2007), action research is a kind of empirical social research which is designed and carried out in close association with an action or to solve a collective problem and in which researchers and participants representative of the situation or the problem are involved in a cooperative and participatory way.

The adopted action-research process was that proposed by Coughlan and Coghlan (2002), which includes planning cycles (context and problem), data collection, data review, data analysis, action planning and evaluation, as Figure 5 shows.

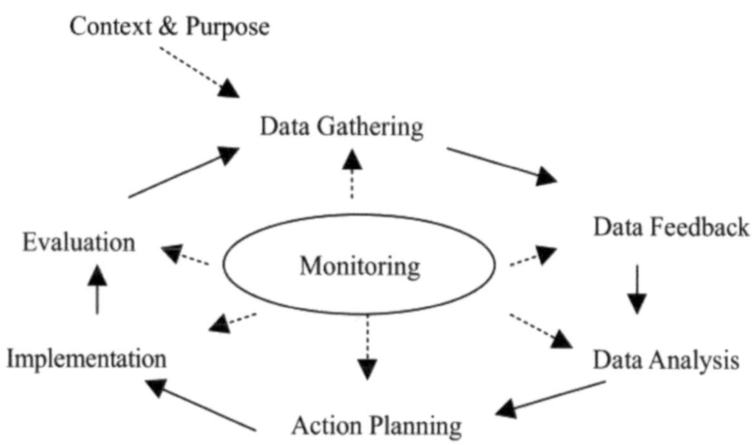

Source: Coughlan and Coghlan (2002)

Fig. 5. Approach to action-research

The following two topics will present the conduction of this research in two companies, located in southeastern Brazil.

3.2 Company A

The company A, founded in 1991, since 1994 successfully manufactures ovens for baking and for industrial kitchens. The company is a Brazilian national leader in the segment of ovens for professional kitchens and a reference in the market it operates.

The research, conducted from January to September 2009, followed the steps of the integrated model, as proposed by Souza (2007), mentioned in section 2.5, in Table 2.

Cycle	Description	Purpose
1	Check the types of lock used in the company, obtaining virtual drawing, access to the lock, take them apart and collect as much data as possible.	Develop a lock system, easy to use, compared to the current model for the oven EC10.
2	Interview the chef cooks of the company. Ask him about the current factory lock system: what´s the best? What are the pros and cons of each one? Do they accomplish or not the expected from the system? What could be changed? What is a good difference?	
3	It´s been sought as much as possible information about industrial ovens available on the market. It´s been got reference locks analysis, according to reverse engineering.	
4	Reference locks have been disassembled and one learned how the systems work. The manufacturing processes were identified, facilities and difficulties to assemble and disassemble were realized. In a word, all the data was collected to start the new design system.	
5	It´s been start the design of parts, with the help of software, taking into account all collected information, as well as the use of DFMA principles to ensure facilities for manufacturing of parts and assembly.	
6	After completing the drawing, they were presented to the engineering manager and to the chef cooks, for the mechanism approval. With the requested items modified, finally came an ideal conceptual design.	
7	The parts have been prototyped for testing.	
8	It´s been made the assembly of the hybrid prototype and verified the validity of the mechanism, which has been presented to the engineering manager, as well as the chef cooks, for approval. It´s been analyzed possible needs for changing and necessary changes made in the conceptual model.	
9	It´s been asked the manufacturing, through machining, of metal parts and springs to the purchases responsible.	
10	A door has been built up with the needed slot for testing with the new locking system. An oven for testing had been set up on the door and the available oven. Alignments and adjustments were necessary in the components. The mechanism has been tested several times. The results were presented to director, engineering manager, chef cooks and the purchases responsible.	
11	Problem were identified and possible needs for improvement. Companies that reduced the samples of springs and machining of parts have been contacted, in order to improve results with the springs and simply machining. The machining company was visited for contacting with the responsible and creation of goal for improvements.	
12	Finally, it´s been chosen the product. More locking prototypes have been made. Pneumatic devices were created for the product prototype wearing. Prices for large-scale production have been negotiate and ordered to produce the locks in the manufacturing process best suitable for each part.	

Table 2. Summary of the conduct action-research cycles in Company A

3.2.1 Identify the opportunity

Two reference ovens have been identified. One from a German company, a direct competitor in Brazil, and another one from an Italian company, that makes different products, including locks. They were also used for comparisons purposes all four different of lock currently used in the company.

There were no problems concerning the acquisition, once the German oven had been previously bought by the factory also in order to make use of the RE technique to other parts of the oven.

The Italian lock was provided for the manufacturer, as a sample for possible future sales. Thus, there was no charge.

3.2.2 Collecting and preparing the initial information

All information has been collected by a employee inside the company, since the availability of the German and the Italian locks, besides the locks used at the factory.

To obtain further information, chef cooks, staff, engineering staff, managers, directors were consulted, as well as collected data from de CS (Customer Service), as well as searching the Internet.

3.2.3 Team building

The formed research team was composed by the chef cooks, engineering manager, plant manager, purchases responsible, and the researcher, who supplied the necessary information in all areas. Each one of the participants of the company has more than five years of experience in the development and manufacturing of ovens.

3.2.4 Disassemble (information about the product)

As for the locks used in the company, their virtual drawing was used, allowing to analyze each one regarding the assembly and each part separately, without having to disassemble the product.

The locks of the German and the Italian ovens were disassembled and analyzed. Through photographs, important information was stored.

Table 3 shows the comparison between the current model EC10 oven lock system and the proposed system. To monitor the work, its whole operation has been registered in virtual drawing, photos and videos, focusing on further analysis.

BEFORE		AFTER	
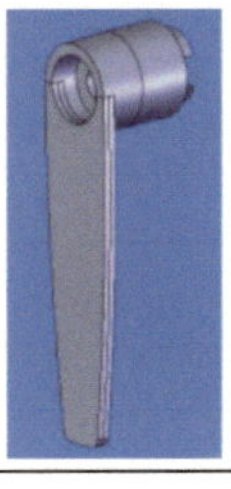	Name: Handle Material: Stainless Steel Manufacture: laser cutting, machining and welding Function/feature: lever to turn the system. Heavy and not ergonomic.	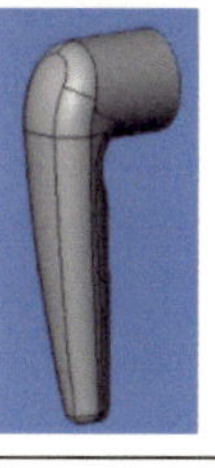	Name: Handle Proposed material: Plastic Manufacturing purpose: Injection Function/feature: lever to turn the ergonomic-shaped system to fit the hand.

BEFORE		AFTER	
	Name: Base Material: Stainless Steel Manufacture: Laser cutting, bending, machining and welding. Function/feature: device to be mounted in the side door. It works as a knocker to stop rotating the drive system, ensure different stage of positioning for the set through the holes and supports other parts of the system.	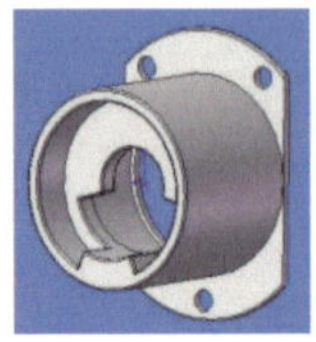	Name: Base Proposed material: Steel Proposed manufacturing: Foundry Function/feature: device to be mounted on the door from inside. It works as a knocker to stop rotating drive system, in addition to host the return spring, nylon bushing component of the spin and snap ring.
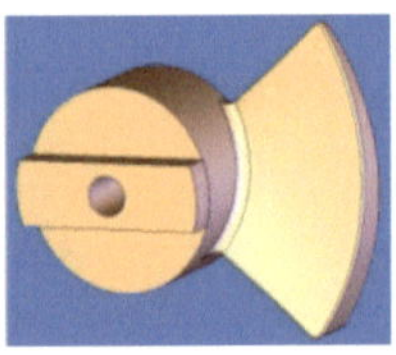	Name: rotating component Material: Bronze Manufacture: machining Function/device: it gets the rotating handle movement and locks the oven door through the conical propeller-shaped shaft.	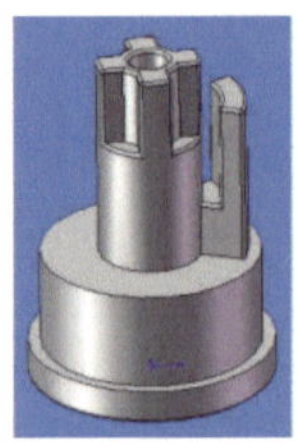	Name: Rotating component Proposed material: Steel Proposed manufacturing: Foundry Function/feature: it remains inside the base of the lock; it moves fast returning springs, it is limited by rotating movements with knockers, it makes connection between the handle and the locking system.
	Name: Machined Allen screw Material: Steel Manufacture: machining Function/feature: machined part serve for fitting the screw fly; it ensures he attachment of the non-rotating component at the base, keeping the clearance for the movement.	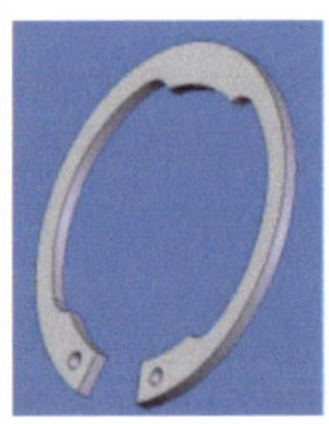	Name: Snap ring Proposed material: Steel Proposed manufacture: on the market Function/feature: it ensures the positioning of the rotating components within the base, while keeping the clearance for the movement.
	Name: Screw fly Material: Steel Manufacture: On the market Function/feature: screwed into the rotating component with the function of limiting the movement of the machined Allen screw, precisely by the machine part.	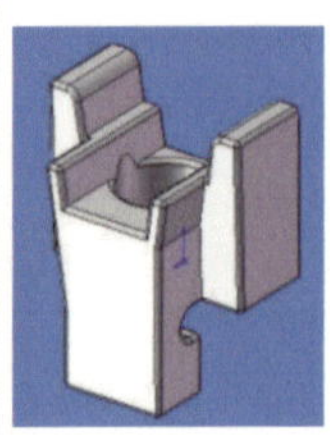	Name: Base of the shaft/spring Proposed material: Steel Proposed manufacture: Foundry Function/feature: fixed on the spinning component through the screw. It ensures the positioning of the shaft/spring, so that it remains the same with the necessary deformation for the locking function.

BEFORE		AFTER	
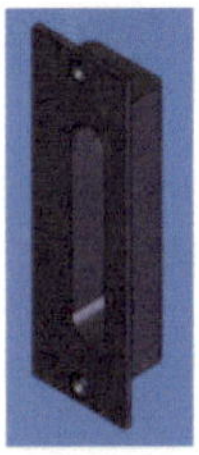	Name: Conical shaft locking component Material: Plastic Manufacture: Foundry Function/feature: set on the side panel with the function of holding the propeller-shaped shaft and through friction, limits the movement and seals the oven chamber.		Name: Two-staged locking screw Proposed material: Steel Proposed manufacture: Foundry and machining Function/feature: fixed in the oven frontal side. It ensures a complete sealing of the oven chamber or a relief stage for releasing steams.
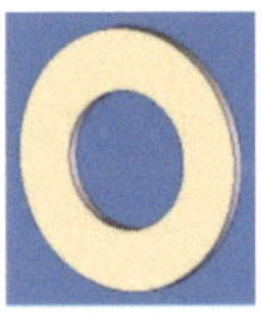	Name: Washer Material: Brass Manufacture: Machining Function/feature: washer function.		Name: Washer Proposed material: Steel Proposed manufacture: On the market Function/feature: Beyond the function of washer, it is used on the two staged lock to ensure positioning adjustment.
	Name: Plate washer Material: Steel Manufacture: on the market Function/feature: to ensure there is no slack in the machined Allen screw and also allows its sliding.		Name: Bushing Proposed material: Nylon Proposed manufacture: Machining Function/feature: to ensure the rotating component positioning inside the base and avoid the friction between both.
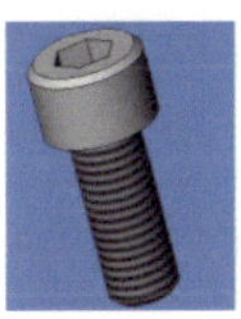	Name: Allen screw Material: Steel Manufacture: on the market Function/feature: to fix the handle on the rotating component.		Name: Allen Screw Proposed material: Steel Proposed manufacture: to fix the shaft/spring base on the rotating component, through the nut on the handle, which will be fixed on the set at this moment.
	Name: Sphere Material: Steel Manufacture: on the market Function/feature: It remains housed in the rotating component, partially occupying the base holes, at the moment the locking function happens at every stage.	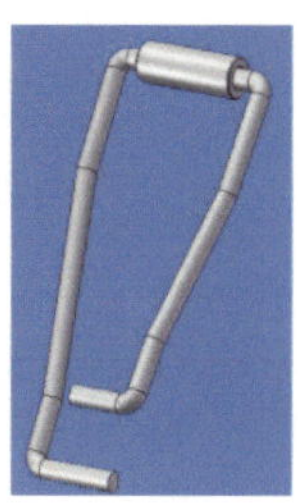	Name: Shaft/spring Proposed material: Stainless steel and spring steel. Proposed manufacture: machining and spring adjustment. Function/feature: next to the two stages lock, it allows the complete sealing of the oven or the lock in the second stage, which allows the door to be relieved for the release of steams.

BEFORE		AFTER	
	Name: Spring Material: Spring steel Manufacture: Spring adjustment Function/feature: to press the housed spheres in the rotating component, so both stages may happens through the holes.	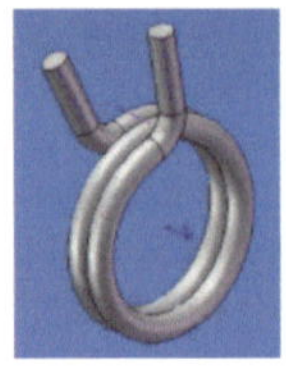	Name: Spring Material: Spring steel Proposed manufacture: Spring adjustment Function/feature: housed in the base and triggered by the rotating component, it makes there is a fast return to the initial position after its drive.

Table 3. Comparison between the current system and the proposed one for the oven lock.

3.2.5 Measure and test (information on the components)

At this phase, we identified the applicability of DFMA during the components analysis, observing:

- premature wear;
- components number reducing;
- alternative materials;
- equipment needed for manufacturing, quality and handling;
- layout of the factory floor.

The operation of the locks used in the company was observed on their own ovens. The German lock was observed as how it works, once it could be assembled on its original oven. As for the Italian lock, it was possible to observe only through a simple manual fitting.

The DFMA applicability analysis were carried out and, once the company doesn´t produce the lock components, it has been asked the expert professionals´ help in manufacturing processes of this kind of component, once they work at two machining companies in the region.

3.2.6 Specify and document

The proposal of a new lock has been modeled through a parametric design software and taking into consideration the information from the previous phases, it has been defined the new product. Each of the new components has been designed, registered and documented accordingly.

3.2.7 Prototyping

All the lock components were prototyped at Federal University of Itajubá (UNIFEI), at the Dimension SST 768 machine, by the Fused Deposition Modeling (FDM), as Figure 6 shows.

3.2.8 Review results

As described in literature, the project went through all the previous phases and, upon completion of these phases, the prototype could be shown to the research team. Having identified new needs, it was necessary to return to some of the previous phases for re-assessment and redesign. After repeating this cycle many times, the final design concept was realized, as shown in Figure 7.

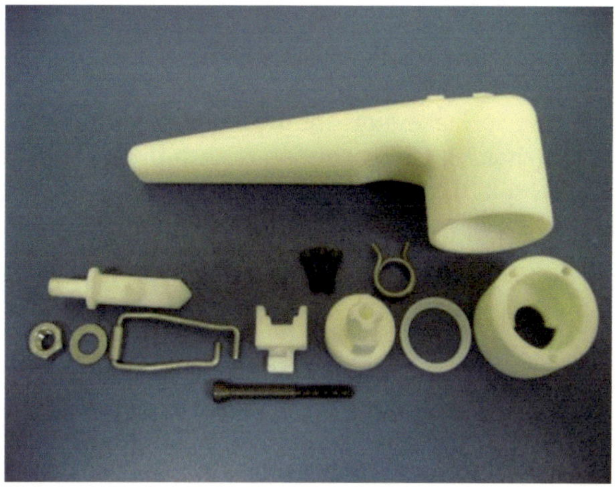

Fig. 6. Prototyped components of the proposed lock system

Fig. 7. Exploded view of the proposed design concept for a locking system

3.3 Company B

Company B is one of three major national suppliers of hour meters for manufacturers of agricultural machinery and parts. The hour meter (a special timer) is an electrical-mechanical device for controlling the length of engagement sessions on machines, equipment and stationary engines.

Among its major applications we find: tractors and general agricultural machinery, forklifts, marine engines, industrial machines and similar mechanisms. This product was chosen for being one of the higher revenue generators for the company, but lately its competitive edge in the market has been threatened by competition from suppliers with more technologically advanced products; as a result, the company is compelled to redesign its product, focusing on reducing its production cost in order to at least maintain its position in the market.

The research followed the steps of the integration model, proposed by Souza (2007), cited in Table 1, presented below.

3.3.1 Identify opportunity

As for the redesign through Reverse Engineering, an hour meter has been chosen as a reference product from a European company, which has commercial dealings in Brazil. This was a joint decision of the production department and the marketing department of the company being studied. The chosen product was considered as a reference for having such high sales in this market.

The technique of redesign, according to Otto and Wood (1998) was adaptive, in view of the need for new subsystems for the redesign of the hour meter to be produced by the company, object of study.

The acquisition of the reference product was possible thanks to the financial support offered by Minas Gerais Research Support Foundation (FAPEMIG), with the announcement "Young Doctors Program", process EDT-538/07, which provided a resource for the research. It is worth notice that the product, result of his research, didn´t break any patent ou commercial property, once que solutions for the generated subsystems were different from those observed on the reference product.

3.3.2 Collecting and preparing the initial information

This phase is the first one with involved technical characteristics. It has been carried out an initial survey of the marked on measuring instrument for machine panels, agricultural equipment and stationary engines.

All information has been brought together, which could contribute for the integration of reverse engineering with DFMA and the RP: elaboration of the product structures (definition of sets and their components), mapping and cronoanalysis of the hour meter assembling process, definition of standard time for each step of the assembling process and the product assembling raising costs.

A series of non structured interviews has been carried out with the mounting employees to identify their major difficulties on the hour meter assembling process. Table 4 shows some of the identified difficulties.

Set/Component	Illustration	Difficulties
Adaptor set		Manual welding of wires on the adaptor (component injected in ABS). During welding, it could happen the melting of the component in ABS because of being close to the welding equipment, causing non-compliance of the component.
Main support and coil support		The sets were assembled through welding, which if underdone could cause non-compliance on some components produced by ABS injection. For being welded linked, when a non-compliance occurs on some components, the disassembling may cause loss of one or two of the sets.
Support plate glass and display		The assemble of steel plate, display and glass is very difficult, once the clean glass can be touched by the assembling employees, being stained, forcing its disassemble for new cleaning. The display is made on aluminum (more expensive than steel, for example) and its manufacturing process needs stamping and a complete silk-screen process for recording of traces of marking time and engraving for the black and white painting.
Mug (external wrapping)		A different model of mug for any of the three models of hour meters, available for trade (one with lighting with rubber cushioning, another without lighting and another with a smaller size for a specific client).

Table 4. Diagnosis of the parts considered in the redesign

3.3.3 Team building

Table 5 shows a group of research formed for the development of work at the company B.

Member	Formation	Experience
Research coordinator	Doctor in industrial engineering	He works on product developing processes for more than 4 years.
Researcher	Doctor in industrial engineering	Mechanical projects expert.
Scientific initiation scholarship (two)	Graduate student in mechanical engineering	Mechanical projects designs.
Sales manager	Business management	More than five years at the trade of the hour meter.
Quality manager	Technician	More than 20 years on the hour meter production and quality control.

Table 5. Research Team at Company B

3.3.4 Disassemble (information about the product)

The studied hour meter has 11 systems and 87 components as a whole. For the redesign of this product, through reverse engineering, the reference product was totally disassembled, so the research group could analyze its constructive aspects, materials, (probable) assembling process, number of components etc.

The reference product analysis revealed several technical information that could be useful in the comparison of the components similar to the studied hour meter. Table 6 shows a comparison between some of these components.

3.3.5 Measure and test (information on the components)

After being disassembled the product, adopted as a reference, has been reassembled and taken to the lab of the company for testing the burn-in, among others. Some tractor model panels have been bought for testing the installation of the redesigned hour meter.

After this analysis, several meetings among the components of the research group were carried out in order to try to incorporate solutions to the current product, based on the reference product analysis and on the DFMA principles, to improve its assembling process and its cost-goal.

3.3.6 Specify and document

The studied company produced three hour meters models, one of them being to serve a client with a smaller mug (the mug is the wrapping that protects all the other components and helps in the fixation of the hour meter on the tractor panel), one with lighting and a damping rubber and another without lighting (for these two, the mugs are different to hold, or not, on their base a socket set for the bulb).

Reference hour meter		**Studied hour meter**	
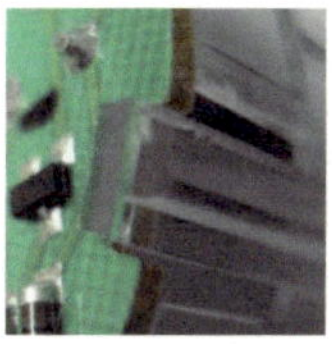	The main support assembling to the coil support is done through a slot, making it easy the disassemble and substitution of any component.	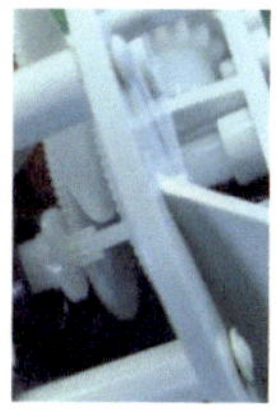	The main support assembling o the coil support is done through welding, making it difficult the disassembling and risky of damages to one of the supports, in case of substitution of any component.
	The display is made out of steel, in one-piece set, and its face in black was composed of a sticking glued to it.		The display is made out of aluminum and it needs a complex process of silkscreen for painting and recording of traces of time and paintings. It is composed of a glass support (steel) plate.
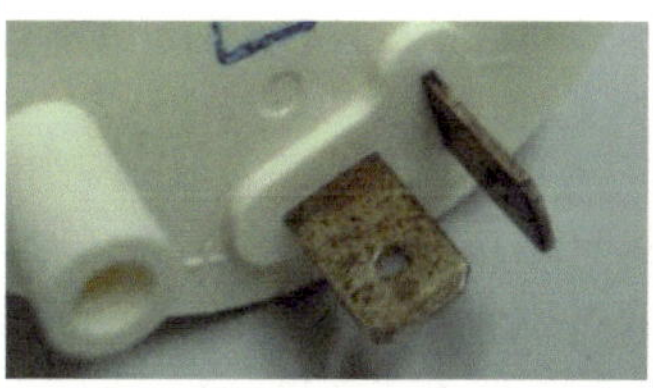	Non-existence of the adaptor. The contact between the hour meter and the panel of the tractor was carried out simply by the terminals without the need of wires, used by hour meters of the studied company.		Adaptor (injected on ABS) with wires manually welded.

Table 6. Comparison of components between the studied hourmeter and the reference one

One of the group suggestions was to propose as well a single mug for the hour meter, to be projected. Other similar analyses were carried out for another sets and components. All the suggestions offered by the research group were documented and the changes on the components or sets were specified. Table 7 shows some of the proposed solutions for the company as a result of the product redesign.

Component	Illustration	Proposed solution
Solution 1: adaptor		- wires elimination; - wires welding process elimination; - contact through terminals.
Solution 2: main support and coil support	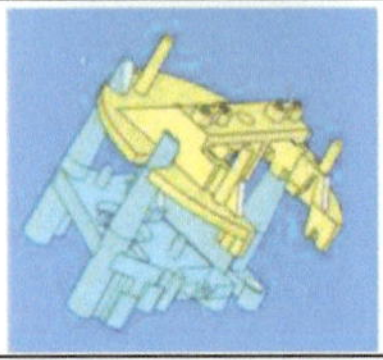	- welding eliminations for the junction of both plates; - ease assembling through fitting.
Solution 3: support plate glass and display	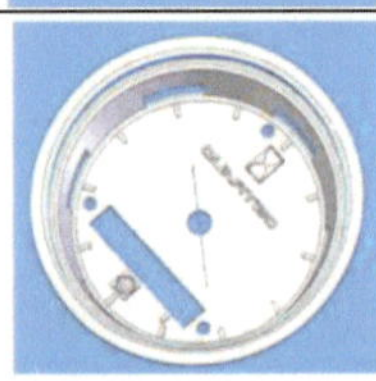	- single component instead of two; - display on steel instead of aluminum; - marking with adhesive instead of silkscreen; - fins to pass lightings (no longer by bulbs, but by leds); - reference fixation points to ease the assembling.
Solution 4: mug		- Possibility of a single mug type, of only one dimension, to serve all the clients and for products with and without lighting.

Table 7. Proposed solutions for the hour meter redesign

3.3.7 Prototyping

For the presentation of the proposed solutions were built rapid prototypes of components, to facilitate understanding by all involved and provide performing tests (dimensional and visual).

The prototypes were made in the rapid prototyping machine Strasys Dimension SST 768, of the Innovation Products Lab (Laboratório de Inovação de Produtos - LIP) from the Optimization of Manufacturing and Technology Innovation Nucleus (NOMATI) of the Federal University of Itajubá (UNIFEI) in Brazil.

For each changed system, it had built its corresponding prototype. Later a hybrid prototype has been built for discussion and the accomplishment of test by the team. Figure 8 shows the hybrid prototype built for the accomplishment of tests.

Fig. 8. Hybrid prototype

3.3.8 Review results

The tests have provided opportunities for improvement on the redesigned components. For example, the vibration test showed that the sets together by snaps showed a performance similar do the original product (union by welding).

This assured the company owners that the alteration proposals could be taken forward, minimizing the risks of failure. This information was registered on the company database as learned lessons.

4. Discussion

According to Coughlan and Coughlan (2002) the data critical analysis aspect in the action-research is that it is cooperative, and the researcher and the members of the client system (for example the managers' team, a group of clients etc.) carry it out together.

Such cooperating approach is based on the supposition that cooperators know much better their company, they know what is going to work and, mainly, they will be the ones to implement and follows the actions to be implemented. So, their involvement is crucial.

In this way, the criteria and tools for analysis were discussed between the researcher and his team of cooperators in the companies, so to be directly linked to the purpose of the research in the core of the interventions.

The following are the research result analysis in the companies A and B.

4.1 Company A

Twelve aspects were identified for comparison of the final results between the current lock system and the new proposed system. Table 8 shows, sparingly, these aspects.

The current lock has 13 components, as it is necessary two spheres and two springs. This is not necessary on the new lock, which has 11 components, representing about 15% reduction on the components number.

As for the current lock they use five manufacturing processes: laser cutting, bending, machining, welding and spring arrangement. As for the new lock, there are only four: plastic injection, machining, spring arrangement and casting, a 20% reduction on the process number. The current lock manufacturing time was informed by the supplier, which makes the product, involving the laser cutting, machining, welding, spring arrangement and finish, resulting in a total time of 220 minutes.

Beyond the manufacturing, the set assemble is also made by this supplier and the lock needs around 480 seconds to be ready for order. This service whole cost is of $ 124.00.

Making contact with suppliers, discussing methods and making estimates for the new lock, one can estimate costs in around $ 45.00 (a 64% cost reduction) involving all the necessary components and the time for manufacturing all the components and the necessary time for manufacturing them in around 20 minutes (a 91% reduction on the manufacturing time). Through the machined assembled prototype, one can estimate a 150 seconds time (reduction of 68%) for the system assembling.

Requisite	**Before**	**After**
Number of components	13	11
Number of manufacturing processes	5	4
Time of manufacturing components (minutes)	220	20
Product costs ($)	124.00	45.00
Time of system assembling (seconds)	480	150
Difficulties/Problems	7	3
Benefits	Robust system, meets the requirements like locks and consolidated in the company.	Innovative lock, easy to use and good resources.
Maintenance	Difficult, normally the system is changed as a whole.	Easy assembling and disassembling.
Functions	3	5
Operation	OPENING: 90 degrees to the left, medium strength. RELIEF: 45 degrees to the left, medium strength. CLOSING: pressure on the door, 90 degrees to the right, great strength.	OPENING: 50 degrees to the left or to the right, maintains a small force. RELIEF: degrees to the left or to the right and release, small force. CLOSING: light pressure or by door slam.
Relief system	Innefficient.	It allows a 20 millimeter relief.
Ergonomics	Tough mechanism, handle with straight edges.	Lightweight mechanism, handle with rounded corners.

Table 8. Lock project system final comparative results analysis

Through a Customer Service system and technical personal assistance one could identify some problems on the current lock:

- expensive manufacturing process, due to the amount and machining complexity of some components;
- leftover material (scrap);
- over time or excessive handling, the system generates a gap caused by swear, once the lever presses the set at every closing of the door;
- for being a locking door system through friction between both parts, until they fit it´s necessary to force a bit to overcome that friction, which makes the system to be a bit tough;
- There is no system to help spring returning movements.
- The existing relief generates a very small opening between the door and the trim, which is not perceived by the client, so it is not used. It also can be used when the client considers it to be inefficient for steams release;

- it is a complicate system for assembling and disassembling, due the presence of screw fly, spheres and springs, which can be used in a proper way for a lay person. Normally when a gap occurs, it is necessary to change the whole lock;
- for being made through the union of a three-millimeter layers, generating a six-millimeter cable, the squares end up being straight, which make the handling a bit painful, once there is the necessity of forcing one of the edges;
- if the lock, after the opening, gets back to the vertical position, after closing the oven the rotating component will crash on the panel and, quite probably, smash it.

After the first tests with the new lock, it was possible to reach preliminary conclusions as to some difficulties: since it is a system in which the shaft/spring must tightly fit into the lock, it is necessary to focus on the door positioning, assuring a perfect alignment; if, due to the oven manufacturing, there is some dimension error, which happens very frequently (due to the existence of processes like punching, bending, fitting with no feedback and welding), it is necessary the use of washers for the correct positioning of the two-stage lock; as some of the proposed components will be machined, it is necessary some big initial investments for the manufacture of machining model, so much for metals as for plastic, in an approximately cost of R$ 35,000.00.

On the other hand to these difficulties, it was possible to see the benefits of each lock. The current one has a robust system, which complies the market demands and it´s consolidated in the company. The new proposal is innovative (in relation to the models used in the company), easy to used and resourceful.

The current system is difficult to maintain, once the exchange of a component rarely solves the problem. Normally the system is substituted as whole, beyond the complexity of assembling and disassembling. The new lock is quite easy to assemble and disassemble, the major components can be exchanged with the removal of a screw. The system has less wear, once it suffers mostly axial strength.

As for its functions, it is possible to observe in the current lock the following: to ensure the oven total sealing; provide relieve system, to serve as a stem for opening and closing of the oven. The new lock closing features include the functions of the current system and more: to open the oven with a twist of the handle, for the right or for the left; to assure a fast return of the handle after been moved.

With regard to the operation, there has been an improvement related to the opening, relieve and closing.

The current lock relieve system is considered to be inefficient, as it allows a very short distance for steam relieve, normally not noticeable by clients. The new lock relieve system allows a 20 mm relieve, and can be used with light touch on the handle. It cannot be driven by choice, in case the handle is activated and remains at 50 degrees of twist at the opening.

The new lock allows the closing (lock) of the door, if it is moved with a light twist of the body when the operator is busy with his hands e doesn´t want to leave the oven door open.

As for ergonomic, the current lock is considered by the team as a tough mechanism, needing to much strength for moving.

The handle has straight corners, which can hurt with daily use. On the new lock the mechanism is light, it can be operated with a single finger; it is easy to be closed and it has rounded square to fit the hand.

After getting all the components in material resistant enough for testing the mechanism, there has been a meeting with all the responsible team for a test. Figure 9 shows the prototype ready for testing.

Fig. 9. New lock assembled for a test

With the use of a new door with proper drilling for the new lock, a mechanism has been assembled in the proposed oven and its operation can be tested.

All the team members handled the lock on different ways, according to their perceptions of the demands the new product must accomplish.

The new lock has been approved by everybody, as some accounts showed. The Major Cook stated: "it doesn´t make any difference for me the kind of lock; I like the current system, but the new one is really easier. The purchase responsible added: I liked it a lot, but now we must choose the materials, manufacturing processes and where it is going to be made. We are on the right path, the competitors are bringing on new things and this lock will be a difference for our oven". Finally, the Plant Director said: "the system is very cool. Let´s define if it is really accomplished in this prototype, to make more functional prototypes and testing. We can use pneumatic actuators to check the wears and go on adjusting till it can be introduced in our line".

4.2 Company B

The proposal of solutions, among those presented at Table 7, provided several benefits for the studied product at Company B.

The **solution 1** (see Table 7) provided the reduction of two components (wires) and their welding onto the adaptor. Previously the adaptor had distinct model for each hourmeter model. Such proposal allowed that only one of the existing models kept on being used, diminishing the components structure and improving their manufacturing planning. The passage of energy between the hour meter plate C1 and the terminal had to be made by two springs, internally assembled in their own accommodations in the mug. This assembling process is much faster than the previous one, beyond spring costs being inferior from the wire costs (including their cutting and preparation), as well as the insertion time to be inferior from that necessary one for the wire welding of the other components.

The **solution 2** provided mainly assembling ease of two sets. The welding process has been eliminated, taking advantage of the assembling concept through fitting of the reference product. However, the used concept in the solution proposal was different from the concept found in the reference product. In the proposal deep changes have been avoided in the components, to prevent the necessity of new models projects for the components injection. With the used concept, some small adjustments were enough in the existing models for the manufacturing of the new components. This proposed solution, beyond reducing the assembly time of these two sets, allows them to be disassembled at any time during the assembly process, in the case of non-compliance in any of the other components.

The **solution 3** helped reduce the cost component, since the display no longer needs to be produced in aluminum, and the new component can be produced in galvanized steel, as was the support of the glass. In addition, the use of an adhesive to the display, eliminating the silk screen process and all the involved sub-processes (cleaning, painting and silk), reducing cost and assembling time. The new component reduces the number of components, as it brought together two components into only one (simplification of product structure).

Finally, the **solution 4** was a natural result from previous ones, once it had been possible to propose only one mug as a wrapping and protection of the hour meter components. This solution simplifies the product structure, favoring a product standardization and reducing the failure possibility in the assembling because of the wrong mug for the right product model.

The proposed improvements will represent a significant reduction in the product several aspects and of its assembling/manufacturing process. Beyond, in case of testing failures, the hour meter can be disassembled and only those failing parts be exchanged, which is not possible in the current hourmeter.

Beyond the improvement on the assembling time, the proposed solutions will allow a significant reduction in the hour meter cost-goal, allowing an increase of its competitiviness on the market.

Table 9 shows a general final summary of he benefits provided with a redesigned product, not only for the four proposal shown in Table 7.

Regarding the reduction of the product cost-goal, the analysis of the research team evaluates a reduction of 33%, providing opportunities to the company to compete with its direct competitors for sharing he market.

In the previous Company B product redesign final results analysis they were not taken into account the improvements made in the product electronics parts, once they were not contemplate in the scope of the accomplished work.

CONJUNTO	COMPONENTS REDUCTION (%)	PROCESS REDUCTION (%)	ASSEMBLING AND MANUFACTURING TIME REDUCTION (%)
Adaptor	29	23	81
Complete plate	29	36	44
Embedding - several	17	0	30
Embedding - box	17	24	62
Embedding - socket	100	100	100
Embedding - accessories	0	8	13
Total	11	15	47

Table 9. Summary of the final results provided in the hour meter redesign

5. Conclusions

It is considered that the goals of this work have been achieved, once from the studied concepts in the theoretical consideration it was possible to analyze a model for the product redesign, which provided reduction in the components number in the assembling processes number, the assembling/manufacturing time and the product redesigning cost-goal.

Preliminary analyzing at Company A the difference between locks costs, manufacturing time, assembling time and facilities by the new model, one sees it will be a very positive change and, although some high cost with the machined model acquisition, such an amount will be rewarding with the time.

The recommendations for the Company B product were made with the care not to significantly alter the current company´s infrastructure in terms of the machines and tools, facilitating the development of the presented solutions and not needing any big investment for its deployment.

The research showed too that the integration of design for manufacturing and assembly (DFMA) with the rapid prototyping, in a reverse engineering approach, as proposed by Souza (2007), is an adequate strategy for the improvement (redesign) of products in small sized companies. The reverse engineering allows the study of other technologies or manufacturing and assembly solutions, components standardization, secondary operations reduction, among others.

The model proposed by Souza (2007) showed consistent for making product redesigns. It is expected that the current work can contribute to the incremental validation of this model. It is advised that other researchers use this same model in another similar research, aiming a possible generalization of the same future.

6. Acknowledgments

The authors would like to thank FAPEMIG (process EDT-538/07 and TEC-PPM-00043-08) and CNPq (project DT 312419/09) for research funding provided by in the form of research projects and scientific initiation scholarship, without which this research would not be possible. Our thanks also to employees and directors of the two researched companies, which allowed us to accomplish the current research.

7. References

Back, N. *Metodologia de projeto de produtos industriais*. Rio de Janeiro, RJ, Editora Guanabara Dois, 1983.

Back, N.; Dias, A.; Silva, J. C.; Ogliari, A. *Projeto Integrado de Produtos: Planejamento, Concepção e Modelagem*. Porto Alegre: Editora Manole, 2008.

Bagci, E. Reverse engineering applications for recovery of broken or worn parts and re-manufacturing: Three case studies. *Advances in Engineering Software*, v. 40, p. 407-418, 2009.

Boothroyd, G.; Dewhurst, P.; Knight, W. *Product development for manufacture and assembly*. Second edition revised and expanded. New York: Marcel Dekker, 2002.

Bourreau, M.; Dogan, P. Cooperation in product development and process R&D between competitors. *International Journal of Industrial Organization*. Doi: 10.1016/j.ijindorg.2009.07.010, 2009.

Chen, L. C. Reverse engineering in the design of turbine blades - a case study in applying the MAMDP. *Robotics and Computer Integrated Manufacturing*, v. 16, n. 2-3, p. 161-167, 2000.

Choi, S. H.; Chan, A. M. M. A virtual prototyping system for rapid product development. *Computer-Aided Design*, v. 36, p. 401-412, 2004.

Cooper, R. G.; Edgett, S. J. *Product Development for de Service Sector. Lessons from market leaders*. New York: Basic Books, 1999.

Coughlan, P.; Coghlan, D. Action research for operations management. *International Journal of Operations & Production Management*, v. 22, n. 2, p.220-240, 2002.

Dufour, C. A. *Estudo do processo e das ferramentas de reprojeto de produtos industriais, como vantagem competitiva e estratégia de melhoria constante*. Dissertação de mestrado. Universidade Federal de Santa Catarina, Florianópolis, 1996, 122p.

Estorilio, C.; Simião, M. C. Cost reduction of a diesel engine using the DFMA method. *Product Management & Development*, v. 4, n. 2, p. 95-103, 2006.

Gautam, N.; Singh, N. Lean product development: Maximizing the customer perceived value through design change (redesign). *International Journal of Production Economics*, v. 114, p. 313-332, 2008.

Hobday, M.; Rush, H.; Bessant, J. Approaching the innovation frontier in Korea: the transition phase to leadership. *Research Policy*, v. 33, p. 1433-1457, 2004.

Huang, G. Q.; Mak, K. L. Design for manufacture and assembly on the Internet. *Computers in Industry*. v. 38, p. 17-30, 1999.

Hüsig, S.; Kohn, S. Computer aided innovation. State of the art from a new product development perspective. *Computers in Industry*, v. 60, p. 551-562, 2009.

InglE, K. A. *Reverse Engineering*. McGraw-Hill, New York, 1994.

Kang, Y.; Park, C.; Wu, C. Reverse-engineering 1-n associations from Java bytecode using alias analysis. *Information and Software Technology*, v. 49, p. 81-98, 2007.

Kim, L.; Nelson, R. *Tecnologia, Aprendizado e Inovação: As Experiências das Economias de Industrialização Recente*. Edição do original estadunidense (2000). Campinas: Unicamp, 2005.

Kochan, A. Rapid prototyping gains speed, volume and precision. *Assembly Automation*, v. 20, n. 4, p. 295-299, 2000.

Mury, L. G. M. *Uma metodologia para adaptação e melhoria de produtos a partir da engenharia reversa.* Dissertação de mestrado. Programa de Pós-Graduação em Engenharia de Produção. Universidade Federal do Rio Grande do Sul - Escola De Engenharia, Porto Alegre, 2000, 89p.

Ogliari, A. *Sistematização da concepção de produtos auxiliada por computador com aplicações no domínio de componentes de plástico injetado.* Tese de Doutorado, PPGEM da Universidade Federal de Santa Catarina, Florianópolis, 1999.

Otto, K. N.; Wood, K. L. Product evolution: a reverse engineering and redesign methodology. *Research in Engineering Design*, v. 10, p. 226-243, 1998.

Pahl, G.; Beitz, W.; Feldhusen, J.; Grote, K. H. *Projeto na Engenharia: fundamentos do desenvolvimento eficaz de produtos, métodos e aplicações.* 6ª edição, São Paulo: Editora Edgard Blücher, 2005.

Rozenfeld, H.; Forcellini, F. A.; Amaral, D. C.; Toledo, J. C.; Silva, S. L.; Alliprandini, D. H.; Scalice, R. K. *Gestão de desenvolvimento de produtos: uma referência para a melhoria do processo.* São Paulo: Editora Saraiva, 2006.

Rosenthal, S. R. *Effective Product Design and Development - How to cut lead time and increase customer satisfaction.* New York, N.Y. Irwin Professional Publishing, 1992.

Salgado, E. G.; Mello, C. H. P.; Silva, C. E. S. Da; Oliveira, E. S.; Almeida, D. A. Análise da aplicação do mapeamento do fluxo de valor na identificação de desperdícios do processo de desenvolvimento de produtos. *Gestão e Produção*, v. 16, n. 3, p. 344-356, 2009.

Silva, C. E. S. *Método para avaliação do desempenho do processo de desenvolvimento de produtos.* Tese (Doutorado em Engenharia de Produção). Universidade Federal de Santa Catarina, Florianópolis, 2001.

Souza, J. F. *Aplicação de projeto para manufatura e montagem em uma abordagem de engenharia reversa: estudo de caso.* Dissertação de Mestrado. Programa de Pós-Graduação em Engenharia de Produção. Universidade Federal de Itajubá, Itajubá/MG, 135p, 2007.

Stephenson, J.; Wallace, K. Design for reability in mechanical systems. *International Conference on Engineering Design, ICED 95.* Praha, August 22-24, 1995.

Thiollent, M. *Metodologia da pesquisa-ação.* 15ª edição, São Paulo: Editora Cortez, 2007.

Toledo, J. C.; Silva, S. L.; Alliprandini, D. R.; Martins, M. F.; Ferrari, F. M. Práticas de gestão no desenvolvimento de produtos em empresas de autopeças. *Produção*, v. 18, n. 2, p. 405-422, 2008.

Vincent, G. *Managing new product development.* New York: Van Nostrand Reinold, 1989.

Wheelwright, S. C.; Clark, K. B. *Revolutionizing product development - Quantum leaps in speed, efficiency, and quality.* New York: Free Press, 1992.

Zhu, J.; Liang, X.; Xu, Q. The cause of secondary innovation dilemma in chinese enterprises and solutions. *Proceedings of the 2005 IEEE International Engineering Conference*, v. 1, p. 297-301, 2005.

Part 3

Reverse Engineering in Medical and Life Sciences

10

Reverse Engineering Gene Regulatory Networks by Integrating Multi-Source Biological Data

Yuji Zhang[1], Habtom W. Ressom[2] and Jean-Pierre A. Kocher[1]
[1]Division of Biomedical Statistics and Informatics, Department of Health Sciences Research, Mayo Clinic College of Medicine, Rochester, MN
[2]Department of Oncology, Lombardi Comprehensive Cancer Center at Georgetown University Medical Center, Washington, DC
USA

1. Introduction

Gene regulatory network (GRN) is a model of a network that describes the relationships among genes in a given condition. The model can be used to enhance the understanding of gene interactions and provide better ways of elucidating environmental and drug-induced effects (Ressom et al. 2006).

During last two decades, enormous amount of biological data generated by high-throughput analytical methods in biology produces vast patterns of gene activity, highlighting the need for systematic tools to identify the architecture and dynamics of the underlying GRN (He et al. 2009). Here, the system identification problem falls naturally into the category of **reverse engineering**; a complex genetic network underlies a massive set of expression data, and the task is to infer the connectivity of the genetic circuit (Tegner et al. 2003). However, reverse engineering of a global GRN remains challenging because of several limitations including the following:

1. Tens of thousands of genes act at different temporal and spatial combinations in living cells;
2. Each gene interacts virtually with multiple partners either directly or indirectly, thus possible relationships are dynamic and non-linear;
3. Current high-throughput technologies generate data that involve a substantial amount of noise; and
4. The sample size is extremely low compared with the number of genes (Clarke et al. 2008).

These inherited properties create significant problems in analysis and interpretation of these data. Standard statistical approaches are not powerful enough to dissect data with thousands of variables (i.e., semi-global or global gene expression data) and limited sample sizes (i.e., several to hundred samples in one experiment). These properties are typical in microarray and proteomic datasets (Bubitzky et al. 2007) as well as other high dimensional data where a comparison is made for biological samples that tend to be limited in number, thus suffering from curse of dimensionality (Wit and McClure 2006).

One approach to address the curse of dimensionality is to integrate multiple large data sets with prior biological knowledge. This approach offers a solution to tackle the challenging task of inferring GRN. Gene regulation is a process that needs to be understood at multiple levels of description (Blais and Dynlacht 2005). A single source of information (e.g., gene expression data) is aimed at only one level of description (e.g., transcriptional regulation level), thus it is limited in its ability to obtain a full understanding of the entire regulatory process. Other types of information such as various types of molecular interaction data by yeast two-hybrid analysis or genome-wide location analysis (Ren et al. 2000) provide complementary constraints on the models of regulatory processes. By integrating limited but complementary data sources, we realize a mutually consistent hypothesis bearing stronger similarity to the underlying causal structures (Blais and Dynlacht 2005). Among the various types of high-throughput biological data available nowadays, time course gene expression profiles and molecular interaction data are two complementary sets of information that are used to infer regulatory components. Time course gene expression data are advantageous over typical static expression profiles as time can be used to disambiguate causal interactions. Molecular interaction data, on the other hand, provide high-throughput qualitative information about interactions between different entities in the cell. Also, prior biological knowledge generated by geneticists will help guide inference from the above data sets and integration of multiple data sources offers insights into the cellular system at different levels.

A number of researches have explored the integration of multiple data sources (e.g., time course expression data and sequence motifs) for GRN inference (Spellman et al. 1998; Tavazoie et al. 1999; Simon et al. 2001; Hartemink et al. 2002). A typical approach for exploiting two or more data sources uses one type of data to validate the results generated independently from the other (i.e., without data fusion). For example, cluster analysis of gene expression data was followed by the identification of consensus sequence motifs in the promoters of genes within each cluster (Spellman et al. 1998). The underlying assumption behind this approach is that genes co-expressed under varying experimental conditions are likely to be co-regulated by the same transcription factor or sets of transcription factors. Holmes et al. constructed a joint likelihood score based on consensus sequence motif and gene expression data and used this score to perform clustering (Holmes and Bruno 2001). Segal et al. built relational probabilistic models by incorporating gene expression and functional category information as input variables (Segal et al. 2001). Gene expression data and gene ontology data were combined for GRN discovery in B cell (Tuncay et al. 2007). Computational methodologies that allow systematic integration of data from multiple resources are needed to fully use the complementary information available in those resources.

Another way to reduce the complexity in reverse engineering a GRN is to decompose it into simple units of commonly used network structures. GRN is a network of interactions between transcription factors and the genes they regulate, governing many of the biological activities in cells. Cellular networks like GRNs are composed of many small but functional modules or units (Wang et al. 2007). Breaking down GRNs into these functional modules will help understanding regulatory behaviors of the whole networks and study their properties and functions. One of these functional modules is called network motif (NM) (Milo et al. 2004). Since the establishment of the first NM in Escherichia coli (Rual et al.

2005), similar NMs have also been found in eukaryotes including yeast (Lee et al. 2002), plants (Wang et al. 2007), and animals (Odom et al. 2004; Boyer et al. 2005; Swiers et al. 2006), suggesting that the general structure of NMs are evolutionarily conserved. One well known family of NMs is the feed-forward loop (Mangan and Alon 2003), which appears in hundreds of gene systems in E. coli (Shen-Orr et al. 2002; Mangan et al. 2003) and yeast (Lee et al. 2002; Milo et al. 2002), as well as in other organisms (Milo et al. 2004; Odom et al. 2004; Boyer et al. 2005; Iranfar et al. 2006; Saddic et al. 2006; Swiers et al. 2006). A comprehensive review on NM theory and experimental approaches could be found in the review article (Alon 2007). Knowledge of the NMs to which a given transcription factor belongs facilitates the identification of downstream target gene modules. In yeast, a genome-wide location analysis was carried out for 106 transcription factors and five NMs were considered significant: autoregulation, feed-forward loop, single input module, multi-input module and regulator cascade.

In this Chapter, we propose a computational framework that integrates information from time course gene expression experiment, molecular interaction data, and gene ontology category information to infer the relationship between transcription factors and their potential target genes at NM level. This was accomplished through a three-step approach outlined in the following: first, we applied cluster analysis of time course gene expression profiles to reduce dimensionality and used the gene ontology category information to determine biologically meaningful gene modules, upon which a model of the gene regulatory module is built. This step enables us to address the scalability problem that is faced by researchers in inferring GRNs from time course gene expression data with limited time points. Second, we detected significant NMs for each transcription factor in an integrative molecular interaction network consisting of protein-protein interaction and protein-DNA interaction data (hereafter called molecular interaction data) from thirteen publically available databases. Finally, we used neural network (NN) models that mimic the topology of NMs to identify gene modules that may be regulated by a transcription factor, thereby inferring the regulatory relationships between the transcription factor and gene modules. A hybrid of genetic algorithm and particle swarm optimization (GA-PSO) methods was applied to train the NN models.

The organization of this chapter is as follows. Section 2 briefly reviews the related methods. Section 3 introduces the proposed method to infer GRNs by integrating multiple sources of biological data. Section 4 will present the results on two real data sets: the yeast cell cycle data set (Spellman et al. 1998), and the human Hela cell cycle data set (Whitfield et al. 2002). Finally, Section 5 is devoted to the summary and discussions.

2. Review of related methods

In recent years, high throughput biotechnologies have made large-scale gene expression surveys a reality. Gene expression data provide an opportunity to directly review the activities of thousands of genes simultaneously. The field of system modeling plays a significant role in inferring GRNs with these gene expression data.

Several system modeling approaches have been proposed to reverse-engineer network interactions including a variety of continuous or discrete, static or dynamic, quantitative or qualitative methods. These include biochemically driven methods (Naraghi and Neher

1997), linear models (Chen et al. 1999; D'Haeseleer et al. 1999), Boolean networks (Shmulevich et al. 2002), fuzzy logic (Woolf and Wang 2000; Ressom et al. 2003), Bayesian networks (Friedman et al. 2000), and recurrent neural networks (RNNs) (Zhang et al. 2008). Biochemically inspired models are developed on the basis of the reaction kinetics between different components of a network. However, most of the biochemically relevant reactions under participation of proteins do not follow linear reaction kinetics, and the full network of regulatory reactions is very complex and hard to unravel in a single step. Linear models attempt to solve a weight matrix that represents a series of linear combinations of the expression level of each gene as a function of other genes, which is often underdetermined since gene expression data usually have far fewer dimensions than the number of genes. In a Boolean network, the interactions between genes are modeled as Boolean function. Boolean networks assume that genes are either "on" or "off" and attempt to solve the state transitions for the system. The validity of the assumptions that genes are only in one of these two states has been questioned by a number of researchers, particularly among those in the biological community. Woolf and Wang 2000 proposed an approach based on fuzzy rules of a known activator/repressor model of gene interaction. This algorithm transforms expression values into qualitative descriptors that is evaluated by using a set of heuristic rules and searches for regulatory triplets consisting of activator, repressor, and target gene. This approach, though logical, is a brute force technique for finding gene relationships. It involves significant computational time, which restricts its practical usefulness. In (Ressom et al. 2003), we proposed the use of clustering as an interface to a fuzzy logic-based method to improve the computational efficiency. In a Bayesian network model, each gene is considered as a random variable and the edges between a pair of genes represent the conditional dependencies entailed in the network structure. Bayesian statistics are applied to find certain network structure and the corresponding model parameters that maximize the posterior probability of the structure given the data. Unfortunately, this learning task is NP-hard, and it also has the underdetermined problem. The RNN model has received considerable attention because it can capture the nonlinear and dynamic aspects of gene regulatory interactions. Several algorithms have been applied for RNN training in network inference tasks, such as fuzzy-logic (Maraziotis et al. 2005) and genetic algorithm (Chiang and Chao 2007).

3. Proposed method

3.1 Overview of the proposed framework

In the proposed framework, we consider two different layers of networks in the GRN. One is the molecular interaction network at the factor-gene binding level. The other is the functional network that incorporates the consequences of these physical interactions, such as the activation or repression of transcription. We used three types of data to reconstruct the GRN, namely protein-protein interactions derived from a collection of public databases, protein-DNA interactions from the TRANSFAC database (Matys et al. 2006), and time course gene expression profiles. The first two data sources provided direct network information to constrain the GRN model. The gene expression profiles provided an unambiguous measurement on the causal effects of the GRN model. Gene ontology annotation describes the similarities between genes within one network, which facilitates further characterization of the relationships between genes. The goal is to discern dependencies between the gene expression patterns and the physical inter-molecular interactions revealed by complementary data sources.

The framework model for GRN inference is illustrated in Figure 1. Besides data pre-processing, three successive steps are involved in this framework as outlined in the following:

Gene module selection: genes with similar expression profiles are represented by a gene module to address the scalability problem in GRN inference (Ressom et al. 2003). The assumption is that a subset of genes that are related in terms of expression (co-regulated) can be grouped together by virtue of a unifying cis-regulatory element(s) associated with a common transcription factor regulating each and every member of the cluster (co-expressed) (Yeung et al. 2004). Gene ontology information is used to define the optimal number of clusters with respect to certain broad functional categories. Since each gene module identified from clustering analysis mainly represents one broad biological process or category as evaluated by FuncAssociate (Berriz et al. 2003), the regulatory network implies that a given transcription factor is likely to be involved in the control of a group of functionally related genes (De Hoon et al. 2002). This step is implemented by the method proposed in our previous work (Zhang et al. 2009).

Network motif discovery: to reduce the complexity of the inference problem, NMs are used instead of a global GRN inference. The significant NMs in the combined molecular interaction network are first established and assigned to at least one transcription factor. These associations are further used to reconstruct the regulatory modules. This step is implemented using FANMOD software (Wernicke and Rasche 2006). We briefly describe it in the following section.

Gene regulatory module inference: for each transcription factor assigned to a NM, a NN is trained to model a GRN that mimics the associated NM. Genetic algorithm generates the candidate gene modules, and particle swarm optimization (PSO) is used to configure the parameters of the NN. Parameters are selected to minimize the root mean square error (RMSE) between the output of the NN and the target gene module's expression pattern. The RMSE is returned to GA to produce the next generation of candidate gene modules. Optimization continues until either a pre-specified maximum number of iterations are completed or a pre-specified minimum RMSE is reached. The procedure is repeated for all transcription factors. Biological knowledge from public databases is used to evaluate the predicted results. This step is the main focus of this chapter.

3.2 Network motif discovery

The NM analysis is based on network representation of protein-protein interactions and protein-DNA interactions. A node represents both the gene and its protein product. A protein-protein interaction is represented by a bi-directed edge connecting the interacting proteins. A protein-DNA interaction is an interaction between a transcription factor and its target gene and is represented by a directed edge pointing from the transcription factor to its target gene.

All connected subnetworks containing three nodes in the interaction network are collated into isomorphic patterns, and the number of times each pattern occurs is counted. If the number of occurrences is at least five and significantly higher than in randomized networks, the pattern is considered as a NM. The statistical significance test is performed by generating 1000 randomized networks and computing the fraction of randomized networks in which the pattern appears at least as often as in the interaction network, as described in (Yeger-Lotem et al. 2004). A pattern with $p \leq 0.05$ is considered statistically significant. This NM discovery procedure was performed using the FANMOD software. For different organisms, different NMs may be identified. As shown in Figure 2 and Figure 3, different sets of NMs were detected in yeast and human. Both NM sets shared some similar NM structures. For example, Figure 2(B) and Figure 3(C) were both feed-forward loops. This NM has been indentified and studied in many organisms including E. coli, yeast, and human. Knowledge of these NMs to which a given transcription factor belongs facilitates the identification of downstream target gene modules.

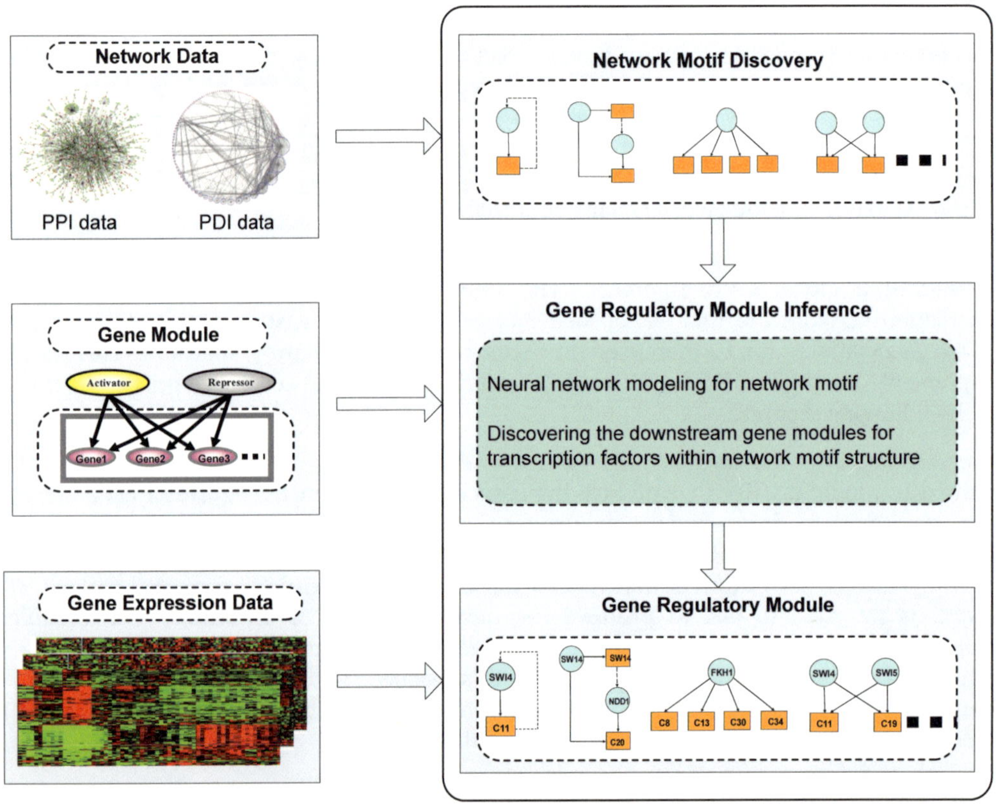

Fig. 1. Schematic overview of the computational framework used for the gene regulatory network inference.

3.3 Reverse engineering transcriptional regulatory modules

In building NNs for inferring GRNs, the identification of the correct downstream gene modules and determination of the free parameters (weights and biases) to mimic the real data is a challenging task given the limited available quantity of data. For example, in inferring a GRN from microarray data, the number of time points is considerably low compared to the number of genes involved. Considering the complexity of the biological system, it is difficult to adequately describe the pathways involving a large number of genes with few time points. We addressed this challenge by inferring GRNs at NM modular level instead of gene level. Neural network models were built for all NMs detected in the molecular interaction data. A hybrid search algorithm, called GA-PSO, was proposed to select the candidate gene modules (output node) in a NN and to update its free parameters simultaneously. We illustrate the models and training algorithm in detail in the following sections.

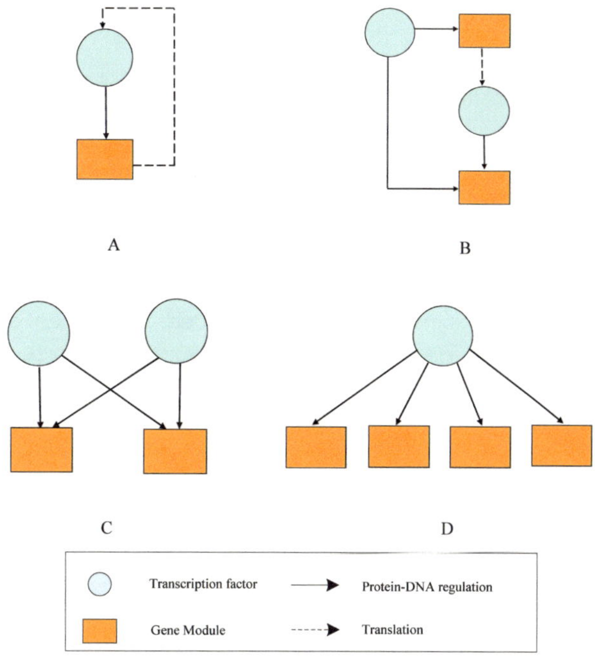

Fig. 2. Four NMs discovered in yeast: (A) auto-regulatory motif; (B) feed-forward loop; (C) single input module; and (D) multi-input module.

3.3.1 Neural network model

The neural network model is based on the assumption that the regulatory effect on the expression of a particular gene can be expressed as a neural network (Figure 4(A)), where each node represents a particular gene and the wirings between nodes define regulatory interactions. Each layer of the network represents the expression level of genes at time *t*. The output of a node at time $t+\Delta t$ is derived from the expression levels at the time *t* and the connection weights of all genes connected to the given gene. As shown in the figure, the output of each node is fed back to its input after a unit delay and is connected to other nodes. The network is used as a model to a GRN: every gene in the network is considered as a neuron; NN model considers not only the interactions between genes but also gene self-regulations.

Figure 4 (B) illustrates the details of the *i*th self-feedback neuron (e.g. *i*th gene in the GRN), where v_i, known as the induced local field (activation level), is the sum of the weighted inputs (the regulation of other genes) to the neuron (ith gene); and $\varphi()$ represents an activation function (integrated regulation of the whole NN on *i*th gene), which transforms the activation level of a neuron into an output signal (regulation result). The induced local field and the output of the neuron, respectively, are given by:

$$v_i(T_j) = \sum_{k=1}^{N} w_{ik} x_k(T_{j-1}) + b_i(T_j) \quad (1)$$

$$x_i(T_j) = \varphi(v_i(T_j)) \quad (2)$$

where the synaptic weights $w_{i1}, w_{i2}, \ldots, w_{iN}$ define the strength of connections between the ith neuron (e.g. ith gene) and its inputs (e.g. expression level of genes). Such synaptic weights exist between all pairs of neurons in the network. $b_i(T_j)$ denotes the bias for the ith neuron at time T_j. We denote $\vec{w}$ as a weight vector that consists of all the synaptic weights and biases in the network. $\vec{w}$ is adapted during the learning process to yield the desired network outputs. The activation function $\varphi()$ introduces nonlinearity to the model. When information about the complexity of the underlying system is available, a suitable activation function can be chosen (e.g. linear, logistic, sigmoid, threshold, hyperbolic tangent sigmoid or Gaussian function.) If no prior information is available, our algorithm uses the hyperbolic tangent sigmoid function.

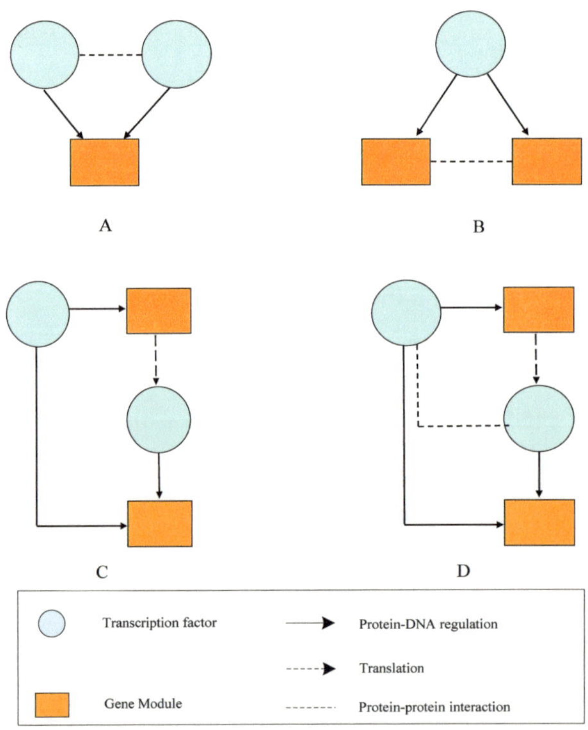

Fig. 3. Four NMs discovered in human: (A) multi-input module; (B) single input module; (C) feed-forward loop - 1; and (D) feed-forward loop - 2.

As a cost function, we use the RMSE between the expected output and the network output across time and neurons in the network. The cost function is written as:

$$E(\vec{w}) = \sqrt{\frac{1}{Nm}\sum_{t=T_i}^{T_m}\sum_{i=1}^{N}[[x_i(t) - \hat{x}_i(t)]]^2} \quad (3)$$

where $x_i(t)$ and $\hat{x}_i(t)$ are the true and predicted values (expression levels) for the ith neuron (gene) at time t. The goal is to determine weight vector $\vec{w}$ that minimize this cost function. This is a challenging task if the size of the network is large and only few samples (time points) are available.

For each NM shown in Figure 2 and 3, a corresponding NN is built. Figure 5 presents the detailed NN model for each NM in Figure 2. For auto-regulatory motif, the NN model is the same as single input module except that its downstream gene module contains the transcription factor itself. Since the expression level of gene module is the mean of expression level of its member genes, the input node and output node have different expression profiles. This avoids an open-loop problem which may cause the stability of the model. For single input and multiple input modules, instead of selecting multiple downstream gene modules simultaneously, we build NN models to find candidate gene modules one at one time. The selected gene modules are merged together to build the final NM gene regulatory modules.

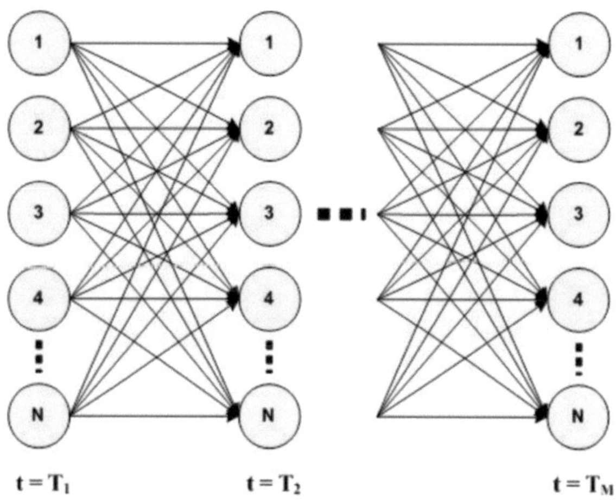

(A)

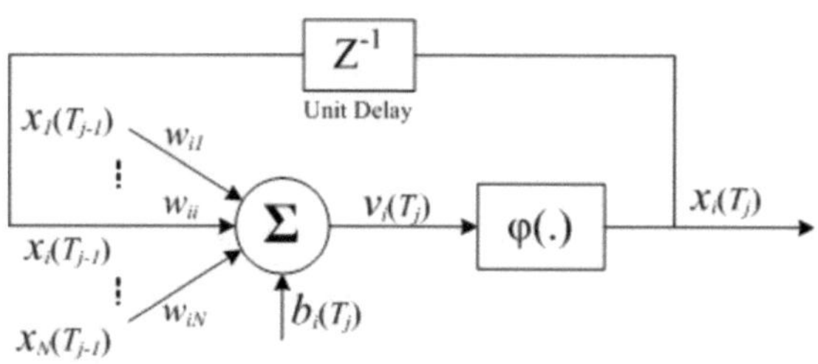

(B)

Fig. 4. Architecture of a fully connected NN (A) and details of a single recurrent neuron (B).

Based on NMs to which a given transcription factor belongs, the next process is to find out the target gene modules and the relationships between them. To resolve this problem, we propose a hybrid GA-PSO training algorithm for NN model.

3.3.2 Genetic algorithm

Genetic algorithms are stochastic optimization approaches which mimic representation and variation mechanisms borrowed from biological evolution, such as selection, crossover, and mutation (Mitchell 1998). In a GA, a candidate solution is represented as a linear string analogous to a biological chromosome. The general scheme of GAs starts from a population of randomly generated candidate solutions (chromosomes). Each chromosome is then evaluated and given a value which corresponds to a fitness level in the objective function space. In each generation, chromosomes are chosen based on their fitness to reproduce offspring. Chromosomes with a high level of fitness are more likely to be retained while the ones with low fitness tend to be discarded. This process is called selection. After selection, offspring chromosomes are constructed from parent chromosomes using operators that resemble crossover and mutation mechanisms in evolutionary biology. The crossover operator, sometimes called recombination, produces new offspring chromosomes that inherit information from both sides of parents by combining partial sets of elements from them. The mutation operator randomly changes elements of a chromosome with a low probability. Over

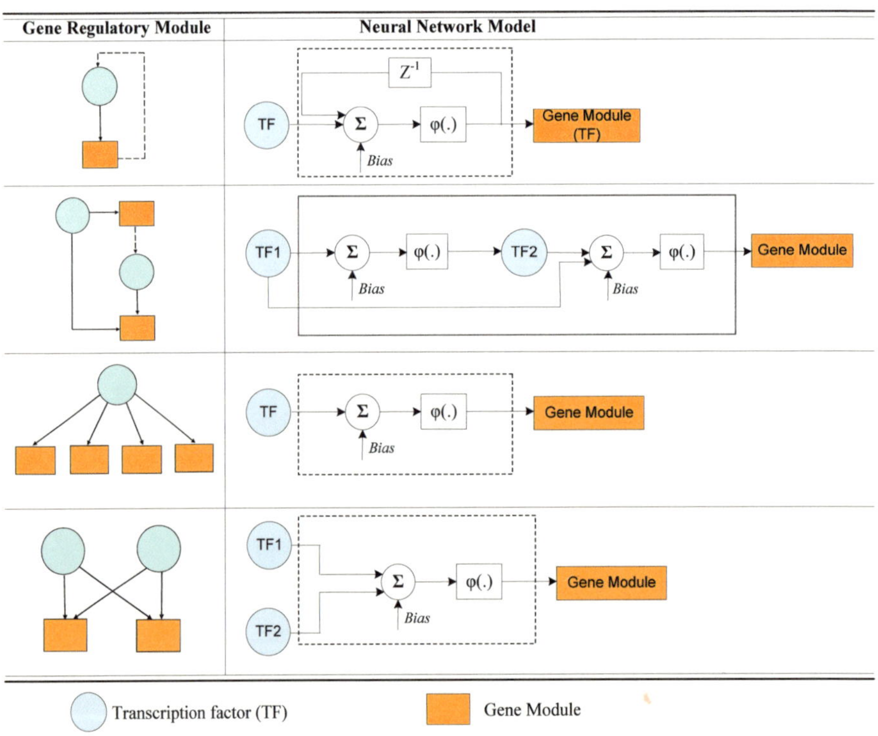

Fig. 5. NN models mimicking the topologies of the four NMs shown in Figure 2. Z^{-1} denotes a unit delay and $\varphi()$ is a logistic sigmoid activation function.

multiple generations, chromosomes with higher fitness values are left based on the survival of the fitness. A detailed description of GA is shown in Figure 6. In this chapter, we propose to apply to GA to select the best suitable downstream gene module(s) for each transcription factor and the NN model(s) that mimic its NM(s). The Genetic Algorithm and Direct Search Toolbox (Mathworks, Natick, MA) is used for implementation of GA.

3.3.3 Particle swarm optimization

After the candidate downstream gene modules are selected by GA, PSO is proposed to determine the parameters in the NN model. Particle swarm optimization is motivated by the behavior of bird flocking or fish blocking, originally intended to explore optimal or near-optimal solutions in sophisticated continuous spaces (Kennedy and Eberhart 1995). Its main difference from other evolutionary algorithms (e.g., GA) is that PSO relies on cooperation rather than competition. Good solutions in the problem set are shared with their less-fit ones so that the entire population improves.

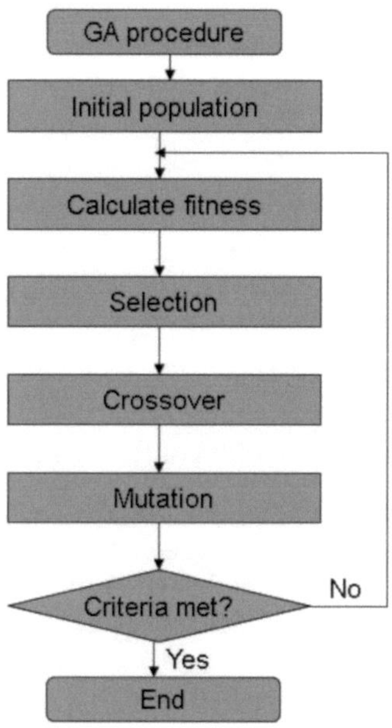

Fig. 6. A detailed description of GA.

Particle swarm optimization consists of a swarm of particles, each of which represents a candidate solution. Each particle is represented as a D-dimensional vector $\vec{w}$, with a corresponding D-dimensional instantaneous trajectory vector $\Delta\vec{w}(t)$, describing its direction of motion in the search space at iteration *t*. The index *i* refers to the *i*th particle. The core of the PSO algorithm is the position update rule (Eq. (4)) which governs the movement of each of the n particles through the search space.

$$\vec{w}_i(t+1) = \vec{w}_i(t) + \Delta\vec{w}_i(t+1) \tag{4}$$

$$\Delta\vec{w}_i(t+1) = \chi[\Delta\vec{w}_i(t) + \Phi_1(\vec{w}_{i,best}(t) - \vec{w}_i(t)) + \Phi_2(\vec{w}_{G,best}(t) - \vec{w}_i(t))] \tag{5}$$

where $\Phi_1 = c_1 \begin{bmatrix} r_{1,1} & & & \\ & r_{1,2} & & \\ & & \ddots & \\ & & & r_{1,D} \end{bmatrix}$ and $\Phi_2 = c_2 \begin{bmatrix} r_{2,1} & & & \\ & r_{2,2} & & \\ & & \ddots & \\ & & & r_{2,D} \end{bmatrix}$

At any instant, each particle is aware of its individual best position, $\vec{w}_{i,best}(t)$, as well as the best position of the entire swarm, $\vec{w}_{G,best}(t)$. The parameters *c1* and *c2* are constants that weight particle movement in the direction of the individual best positions and global best positions, respectively; and $r_{1,j}$ and $r_{2,j}$, $j = 1,2,...D$ are random scalars distributed uniformly between 0 and 1, providing the main stochastic component of the PSO algorithm. Figure 7 shows a vector diagram of the contributing terms of the PSO trajectory update. The new change in position, $\Delta\vec{w}_i(t+1)$, is the resultant of three contributing vectors: (i) the inertial component, $\Delta\vec{w}_i(t)$, (ii) the movement in the direction of individual best, $\vec{w}_{i,best}(t)$, and (iii) the movement in the direction of the global (or neighborhood) best, $\vec{w}_{G,best}(t)$.

The constriction factor, χ, may also help to ensure convergence of the PSO algorithm, and is set according to the weights *c1* and *c2* as in Eq.(6).

$$\chi = \frac{2}{\left|2 - \varphi - \sqrt{\varphi^2 - 4\varphi}\right|}, \varphi = c_1 + c_2, \varphi > 4 \tag{6}$$

The key strength of the PSO algorithm is the interaction among particles. The second term in Eq. (5), $\Phi_2(\vec{w}_{G,best}(t) - \vec{w}_i(t))$, is considered to be a "social influence" term. While this term tends to pull the particle towards the globally best solution, the first term, $\Phi_1(\vec{w}_{i,best}(t) - \vec{w}_i(t))$, allows each particle to think for itself. The net combination is an algorithm with excellent trade-off between total swarm convergence, and each particle's capability for global exploration. Moreover, the relative contribution of the two terms is weighted stochastically.

The algorithm consists of repeated application of the velocity and position update rules presented above. Termination occurs by specification of a minimum error criterion, maximum number of iterations, or alternately when the position change of each particle is sufficiently small as to assume that each particle has converged.

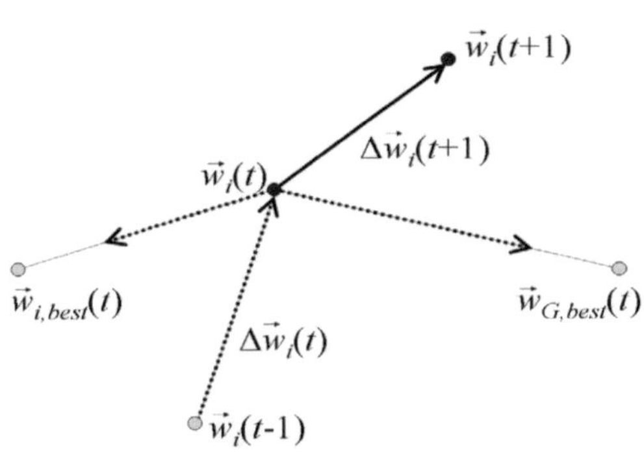

Fig. 7. Vector diagram of particle trajectory update.

A pseudo-code description of the PSO algorithm is provided below:

1. Generate initial population of particles, $\vec{w}_i$, i=1,2,...,n, distributed randomly (uniform) within the specified bounds.
2. Evaluate each particle with the objective function, $f(\vec{w}_i)$; if any particles have located new individual best positions, then replace previous individual best positions, $\vec{w}_{i,best}$, and keep track of the swarm global best position, $\vec{w}_{G,best}$.
3. Determine new trajectories, $\Delta\vec{w}_i(t+1)$, according to Eq. (5).
4. Update each particle position according to Eq. (4).
5. Determine if any $\vec{w}_i(t+1)$ are outside of the specified bounds; hold positions of particles within the specified bounds.

If termination criterion is met (for example completed maximum number of iterations), then $\vec{w}_{G,best}$ is the best solution found; otherwise, go to step (2).

Selection of appropriate values for the free parameters of PSO plays an important role in the algorithm's performance. In our study, the parameters setting is presented in Table 1, and the constriction factor χ is determined by Eq.(6). The PSOt Toolbox (Birge 2003) was used for implementation of PSO.

Parameter	Value
Maximum velocity, Vmax	2
Maximum search space range, |Wmax|	[-5,5]
Acceleration constants, c1 & c2	2.05, 2.05
Size of Swarm	20

Table 1. PSO parameter setting

3.3.4 GA-PSO training algorithm

A hybrid of GA and PSO methods (GA-PSO) is applied to determine the gene modules that may be regulated by each transcription factor. Genetic algorithm generates candidate gene modules, while the PSO algorithm determines the parameters of a given NN represented by a weight vector . The RMSE between the NN output and the measured expression profile is returned to GA as a fitness function and to guide the selection of target genes through reproduction, cross-over, and mutation over hundreds of generations. The stopping criteria are pre-specified minimum RMSE or maximum number of generations. The GA-PSO algorithm is run for each transcription factor to train a NN that has the architecture mimicking the identified known NM(s) for the transcription factor. Thus, for a given transcription factor (input), the following steps are carried out to identify its likely downstream gene modules (output) based on their NM(s):

1. Assign the NM to the transcription factor it belongs to.
2. Use the following GA-PSO algorithm to build a NN model that mimics the NM to identify the downstream gene modules.
   a. Generate combinations of M gene modules to represent the target genes that may be regulated by the transcription factor. Each combination is a vector/chromosome. The initial set of combinations is composed of the initial population of chromosomes.
   b. Use the PSO algorithm to train a NN model for each chromosome, where the input is the transcription factor and the outputs are gene modules. The goal is to

determine the optimized parameters of the NN that maps the measured expression profiles of the transcription factor to the gene modules.

c. For each chromosome, calculate the RMSE between the predicted output of the NN and measured expression profiles for the target gene modules.
d. Apply GA operators (reproduction, cross-over, mutation) based on the RMSE calculated in Step 2.3 as a fitness value. This will generate new vectors/chromosomes altering the choice of output gene module combinations.
e. Repeat steps 2.1 - 2.4 until stop criteria are met. The stopping criteria are numbers of generations or minimum RMSE, depending on which one is met first.
f. Repeat Steps 2.1 - 2.5 for each NM the transcription factor is assigned to.

3. Repeat Steps 1 and 2 for each transcription factor.

When the process is completed, NM regulatory modules are constructed between transcription factors and their regulated gene modules.

4. Results

4.1 Yeast cell cycle dataset

4.1.1 Data sources

Gene expression dataset: the yeast cell cycle dataset presented in (Spellman et al. 1998) consists of six time series (*cln3, clb2, alpha, cdc15, cdc28,* and *elu*) expression measurements of the mRNA levels of *S. cerevisiae* genes. 800 genes were identified as cell cycle regulated based on cluster analysis in (Spellman et al. 1998). We used the *cdc15* time course data of the 800 genes since it has the largest number of time points (24). Missing values in the data were imputed using KNN imputation (Troyanskaya et al. 2001). The expression pattern of each gene was standardized between 0 and 1.

Molecular interaction data: data of transcription factors and their target genes were extracted from the SCPD database (Zhu and Zhang 1999), from the YPD database (Costanzo et al. 2001), and from recent publications on genome-wide experiments that locate binding sites of given transcription factors (Ren et al. 2000; Iyer et al. 2001; Simon et al. 2001; Lee et al. 2002). For data extraction from the latter we used the same experimental thresholds as in the original papers. Protein-protein interaction data was extracted from the DIP database (Przulj et al. 2004), from the BIND database (Bader et al. 2003), and from the MIPS database (Mewes et al. 2002). In total the molecular interaction dataset consisted of 8184 protein pairs connected by protein-protein interactions and 5976 protein pairs connected by protein-DNA interactions.

4.1.2 Gene module Identification

We grouped 800 cell cycle-regulated genes into clusters by Fuzzy c-means method, where genes with similar expression profiles are represented by a gene module. The optimal cluster number was determined by the proposed method in (Zhang et al. 2009). The highest *z* score was obtained when the number of clusters was 34 by Fuzzy c-means clustering with optimal parameter m = 1.1573. We evaluated the resulting clusters through the gene set enrichement analysis method. All clusters except 10, 18, 21, 22, 25 and 26 are enriched in some gene ontology categories (data not shown). We used these clusters as candidate gene modules in our subsequent analyses to reduce the search space for gene regulatory module inference.

4.1.3 Network motif discovery

Among the 800 cell cycle related genes, 85 have been identified as DNA-binding transcription factors (Zhang et al. 2008). Four NMs were considered significant: auto-regulatory motif, feed-forward loop, single input module, and multi-input module (Figure 2). These NMs were used to build NN models for corresponding transcription factors.

4.1.4 Reverse engineering gene regulatory networks

Neural network models that mimic the topology of the NMs were constructed to identify the relationships between transcription factors and putative gene modules. The NN models

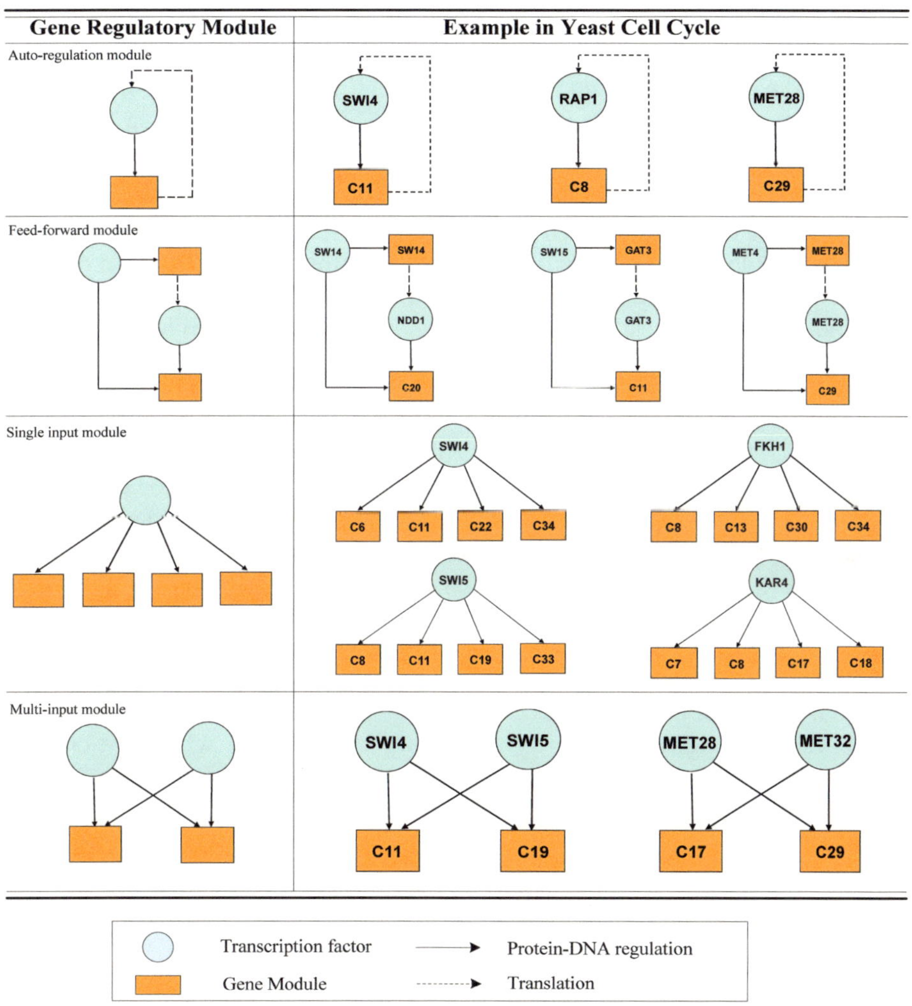

Fig. 8. Predicted gene regulatory modules from eight known cell cycle dependent transcription factors in yeast cell cycle dataset. The left panel presents the four gene regulatory modules, and the right panel depicts inferred gene regulatory modules for eight known cell cycle dependent transcription factors.

were trained to select for all 85 transcription factors the downstream targets from the 34 gene modules. The parameter settings of GA-PSO algorithm are set as described in our previous work (Ressom et al. 2006). Our inference method mapped all 85 transcription factors to the target gene modules and inferred the most likely NMs.

We evaluated the predicted gene regulatory modules for the following eight well known cell cycle related transcription factors: *SWI4, SWI5, FKH1, NDD1, ACE2, KAR4, MET28* and *RAP1*. Since the "true" GRN is not available, the accuracy of putative regulatory relationship was determined by searching known gene connections in databases. Based on the results of the NM module prediction, we collected literature evidences from SGD (Cherry et al. 1997) and BIND (Bader et al. 2003) databases. We examined the inferred relationships for each of the eight transcription factors. An inferred relationship is assumed to be biologically significant if the transcription factors are correlated with the biological functions associated with the critical downstream cluster(s). Figure 8 lists the significant relationships; the eight transcription factors yielded an average precision of 82.9%. NMs for four of these transcription factors were identified in Chiang et al. (Chiang and Chao 2007) together with other four transcription factors. The eight transcription factors in Chiang et al. yielded an average precision of 80.1%.

The regulatory relationships inferred by the proposed method are expected to correspond more closely to biologically meaningful regulatory systems and naturally lead themselves to optimum experimental design methods. The results presented in Figure 8 are verified from previous biological evidences. For example, *FKH1* is a gene whose protein product is a fork head family protein with a role in the expression of G2/M phase genes. It negatively regulates transcriptional elongation, and regulates donor preference during switching. To further investigate the possibilities that the predicted downstream gene clusters are truly regulated by *FKH1*, we applied the motif discovery tool, WebMOTIFS (Romer et al. 2007) to find shared motifs in these gene clusters (data not shown). The results revealed that a motif called Fork_head, GTAAACAA, is identified as the most significant motif among these gene clusters (Weigel and Jackle 1990). This finding strongly supports our NM inference results. Another example is the FFL involving *SWI5, GAT3* and Gene Cluster 10. *SWI5* has been identified as the upstream regulator of *GAT3* (Simon et al. 2001; Lee et al. 2002; Harbison et al. 2004). Genes in cluster 10 are mostly involved in DNA helicase activity and mitotic recombination, both of which are important biological steps in the regulation of cell cycle. Although no biological evidences have shown that *SWI5* and *GAT3* are involved in these processes, there are significant numbers of genes in cluster 10 which are characterized (according to yeastract.com) as genes regulated by both transcription factors (24 for *GAT3* and 23 for *SWI5* out of 44 genes in cluster 10, respectively).

4.2 Human hela cell cycle dataset

4.2.1 Data sources

Gene expression dataset: the human Hela cell cycle dataset (Whitfield et al. 2002) consists of five time courses (114 total arrays). RNA samples were collected for points (typically every 1-2 h) for 30 h (Thy- Thy1), 44 h (Thy-Thy2), 46 h (Thy-Thy3), 36 h (Thy-Noc), or 14 h (shake) after the synchronous arrest. The cell-cycle related gene set contains 1,134 clones corresponding to 874 UNIGENE clusters (UNIGENE build 143). Of these, 1,072 have corresponding Entrez gene IDs, among which 226 have more than one mapping to clones. In total, 846 genes were used for GRN inference. We chose the Thy-Thy3 time course gene expression pattern for 846 genes, since it has the largest number of time points (47). Missing values in the data were imputed using KNN imputation (Troyanskaya et al. 2001). The expression pattern of each gene was standardized between 0 and 1.

Molecular interaction data: Protein-protein interactions were extracted from twelve publicly available large-scale protein interaction maps, seven of which are based on information from scientific literature literature-based, three on orthology information, and two on results of

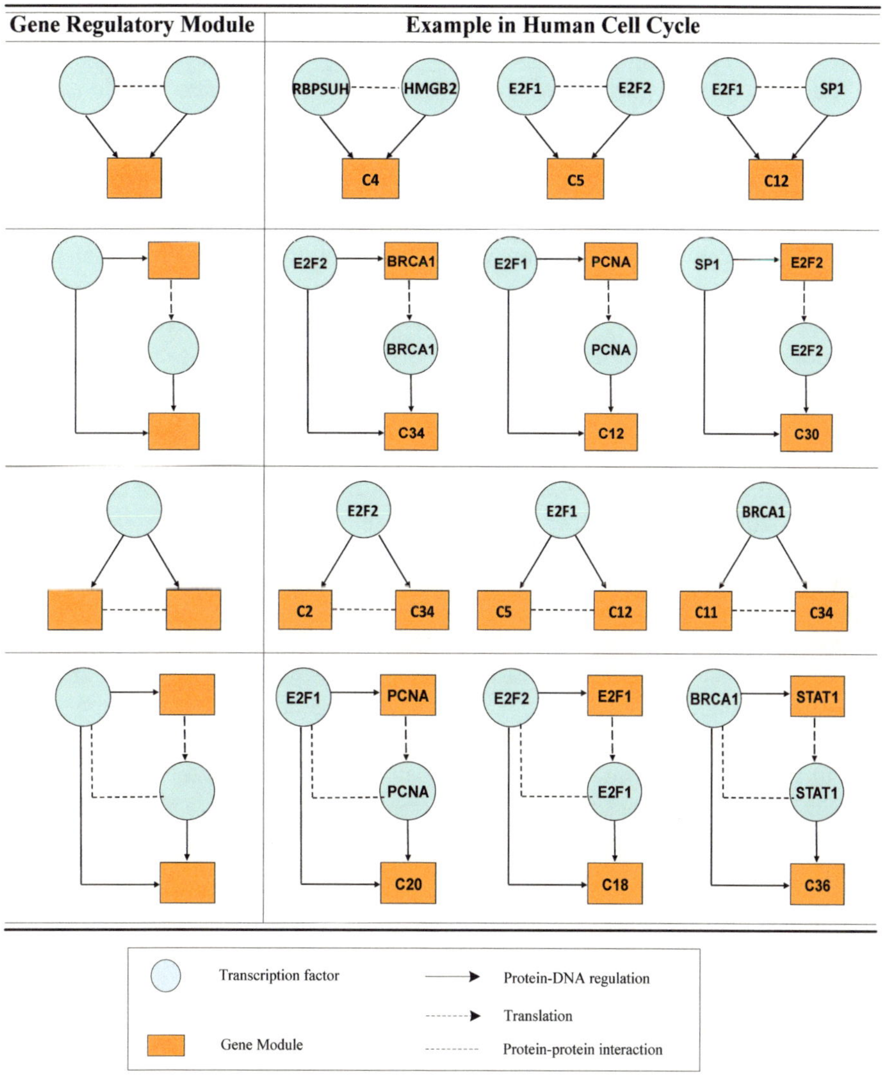

Fig. 9. Predicted gene regulatory modules from known human cell cycle dependent genes. The left panel presents the four gene regulatory modules, and the right panel depicts inferred transcription factor-target gene relationships for eight cell cycle dependent transcription factors.

previous yeast two-hybrid (Y2H) analyses (Zhang et al. 2010). The analysis was restricted to binary interactions in order to make consistent between Y2H-based interactions and the remaining maps. To merge twelve interaction maps into one combination map, all proteins were mapped to their corresponding Entrez gene IDs. The protein-DNA interaction data was extracted from the TRANSFAC database (Wingender et al. 2001). In total the molecular interaction data consisted of 20,473 protein pairs connected by protein-protein interactions and 2,546 protein pairs connected by protein-DNA interactions.

4.2.2 Gene module identification

A total of 846 genes associated with the control of cell cycle have been identified previously in Hela cells. We further partitioned these genes into more specific functional groups by Fuzzy c-means. The optimal value of m for the dataset used in this study was 1.1548. The highest *z* score was obtained with 39 clusters, indicating an optimal condition to reduce the search space for GRN inference. To evaluate the optimal clusters selected based on gene ontology, gene set enrichment analysis was applied using the optimal value. The total set of genes involved in cell cycle regulation was further subdivided into 39 clusters. Of these clusters, 31 were clearly associated with gene ontology categories that imply a more specific function that unifies the members of one but not other clusters, thereby establishing more direct relationships among certain smaller sub-groups of genes. For example, clusters 8 and 29 are both associated with pre-mitotic, mitotic and post-mitotic events (M-phase). However, members of cluster 8 are distinguished from the members of cluster 29 by virtue of their specific roles in chromosome doubling (DNA replication) and cytokinesis. Conversely, members of cluster 29 are distinguished from the members of cluster 8 by virtue of their specific roles in spindle fiber assembly and disassembly.

Biological significance of these highly specific functional relationships, established by our clustering scheme, can further be extended in terms of relationships within the regulatory context. For instance, members of both gene modules 8 and 29 have been identified previously as direct downstream targets of *E2F* factors (Ren et al. 2002). Similar relationships are established with other clusters such as gene module 32, which is comprised of genes with biochemical roles of a DNA ligase. Thus, the genes in gene module 32 are involved in processes associated with gap repair or Okazaki fragment processing during DNA replication and chromosome doubling. Previous studies have established that genes associated with this function are under the regulatory control of *E2F1* and *PCNA* (Shibutani et al. 2008).

Based on all these relationships, we demonstrated that one specific strength of the proposed method is its ability to distinguish genes that are related by function in a broad sense and sub-categorize them into highly specific (narrow) functional categories, resulting in the prediction of regulatory relationships that are consistent with biologically validated relationships.

4.2.3 Network motif discovery

All genes with either direct or indirect roles in the regulation of transcription were first identified from the total set of 846 cell cycle associated genes according to gene ontology categories that denote possible roles in transcription (Ashburner et al. 2000). Candidate genes that remained after filtering other gene function categories are those that are assigned to the following putative functions: transcription factor activity (GO: 0003700), regulation of transcription (GO: 0061019), and transcription factor complex (GO: 0005667). Since gene ontology information alone may not be sufficient to identify the genes with bona fide roles as transcription factors, we further filtered our list of candidate transcription factors by adding another layer of confirmatory information based on the results of PubMed database searches. This additional annotation allowed us to validate the gene ontology classification of our candidate genes. Among the 846 cell cycle related genes, 46 were annotated with functions related to transcriptional regulation based on both gene ontology and PubMed databases. These genes were considered as putative transcription factors (Zhang et al. 2010).

In the microarray gene expression data, genes are often represented by multiple oligonucleotide probes. Genes represented by probe sets with larger variance were further considered in this study. We decomposed the collected human molecular interaction network into several NMs, with each NM potentially associated with a given transcription factor(s). A total of four NMs were found to be significant in the combined molecular interaction network (Figure 3), thus each transcription factor was assigned to at least one of these NMs.

4.2.4 Reverse engineering gene regulatory networks

The relationships between transcription factors and gene modules were determined based on NN models. For each of the four NMs (Figure 3), a suitable NN was built as we previously described (Zhang et al. 2008). The NN models were trained using the GA-PSO algorithm to find the downstream gene clusters for all 46 putative transcription factors. Associations between each transcription factor and 39 gene modules was determined by training the NN model that mimics the specific NM for a given transcription factor. Due to a reduction in the computational complexity (mapping between 46 transcription factors and 39 gene clusters instead of 846 genes), the numbers of GA and PSO generations needed to reach the pre-specified minimum RMSE was significantly reduced. The proposed inference method successfully assigned all 46 putative transcription factors to their target gene modules and inferred the most likely gene regulatory modules (see Figure 9 for representative gene regulatory modules).

The validity and accuracy of the network depicted by the gene regulatory modules are assessed by comparison with a network model constructed based on actual biological data. In the absence of such information, we performed an initial validation of the network by searching for known gene connections in databases. Based on the prediction results, we collected literature evidence from the NCBI and TRANSFAC databases. We reviewed each predicted NM and examined the relationships between the transcription factor and its target gene module(s). Subsequent analysis was performed under the basic assumption that the inferred NM is more likely to be biologically meaningful if the transcription factors therein are correlated with the enriched biological functions in the downstream clusters.

Significant NMs resulting from the survey of available literature cell cycle dependent genes such as *E2F1*, *E2F2*, *SP1*, *BRCA1*, *STAT1*, *PCNA*, *RBPSUH*, and *HMGB2* are listed in Figure 9. Based on the combined information, the biological implication of the network is further explained. For instance, *E2F* is a transcription factor that plays a crucial role in cell-cycle progression in mammalian cells (Takahashi et al. 2000). *E2F1*, which contains two overlapping *E2F*-binding sites in its promoter region, is activated at the G1/S transition in an *E2F*-dependent manner. *E2F2* interacts with certain elements in the *E2F1* promoter and both genes are involved in DNA replication and repair (Ishida et al. 2001), cytokinesis, and tumor development (Zhu et al. 2001). According to the gene set enrichment analysis results, gene module 8 is enriched with genes involved in mitosis and cytokinesis, and gene module 34 is enriched with genes involved in several functional categories associated with tumor development. As shown in Figure 9, both gene module 8 and 34 are predicted to be regulated by *E2F1* and *E2F2*, and these results are in agreement with previous reports based on biological data.

Our analysis predicts that *E2F1* and *PCNA* are components of the same network. Both of these genes are involved in the regulation of gene modules 32 and 34. The best understood molecular function of the *PCNA* protein is its role in the regulation of eukaryotic DNA polymerase delta processivity, which ensures the fidelity of DNA synthesis and repair (Essers et al. 2005). However, recent studies have provided evidence that the *PCNA* protein also functions as a direct repressor of the transcriptional coactivator p300 (Hong and Chakravarti 2003). Another study shows that *PCNA* represses the transcriptional activity of retinoic acid receptors (RARs) (Martin et al. 2005). Thus, the involvement of these genes in the same network, as predicted by our network inference algorithm, is strongly supported by knowledge of regulatory relationships already established in experimental data. The results of our prediction are in agreement with these reports since both gene modules 8 and 32 are enriched with genes involved in DNA synthesis and regulatory processes.

We proposed three approaches to investigate further whether the genes predicted to be regulated by *E2F* genes in gene modules 8, 32 and 34 are validated in classical non-genome wide methods. First, we investigated how many "known" *E2F1* and *E2F2* targets are predicted by our proposed method. According to Bracken et al. (Bracken et al. 2004), 130 genes were reviewed as *E2F* targets, 44 of which were originally identified by classical, non-genome-wide approaches. Since we restricted our analysis to the 846 cell cycle related genes, 45 genes matched the *E2F* target genes listed in Bracken et al., 21 of which were known from studies using classical molecular biology analyses. The gene targets predicted by our method match 15 of 45 genes, all 15 of which are among those found originally using standard molecular biology experiments. One possible reason is that genome-wide approaches are usually highly noisy and inconsistent across different studies.

Second, we wanted to see whether our predicted gene target clusters are enriched in the corresponding binding sites for the transcription factors in their upstream region. For both *E2F1* and *E2F2*, 7 out of 17 genes in gene module 8 contain binding sites in their upstream regions as confirmed by data in the SABiosciences database[1].

Finally, we determined how many genes in the gene clusters have *E2F* binding sites. We applied WebMOTIFS to find shared motifs in the gene modules predicted to the *E2F* targets using binding site enrichment analysis. The results revealed that a motif called E2F_TDP, GCGSSAAA, is identified as the most significant motif amon[1]g gene modules 2, 8, 29, 31, 32 and 34. Unfortunately, for gene modules 30 and 36 the number of genes in these clusters is

[1] http://www.sabiosciences.com/

too small for WebMOTIFS analysis. All these gene modules are predicted to the downstream targets of E2F. For instance, 43 out of 52 genes in gene module 2 have putative *E2F* binding sites in their upstream regions. The detailed information of binding site enrichment analysis results is shown in Table 2. For those gene regulatory networks where two transcription factors are involved in, the downstream gene modules are found to be enriched in both the binding site sequence motifs. For instance, gene module 32 is enriched in both E2F_TDP and MH1 motifs, corresponding to the two transcription factors in the gene regulatory module: *E2F1* and *SP1*. These binding site enrichment analysis results strongly support our inference results.

Cluster #	Sequence logo[a]	Binding domain (Pfam ID)	Corresponding transcription factor	Conserved binding motif[b]
Cluster 2		E2F_TDP (PF02319)	E2F1 E2F2	GCGssAAa
Cluster 8		E2F_TDP (PF02319)	E2F1 E2F2	GCGssAAa
Cluster 29		zf-C4 (PF00105)	BRCA1	TGACCTTTG ACCyy
		E2F_TDP (PF02319)	E2F1 E2F2	GCGssAAa
Cluster 31		HMG_box (PF00505)	HMGB2	AACAAwRr
Cluster 32		MH1 (PF03165)	SP1	TGGc.....gCCA
		E2F_TDP (PF02319)	E2F1 E2F2	GCGssAAa
Cluster 34		E2F_TDP (PF02319)	E2F1 E2F2	GCGssAAa
Cluster 38		zf-C4 (PF00105)	BRCA1	TGACCTTTG ACCyy
		E2F_TDP (PF02319)	E2F1 E2F2	GCGssAAa

Table 2. Binding site enrichment analysis for gene modules identified in human Hela cell cycle dataset. [a]Sequence logos represent the motif significantly overrepresented in individual gene cluster associated with their predicted upstream transcription factors, according to the WebMOTIFS discovery algorithm. Individual base letter height indicates level of conservation within each binding site position; [b]Conserved binding motifs are the conserved binding sequences used in the WebMOTIFS discovery algorithm.

5. Summary and discussions

Reverse engineering GRNs is one of the major challenges in the post-genomics era of biology. In this chapter, we focused on two broad issues in GRN inference: (1) development of an analysis method that uses multiple types of data and (2) network analysis at the NM modular level. Based on the information available nowadays, we proposed a data integration approach that effectively infers the gene networks underlying certain patterns of gene co-regulation in yeast cell cycle and human Hela cell cycling. The predictive strength of this strategy is based on the combined constraints arising from multiple biological data sources including time course gene expression data, combined molecular interaction network data, and gene ontology category information.

This computational framework allows us to fully exploit the partial constraints that can be inferred from each data source. First, to reduce the inference dimensionalities, the genes were grouped into clusters by Fuzzy c-means, where the optimal fuzziness value was determined by statistical properties of gene expression data. The optimal cluster number was identified by integrating gene ontology category information. Second, the NM information established from the combined molecular interaction network was used to assign NM(s) to a given transcription factor. Once the NM(s) for a transcription factor was identified, a hybrid GA-PSO algorithm was applied to search for target gene modules that may be regulated by that particular transcription factor. This search was guided by the successful training of a NN model that mimics the regulatory NM(s) assigned to the transcription factor. The effectiveness of this method was illustrated via well-studied cell cycle dependent transcription factors (Figure 3.10 and 3.11). The upstream BINDING SITE ENRICHMENT ANALYSIS indicated that the proposed method has the potential to identify the underlying regulatory relationships between transcription factors and their downstream genes at the modular level. This demonstrates that our approach can serve as a method for analyzing multi-source data at the modular level.

Compared to the approach developed in [148], our proposed method has several advantages. First, our method performs the inference of GRNs from genome-wide expression data together with other biological knowledge. It has been shown that mRNA expression data alone cannot reflect all the activities in one GRN. Additional information will help constrain the search space of causal relationships between transcription factors and their downstream genes. Second, we decompose the GRN into well characterized functional units - NMs. Each transcription factor is assigned to specific NM(s), which is further used to infer the downstream target genes. We not only reduce the search space in the inference process, but also provide experimental biologists the regulatory modules for straightforward validation, instead of one whole GRN containing thousands of genes and connections as is often generated by IPA. Third, we group the genes into functional groups that are potentially regulated by one common transcription factor. The proposed approach reduces the noise in mRNA expression data by incorporating gene functional annotations.

In summary, we demonstrate that our method can accurately infer the underlying relationships between transcription factor and the downstream target genes by integrating multi-sources of biological data. As the first attempt to integrate many different types of data, we believe that the proposed framework will improve data analysis, particularly as more data sets become available. Our method could also be beneficial to biologists by predicting the components of the GRN in which their candidate gene is involved, followed by designing a more streamlined experiment for biological validation.

6. References

Alon, U. (2007). "Network motifs: theory and experimental approaches." Nat Rev Genet 8(6): 450-461.

Ashburner, M., C. A. Ball, et al. (2000). "Gene ontology: tool for the unification of biology. The Gene Ontology Consortium." Nat Genet 25(1): 25-29.

Bader, G. D., D. Betel, et al. (2003). "BIND: the Biomolecular Interaction Network Database." Nucleic Acids Res 31(1): 248-250.

Berriz, G. F., O. D. King, et al. (2003). "Characterizing gene sets with FuncAssociate." Bioinformatics 19(18): 2502-2504.

Birge, B. (2003). PSOt - a particle swarm optimization toolbox for use with Matlab. Swarm Intelligence Symposium, 2003. SIS '03. Proceedings of the 2003 IEEE.

Blais, A. and B. D. Dynlacht (2005). "Constructing transcriptional regulatory networks." Genes Dev 19(13): 1499-1511.

Boyer, L. A., T. I. Lee, et al. (2005). "Core transcriptional regulatory circuitry in human embryonic stem cells." Cell 122(6): 947-956.

Bracken, A. P., M. Ciro, et al. (2004). "E2F target genes: unraveling the biology." Trends Biochem Sci 29(8): 409-417.

Bubitzky, W., M. Granzow, et al. (2007). Fundamentals of Data Mining in Genomics and Proteomics. New York, Springer.

Chen, T., H. L. He, et al. (1999). "Modeling gene expression with differential equations." Pac Symp Biocomput: 29-40.

Cherry, J. M., C. Ball, et al. (1997). "Genetic and physical maps of Saccharomyces cerevisiae." Nature 387(6632 Suppl): 67-73.

Chiang, J. H. and S. Y. Chao (2007). "Modeling human cancer-related regulatory modules by GA-RNN hybrid algorithms." BMC Bioinformatics 8: 91.

Clarke, R., H. W. Ressom, et al. (2008). "The properties of high-dimensional data spaces: implications for exploring gene and protein expression data." Nat Rev Cancer 8(1): 37-49.

Costanzo, M. C., M. E. Crawford, et al. (2001). "YPD, PombePD and WormPD: model organism volumes of the BioKnowledge library, an integrated resource for protein information." Nucleic Acids Res 29(1): 75-79.

D'Haeseleer, P., X. Wen, et al. (1999). "Linear modeling of mRNA expression levels during CNS development and injury." Pac Symp Biocomput: 41-52.

De Hoon, M. J., S. Imoto, et al. (2002). "Statistical analysis of a small set of time-ordered gene expression data using linear splines." Bioinformatics 18(11): 1477-1485.

Essers, J., A. F. Theil, et al. (2005). "Nuclear dynamics of PCNA in DNA replication and repair." Mol Cell Biol 25(21): 9350-9359.

Friedman, N., M. Linial, et al. (2000). "Using Bayesian networks to analyze expression data." J Comput Biol. 7: 601-620.

Harbison, C. T., D. B. Gordon, et al. (2004). "Transcriptional regulatory code of a eukaryotic genome." Nature 431(7004): 99-104.

Hartemink, A. J., D. K. Gifford, et al. (2002). "Combining location and expression data for principled discovery of genetic regulatory network models." Pac Symp Biocomput: 437-449.

He, F., R. Balling, et al. (2009). "Reverse engineering and verification of gene networks: principles, assumptions, and limitations of present methods and future perspectives." J Biotechnol 144(3): 190-203.

Holmes, I. and W. J. Bruno (2001). "Evolutionary HMMs: a Bayesian approach to multiple alignment." Bioinformatics 17(9): 803-820.

Hong, R. and D. Chakravarti (2003). "The human proliferating Cell nuclear antigen regulates transcriptional coactivator p300 activity and promotes transcriptional repression." J Biol Chem 278(45): 44505-44513.

Iranfar, N., D. Fuller, et al. (2006). "Transcriptional regulation of post-aggregation genes in Dictyostelium by a feed-forward loop involving GBF and LagC." Dev Biol 290(2): 460-469.

Ishida, S., E. Huang, et al. (2001). "Role for E2F in control of both DNA replication and mitotic functions as revealed from DNA microarray analysis." Mol Cell Biol 21(14): 4684-4699.

Iyer, V. R., C. E. Horak, et al. (2001). "Genomic binding sites of the yeast cell-cycle transcription factors SBF and MBF." Nature 409(6819): 533-538.

Kennedy, J. and R. C. Eberhart (1995). "Particle swarm optimization." Proceedings of the 1995 IEEE International Conference on Neural Networks (Perth, Australia) IV: 1942-1948.

Lee, T. I., N. J. Rinaldi, et al. (2002). "Transcriptional regulatory networks in Saccharomyces cerevisiae." Science 298(5594): 799-804.

Mangan, S. and U. Alon (2003). "Structure and function of the feed-forward loop network motif." Proc Natl Acad Sci U S A 100(21): 11980-11985.

Mangan, S., A. Zaslaver, et al. (2003). "The coherent feedforward loop serves as a sign-sensitive delay element in transcription networks." J Mol Biol 334(2): 197-204.

Maraziotis, I., A. Dragomir, et al. (2005). "Gene networks inference from expression data using a recurrent neuro-fuzzy approach." Conf Proc IEEE Eng Med Biol Soc 5: 4834-4837.

Martin, P. J., V. Lardeux, et al. (2005). "The proliferating cell nuclear antigen regulates retinoic acid receptor transcriptional activity through direct protein-protein interaction." Nucleic Acids Res 33(13): 4311-4321.

Matys, V., O. V. Kel-Margoulis, et al. (2006). "TRANSFAC and its module TRANSCompel: transcriptional gene regulation in eukaryotes." Nucleic Acids Res(34 Database): D108 - 110.

Mewes, H. W., D. Frishman, et al. (2002). "MIPS: a database for genomes and protein sequences." Nucleic Acids Res 30(1): 31-34.

Milo, R., S. Itzkovitz, et al. (2004). "Superfamilies of evolved and designed networks." Science 303(5663): 1538-1542.

Milo, R., S. Shen-Orr, et al. (2002). "Network motifs: simple building blocks of complex networks." Science 298(5594): 824-827.

Mitchell, M. (1998). An introduction to genetic algorithm, MIT Press.

Naraghi, M. and E. Neher (1997). "Linearized buffered Ca2+ diffusion in microdomains and its implications for calculation of [Ca2+] at the mouth of a calcium channel." J Neurosci 17(18): 6961-6973.

Odom, D. T., N. Zizlsperger, et al. (2004). "Control of pancreas and liver gene expression by HNF transcription factors." Science 303(5662): 1378-1381.

Przulj, N., D. A. Wigle, et al. (2004). "Functional topology in a network of protein interactions." Bioinformatics 20(3): 340-348.

Ren, B., H. Cam, et al. (2002). "E2F integrates cell cycle progression with DNA repair, replication, and G(2)/M checkpoints." Genes Dev 16(2): 245-256.

Ren, B., F. Robert, et al. (2000). "Genome-wide location and function of DNA binding proteins." Science 290(5500): 2306-2309.

Ressom, H., R. Reynolds, et al. (2003). "Increasing the efficiency of fuzzy logic-based gene expression data analysis." Physiol Genomics 13(2): 107-117.

Ressom, H. W., Y. Zhang, et al. (2006). "Inference of gene regulatory networks from time course gene expression data using neural networks and swarm intelligence." Proceedings of the 2006 IEEE Symposium on Computational Intelligence in Bioinformatics and Computational Biology, Toronto, ON: 435-442.

Ressom, H. W., Y. Zhang, et al. (2006). Inferring network interactions using recurrent neural networks and swarm intelligence. Conf Proc IEEE Eng Med Biol Soc (EMBC 2006), New York City, New York, USA.

Romer, K. A., G. R. Kayombya, et al. (2007). "WebMOTIFS: automated discovery, filtering and scoring of DNA sequence motifs using multiple programs and Bayesian approaches." Nucleic Acids Res 35(Web Server issue): W217-220.

Rual, J. F., K. Venkatesan, et al. (2005). "Towards a proteome-scale map of the human protein-protein interaction network." Nature 437(7062): 1173-1178.

Saddic, L. A., B. Huvermann, et al. (2006). "The LEAFY target LMI1 is a meristem identity regulator and acts together with LEAFY to regulate expression of CAULIFLOWER." Development 133(9): 1673-1682.

Segal, E., B. Taskar, et al. (2001). "Rich probabilistic models for gene expression." Bioinformatics 17 Suppl 1: S243-252.

Shen-Orr, S. S., R. Milo, et al. (2002). "Network motifs in the transcriptional regulation network of Escherichia coli." Nat Genet 31(1): 64-68.

Shibutani, S. T., A. F. de la Cruz, et al. (2008). "Intrinsic negative cell cycle regulation provided by PIP box- and Cul4Cdt2-mediated destruction of E2f1 during S phase." Dev Cell 15(6): 890-900.

Shmulevich, I., E. R. Dougherty, et al. (2002). "Probabilistic Boolean Networks: a rule-based uncertainty model for gene regulatory networks." Bioinformatics 18(2): 261-274.

Simon, I., J. Barnett, et al. (2001). "Serial regulation of transcriptional regulators in the yeast cell cycle." Cell 106(6): 697-708.

Spellman, P. T., G. Sherlock, et al. (1998). "Comprehensive identification of cell cycle-regulated genes of the yeast Saccharomyces cerevisiae by microarray hybridization." Mol Biol Cell 9(12): 3273-3297.

Swiers, G., R. Patient, et al. (2006). "Genetic regulatory networks programming hematopoietic stem cells and erythroid lineage specification." Dev Biol 294(2): 525-540.

Takahashi, Y., J. B. Rayman, et al. (2000). "Analysis of promoter binding by the E2F and pRB families in vivo: distinct E2F proteins mediate activation and repression." Genes Dev 14(7): 804-816.
Tavazoie, S., J. D. Hughes, et al. (1999). "Systematic determination of genetic network architecture." Nat Genet 22(3): 281-285.
Tegner, J., M. K. Yeung, et al. (2003). "Reverse engineering gene networks: integrating genetic perturbations with dynamical modeling." Proc Natl Acad Sci U S A 100(10): 5944-5949.
Troyanskaya, O., M. Cantor, et al. (2001). "Missing value estimation methods for DNA microarrays." Bioinformatics 17(6): 520-525.
Tuncay, K., L. Ensman, et al. (2007). "Transcriptional regulatory networks via gene ontology and expression data." In Silico Biol 7(1): 21-34.
Wang, E., A. Lenferink, et al. (2007). "Cancer systems biology: exploring cancer-associated genes on cellular networks." Cell Mol Life Sci 64(14): 1752-1762.
Weigel, D. and H. Jackle (1990). "The fork head domain: a novel DNA binding motif of eukaryotic transcription factors?" Cell 63(3): 455-456.
Wernicke, S. and F. Rasche (2006). "FANMOD: a tool for fast network motif detection." Bioinformatics 22(9): 1152-1153.
Whitfield, M. L., G. Sherlock, et al. (2002). "Identification of genes periodically expressed in the human cell cycle and their expression in tumors." Mol Biol Cell 13(6): 1977-2000.
Wingender, E., X. Chen, et al. (2001). "The TRANSFAC system on gene expression regulation." Nucleic Acids Res 29(1): 281-283.
Wit, E. and J. McClure (2006). Statistics for Microarrays: Design, Analysis and Inference, John Wiley & Sons.
Woolf, P. J. and Y. Wang (2000). "A fuzzy logic approach to analyzing gene expression data." Physiol Genomics 3(1): 9-15.
Yeger-Lotem, E., S. Sattath, et al. (2004). "Network motifs in integrated cellular networks of transcription-regulation and protein-protein interaction." Proc Natl Acad Sci U S A 101(16): 5934-5939.
Yeung, K. Y., M. Medvedovic, et al. (2004). "From co-expression to co-regulation: how many microarray experiments do we need?" Genome Biol 5(7): R48.
Zhang, Y., J. Xuan, et al. (2008). "Network motif-based identification of transcription factor-target gene relationships by integrating multi-source biological data." BMC Bioinformatics 9: 203.
Zhang, Y., J. Xuan, et al. (2009). "Reverse engineering module networks by PSO-RNN hybrid modeling." BMC Genomics: In Press.
Zhang, Y., J. Xuan, et al. (2010). "Reconstruction of gene regulatory modules in cancer cell cycle by multi-source data integration." PLoS One 5(4): e10268.
Zhu, J. and M. Q. Zhang (1999). "SCPD: a promoter database of the yeast Saccharomyces cerevisiae." Bioinformatics 15(7-8): 607-611.
Zhu, J. W., S. J. Field, et al. (2001). "E2F1 and E2F2 determine thresholds for antigen-induced T-cell proliferation and suppress tumorigenesis." Mol Cell Biol 21(24): 8547-8564.

11

Reverse-Engineering the Robustness of Mammalian Lungs

Michael Mayo[1], Peter Pfeifer[2] and Chen Hou[3]
[1]*Environmental Laboratory, US Army Engineer Research and Development Center, Vicksburg, MS*
[2]*Department of Physics, University of Missouri, Columbia, MO*
[3]*Department of Biological Sciences, Missouri University of Science and Technology, Rolla, MO, USA*

1. Introduction

This chapter is devoted to reverse-engineering the cause of a dramatic increase in the total oxygen uptake rate by the lung, wherein oxygen is supplied to the blood to meet the increasing energetic demands between rest and exercise. This uptake rate increases despite a much smaller increase in the oxygen partial pressure difference across the lung's exchange tissues (e.g. alveolar membranes), thought to mainly drive the oxygen-blood transfer in a similar way that electric currents are driven by voltage differences according to Ohm's law. As we explain below, a full understanding of this special property has the potential to improve various engineering processes, such as stabilizing chemical yields in heterogeneous catalysis, improving the efficiency of heat-transporters, and improving energy generation in electrochemical reactors.

To reverse-engineer the cause of this mostly pressure-independent increase in the oxygen uptake rate, we focus on the development of mathematical models based on the rate-limiting physical transport processes of i) diffusion through the airway spaces, and ii) "reaction" of the oxygen molecules across the surface of permeable membranes responsible for transferring oxygen from air to blood. Two of these mathematical models treat the terminal, or acinar, airways of mammalian lungs as hierarchical trees; another treats the entire permeable surface as fractal. By understanding how the parameters of these mathematical models restrict the overall oxygen uptake rate, we infer how the lung preserves its function when exposed to environmental hazards (e.g. smoking), damage (e.g. surgery), or disease (e.g. emphysema). The focus of our work here is to discover, or reverse engineer, the operational principles that allow mammalian lungs to match increased oxygen demands with supply without any significant alteration of its "hardware."

We first begin with a mathematical description of oxygen diffusion as the primary transport mechanism throughout the airways responsible for the oxygen uptake in the deep regions of the mammalian lungs studied here. We then discuss several different, but complementary analytical models that approach the oxygen-transport problem from different directions, while also developing a new one. Although these models are different from one another

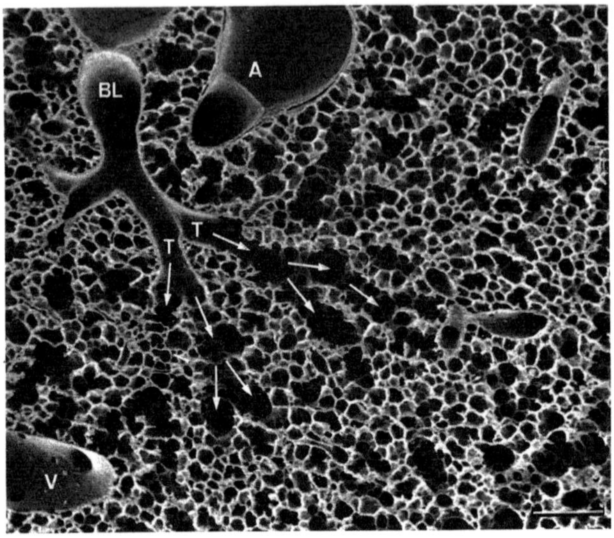

Fig. 1. Scanning electron micrograph of the perfusion-fixed lung tissue (Weibel, 1984), showing transition between peripheral bronchiole (BL) and terminal bronchiole (T). Alveolar ducts are denoted by arrows in the direction of downstream flow, near pulmonary arteries (A) and veins (V). Scale marker is 200 μm.

in how they treat the exchange-surface, they all consistently predict a region of the parameter space in which the current is "robust;" i.e. changes or error in the parameters do not affect the functional state of the system. Finally, we apply physiological data for the human lung–the prototypical mammalian lung studied here–to validate these models against experimental measurements; we use them as a tool to reverse-engineer how the human lung supplies the body with increasing oxygen currents under the body's increasing oxygen demands that occur, for example, during heavy exercise.

2. Motivation

Mammalian lungs regulate the exchange of respiratory gases (here we focus on molecular oxygen, O_2) between air and pulmonary blood, delivering oxygen to cells that use it to drive energy metabolism, such as glycolysis. Beginning from the trachea, these gases are transported downstream throughout the bronchial tree by convection until their speed drops drops below the local diffusion speed, wherein further transport toward the periphery of the lung occurs by stationary diffusion. As shown in Fig. 1, the airways in which this transition occurs, termed the transitional bronchioles, are defined by the appearance of air sacs, or alveoli, that appear along the walls of the airway channels, termed acinar ducts (Weibel, 1984). While only sparsely populating the walls of the transitional bronchioles, these alveoli dominate the walls of the acinar airways, which lay only a few branch generations downstream of the transitional bronchioles. The epithelial cells lining the alveoli are tightly packed, so they form a jointless surface of alveolar membranes across which the gas exchange almost entirely occurs (Weibel, 1984).

The oxygen uptake rate, I, measured in units of moles of gas transferred across the entire surface of alveolar membranes of the lung per unit time, measures the ability of the body to meet the changing energetic demands of its tissues under changing physiological conditions, such as foraging or predation. For example, altering cell metabolism increases/decreases oxygen demands (as a vital component in glycolysis), and the mammalian lung, as a whole, responds by automatically increasing/decreasing this current without invoking any biochemical feedback loops.

There are several steps between oxygen in the air and its final delivery to the cell. The rate-limiting step is its diffusion to, and across, the surface of alveolar membranes that collectively serve as the gas-exchange surface. It then binds with the erythrocytes, or red blood cells in the pulmonary arteries, to any of the four binding sites on hemoglobin, which allows for its dissolution in blood plasma. An oxygen partial pressure difference between air, p_a, and erythrocytes, p_e, serves as the driving force in the oxygen uptake rate across the membranes, and can be written as (Comroe, 1962; Weibel, 1984):

$$I = T_{lung}\left(p_a - p_e\right), \tag{1}$$

wherein T_{lung} is the total diffusing capacity of the mammalian lung (in units of oxygen molecules transferred to erythrocyte per unit time and pressure). Because diffusing oxygen moves first across a barrier of alveolar membranes and then through the blood plasma, they can be viewed as resistors connected in series (Hou et al., 2010), in which the same current flows through each biological "resistor." Equation 1 can then be rewritten in terms of only the oxygen partial pressure difference across the membranes alone, $p_a - p_b$ (Weibel, 1984):

$$I = T_m\left(p_a - p_b\right), \tag{2}$$

wherein T_m is the membrane's diffusing capacity for oxygen.

As the body increasingly demands more oxygen to supply muscles and other tissues with chemical energy, the uptake rate, as given by Eqn. 2, increases 20-fold under the most strenuous exercise and breathing conditions as compared to the resting state, although the driver of the oxygen current–the partial pressure difference–increases only 2–fold under these same conditions (Weibel, 1992). The diffusing capacity of the membranes is, T_m, therefore, is almost entirely responsible for this increase in oxygen uptake rate; not the partial pressure difference.

To put this result in perspective, consider an analogy between electrical and biological circuits, wherein biological surface areas and permeabilities play the role of electrical impedance, chemical/nutrient exchange and uptake rates across these biological surfaces (e.g. oxygen uptake rates) play the role of electric currents, and partial pressure differences across biological surfaces play the role of voltage differences across electrical components. Relationships of the type given by Eqn. 2 are therefore analogous to Ohm's law in electric circuits. To say that the oxygen partial pressure difference does not, in effect, provide for the entirety of the observed increase in oxygen current supplied to the body by the lung, is equivalent to stating that a voltage difference is not entirely responsible for increasing the electrical current through a circuit's component, such as a resistor. Here we use mathematical modeling to explain this phenomenon, and use it to determine the cause of the lung's robustness–it's ability to provide a constant oxygen current to the blood despite disease or damage to its exchange tissues.

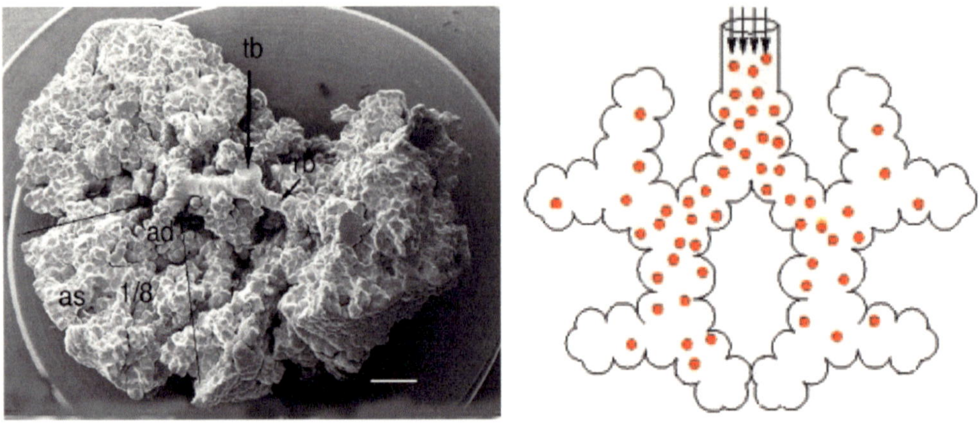

(a) (b)

Fig. 2. (a) Silicon rubber case of a rabbit lung acinus (Sapoval et al., 2002); (b) illustration of a model mammalian lung acinus, wherein oxygen (red) concentration gradients are established by limited access to the acinar volume by by diffusion throughout the airways (Sapoval et al., 2002).

3. Mathematical modeling of mammalian lungs

3.1 Transitions between rest and exercise determine the size of the physiological diffusion space

Oxygen uptake in mammalian lungs occurs across the alveolar ducts of the acinar airways–the elementary gas exchange unit of mammalian lungs–which host the alveoli (Weibel, 1984), as illustrated in Figs. 1 and 2. These are the airways in which oxygen is transported entirely by diffusion in the resting state, and there are $\sim 10^5$ of them in human lungs under these conditions (Hou et al., 2010). The branching generation at which the tracheobronchial tree ends defines the entrance to the acinar airways, and is marked by the convection-diffusion transition in the resting state, which can be located through mass-balance considerations.

The mass flow-rate through a duct of the ith generation of bronchial tree, $\dot{M} = \rho v_i A_i$ (in units of mass per time), is written in terms of the cross-sectional area of the duct, $A_i = \pi r_i^2$, the speed of the gases across this area, v_i and the local oxygen density, ρ. No molecules of the gas is lost across a branching point, the point in which a parent duct extends into m-many daughter ones, because there are no alveoli lining them. Mass-balance in this branch gives $\dot{M}_i = m\dot{M}_{i+1}$, so that the transport speed can be written in terms of its speed at the trachea, v_0:

$$v_i = \frac{v_0}{\sum_{j=0}^{i} m^{j/3}} = \frac{m-1}{m^{(i+1)/3}} v_0. \tag{3}$$

Here, we have applied Murray's law for the bronchial tree, $r_i = r_0 m^{-i/3}$ (Weibel, 1984), connecting radii of downstream branches, r_i, to that of the trachea, r_0. Note that $m = 2$ for mammalian lungs. The tree's total cross-sectional area therefore increases exponentially with branching generation according to Eqn. 3, resulting in a drastic decrease of the oxygen velocity within the deeper airway branches as compared to the trachea.

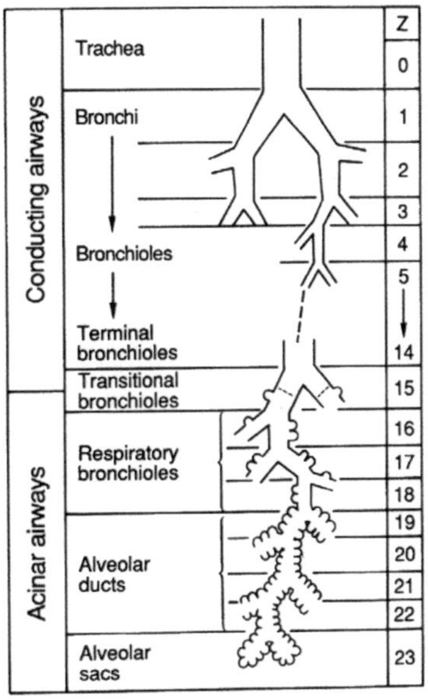

(a)

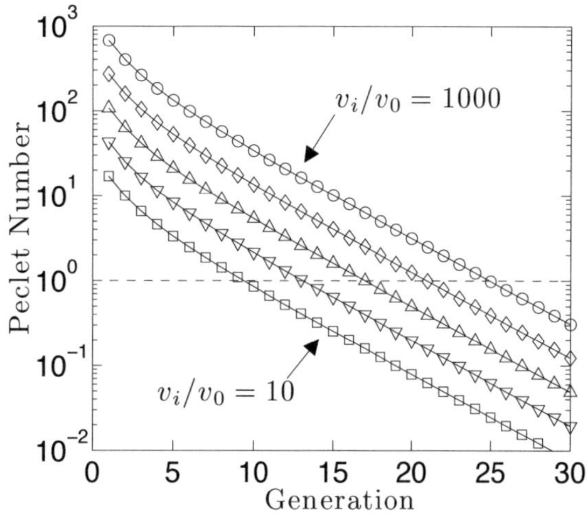

(b)

Fig. 3. (a) Branching hierarchy of mammalian lungs (Weibel, 1984); (b)Velocity of respiratory gases, such as molecular oxygen, decrease with increasing depth into the bronchial tree. The convection-diffusion transition occurs when these gas velocities fall below the local diffusion speed.

The Peclet number gives the ratio of diffusive to convective flow rate, and the branching generation at which the Peclet number equals 1 gives the convection-diffusion transition. In the human lung, for example, this transition occurs at approximately the 18th branching generation in the resting state (Hou 2005; Hou et al., 2010). The airway "unit" defined by the remaining five generations are termed a 1/8 subacinus (Haefeli-Bleuer and Weibel, 1988). For different exercise states, however, this transition occurs deeper than generation 18, because the inspiration speed at the trachea increases. This effect is illustrated in Fig. 3 by evaluating Eqn. 3 for varying speeds at the trachea in units of the diffusional speed of oxygen in air.

In reality, transitions between exercise conditions is smooth; however, in light of Fig. 3, we refer herein to an "exercise state" in terms of how the exercise conditions affect the lung's convection-diffusion transition. In this context, four distinct exercise states can be identified in humans (Sapoval et al., 2002; Felici et al., 2004; Grebenkov et al., 2005; Hou 2005; Hou et al., 2010), which serve as the exemplary mammalian lung system for remainder of this article. These regimes are *rest* ($i = 18$), *moderate exercise* ($i = 19$), *heavy exercise* ($i = 20$), and *maximum exercise* ($i = 21$). On average, the human lung terminates with a total depth of 23 branching generations, giving an approximately equal length to all downstream branching paths. In terms of subacinar trees, these exercise states can be associated to airways of depth $n = 23 - 18 = 5$ (rest), $n = 23 - 19 = 4$ (moderate exercise), $n = 23 - 20 = 3$ (heavy exercise), and $n = 23 - 21 = 2$ (maximum exercise) (Hou et al., 2010).

The subacinar trees identified in terms of these four discrete "exercise states," define the corresponding diffusion space relevant for each breathing regime. Because diffusion occurs at rest in the network of alveolar ducts, rather than the respiratory bronchioles, we consider an elementary airway unit to be a "1/8 subacinus" (Weibel, 1984) that begins with branching generation 18, instead of an entire lung acinus that includes respiratory bronchioles, and supports a network of alveolar ducts spanning 5 generations. Successive subacinii corresponding to the other exercise states are termed 1/16- (moderate exercise), 1/32- (heavy exercise), and 1/64-subacinii (maximum exercise).

3.2 Equations for oxygen transport throughout and across the acinar tree

While strenuous exercise pushes the diffusion source deeper into the lung, as evidenced by Eqn. 3 and Fig. 3, the evolution of the oxygen concentration difference between the subacini entrance and the blood side of the membranes, $c(\mathbf{x})$, obeys the stationary diffusion equation (Felici et al., 2003):

$$\nabla^2 c(\mathbf{x}) = 0, \text{ with } \mathbf{x} \in \text{diffusion space.} \tag{4}$$

The concentration across the tree's entrance (the diffusional "source") gives the first boundary condition,

$$c(\mathbf{x}) = c_a, \text{ with } \mathbf{x} \in \text{source.} \tag{5}$$

The oxygen flux entering the gas-exchange (the diffusional "receptor") surface is matched with the flux moving through it (Hou, 2005):

$$\nabla c(\mathbf{x}) \cdot \mathbf{n}(\mathbf{x}) = \frac{c(\mathbf{x}) - c_b \beta_a / \beta_b}{\Lambda}, \text{ with } \mathbf{x} \in \text{boundary,} \tag{6}$$

wherein the β_a and β_b are the solubility of oxygen in air and blood, respectively.

The parameter $\Lambda = D_a/W$ is the ratio of the diffusivity of oxygen in air, D_a, to the surface permeability, W, has units of length, and is the only length scale for the boundary-valued problem defined by Eqns. 4 to 6. Moreover, it has an elegant physical interpretation: it measures the length along the surface a diffusing molecule visits before it is absorbed by the surface, and for this reason is termed the exploration length (Pfeifer & Sapoval, 1995).

3.3 The effective surface area: area of the active zones involved in the oxygen transport

Although the diffusion-reaction problem defined by Eqns. 4 to 6 give concentrations across the tree's exchange surface, we are instead interested in the *total* current of molecules supplied to the blood by the whole of the airway tree. Computing this current for a single subacinus, I_g, from Eqns. 4 to 6 can be carried out by integrating the concentrations over its entire surface, S_g (Hou et al., 2010):

$$I_g = W \int_{\mathbf{x} \in S_g} \left(c(\mathbf{x}) - c_b \beta_a / \beta_b \right) dS \tag{7}$$

Manipulating this equation leads to an expression for the current in terms of a constant concentration difference:

$$I_g = W S_{eff,g} \left(c_a - c_b \beta_a / \beta_b \right), \tag{8}$$

wherein $S_{eff,g}$ is a function of the exploration length (Hou, 2005):

$$S_{eff,g}(\Lambda) = \int_{\mathbf{x} \in S_g} \frac{c(\mathbf{x}; \Lambda) - c_b \beta_a / \beta_b}{c_a - c_b \beta_a / \beta_b} dS. \tag{9}$$

This quantity, termed the effective surface area (Felici et al., 2003; Felici et al., 2004; Grebenkov et al., 2005; Hou, 2005; Hou et al., 2010), measures the "active" portion of the tree's surface, and is generally less than its total, i.e. $S_{eff,g} \leq S_g$. The difference in these areas is unused in any molecular transport, and is "inactive," or *screened* from molecular access to it.

This screening can be conceptualized in terms of the exploration length (see below). For example, $\Lambda = 0$ (i.e. permeability is infinite) describes a situation in which no molecules explore areas of the tree beyond the entrance, being immediately absorbed by the surface on their first contact with it. This regime is termed *complete screening*. In contrast, $\Lambda = \infty$ (i.e. permeability is zero) implies that oxygen molecule hits the surface many times and eventually visits the entire surface, marking the regime of *no screening*. These facts provide a powerful conceptual picture of the lung's operational principles: to increase the current under constant conditions of membrane permeability and concentration difference, the effective surface area must increase proportionally. So, for breathing/exercise states of increasing exercise intensity, ever larger fractions of the lung's exchange area must be recruited for the molecular transport across it.

3.4 Total current into the tree

The current crossing the lung's exchange areas is the sum of currents contributed from each individual branch of the subacinar tree, given by Eqn. 8:

$$I = \sum_{i=1}^{N_g} I_{g,i}, \tag{10}$$

wherein N_g gives the number of gas exchangers in the lung in the current exercise state (explained below). Taking an average of both sides of Eqn. 10 over all such gas-exchangers gives $I = N_g I_g$, wherein I_g is the average current supplied by a single subacinus. The total current can then be written as

$$I = N_g W S_{eff,g} \left(c_a - c_b / \beta_a / \beta_b \right). \tag{11}$$

This equation, Eqn. 11, can be rewritten in terms of the physiological variables of Eqn. 2:

$$I = \frac{D_m \beta_m S_{eff}}{\tau} \left(p_a - p_b \right) = W S_{eff} \left(c_a - c_b \beta_b / \beta_a \right), \tag{12}$$

wherein the diffusing capacity of the lung has been replaced by the diffusion coefficient of oxygen through the surface of alveolar membranes, D_m, the thickness of the membrane-barrier, τ, the solubility of oxygen in the membranes, β_m , and the effective surface area of the entire lung, S_{eff}. The permeability can itself be expressed in terms of measurable quantities, and dependent upon the thickness of the membranes:

$$W = \frac{D_m \beta_m}{\tau}. \tag{13}$$

To good approximation, the thickness of the membranes is constant and the permeability is position-independent.

The total current, Eqn. 11, crucially depends on how the effective surface area responds to the current physiological conditions. Integrating directly from the concentrations, as in Eqn. 9, requires a solution to the difficult boundary-valued diffusion-reaction problem defined above (Eqns. 4 to 6). In the next section, we review an entirely geometrical method, termed the Rope-Walk Algorithm, permitting us to side-step the difficult integration required by equation 9, and, through Eqn. 11, allows for a solution of Eqns. 4 to 6 to be found without directly solving the full diffusion-reaction problem.

3.5 Rope-Walk algorithm: solving the diffusion equation without solving the diffusion equation

We consider a self-similar surface with fractal dimension D_f, surface area S, and composed of cubic elementary units of side length, l, which serves as a molecular "receptor" in the diffusion-reaction problem. Molecules encounter this surface after diffusing from the source with area S_s, which is much smaller than the receptor's total surface area $S_s << S$. Only surface sites that such diffusing molecules visit while "walking" along it, even if the exploration length is zero, are considered here. Such sites are very close to the diffusion source. A rope of length Λ is rolled out along the surface as diffusing molecules "walk" along it, which determines the diameter of the profile so covered/explored by ropes, from which the effective surface area explored by diffusing molecules is found, S_{eff} (Hou, 2005; Hou et al., 2010):

$$S_{eff} = \begin{cases} S_s & \Lambda < l \\ S_s \left(\Lambda / l\right)^{(D_f-2)/(D_f-1)} & l \leq \Lambda \leq l\left(S_s^{1/2}/l\right)^{D_f-1} \\ S_s^{1/2}\Lambda & l\left(S_s^{1/2}/l\right)^{D_f-1} \leq \Lambda \leq S_s^{1/2} S \\ S & S_s^{1/2} S \leq \Lambda \end{cases}, \tag{14}$$

describing four screening regimes, respectively given as: *complete screening*, *strong partial screening*, *weak partial screening*, and *no screening*.

These ropes decompose the total surface into regions accessible to the diffusing molecule, and regions inaccessible, which are determined by how the rope length compares with other three length scales: side lengths of the elementary unit, the size of the diffusion source, and the "perimeter" of the membrane surface. If the rope length is smaller than an elementary block unit, $\Lambda < l$, then only the region very close to the source, with area S_s, is active in transport, which marks the regime of complete screening. If the rope is longer than the perimeter of the surface profile, then molecules explore the entire surface before they cross it, and this is the case of no screening. In between, there are two partial screening cases, in which the rope is longer than the elementary block but not long enough to wrap the whole surface.

4. Mathematical models of gas-exchangers

Several mathematical models describing molecular transport across reactive surfaces have been used to study the response of the oxygen current across mammalian lungs at physiological conditions (Hou et al., 2010; Mayo, 2009; Grebenkov et al., 2005). Although each model treats the exchange surface differently, they each provide similar predictions of, and independently verify, the "robustness" of the human lung (described below). More importantly, these models provide fully analytic formulas of the total current, allowing for transparent relationships to be derived between this robustness and the model's parameters.

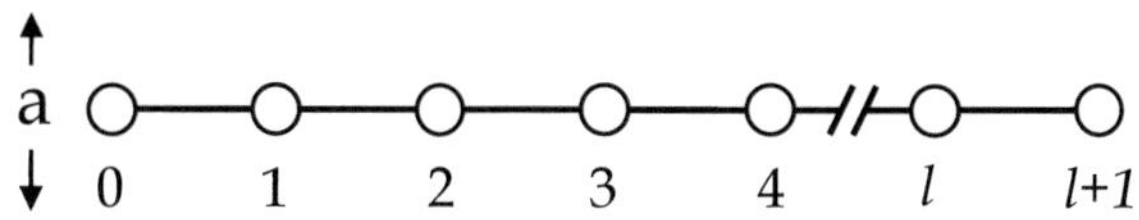

Fig. 4. Discretized branch of an alveolar duct in the square-channel model.

Together with Eqn. 11, the Rope-Walk algorithm serves as the first of three predictive mathematical models we describe here. The next model is the square-channel model proposed by Grebenkov and his collaborators (Grebenkov et al., 2005). The third model, the Cayley tree model, is a new model of the acinar tree we present here.

4.1 Square-channel model

4.1.1 Modeling a single alveolar duct

In an approach developed by Grebenkov and his collaborators (Grebenknov et al., 2005), a single branch of the subacinar tree is modeled discretely, as a square channel, from which the entire acinar tree is assembled. Figure 4 illustrates a single branch in this model, wherein oxygen molecules diffuse throughout a channel of $d = 3$ dimensions. These molecules begin diffusion from a square cross-section of area a^2 to ultimately "react" with the exchange surface along the channel walls, which occurs at discrete intervals separated by a distance a.

The full diffusion-reaction problem is therefore mapped onto a discrete, one-dimensional process that evolves according to the following diffusion "rules" (Grebenkov et al., 2005). Molecules currently at site i move to the left (site $i-1$) or right (site $i+1$) with probability $1/2d$, or stay on the current site with probability $(1-\sigma)(1-1/d)$, wherein $\sigma = 1/(1+\Lambda/a)$ is the absorption probability of the molecule with the surface. Finally, the molecule crosses the surface with probability $\sigma(1-1/d)$. Collectively, these rules can be written as a finite difference equation (Grebenkov et al., 2005), which is a discretized version of Eqns. 4 to 6:

$$\frac{1}{2}(c_{i-1}+c_{i+1}) - c_i = \sigma(d-1)c_i, \tag{15}$$

wherein $i = 0, 1, \ldots, l$.

Equation 15 can be solved by applying the discrete Fourier transform, with boundary conditions $c_0 = c_{ent}$ and $c_{l+1} = c_{ext}$ (Grebenkov et al., 2005). These solutions can be expressed in terms of linear relationships between concentrations at lattice sites 0,1,l, and $l+1$, shown in Fig. 4:

$$c_1 = (1-u_{\sigma,k})\, c_{ent} + v_{\sigma,k} c_{ext}, \text{ and} \tag{16}$$

$$c_k = v_{\sigma,k} c_{ent} + (1-u_{\sigma,k})\, c_{ext}. \tag{17}$$

Here, the coefficients $u_{\sigma,k}$ and $v_{\sigma,k}$ depend only on the dimension of the diffusion space, d, and the absorption probability, σ (Grebenkov et al., 2005):

$$u_{\sigma,k} = 1 - \frac{s_{\sigma,k}}{([1+(d+1)\sigma]s_{\sigma,k}+1/2)^2 - s_{\sigma,k}^2}, \text{ and} \tag{18}$$

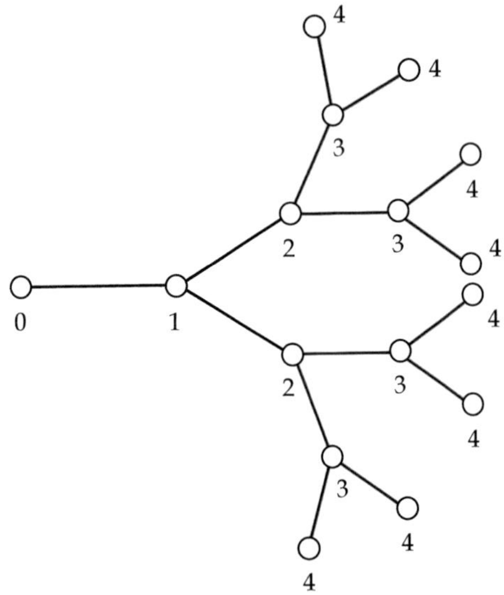

Fig. 5. Exemplary hierarchical bifurcating tree of depth $n = 3$.

$$v_{\sigma,k} = 1 - \frac{[1 + (d+1)\,\sigma]s_{\sigma,k} + 1/2}{\left([1 + (d+1)\,\sigma]s_{\sigma,k} + 1/2\right)^2 - s_{\sigma,k}^2}, \tag{19}$$

wherein the sum, $s_{\sigma,k}$, is given by

$$s_{\sigma,k} = \frac{1}{2k}\sum_{j=0}^{k-1}[1 + (d-1)\,\sigma - \cos\,(2\pi j/k)]^{-1}. \tag{20}$$

Equations 16 through 20 give the concentrations in a single duct near its ends. In the following sections this result is extended to describe the oxygen currents crossing the exchange surface of alveolar membranes lining these ducts.

4.1.2 Building the tree from a single branch

A treelike structure can be assembled from the individually modeled branches of the previous section, and Fig. 5 illustrates of an exemplary bifurcating tree. Its branching hierarchy is conceptualized by parent and daughter branches, in which m-many daughter branches extend from each parent branch at the branch points. In this model, the branches are subscripted according to whether they are an entrance or exit quantity of a branch in a given generation, i.e. $c_{ent,i}$ is the entrance concentration of a branch in the ith generation along any path from leaf to root. The problem, then, is to compute the current, I, leaving the surface of the entire tree, which is the sum of the contributions from each individual branch, $I_i = I_{ent,i} - I_{ext,i}$:

$$I = \sum_{k=0}^{n} m^k\left(I_{ent,k} - I_{ext,k}\right) + m^n I_{ext,n} = I_{ent,0}, \tag{21}$$

wherein we have used $I_{ext,k-1} = mI_{end,k}$. From Eqn. 21, we only need compute the current entering the tree by its root to find the current leaving the effective area of the reactive surface. A branch-by-branch renormalization procedure is now used to calculate this quantity.

4.1.3 Branch-by-branch calculation of the total current into the tree

The currents entering and leaving any branch of the tree can be written in terms of concentrations there (Grebenkov et al., 2005):

$$I_{ent} = DS_0 \frac{c_0 - c_1}{a}, \text{ and } I_{ext} = DS_0 \frac{c_l - c_{l+1}}{a}, \tag{22}$$

wherein $S_0 = a^{d-1}$ is the area of a square cross-section for the channel. Applying these expressions to Eqns. 16 and 17 relates the entrance and exit currents with their respective concentrations (Grebenkov et al., 2005):

$$c_{ent} = \frac{u_{\sigma,l}}{v_{\sigma,l}} c_{ext} + \frac{a}{DS_0 v_{\sigma,l}} I_{ext}, \text{ and } I_{ent} = \frac{u_{\sigma,l}}{v_{\sigma,l}} I_{ext} + \frac{DS_0}{a} \frac{u_{\sigma,l}^2 - v_{\sigma,l}^2}{v_{\sigma,l}} c_{ext}. \tag{23}$$

Beginning with a terminal branch, the current leaving its end cross-section can be written in terms of the exploration length (Grebenkov et al., 2005):

$$I_{ext,n} = \frac{DS_0}{\Lambda} c_{ext,n}, \tag{24}$$

allowing for the current entering the branch to be given by

$$I_{ent,n} = DS_0 \frac{(\Lambda/a)\left[u_{\sigma,l}^2 - v_{\sigma,l}^2\right]}{\Lambda u_{\sigma,l} + a} c_{ent,n}. \tag{25}$$

Since a terminal branch is the daughter branch to one in the $n-1$ generation, and noting both mass conservation at the branch point, $I_{ext,n-1} = m I_{ent,n}$, and that concentrations are independent of the labeling there, $c_{ext,n-1} = c_{ent,n}$, we find that

$$I_{ext,n-1} = \frac{DS_0}{f(\Lambda)} c_{ext,n-1}, \tag{26}$$

wherein

$$f(\Lambda) = \frac{a}{m} \left(\frac{(\Lambda/a)\, u_{\sigma,l} + 1}{(\Lambda/a)\left(u_{\sigma,l}^2 - v_{\sigma,l}^2\right) u_{\sigma,l}} \right). \tag{27}$$

Comparing Eqns. 26 to 27 to Eqn. 24, it is clear that the current leaving a branch in the $n-1$ generation can be viewed as a boundary condition across the leaves of a "reduced" tree of depth $n-2$. This procedure can be continued until the current entering the tree by its root is expressed in terms of the concentration there, c_0 (Grebenkov et al., 2005):

$$I = \frac{DS_0}{m f^{n+1}(\Lambda)} c_0, \tag{28}$$

wherein $f^{n+1}(\Lambda) = f \circ \cdots \circ f(\Lambda)$ gives the $n+1$–fold functional composition of Eqn. 27, and, with $d = 3$, $S_0 = a^2$ is the cross-section of the square channel.

4.2 Cayley tree model

Instead of modeling an acinus as a hierarchical tree of square channels, here we consider these branches as cylinders; this symmetry allows for a continuous description of the concentrations along its branches (Mayo 2009; Mayo et al., 2011). This model is flexible enough to include scaling relationships between parent and daughter branches, giving the total current in terms of the tree's fractal dimension.

4.2.1 Scaling relationships and fractal dimensions of the fractal Cayley tree

To account for scaling between the tree's branches, we adopt the following labeling scheme. The width and length of each branch is given by $2r_{e_i}$ and L_{e_i}, respectively, wherein $e_i = (i, i+1)$ label the edges of the Cayley graph in terms of its node, as illustrated by Fig. 5, and $i = 0, 1, \ldots, n, n+1$, with n being the depth of the tree. The single entrance branch, $e_0 = (0, 1)$, is termed the "trunk," whereas the m^n-many terminal branches, each labeled by $e_n = (n, n+1)$, are those composing its canopy, or "leaves."

We decompose the tree's surface into two parts: i) the canopy, or the surface composed of the union of end-caps of the terminal branches, and ii) the tree's cumulative surface area, or the sum of all surfaces minus the end cross-sections. The width and length of daughter branches can be expressed in terms of the those quantities for the parent branch through scaling relationships for their length, $m\left(L_{e_i}\right)^{D_{tree}} = L_{e_{i-1}}^{D_{tree}}$ and width, $m\left(r_{e_i}\right)^{D_{canopy}} = r_{e_{i-1}}^{D_{canopy}}$ (Mandelbrot, 1982). The ratios of these quantities across successive generations can be expressed in terms of the scaling exponents for the cumulative surface of the tree, D_{tree} , and its canopy, D_{canopy}:

$$p = m^{-1/D_{tree}}, \text{ and } q = m^{-1/D_{canopy}}. \tag{29}$$

For simplicity, we assume the length and width of branches in the same generation are of equal length and width; however, we allow branches to scale in width or length across generations: $p = p_{e_i} = L_{e_i}/L_{e_{i+1}}$ and $q = q_{e_i} = r_{e_i}/r_{e_{i+1}}$ for $i = 0, 1, \ldots, n-1$. These scaling exponents can be equated with the fractal dimension of the tree's cumulative and canopy surface areas (Mandelbrot, 1982; Mayo, 2009).

4.2.2 Helmholtz approximation of the full diffusion-reaction problem in a single branch

For cylindrical branches in which the ratio of radius to length, termed the aspect ratio, r/L, is "small," the oxygen concentration is, to very good approximation, dependent only on the variable describing its axis, x (Mayo, 2009). Mass-balance of the oxygen flux in the cylinder gives a Helmholtz-style equation for the concentration in the tube (Mayo et al., 2011):

$$\frac{d^2}{dx^2} c\left(x\right) - \left(\frac{\phi}{L}\right)^2 c\left(x\right) = 0. \tag{30}$$

wherein the Thiele modulus of the branch is given in terms of the exploration length:

$$\phi = L\sqrt{\frac{2}{r\Lambda}}. \tag{31}$$

The tree is composed of three classes of branches, each defined by type of boundary condition given across the beginning and end of the tube. Giving an exit concentration (written in terms of the exit current) and an entrance current for a terminal branch, $c(x=L) = I_{ext}/W\pi r^2$ and $d/dxc(x=0) = -I_{ent}/D\pi r^2$, gives a solution to Eqn. 30 connecting the entrance and exit currents (Mayo, 2009):

$$c(x) = \frac{I_{ent}\sinh[\phi(1-x/L)] + I_{ext}\phi\cosh(\phi x/L)}{(\pi\rho^2 D/L)\,\phi\cosh\phi}. \tag{32}$$

Similar equations can be found for the trunk and "intermediate branches," resulting in equations that link entrance and exit concentrations, or a mixture of concentrations and currents (Mayo et al., 2011). These equations are used in a renormalization calculation, similar to the branch-by-branch calculation of the square-channel model above, to compute the total current entering the tree by its root.

4.2.3 Total current into the tree

Elsewhere we demonstrate how equations of the type described by Eqn. 32 can be employed for a branch-by-branch calculation of the total current, similar to that of the square-channel model described above, and written in terms of the scaling ratios of Eqn. 29 (Mayo et al., 2011). This calculation results in

$$I = \frac{D\pi r_0^2}{mq^2\Lambda_{eff}}c_0, \tag{33}$$

wherein $c_0 = c_{ent,0}$ denotes the concentration across the entrance of the trunk, consistent with the terminology of Eqn. 28 and $r_0 = r_{e_0}$ is the radius of the trunk. So, the effective exploration length, Λ_{eff} is a p,q–dependent expression,

$$\frac{\Lambda_{eff}}{L_0} = \frac{g_0}{q^2}\circ\frac{g_1}{q^2}\circ\cdots\circ\frac{g_n(\Lambda/L_0)}{q^2}, \tag{34}$$

wherein $L_0 = L_{e_0}$ is the length of the trunk. Equation 34 is the $n+1$–fold functional composition of a branch-wise attenuating function $g_i = g_{e_i}$. This function itself is given by the formula

$$\frac{g_i(\Lambda/L_0)}{q^2} = \frac{(\Lambda/L_0)\,q^{-i/2}\phi_0 + \tanh\left[(p/\sqrt{q})^i\,\phi_0\right]}{(\Lambda/L_0)\,q^{2-i}m\phi_0^2\tanh\left[(p/\sqrt{q})^i\,\phi_0\right] + q^{2-i/2}m\phi_0}, \tag{35}$$

wherein $\phi_0 = L_0\sqrt{2/r_0\Lambda}$ is the Thiele modulus of the entrance branch, but depends on the exploration length penetrating into the tree.

4.2.4 Attenuating function as a Möbius transformation

Equation 35 is a Möbius transformation (Needham, 2007), and using this fact, Eqn. 34 can be expressed analytically. Möbius transformations, denoted by μ, are mappings that rotate, stretch, shrink, or invert curves on the complex plane, and take the following form (Needham, 2007): $\mu(z) = az + b/cz + d$, wherein a, b, c, d, and z are complex numbers. Remarkably, functional compositions of μ can also be calculated by multiplying matrices derived from it, termed Möbius matrices, drastically reducing the complexity of the functional-composition problem.

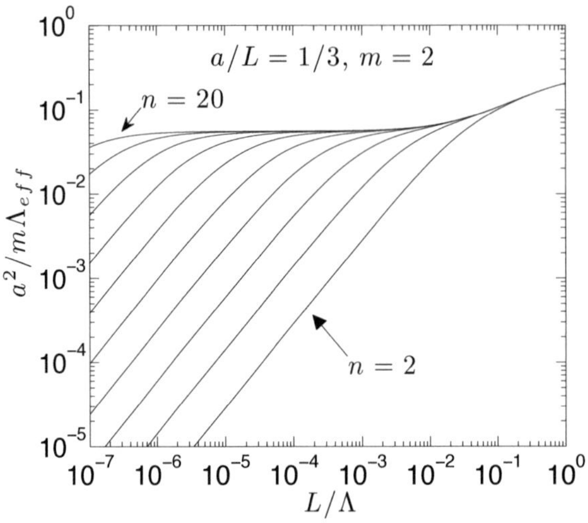

Fig. 6. Scaled currents as given by the square-channel model for trees of differing depth, n. Here, lengths are scaled in units of channel length, $L = 3a$.

Denoting the branch-wise Möbius matrix of g_i/q^2 by G_i, we construct

$$G_i = \begin{pmatrix} q^{-i/2}\phi_0 & \tanh\left[\left(p/\sqrt{q}\right)^i \phi_0\right] \\ q^{2-i} m\phi_0^2 \tanh\left[\left(p/\sqrt{q}\right)^i \phi_0\right] & q^{2-i/2} m\phi_0 \end{pmatrix}. \tag{36}$$

The effective exploration length, $\Lambda_{eff}/L_0 = D_{eff}/L_0 W_{eff}$, can be calculated according to

$$\prod_{i=0}^{n} G_i \begin{pmatrix} D/L_0 \\ W \end{pmatrix} = \begin{pmatrix} D_{eff}/L_0 \\ W_{eff} \end{pmatrix}. \tag{37}$$

In the special case of a "symmetric" tree, i.e. $p = q = 1$, the fully fractal Möbius matrix, Eqn. 37, reduces to

$$G_i = \begin{pmatrix} \phi_0 & \tanh\phi_0 \\ m\phi_0^2 \tanh\phi_0 & m\phi_0 \end{pmatrix}. \tag{38}$$

A fully analytical formula can be derived from this simplification by diagonalizing this 2×2 matrix, but this procedure and its implications will be presented elsewhere (Mayo et al., 2011).

Note that Eqns. 33 to 35 of the Cayley tree model, and Eqns. 27 and 28 of the square-channel model are predictions for the same quantity: the total current leaving the tree through its "reactive" side-walls. While the square-channel model is restricted to describe branches of equal width and length, the Cayley the model carries no such limitation. This scaling is quantified by inclusion of the trees' two fractal dimensions, D_{tree} and D_{canopy}, implied by the length and width ratios p and q, respectively.

Although the Cayley tree model is more general than the square-channel model in this respect, there are firm physiological data demonstrating the length and width of alveolar ducts remain constant with increasing generation in the human lung, i.e. $p = q = 1$ (Weibel, 1984), allowing for a direct comparison between the Cayley tree and square-channel models under application of this data to these models. The implications of the fracticality of the Cayley tree model will be discussed elsewhere.

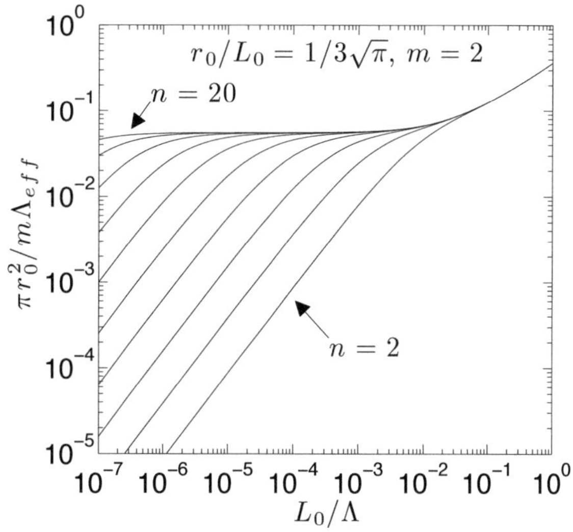

Fig. 7. Scaled currents given by the Cayley tree model for trees of varying depth, n. Here, r_0 and L_0 are the radius and length of the tree's entrance branch, respectively.

5. Reverse-engineering the robustness of mammalian lungs

5.1 Plateaus in the oxygen current associated with "robustness" to changing parameters

Despite differences in their geometrical treatment of the exchange surface, each of the models presented here (Rope-walk, square-channel, and Cayley tree models) predict the existence of a broad region in the exploration length, defined by $\partial I/\partial W = 0$, wherein the current entering the tree remains unchanged with respect to the surface's permeability.

Figure 6 illustrates this current, scaled in units of Dc_0 (fixed diffusivity), in the square-channel model. Here, L is the length of each channel, expressed in units of lattice constant a, and trees of differing depth, ranging from $n = 2$ to $n = 20$, in steps of two, are compared against one another. For smaller trees, the plateau is shorter, but the plateau is the largest for the larger trees (n or m large). Figure 7 illustrates the scaled current computed for the Cayley tree model. Plateaus similar to the square-channel model are presented, with the diameter of the source chosen by equating trunk cross-sectional areas with the square-channel model. Finally, figure 8 depicts currents computed using the Rope-Walk Algorithm, wherein the plateau widths are more clearly defined.

These plateaus describe a reduction in the active zones that is exactly matched by an increase in the permeability, or vice versa, keeping the current constant. Operation of mammalian lungs near the onset of these plateaus allows for the maximum current to be supplied to the blood by the lung while maintaining "robustness" necessary to mitigate any reduction in permeability that might occur from, for example, disease.

5.2 Screening regimes induced by diffusion of respiratory gases

These models each predict the existence of various screening regimes, which limit molecular access to the exchange area for different values of the surfaces' permeability. In the regime $\Lambda = 0$ ($W = \infty$), termed *complete screening* above, molecules do not explore further than the

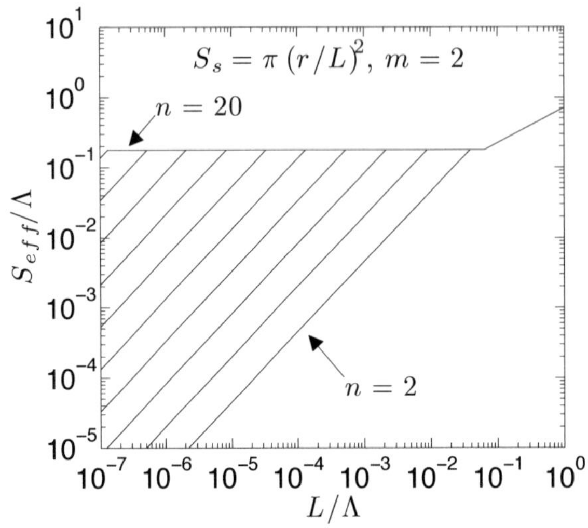

Fig. 8. Scaled currents in the Rope-Walk model for airway trees of varying size. Here, *r* and *L* denotes the radius and length of branches in the tree used to model the total gas-exchanger area.

entrance to the diffusion space, being absorbed by the exchange surface on their first contact with it. In the case of the Rope-Walk Algorithm model, this results in deep surface crevices possessing vanishing probability to admit any molecules. In both the Cayley tree and square channel models, this regime paints a picture in which vast amounts of surface area go unused, so that any effort in maintaining or creating the size and shape of the tree is wasted. In the opposite regime, $\Lambda = \infty$ ($W = 0$), the entire surface is visited by molecules, although they never cross it. Between these two extremes lies a region in which some, but not all, of the surface is explored. In this region, a balance between maximizing both the area of the active zones and the current crossing them guarantees that a minimum of the surface area is unused in the transport across it. Furthermore, direct validation of the partial screening regimes may be difficult, as the region of constant current cannot provide a unique value for the exploration length (or permeability) when measured under experimental conditions.

5.3 Efficiency of the gas-exchanger

The efficiency of the gas-exchanger, η_g, is defined as the ratio of current crossing the exchange surface to the total available current: $\eta_g = I/WS_gc_0 = S_{eff,g}/S_g$, giving a dimensionless measure of the gas-exchangers' performance, and can also be computed as the ratio of effective to total surface area (Hou, 2005; Grebenkov et al., 2005). Applied to the square-channel model, this efficiency is given by:

$$\eta_g = \frac{a^2}{mS_g}\left(\frac{\Lambda}{f^{n+1}(\Lambda)}\right). \tag{39}$$

wherein the total surface area of the square-channel tree is $S_g = 4a^2\,(l+1)\sum_{i=1}^{n} m^i + m^n a^2$. In the Cayley tree model, this efficiency is given by

$$\eta_g = \frac{\pi\rho^2}{mq^2S_g}\left(\frac{\Lambda}{L_0\Lambda_{eff}}\right), \tag{40}$$

Parameter	Unit	Value			
		Rest	Moderate	Heavy	Maximum
Convection-diffusion transition	n/a	18	19	20	21
S_g	cm^2	6.75	3.36	1.69	0.844
N_g	$\times 10^5$	1.81	3.63	7.26	14.5
$c_a - c_b\beta_a/\beta_b$	$\times 10^{-7}$ moles/ml	1.97	4.10	4.97	4.51

Table 1. Data used for evaluating the mathematical models at varying levels of exercise, from ref. (Hou et al., 2010).

with the surface area of the fractal tree given by $S_g = 2\pi r_0 L_0 \sum_{i=0}^{n} (pqm)^i + (q^2 m)^n \pi r_0^2$ (Mayo, 2009). Finally, the efficiency of the Rope-Walk Algorithm is easily computed from Eqns. 14 by dividing them by the measured area of a gas exchanger, which serves as the area of the fractal surface across which the oxygen transport occurs.

To compute the current crossing the exchange surface in the human lung, the efficiency of a single gas exchanger is considered to be the same for all N_g–many gas-exchangers of the lung. This approximation gives:

$$I = N_g W \eta_g S_g \left(c_{air} - c_{blood}\beta_{air}/\beta_{air} \right), \tag{41}$$

wherein the values for the physiological parameters N_g, S_g, and $c_{air} - c_{blood}\beta_{air}/\beta_{blood}$ depend on the exercise state (Hou et al., 2010).

6. Validating these models against experimental data

The experimental data necessary to evaluate Eqn. 41 have been recently tabulated (Sapoval et al., 2005; Hou et al., 2010), from which exercise-independent parameters, valid for all models, are found. Here, the diameter of an single alveoli, $l_a = 0.0139$ cm (Hou et al., 2010), serves as the inner cut-off of the fractal surface in the Rope-Walk model, but is also taken as the smallest length scale in both the Cayley tree and square-channel models, i.e. $l_a = 2r_0$. Moreover, the permeability of the alveolar membranes to molecular oxygen, $W = 0.00739$ cm/sec (Hou et al., 2010), and its diffusivity of oxygen in air, $D_a = 0.243$ cm^2/sec (Hou et al., 2010), can be used to estimate the physiological value of the exploration length $\Lambda = D_a/W = 32.88$ cm. Finally, the Cayley tree and square-channel models must also include the length of their branches, taken in both models as the averaged length of an alveolar duct, $L_0 = 0.0736$ cm (Sapoval et al., 2005). Previous measurements firmly establish that the actual duct-length and -radius do not appreciably change with acinar branching generation (Haefeli-Bleuer & Weibel, 1988). In the Cayley tree model, this fact sets the branch-scaling parameters $p = q = 1$, corresponding to diverging fractal dimensions. The acinar tree, therefore, completely overfills the available space, packing the most exchange area into the pleural cavities in the fewest branching generations.

Exercise-dependent parameters are given in Table 1, tabulated from ref. (Hou et al., 2010) for all four exercise regimes considered here (rest, moderate, heavy, and maximum exercise). In the Rope-Walk model, these regimes conceptualize an increase in the active zones, resulting in the oxygen penetrating increasingly deeper crevices of the fractal surface. In the Cayley tree and square-channel models, these changing parameters associate with an oxygen source being pushed deeper into the tree, leaving a "smaller" gas-exchanger/subacinus for increasing

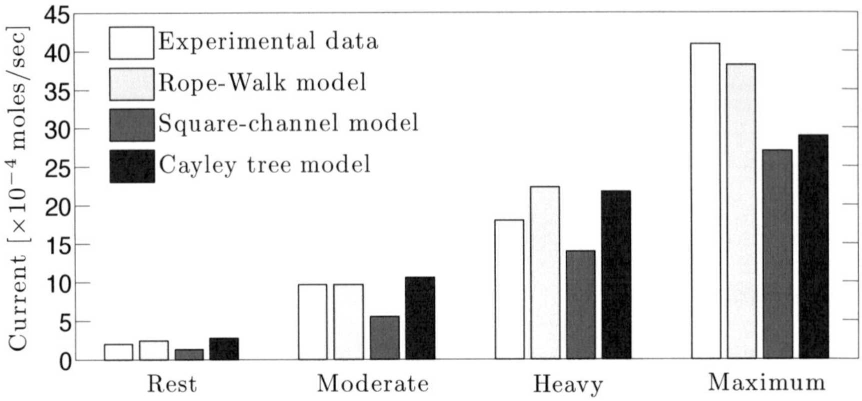

Fig. 9. Comparison between predicted values and the means of the measured oxygen uptake rates/currents at varying exercise levels.

exercise levels. This is reduction is balanced, however, with a drastic increase in the number of activated gas exchangers (Hou et al., 2010).

Figure 9 compares the predictions of these models to the measured currents for each exercise regime as reported by (Hou et al., 2010). Due to the discrete nature of the square-channel model, the length of a channel is restricted to be an integer multiple of its diameter (Grebenkov et al., 2005). So, setting $a = 0.0139$ cm requires that $l = 0.0760$ cm $/0.0139$ cm $= 5.47$; however, we rounded this value down to $l = 5$. Nevertheless, all models give reasonable agreement with the available data for the currents, with the Rope-Walk model giving closest agreement. This should be contrasted with the entirely different treelike models. We find the Cayley model to perform better than the square-channel model when equating their smallest length scales.

7. Industrial applications of lung-derived robustness

In this reverse engineering study, a finished product, the human lung, was deconstructed into its elementary processes/structures using mathematical modeling as the main investigative tool. Using this process, we uncovered a mechanism, termed diffusional screening, responsible for robustness of the prototypical lung studied here that functions by adjusting the area of the active zones in response to any loss of surface permeability, without any feedback loops or addition of any extra "hardware." Because aspects of some engineered processes evolve according to Eqns. 4 to 6, such as voltages, chemicals, or temperatures, they may also benefit from similar robustness derived, in part, from a treelike/fractal exchange surface. Here we briefly review just few examples.

7.1 Fuel cells

Fuel cells transduce chemical energy from a fuel (e.g. hydrogen, methane) into electrical energy through catalysis with an oxidizing agent (e.g. oxygen). Unfortunately, current devices lack the efficiency necessary to support wide-spread implementation in areas such as the transportation sector. Recent work, however, shows such efficiency can be improved 10-20% for a single cell of a stack-based setup using lung-inspired designs (Kjielstrup et al., 2010).

7.2 Heterogeneous catalysis

An active area of research in chemical engineering concerns the study of the chemical yield, and other properties, resulting from a gas or liquid reactant in contact with a solid nanoporous catalyst. It is known, for example, that the pore-size distribution influences the catalytic efficiency, wherein the reaction proceeds according to first-order kinetics (Gheorghui & Coppens, 2004). In this context Eqns. 4 to 6 describe the steady-state reactant concentration, while the total current, Eqn. 7, gives the yield. Although the resulting robustness of the lung's treelike "design" might protect against potential problems such as catalytic poisoning, it is not optimal in the sense of maximizing the reaction yield (Gheorghiu & Coppens, 2004).

7.3 Heat distribution systems

A nontrivial problem in thermal conduction is to efficiently distribute a localized heat source throughout a dissipation volume, preventing temperature increases at the source. Recent results from optimization analysis demonstrate the most efficient configuration of such a heat-transport network is treelike (Bejan, 2006). In many circumstances, temperature gradients evolve according to equations of the type in Eqns. 4 to 6, when heat is allowed to leak through the materials and into the environment (Carslaw & Jaeger, 1986). Results shown in Figs. 6 through 8 therefore equally describe heat transport across treelike and fractal surfaces, and suggest that treelike heat-pipe networks may be more tolerant to variations in material and manufacturing quality.

8. Conclusions

Although the partial pressure difference of oxygen in the gas-exchange regions of mammalian lungs increases only two-fold under the heaviest exercise conditions, the actual current increases approximately 20–fold, leaving another mechanism to supply the difference. Reverse engineering using mathematical modeling revealed that, depending on the exercise level, portions of the exchange surface of alveolar membranes remain "inactive" in any oxygen transport, so that a smaller effective area is responsible for supplying the oxygen current to the blood. With increasing exercise/breathing states, increasing surface areas are activated, drastically increasing the total oxygen uptake rate. This screening mechanism is termed "diffusional screening." Transitions between no- and partial-screening regimes mark a region in which the exploration length matches any decrease in the active zones due to oxygen inaccessibility to the exchange surface, establishing a broad plateau in the total current indicative of robustness. That is, altered diffusivity or permeability produces no change to the total current across several orders of magnitude, without the addition of any extra "hardware."

Other engineered systems, such as fuel cells, heterogeneous catalytic reactors, and heat pipes are described by the same fundamental processes: diffusion through a service volume and "reaction" along its surface. Using this information, structural designs of these industrial systems might be reengineered to mitigate the effects of uncertainties in manufacturing processes or material properties.

9. References

[1] Bejan, A., and Lorente, S. (2006). Constructal theory of generation of configuration in nature and engineering. *J. Appl. Phys.*, Vol. 100, pp. 041301.

[2] Carslaw, H.S., and Jaeger, J.C. (2000). *Conduction of Heat in Solids*, Oxford University Press Inc., New York, NY.
[3] Comroe, J.H. (1962). *The lung; clinical physiology and pulmonary function tests*, Year Book Medical Publishers, Chicago, IL.
[4] Felici, M. and Filoche, M. and Sapoval, B. (2003). Diffusional screening in the human pulmonary acinus. *J. Appl. Physiol.*, Vol. 94, pp. 2010.
[5] Felici, M. and Filoche, M. and Sapoval, B. (2004). Renormalized Random Walk Study of Oxygen Absorption in the Human Lung. *Phys. Rev. Lett.*, Vol. 92, pp.068101.
[6] Gheorghiu, S., and Coppens, M.-O. (2004). Optimal bimodal pore networks for heterogeneous catalysis. *AIChE J.*, Vol. 50, pp. 812.
[7] Grebenkov, D. S. and Filoche, M. and Sapoval, B. and Felici, M. (2005). Diffusion-Reaction in Branched Structures: Theory and Application to the Lung Acinus. *Phys. Rev. Lett.*, Vol. 94, pp. 050602.
[8] Haefeli-Bleuer, B., and Weibel, E.R. (1998). Morphometry of the human pulmonary acinus *Anat. Rec.*, Vol. 220, pp. 401.
[9] Hou, C. (2005). *Scaling laws for oxygen transport across the space-filling system of respiratory membranes in the human lung*, PhD thesis, University of Missouri, Columbia, MO.
[10] Hou, C., Gheorghiu, S., Huxley, V.H., and Pfeifer, P. (2010). Reverse Engineering of Oxygen Transport in the Lung: Adaptation to Changing Demands and Resources through Space-Filling Networks. *PLoS Comput. Biol.*, Vol. 6, No. 8, pp. e1000902.
[11] Kjelstrup, S., Coppens, M.-O., Pharoah, J.G., and Pfeifer, P. (2010). Nature-Inspired Energy- and Material-Efficient Design of a Polymer Electrolyte Membrane Fuel Cell. *Energy Fuels*, Vol. 24, pp. 5097.
[12] Mayo, M. (2009). *Hierarchical Model of Gas-Exchange within the Acinar Airways of the Human Lung*, PhD thesis, University of Missouri, Columbia, MO.
[13] Mayo, M. Gheorghiu, S., and Pfeifer, P. (2011). *Diffusional Screening in Treelike Spaces: an Exactly Solvable Diffusion-Reaction Model, Submitted.*
[14] Mandelbrot, B. (1982). *The Fractal Geometry of Nature*, W.H. Freeman, USA.
[15] Needham, T. (2007). *Visual Complex Analysis*, Oxford University Press, USA.
[16] Pfeifer, P., and Sapoval, B. (1995). Optimization of diffusive transport to irregular surfaces with low sticking probability. *Mat. Res. Soc. Symp. Proc.*, Vol. 366, pp. 271.
[17] Sapoval, B., Filoche, M., and Weibel, E.R. (2002). Smaller is better–but not too small: A physical scale for the design of the mammalian pulmonary acinus. *Proc. Natl. Acad. Sci. USA*, Vol. 99, No. 16, pp. 10411.
[18] Weibel, E.R. (1984). *The Pathway for Oxygen*, Harvard University Press, Cambridge, MA.
[19] Weibel, E.R., Taylor, C.R., and Hoppeler, H. (1992). Variations in function and design: Testing symmorphosis in the respiratory system. *PLoS Comp. Biol.*, Vol. 6, No. 8, pp. e1000902
[20] Weibel, E.R., Sapoval, B., and Filoche, M. (2005). Design of peripheral airways for efficient gas exchange. *Respir. Physiol. Neurobiol.*, Vol. 148, pp. 3.

12

Reverse Engineering and FEM Analysis for Mechanical Strength Evaluation of Complete Dentures: A Case Study

A. Cernescu[1], C. Bortun[2] and N. Faur[1]
[1]*Politehnica University of Timisoara*
[2]*"Victor Babes" University of Medicine and Pharmacy of Timisoara*
Romania

1. Introduction

Complete dentures are used in social healthcare of the seniors. These frequently deteriorate, due to the fragility and structural defects of the materials from which are realized, and also due to the accidents produced because of the patients disabilities. The loss of teeth impairs patients' appearance, mastication ability and speech, thus upsetting the quality of their social and personal life (Mack F., 2005). The selection of materials used in complete dentures technology is crucial, because this directly relates to its performance and life span. Generally, the complete dentures bases are made from acrylic resins - heat curing, light curing, casting, injection, microwaves technologies. Processing technology of these materials sometimes lead to complete dentures with small defects, which can initiate cracks; these are responsible for failure of the complete denture before the expected lifetime. The relative short lifetime of the complete dentures has led researchers to investigate the causes of fracture by studying the stress distribution upon mastication and to find ways to improve their mechanical performance. The finite element method (FEM) has been used for five decades for numerical stress analysis (N. Faur, 2002). The advent of 3D FEM further enables researchers to perform stress analysis on complicated geometries such as complete dentures, and provides a more detailed evaluation of the complete state of stress in their structures.

1.1 The aim of the work

Due to developing technologies of acrylic resins, the complete dentures have a high degree of porosity (defects). These defects in material structure, together with brittle fracture behavior, can cause failure of the complete denture before the expected lifetime.

The aim of this paper is to perform a numerical analysis which emphasize the high risk of denture degradation due to presence of defects. Numerical analysis was performed by applying finite elements method on a three-dimensional geometric model resulted by 3D scanning of a real denture. The scanned model, as a point cloud, has been processed and converted into a solid geometric model using „reverse engineering" techniques. Through the subject approached, this paper wants to inform about the reverse engineering tehniques and also presents their usefulness by a numerical analysis.

Based on FEM analysis have been investigated the stress distribution and structural integrity of a maxillary complete denture. The study focused on fracture resistance evaluation of dentures, in the presence of structural defects of materials, which initiates denture's cracking or fracture, before the estimated lifetime. Also, was analysed, through defectoscopy method, the porosity degree of dentures depending on the material they are made, and the influence of the defect size and location in denture, on the stress and strain state.

2. Material and methods

2.1 Mechanical properties of the material

For this study, have been selected maxillary complete dentures from different acrylic resins obtained by two technologies: heat-curing material - Meliodent (Heraeus Kulzer, Senden, Germany) and light curing material - Eclipse Resin System (Dentsply International Inc.-DeguDent GmbH, Hanau Germany). The dentures were non-destructively evaluated using an Olympus stereomicroscope, Type SZX7, locating the defects and micro-cracks resulted from their technology, fig. 1-a, b. In most of dentures assessed, defects were located in the area indicated in Figure 1. Using an image processing system, QuickphotoMicro 2.2, was made an assessment of defects size, fig. 1-b. In the next step of the study, was performed an experimental program to determine the mechanical properties of the materials involved in the analysis. The materials have been prepared in accordance to the manufacturer's recommendations, Table 1. The mechanical properties were determined by tensile tests on a testing machine, model Zwick Roell (Zwick GmbH & Co. KG, Ulm, Germany), according to ISO 527 standard and bending tests according to ASTM D 790 standard. The test results showed a brittle fracture behavior, which may indicate some vulnerabilty of this materials in the presence of defects.

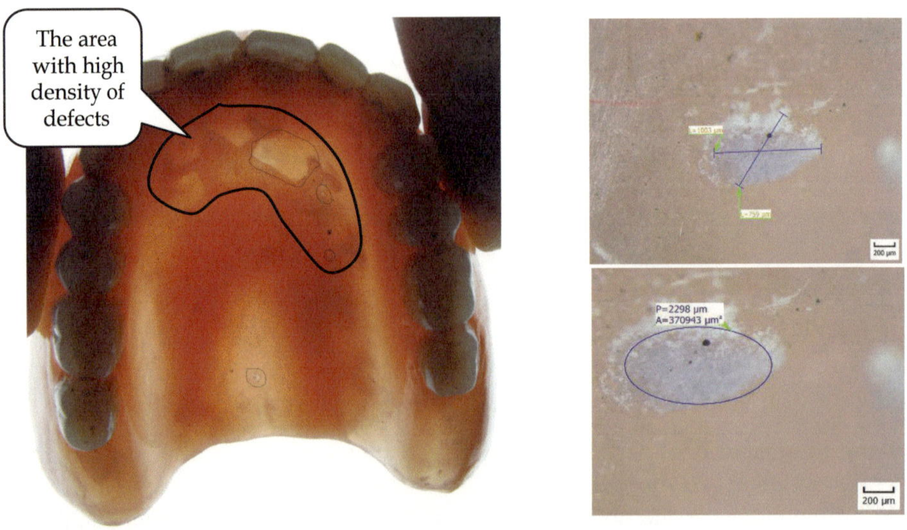

a) b)

Fig. 1. Non-destructive evaluation of maxillary complete dentures: a) locating defects in denture; b) measurement of localised defects.

Brand Name	Polymer: monomer ratio	Batch No. (polymer/monomer)	Description	Polymerization procedure
Meliodent Heat Cure	34g:17mL	64713213/64713308	Heat polymerized	7 hrs at 70° C and 1 hr at 100° C
Eclipse Prosthetic Resin System	Base plate supplied as pre-packed material	030822	Light - activated	Visible blue light

Table 1. The characteristics of acrylic resins included in this study

2.2 Geometric modeling of the upper complete denture

Finite element analysis was performed on geometric models, resulted after the complete dentures' 3D scanning (with 3D laser scanner LPX1200, Roland) and image processing by „reverse engineering", taking into consideration the located defects. A thin layer of green dye (Okklean, Occlusion spray, DFS, Germany) was sprayed on the surface of the denture to increase its contrast for scanning. The denture was positioned on the rotating table of the 3D scanner and scanned with a scanning pitch of 0.1 x 0.1 mm.

Scanning technique used is that of triangulation which is based on using a 3D non-contact active scanner. Non-contact active scanners emit some kind of radiation or light and exploit a camera to look for the location of the laser dot. Depending on how far away the laser strikes a surface, the laser dot appears at different places in the camera's field of view. This technique is called triangulation because the laser dot, the camera and the laser emitter form a triangle, fig. 2.

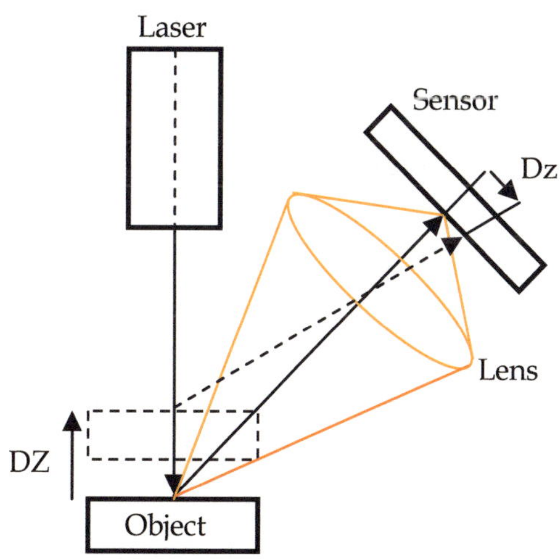

Fig. 2. Principle of laser triangulation sensor

The results of scanning process may be a point cloud (fig. 3) or a polygon mesh (fig. 4) having the shape of the scanned object. In a polygonal representation, the registered points are connected by straight edges forming a network of small plane triangular facets. After 3D scanning, the point cloud or polygon mesh are processed by reverse engineering technique and converted into a solid geometric model, fig. 5.

Fig. 3. The point cloud resulted from 3D scanning of the maxillary denture

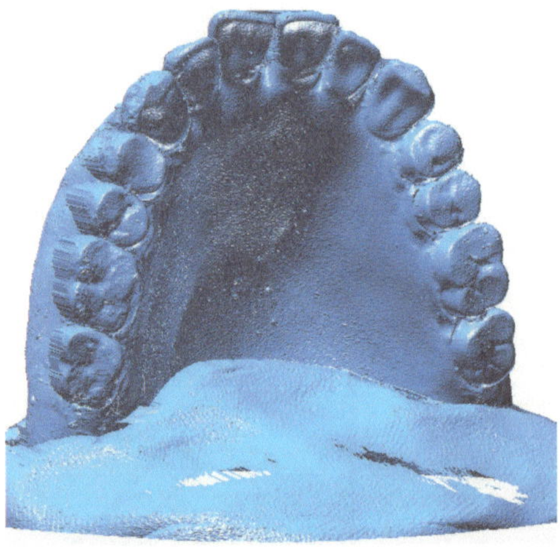

Fig. 4. The polygon mesh resulted from 3D scanning of the maxillary complete denture

The first step in converting a point cloud is processing and polygonization. This stage may include operations such as:

- Filter noise - removing the points placed in undesirable regions due to measurement errors, this can be done automatically;
- Filter redundancy - uniformly reducing the number of points in a point set where the points are too close or overlapped each other;
- Triangulation 3D - this operation converts a point cloud to a polygonal model.

If an object is scanned from several angles and resulting in more scanned surfaces, they must be registered and merged in a single polygon mesh.

After 3D scanning of a maxillary complete denture, a point cloud (fig. 3) was imported into the Pixform Pro software (INUS Technology, Seoul, Korea), and processed to create a fully closed polygon mesh. To create a continuous polygon mesh the point cloud of the scanned denture was triangulated and converted into a polygonal model. This polygonal model has

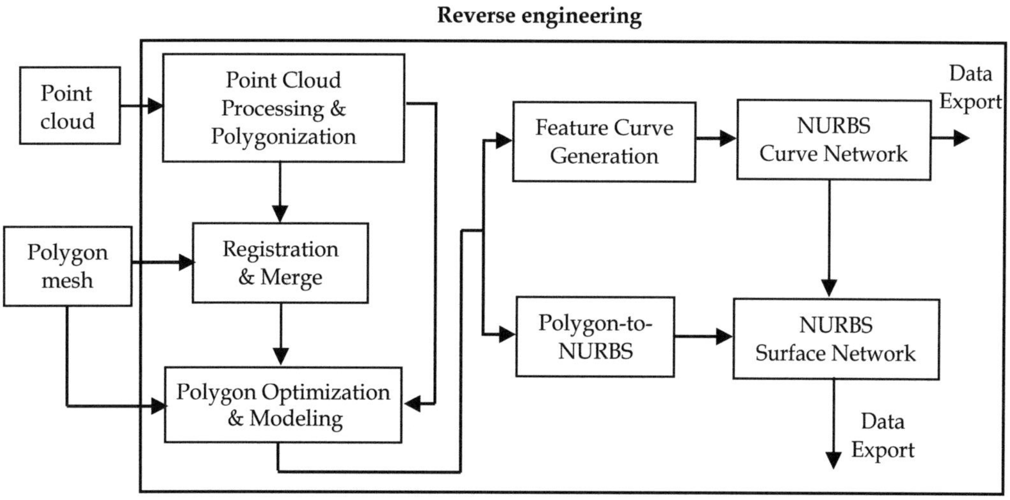

Fig. 5. The work process of reverse engineering technique

gone through a set of operations in the order they are listed: cleaning abnormal polygon meshes, refining the surface by smoothing and fill holes.

The smooth operation smoothes the surface of the polygonal model by changing the coordinates of the input vertices. The operation can be done automatically and provides three methods: Laplacian, Loop and Curvature. The Laplacian method is a tool for enhance global smoothness wile Loop method is a kind of local smoothing tool for keeping details of model. The Curvature method is used for curvature based smoothing. For this work was chosen the Laplacian smoothing method because it has the smallest deviations from the scanned model.

Another important operation in polygon mesh optimization is to fill holes in a model that may have been introduced during the scanning process. This operation can be done automatically or manually and constructs a polygonal structure to fill the hole, and both the hole and the surrounding region are remeshed so the polygonal layout is organized and continuous (Pixform Pro, 2004).

The result of polygon mesh optimization stage is a fully closed model (fig. 6) ready to generate NURBS (Non-uniform Rational B-Spline) curves or surfaces network.

The surface creation process begins by laying down curves directly on the polygonal model to define the different surfaces to be created. The curves network created on model (fig. 7) can be the basis for subsequent realization of the surfaces.

Once the curves network is created, the model is ready to generate NURBS surfaces (fig. 8). This can be done automatically or manual. Automatic surface generation doesn't need to draw a curve, while manual surface generation can completely maintain the flow line of the original polygon surface. Manual generation of surfaces is related to the network of curves.

For this case, because the scanned denture has a complex geometry, was chosen automatic generation of NURBS surfaces on the polygonal model. To obtain the geometric model of the maxillary complete denture the NURBS surfaces network was exported in initial graphics exchange specification (IGES) format and then imported into Solid Works 2007 for conversion into a solid model, fig. 9.

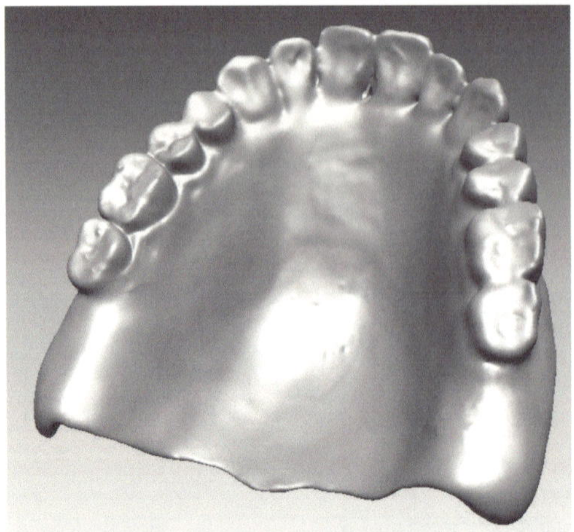

Fig. 6. A closed polygon mesh resulted after the optimization stage

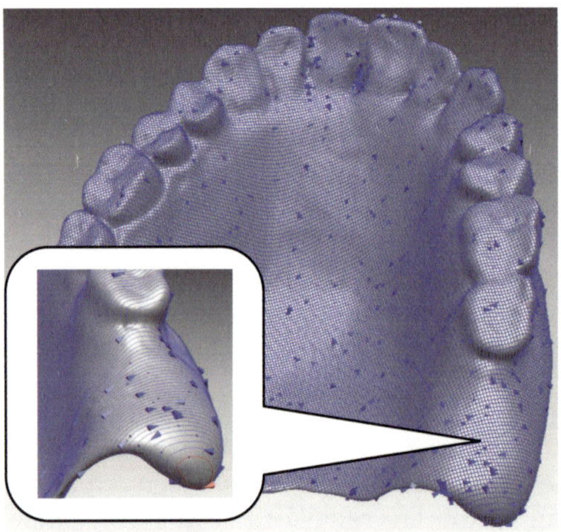

Fig. 7. The NURBS curve network generated on polygonal model

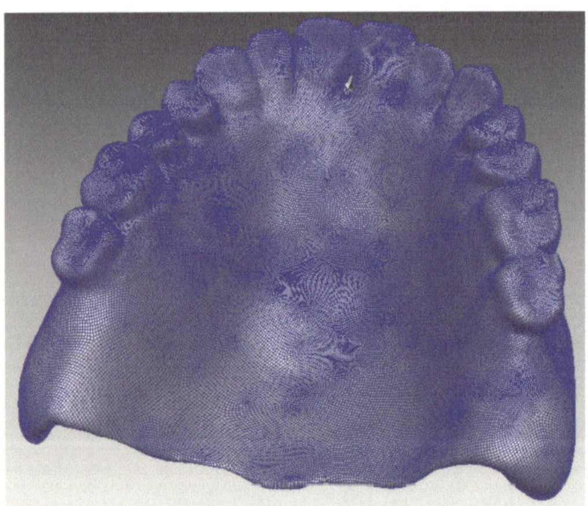

Fig. 8. The NURBS surface network generated on polygonal model

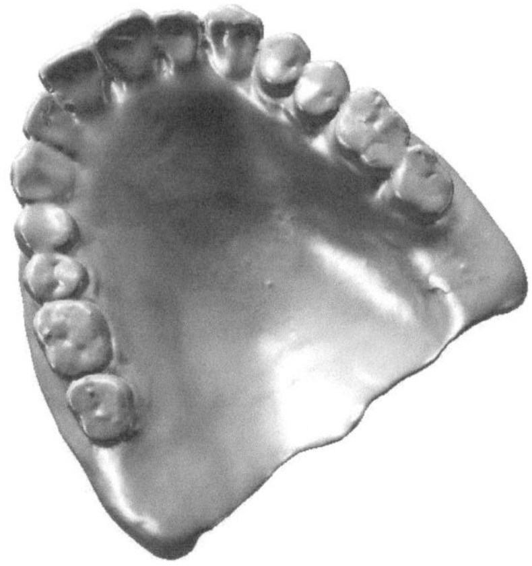

Fig. 9. The solid geometric model of complete denture

The NURBS tools (curves and surfaces) are commonly used in computer-aided design (CAD) and also found in various 3D modeling and animation software packages. They allow representation of geometrical shapes in a compact form. NURBS surfaces are functions of two parameters mapping to a surface in three-dimensional space. The shape of the surface is determined by control points.

2.3 The FEM analysis

Using the FEM software package, ABAQUS v6.9.3, on the geometric model of complete denture, was performed an analysis of the stress and strain field, taking into consideration different located defects. Based on non-destructive evaluation were carried out four models of analysis. At each model was considered a defect as a material hole with a diameter of 2 mm and 1 mm depth, in the area indicated in figure 1.

In the first model the fault was introduced near the midlle of the denture thickness, fig. 10. In the second and third model the faults were considered near the top surface of the denture and bottom respectively, fig. 11 and 12, and the fourth model shows a situation with a fault located in the thickness of the denture, with an irregular shape and a total surface twice that the faults defects of previous models, fig. 13. The fault depth of the fourth model is about 1 mm.

All four models were analyzed in two situations, in the first case we consider that the material of maxillary denture is Eclipse and the second case when the material is Meliodent.

The maximum force of mastication at a patient with complete denture is between 60-80 N (Zarb G, 1997). For this study was considered a mastication force of 70 N distributed on palatal cusps of the upper teeth, fig. 14. The areas with distributed force are about 46.666 mm^2 and the result is a normal pressure of 1.5 MPa. To fix the model, there have been applied supports on surfaces shown in fig. 15.

The supports from denture channel allow a 0.2 mm displacement in vertical direction and stop the displacements in horizontal plane. Also, the supports from palatal vault allow a 0.1 mm displacement in vertical direction and stop the displacements in horizontal plane. Allowed displacements were considered to replace the deformations of the oral mucosa.

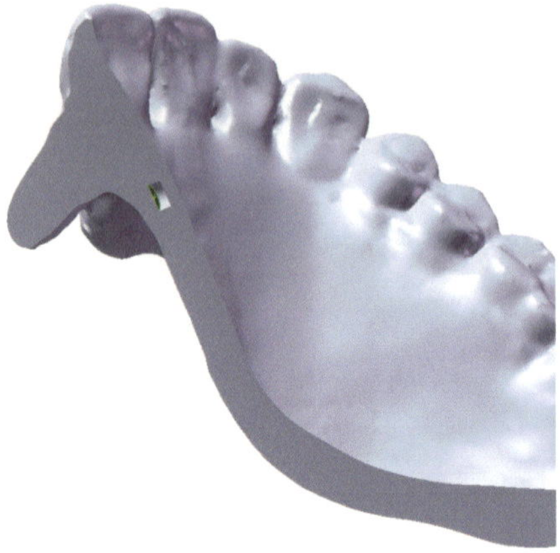

Fig. 10. The first analysis model: the fault is considered near the midlle of the denture thickness

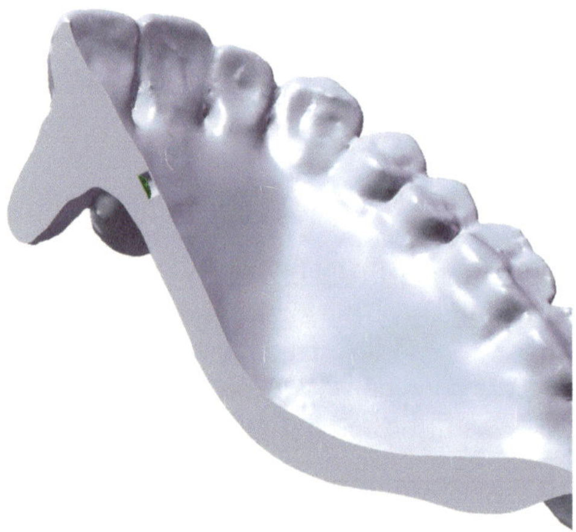

Fig. 11. The second analysis model: the fault is considered near the top surface of the denture

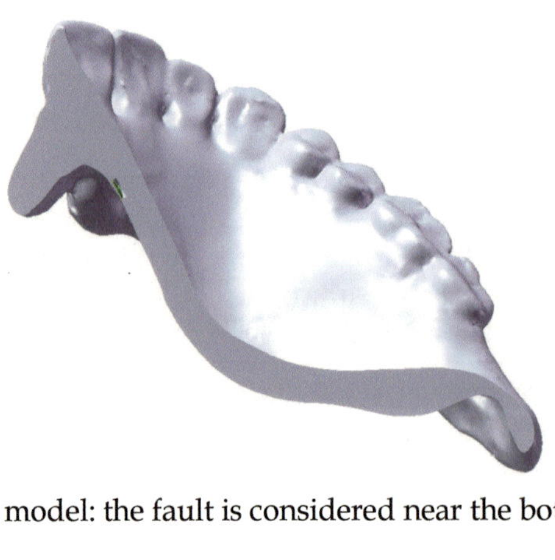

Fig. 12. The third analysis model: the fault is considered near the bottom of the denture

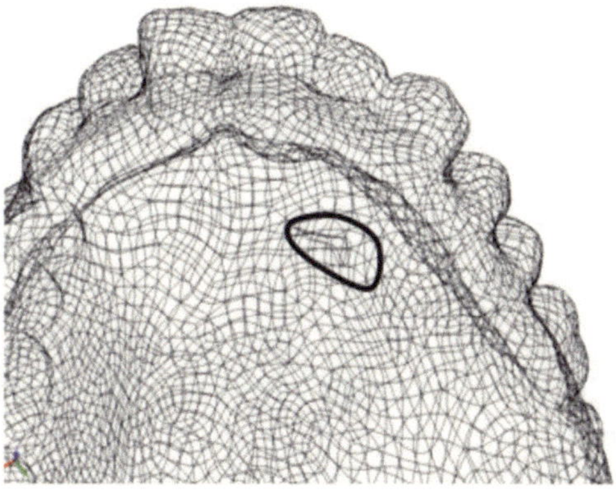

Fig. 13. The fourth analysis model: the fault is considered in the thickness of the denture

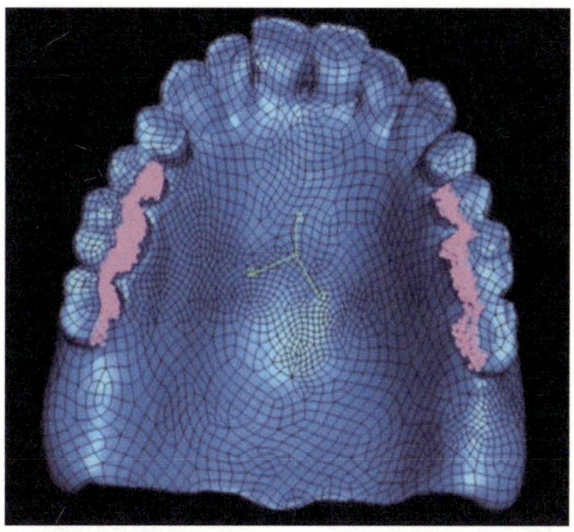

Fig. 14. The applied pressure on palatal cusps

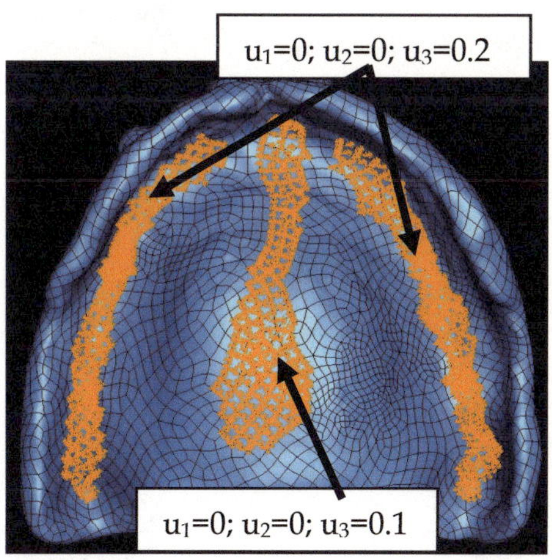

Fig. 15. Applied boundary conditions on complete denture model

All the analysis models have been meshed in tetrahedral finite elements, C3D4, accounting for a total of 243032 elements and 49154 nodes.

3. Results

In most assessed dentures was observed that the faults occurs mainly in the area where the thickness of denture is high, as indicated in figure 1. It was also noticed that, in the Eclipse dentures the density of defects may be higher than in the Meliodent dentures, but the defects in Eclipse may be smaller in size than those in Meliodent. This is due to different technologies for developing materials (heat curing polymerization - Meliodent and light curing polymerization - Eclipse).

The mechanical properties resulted after the experimental programs were given in table 2. The results show that, Eclipse Base Plate has a better elasticity compared to Meliodent and also a better fracture strength.

Material	Ultimate Tensile Strength σ_{uts} [MPa]	Tensile Young's modulus, E [MPa]	Total Elongation A_t [%]	Flexural Strength σ_f [MPa]
Eclipse	80.16	3390	4.06	127
Meliodent	68.62	1215	8.76	118

Table 2. Mechanical properties of the materials used for FEM analysis

For finite element analysis were considered four analysis models, each of them having a defect located in different areas of the denture. For all these cases have been evaluated the stress and strain states (fig. 16 - 24).

Since the materials have a brittle fracture behavior it was considered for this analysis the fracture criterion which takes into account the Maximum Principal Stress.

In all analyzed models, the presence of the faults has increased the stress and strain state, compared to the situation they are not considered. Moreover, this defects increased the fracture risk of denture. Thus, in case of model I the fracture risk of denture has increased by almoust 29 % due to present defect, in the second model the fracture risk increased by almost 14 %, in the third case was an increase of almost 90 % and in the latter case (the fourth model) the fracture risk increased with 18 %. The increased rates of fracture risk of denture were determined reporting the actual stress states to the stress state of the same

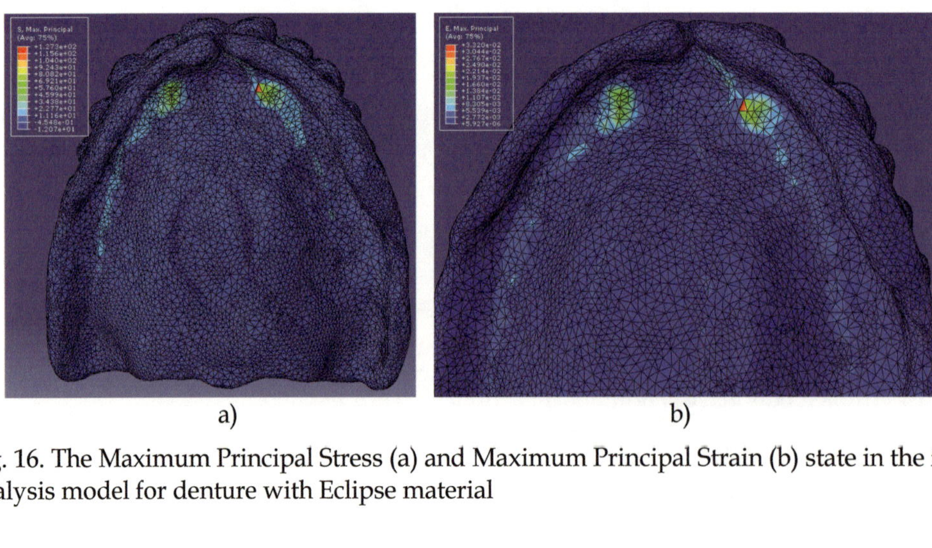

a) b)

Fig. 16. The Maximum Principal Stress (a) and Maximum Principal Strain (b) state in the first analysis model for denture with Eclipse material

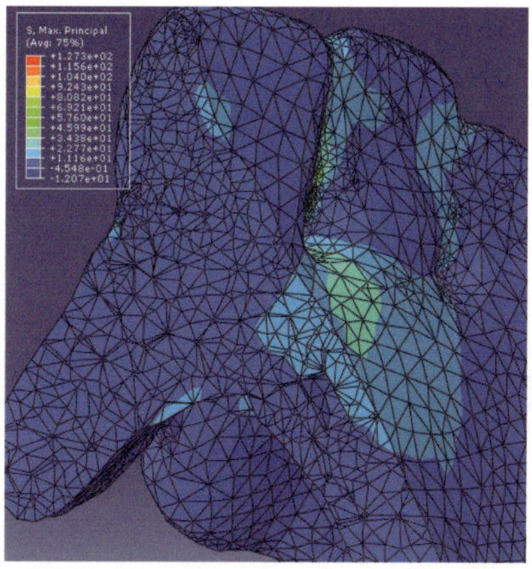

Fig. 17. The Maximum Principal Stress around the defect in the first analysis model for denture with Eclipse material

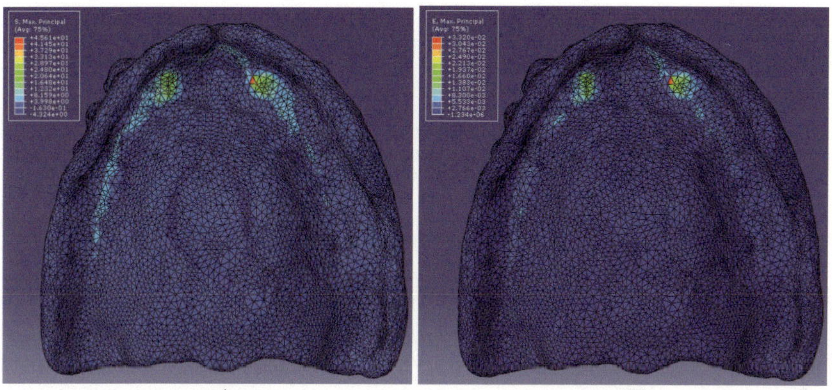

a) b)

Fig. 18. The Maximum Principal Stress (a) and Maximum Principal Strain (b) state in the first analysis model for denture with Meliodent material

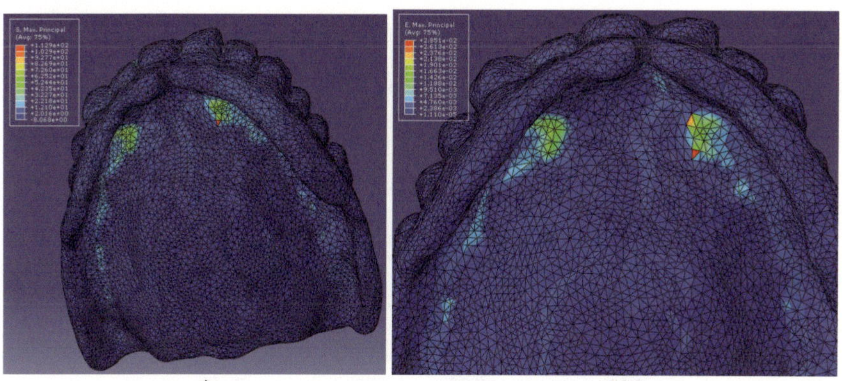

a) b)

Fig. 19. The Maximum Principal Stress (a) and Maximum Principal Strain (b) state in the second analysis model for denture with Eclipse material

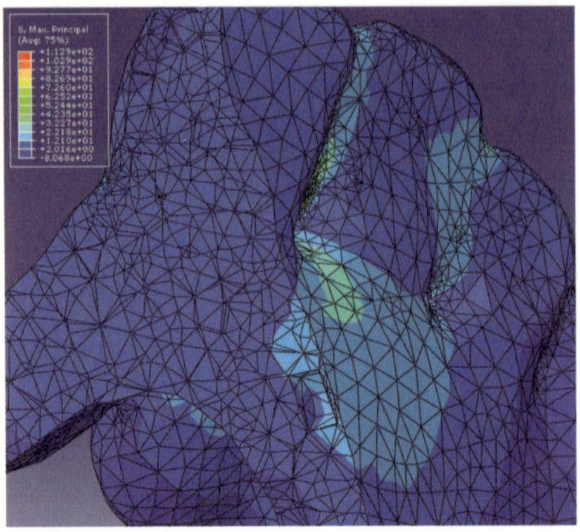

Fig. 20. The Maximum Principal Stress around the defect in the second analysis model for denture with Eclipse material

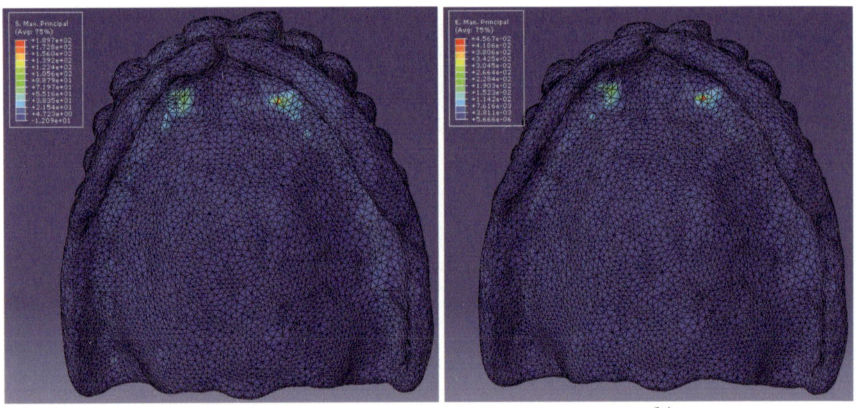

a) b)

Fig. 21. The Maximum Principal Stress (a) and Maximum Principal Strain (b) state in the third analysis model for denture with Eclipse material

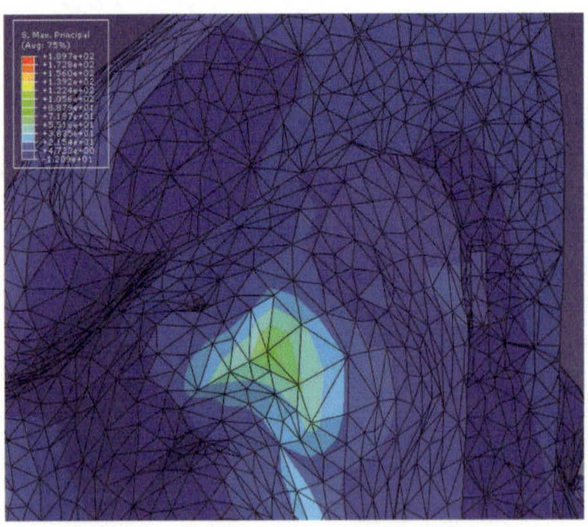

Fig. 22. The Maximum Principal Stress around the defect in the third analysis model for denture with Eclipse material

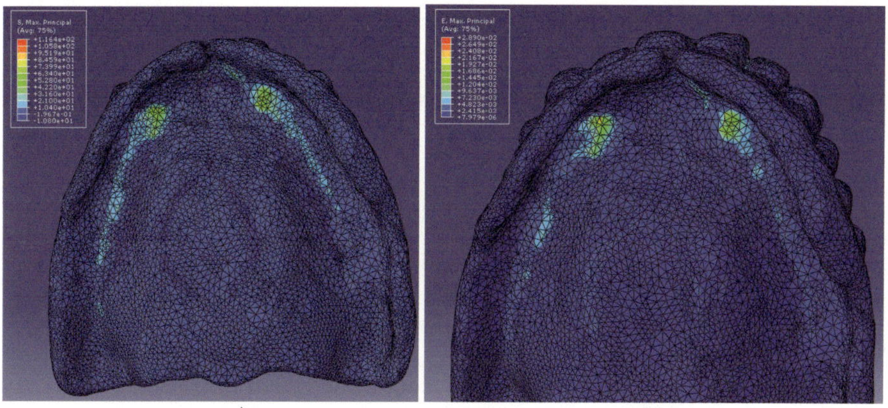

a) b)

Fig. 23. The Maximum Principal Stress (a) and Maximum Principal Strain (b) state in the fourth analysis model for denture with Eclipse material

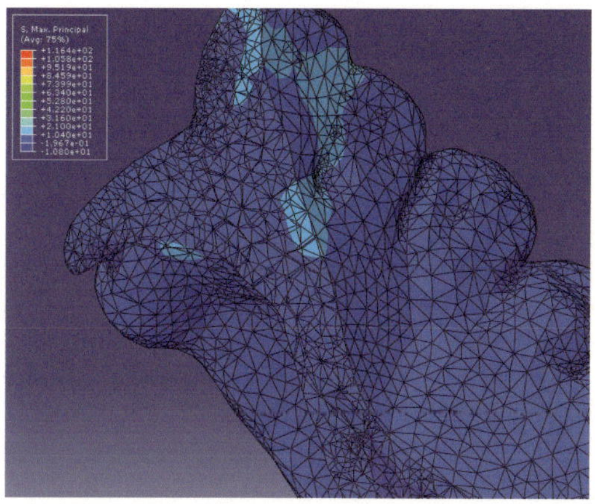

Fig. 24. The Maximum Principal Stress around the defect in the fourth analysis model for denture with Eclipse material

denture, loaded in the same way but without defects. These results indicate a greater influence on the stress state when the defect is closer to the bottom of the denture and less if the defect is almost to the upper surface of the denture. Defect in the fourth model, although it has a large surface area, is at the limit of the area indicated as the highest density of defects and because of this it not influence too much the stress and strain state.

In the case of Meliodent denture was observed the same influence of presence defects on stress state and fracture strain.

4. Conclusions

The methodology presented in this paper consist in 3D scanning of a real object, processing of the scanned results by reverse engineering and obtaining a digital geometric model and conducting numerical analysis. This methodology can by successfully applied in design optimization, especially in objects with complex geometry.

An important role in fracture strength evaluation of the dentures plays the material's defects and their localization towards the most loaded areas of the denture.

The structural defects located inside the model have a smaller influence on the state of stress than those located on the exterior surface. Also, very relevant for the fracture of the denture is the stress field around the crack, which can either close or open the crack.

The defects in the material's structure may have a negative impact on denture's mechanical resistance. Complete dentures' defects can initiate cracks that are responsible for their failure before the expected lifetime.

5. Acknowledgment

This work was supported by the strategic grant **POSDRU/89/1.5/S/57649**, Project **ID-57649** (PERFORM-ERA), co-financed by the European Social Fund-Investing in People, within the Sectoral Operational Programme Human Resources Development 2007-2013 and by the **IDEAS Grant CNCSIS, 1878/2008**, contract no. 1141/2009.

6. References

A. Cernescu, N. Faur, C. Bortun, M. Hluscu (2011). A methodology for fracture strength evaluation of complete denture, *Engineering Failure Analysis*, Vol. 18, 1253-1261 p.;

ABAQUS Version 6.9.3. Documentation Manual;

ASTM D790. Standard Test Methods for Flexural Properties of Unreinforced and Reinforced Plastics and Electrical Insulating Materials;

Darbar UR, Hugget R, Harrison A, Williams K. (1995). Finite element analysis of stress distribution at the tooth-denture base interface of acylic resin teeth debonding from the denture base, *J Prosthet Dent*, 74:591-4;

Darbar UR, Huggett R, Harrison A (1994). Denture fracture - a survey, *Br Dent J.*, 176:342-5;

Dorner S, Zeman F, Koller M et al. (2010). Clinical Performance of complete denture: A retrospective study, *Int J Prosthodont*, 23(5): 410-417;

Hargreaves AS (1969). The prevalence of fractured dentures. A survey, *Br Dent J.*, 126:451-5;

Mack, F.; Schwahn, C., Feine, J.S., et al. (2005). The impact of tooth loss on general health related to quality of life among elderly Pomeranians: results from the study of health in Pomerania (SHIP-O), *International Journal of Prosthodontic*, Vol.18, 414-9;

N. Faur, C. Bortun, L. Marsavina et al. (2010). Durability Studies for Complete Dentures, *ADVANCES IN FRACTURE AND DAMAGE MECHANICS VIII*, Key Engineering Materials, Vol. 417-418, 725-728 p.

N. Faur; (2002). Elemente finite - fundamente, Politehnica Timisoara, Romania, ISBN 973-8247-98-5;

Pixform Pro (2004). Tutorial, Powered by RapidForm™ Technology from INUS Technology; Roland DG Corporation;

Reddy, I.N., (1993). An introduction to the Finite Elemente Method. Mc Graw Hill Inc.;

Rees Js, Huggett R, Harrison A. (1990). Finite element analysis of the stress-concentrating effect of fraenal notches in complete dentures, *Int J Prosthodont*, 3:238-40;

SR EN ISO 527. Standard Test Method for Tensile Properties of Plastic Materials;

Y.Y. Cheng, J.Y. Lee et al. (2010). 3D FEA of high-performance polyethylene fiber reinforced maxillary denture, *Dental Materials*, article in press;

Zarb, G., Bolender, C.H., Carlsson, (1997). G. Boucher's Prosthodontic Treatment for Edentulous Patients, Mosby;